TAYLORED LIVES

Martha Banta

TAYLORED LIVES

Narrative
Productions
in the Age of
Taylor, Veblen,
and Ford

THE UNIVERSITY OF CHICAGO PRESS CHICAGO & LONDON

MARTHA BANTA is professor of English at the University of California, Los Angeles.

The University of Chicago Press, Chicago 60637
The University of Chicago Press, Ltd., London
© 1993 by The University of Chicago
All rights reserved. Published 1993
Printed in the United States of America
02 01 00 99 98 97 96 95 94 93   1 2 3 4 5

ISBN: 0-226-03701-0 (cloth)

Library of Congress Cataloging-in-Publication Data

Banta, Martha.
    Taylored lives : narrative productions in the age of Taylor,
Veblen, and Ford / Martha Banta.
        p.   cm.
    Includes bibliographical references (p.   ) and index.
    1. United States—Civilization—1865–1918.   2. United States—
Civilization—1918–1945.   3. Efficiency, Industrial—Social
aspects—United States.   4. American fiction—History and criticism.
5. Narration (Rhetoric)   I. Title.
E168.B22   1993
973—dc20   92-38609
                                                                       CIP

The illustration used on the title page spread of this book is drawn from *Sears Modern Homes* (1915), courtesy of Sears, Roebuck and Company.

⊗The paper used in this publication meets the minimum requirements of the American National Standard for Information Sciences—Permanence of Paper for Printed Library Materials, ANSI Z39.48–1984.

CONTENTS

ILLUSTRATIONS

PREFACE

FOLLOWING THROUGH ON THE PROJECT I began in my last book, *Imaging American Women*, *Taylored Lives* is intensely *about theory-making*. It is about how a culture is shaped by those who convinced themselves that they had finally accomplished what Emerson says we all set out to do in our rage for control—to discover "a true theory" that will "explain all phenomena." "Language, sleep, madness, dreams, beasts, sex" were the "inexplicable" things Emerson singled out for mastery by whoever could grasp the all-encompassing "true theory." It is precisely these items of concern—subsumed under alternative terms more familiarly used by businessmen, women's rights advocates, sociologists, labor agitators, economists, and muckrakers—that Frederick Winslow Taylor and his cohorts aspired to explain, and by explaining, to control.

If the practical visionaries of the late capitalist era initially set out to determine "the one best way" to increase industrial productivity or to clarify the vagaries of human behavior by means of the newly institutionalized social sciences, they quickly took upon themselves a far greater aim: that of bringing order, rationality, and efficiency out of the disorder, the irrationality, and the wastefulness of the times. Not devoid of conceit, they believed that *their* theory-making would resolve whatever was generally ungovernable in government procedures, business enterprises, household arrangements, and the workplace (which was always unruly, but increasingly so with the influx of all the new "others"), as well as (why stop before tidying up *everything?*) the conduct of everyday life.

One striking consequence of their concerted effort to fill every corner of social space with the blandishments of management theory was the creation of countless stories about lives uplifted by the gospel of Taylorism, stories directed at a variety of audiences. Just as striking was the urgency with which contrary stories, ones that destabilized myths of the efficient life born of self-deluded trust in any "one best way," were rushed into print. By analyzing the critical, symbiotic mass formed of both theories and stories, we learn about the obsessive need to create "rationalizing" models during the age of Taylor, Veblen, and Ford. We also discover eerily instructive resemblances to those enterprises by which we, today, try to make some sense of the buzzing, booming chaos of our times.

The activities of our leading narratologists, historiographers, and others who propound highly structured literary and cultural theories yield close parallels to the paradigm of activity introduced as "Taylorism" in the first years of this century. Whatever the consequences to the social central nervous system, faith in "the one best way" of theory-making flourishes even among those (especially among those) who fiercely rebuke philosophical absolutes or any leaning toward cognitive certainties. How frequently we face the consequences of "the paradoxes that make theory—specifically the theory of narrative—into an authoritarian antiauthoritarianism."[1]

Indeed we have before us a repatterning of many of the arguments left over from that earlier culture, a culture that aspired to manage every detail of quotidian existence. Granted that we need theory, need it mightily in order to extend some ordering power over our hectic lives; granted that we profit greatly from employing conceptual models that enable us to project solutions to our future needs; granted that theory-making is what we do every day in our own day, just as people did in those years when Taylor's name was as significant (and to many more people) as the names of Foucault, Lacan, and Derrida; granted all the cultural advantages and intellectual pleasures that systems-making provides, it still remains a potentially dangerous enterprise. Or rather, as *Taylored Lives* will show, the enterprise was "dangerous" all along, not because people discovered that system overwhelmed life, but because system and life were revealed to be nearly one and the same.

This book is about matters that cross the line between (1) Taylorism as a historical "given" of the early twentieth century, which fostered the dream of a "contained" (often excessively controlled) society, and the narratives (also often excessively controlled) that sprang up out of the sense of urgency either to defend or to deny flat-out assertions that the Answer to All had been found at last; and (2) Taylorism as a paradigm for contemporary socioliterary theory, a paradigm marked by strong traces of the constant tension between containment and resistance to any damn-fool notion that there ever can be "one best way."

Taylored Lives examines and interrogates examples from the extraordinary range of stories that once were told in the pages of the popular press, journals both high and low, and book-length narratives both literary and extraliterary. It treats what we do as practicing narratologists (then and now) in our eager efforts to get at the substance of tale-bearing structures, self-defined as ideological either by intention or consequence.

The apparatus I myself bring to these appraisals is twofold: (1) theories characterized by their conscious desire to undermine systems that (however inadvertently) nourish "theory desire," that is, theories that act as stubborn adversaries to Taylorism in whichever guise it takes—William James's pragmatism or Stuart Hall's Gramscian analysis, to name but two—and, since one needs more than one's own pet theories to take on another's pet theories, (2) masses of empirical data that ground theory-making within history. For do we not need to convey the episodic texture of the times (details about how people felt and lived) in order to scrutinize the layers of authority imposed by the charts and diagrams created by efficiency experts of every stripe, whether they are engineers, psychologists, business pundits, house builders, anthropologists, political strategists, domestic scientists, product designers, or literary critics?

What is on display, therefore, is a "history" of the culture of theorizing—one that came into being a century ago in the steel mills of Pennsylvania in the hope, first, of controlling modes of productivity (i.e., the labor force), then proceeded to spread itself across the American terrain in an interlocking series of social systems and everyday practices masquerading as the ideology of choice. It is a history that continues to replicate itself in our own desire to gain totalizing control over literary structures, by whose means we might gain control (we ardently believe, we perhaps kid ourselves) over the systematized worlds in which we speak, make money, wield power, love, live, and die.

ACKNOWLEDGMENTS

CHAPTERS 3 and 4 of this book incorporate material that first appeared in
" 'At Odds/In League': Brutality and Betterment in the Age of Taylor,
Veblen, and Ford," in *Prospects 14. The Annual of Cultural History,* edited
by Jack Salzman (New York: Cambridge University Press, 1989). I am
grateful to the publisher for permission to reproduce this material here.

My thanks go to the UCLA Academic Senate Research Grant program for its support of my research, and to the attentive staffs of the University Library of UCLA and the Ford Motor Company Archives and
Library of the Henry Ford Museum and Greenfield Village, Dearborn,
Michigan.

My gratitude also goes to Cecelia Tichi and Mark Seltzer, who lavished their time and attention upon my manuscript, thereby giving me a
fuller sense of the achievements I might be making and the blunders or
omissions against which I must guard myself.

Alan Thomas, Ellen Feldman, and other members of the University
of Chicago Press merit my most sincere appreciation for the tender loving
care they showed my work in moving it from inception toward publication. And I am grateful to Janet Sarbanes, my UCLA research assistant,
who helped me survive the horrors of reading proofs.

On an even more personal note, I conclude this little review of ac-
knowledgments for services rendered with my heartfelt thanks to Mar-
jorie and Joe, Nancy and Rob, for having furnished me with such a richly
managed culture of friendship.

TAYLORED LIVES

When ideologies are formulated to defend a set of economic interests, it is more illuminating to examine the strategy of argument than to insist that the argument is selfish.

> Reinhard Bendix, *Work and Authority in Industry: Ideologies of Management in the Course of Industrialization*

Our narratives can be interpreted as negotiations and renegotiations over the legitimacy of given versions of professional expertise.

> Bruce Robbins, "Death and Vocation: Narrativizing Narrative Theory"

INTRODUCTION

The Rage for Narrativization

When Frederick Winslow Taylor came to Harvard University in 1909 to speak to the members of the newly opened School of Business, he told a story. This was not unusual for Taylor. He had many stories to tell. Although each had the same thrust—the need to apply the guiding hand that is simultaneously visible and invisible (now you see it, now you feel it)— his stories incorporated a variety of narrative structures, plot devices, and discourse systems, depending upon whether the Father of Scientific Management believed he had to explain or to justify "the one best way" (the way of "predetermined routine" aided by "the best tools" and the "best machines") to tightly fit factory workers to their assigned tasks.[1]

Taylor doubtless assumed that the particular tale he told that day in Cambridge was a simple one, Aristotelian in regard to the cause-effect relations essential to the poetics of dramatic conflict and the management principles of boss-worker dynamics. As far as he was concerned, its plotting strategy presented listeners with the choice of two plots, old and new. The one was a tragicomedy of errors occasioned by wasted effort; the other was an ameliorating melodrama by means of which virtue (the right that is might) is triumphant. Taylor the narrator made it clear which denouement the narratology of Taylorism has to offer.

> The management of workmen consists mainly in the application of three elementary ideas:
> *First:* Holding a plum for them to climb after.
> *Second:* Cracking the whip over them, with an occasional touch of the lash.
> *Third:* Working shoulder to shoulder with them, pushing in the same direction, and all the while teaching, guiding, and helping them.
> The management of the present consists of a continuation of the first two of these elements, and of these the plum is more effective than the lash, although the latter is too often applied. Scientific management, the management of the future, consists in the application of all three elements, the lash, however, being left almost out of sight, while the close, hearty co-operation of the management with the workmen becomes the most prominent feature, and a good big plum is kept always in sight. This is the sum and substance of what I shall try to tell you today.[2]

The erstwhile engineer, who soon became his generation's foremost
management expert, continually assumed dual roles: the narratologist
who formulates principles and the narrator who practices his art. Out of
the urgency to demonstrate "the one best way" to possess the efficient life
and to create a harmonious society of workmen and bosses, Taylor devised stories that illustrated the narratological theories lying behind the
management principles he was introducing into the workplace. For what
is Taylorism but an extended narrative structure and discourse system,
one that extends far beyond the factory floor to encompass every aspect of
cultural existence?

Taylored Lives focuses upon the historical moments when Frederick
Winslow Taylor told his stories and practiced his theories between the
mid-1880s and 1915, then follows them into the 1930s, when his disciples
provided the sequels to his urtext for workplace control. This account
deals primarily with the United States as the site of the dramas concerning
"the managed life," but it also makes references to transnational events
taking place just off stage: narrative romps centered upon the Rough Riders in Cuba and mining engineers in Latin America, and the plot twists
introduced to *Taylorismus* by Lenin and Gramsci. It locates narratives of
the managerial ethos within diverse areas of domestic and national activity, such as the imperialist project, the machine process, and the business
enterprise; the science of households; and the making of ready-made garments, ready-made houses, and ready-made work environments. As for
the protagonists, they include owners, managers, and workers; women
and men; old-stock Americans, immigrants, and minorities; producers
and consumers; and representatives of almost every class and caste.

It would be misleading to imply that Taylor remained in full command of either the practices of narrativization or the theoretical analysis
that gives the stories unearthed in *Taylored Lives* their significance. If Taylor's successors had to struggle anxiously against the influence of their
strong father, Taylor himself was surrounded by strong tellers and forceful theorizers, among them Theodore Roosevelt and Henry Adams,
Thorstein Veblen and Charlotte Perkins Gilman, Henry Ford and Lillian
Gilbreth, Christine Frederick and Melusina Fay Peirce, not to mention
scores of others who supported or condemned "the one best way," others
who will insist upon being heard throughout this book.

For example, this is the Ford production line propelled by "the Taylorized speed-up" as John Dos Passos flings it across the page:

> reachunder, adjustwasher, screwdown bolt, shove in cofferpin,
> reachunder, adjustwasher, screwdown bolt, reachunderadjustscrew-
> downreachunderadjust, until every ounce of life was sucked off into

production and at night the workmen went home gray shaking husks.[3]

There will be other instances of melodrama packed into one prolonged screech of printed text—"reachunderadjustscrewdown-reachunderadjust"—but this is not the only kind of story to be told or the only way to tell it. Throughout its interrogation of an era characterized by patterned lives and systems of control, *Taylored Lives* seeks to discover what kinds of narrative patterns were already available for use and what new strategies for expression ached to be brought into being. It argues that just such diversity of responses to the culture of management made that culture what it was. It is not merely that Taylor, in defining Taylorism, creates narratives of power relations and a mode of narratology for their analysis. It is that everyone caught up in the times had tales to tell that "spoke" the times into being.[4]

There would be no point (although some studies draw different conclusions) for this book to lay out nine chapters dedicated to the predictable: one crushing narrative after another of the sufferings of powerless victims on the one hand, and, on the other hand, the triumphs of a "control society" tapped into place by crafty bastards or befuddled ameliorists.[5] Without letting anyone "off the hook,"[6] it is more instructive to demonstrate the narrative productions that entered the marketplace during the age of Taylor, Veblen, and Ford, shaped by authors in reaction to the culture of management they were both making and being made by.[7]

Sample Narratives

Details about the social and historical conditions affecting the culture of management as well as discussions of the terms that bonded the narrativization of history, science, fiction, and business into a corporate entity lie ahead. At this juncture, however, it is important to underscore the unpredictable nature of the narratives that surfaced under these circumstances. Here, then, are a few examples of the manner in which certain high-stakes issues were being plotted once control systems and the vagaries of modern American life began to merge.

Taylorism and the Children of Time

The two passages below have been taken from well-known literary texts. The first contains an absence that distinguishes it from narratives formulated strictly according to the principles that govern Taylorism and the methods that made Fordism famous; the second comes closer to qualifying its narrator as a true child of Taylorized time, but even here something is missing.

The passage from William Faulkner's *The Hamlet* describes the acts of sweeping and bed-making the idiot Ike Snopes performs under the kindly managerial eye of Mrs. Littlejohn.

> There is no work, no travail, no muscular and spiritual reluctance to overcome, constantly war against; yesterday was not, tomorrow is not, today is merely a placid and virginal astonishment at the creeping ridge of industry and trash in front of the broom, at sheets coming smooth and taut at certain remembered motions of the hands— a routine grooved, irkless; a firm gentle compelling hand, a voice to hold and control him through joy out of kindness as a dog is taught and held.[8]

The following passage excerpts the story of Booker T. Washington's arrival at the Hampton Institute, the fear and trembling the child feels about whether he will gain admission, and the means he is offered to prove his worth when the head teacher says, " 'The adjoining recitation-room needs sweeping. Take the broom and sweep it.' "

> I swept the recitation-room three times. Then I got a dusting-cloth and I dusted it four times. All the wood-work around the walls, every bench, table, and desk, I went over four times with my dusting-cloth. . . . When I was through, I reported to the head teacher. She was a "Yankee" woman who knew just where to look for dirt. . . . When she was unable to find one bit of dirt on the floor, or a particle of dust on any of the furniture, she quietly remarked, "I guess you will do to enter this institution."[9]

Champions of Taylorism and Fordism find much to commend in the behavior of the idiot and the ex-slave boy. There is little to fault in either laborer's thoroughness, effective use of motor skills, unquestioning dedication to the completion of the task, or obedience to competent quality control managers. What disqualifies both the boy and the idiot from full adherence to "the one best way" is their disregard of time as time is annotated by Taylor and Ford.

The preindustrial child *takes too much time* at his broom; the ahistorical idiot *knows no time* as he sweeps. Neither acts (or is made to act) out of the dread consciousness that time is both the greatest enemy of efficient work and the instrument with which to master effective production. Time used (as Booker does) as though it were conspicuous leisure leagued with virtuous excess, or time experienced (as Ike does) as preconscious sensory force, is time wasted on the modern production line. Time wasted is the mark of the pervasive entropic loss of energy that threatens the children of time. Only if time's space were crammed with as many repetitious movements as machinery allows might the terrors of industrial, social, and cosmic waste be assuaged.[10]

Ike the idiot and Booker the black boy are special cases. On the surface they appear to fit Taylor and Ford's general notion that the best workers for the modern industrial shop are strong of body and like patient animals, but complicating factors lie beneath the surface of Ike's and Booker's inability to adapt fully to the specific demands of the early twentieth-century culture of management.

Taylor and Ford were convinced that money is the sole motive that drives workers forward.[11] They could not acknowledge that other realm of existence Ike Snopes inhabits—eased into "a routine grooved, irkless," untouched by theories of use value, exchange value, or alienation. Nor is the money motive enough to satisfy Booker. Self-esteem gained through self-driven productivity is as important to this small black boy as the "college examination" that wins whites "entrance into Harvard or Yale."[12]

Of course, neither Ike nor Booker remains untouched by their generation's passionate concern about the efficient management of time and matter. Ike's time-free love for the heifer is managed by those around him so that nothing (not even the beef from his slaughtered amorosa) will go to waste. Booker grows up to manage the Tuskegee Institute according to principles that we might call Bookerism.[13] His lauded management system appropriates the obsession of white men with white time and motion so skilfully that, later on, Nella Larsen's Helga Crane and Ralph Ellison's Invisible Man will be obliged to recoil against it.[14]

Production Systems and Consumer Desires

People tied to clock time are certain to be affected by consumer desires. Long before Booker T. Washington became a powerful spokesman for a policy of efficient labor power directed at resolving immediate socioeconomic problems between the races, Washington the child had an experience that Washington the adult never forgot. As a slave dressed in rags, his native talents wasted, he could only look forward to Sundays. On that day, molasses was sent to the slave quarters from "the big house" as a special treat.

> I would get my tin plate and hold it up for the sweet morsel, but I would always shut my eyes while the molasses was being poured out into the plate, with the hope that when I opened them I would be surprised to see how much I had got. When I opened my eyes I

would tip the plate in one direction and another, so as to make the molasses spread all over it, in the full belief that there would be more of it and that it would last longer if spread out in this way.[15]

Spreading the molasses around became the impetus to Washington's later systems-making. Neither he nor the people he managed would ever miss out on the opportunity to have that extra "sweet morsel" that comes from seizing the chance to make a little seem like more.

Creating the sense of abundance in the midst of lack allows for consumer manipulation, but it hardly decreases cravings that are there in the first place.[16] When Faulkner's Mink Snopes is released from the time warp of Parchman Prison where he has spent the last thirty-eight years, he is completely unprepared for what he finds. A work farm like Parchman is isolated from the irregularities of the outside world that disturb careful control over timed functions. It is a perfect mechanism for the negation of production waste: the bodies of its inmates are provided with just enough sustenance to do the field labor that brings profit to the state (and to any individual along the way who makes a snatch with his invisible hand). Under these conditions, the economic balance is exquisitely maintained. There are only producers at Parchman, no consumers.

Mink Snopes is suddenly thrust out of this closed world into the highly rationalized consumer society of 1946, a society made up of "repetitive Dixie Cafes or Mac's or Lorraine's" with "machine-made prefrozen pie and what they would call coffee—the food perfectly pure and perfectly tasteless except for the dousing of machine-made tomato ketchup."[17] This is not the cause of the terror that seizes him. It is when Mink sees a stack of soft drink cases that "something terrible happened inside his mouth and throat." Here is a man who has just enough money to buy the pistol he needs for the revenge he has waited almost four decades to carry out, but he still craves a "sweet morsel" that has no efficient place in his plan.

> the first swallow coldly afire and too fast to taste until he could curb, restrain the urgency and passion so he could taste and affirm that he had not forgot the taste at all in the thirty-eight years: only how good it was, draining that bottle in steady controlled swallows now and only then removing it and in horror hearing his voice saying, "I'll have another one," even while he was telling himself *Stop it! Stop it!*[18]

In the Snopes trilogy Faulkner produces a series of narratives constructed around the waste and need introduced by the uncontrollable "human element," which no principle of scientific management can completely rationalize or control. In *The Hamlet* he portrays the madness of Henry Armstid's unproductive labor of digging, digging, digging in the voided earth, driven by his dream of the "sweet morsel" of buried gold. In *The Mansion* he portrays Mink's unruly desire for what memory recalls as thirst for the long-absent bottle of soda pop, a desire that threatens the successful fulfillment of a carefully managed plan of revenge. Whereas Brookerism banks on its faith that one can spread things around by imposing reasoned self-discipline and carefully managed time schedules, cravings can never be satisfied through controlling systems in Faulkner's world, managed as it is by "the unmathematical, the overfecund, the prime disorderly and illogical and patternless spendthrift."[19]

We may recognize that matters are never as simple as Faulkner seems to make them when he gets going on his nature-versus-machinery polemic, but then Faulkner is not as simplistic on this score as he is too frequently taken to be. Succeeding chapters will suggest the ways in which he (and others like him who harbor feelings of resentment and resistance to forms of collective control) tussles with the complicitous relations between guts and grids that collapse their status as easy oppositions.[20]

Domestic Sciences

The site of the dastardly deeds Taylorism and Fordism have done to "the little people" in their grip is commonly allegorized in terms of that claustrophobically enclosed factory environment for robotic motions, giant gears, and surveillance monitors for which Charlie Chaplin's *Modern Times* is everyone's first point of reference.[21] However, *One Week,* produced in 1920 by Buster Keaton and Eddie Cline, provides a more accurate index of an era during which management methods for efficient production were inspiring, and complicating, every phase of diurnal experience. Located outside the factory in a raw new residential neighborhood, it tells its story by means of melodrama, domestic romance, time-motion study, and revenge comedy, wrapping up the traumatic production of house-lives within a few effectively utilized cinematic minutes.

As a wedding present, Buster and his bride receive a house lot and a set of crates containing ready-made parts manufactured by the Portable House Company. As chapter 7 details, the ready-made house was one of the prizes scientifically managed production systems offered to the general public in the first decades of the twentieth century. Families were meant to be masters of their own do-it-yourself fate. Mail-order catalogues promised dream houses that could be assembled in record time and for a fraction of the cost of a custom-built home. Keaton's film demystifies this perfect system by introducing the unpredictable in forms human, natural, and mechanistic, showing at the same time how unpredictability itself is in league with the all-pervasive systems that constitute both *the told-about* and *the telling*.

A rejected suitor alters the identifying numbers on the house-part crates without the newlyweds' knowledge. We view the process as, day by day over one week's time, Buster energetically assembles the misnumbered parts into a structure perplexed by the same vertigo as Dr. Caligari's village (see figure 1). Human error is compounded by natural disaster. First the structure is smashed by a violent storm, then Buster learns this monstrosity sits on the wrong lot. In his attempt to move the house to its rightful location, his car (one of Mr. Ford's finest) stalls on the railroad tracks with the house in tow and everything is demolished by a speeding train.

In *One Week,* nature, the machine, and the human element conspire to overwhelm our honeymoon couple with a series of mishaps no scientific management practices can offset. Through it all, Keaton's face conveys that "stark grandeur," that "philosophical pessimism," which radicals of the time found unacceptable in a society in urgent need of revolutionary change.[22] Nonetheless, his constant busyness and inventiveness hardly make him a passive victim. That his blank countenance and the smoothly jerky motions of his perfectly coordinated limbs make him the living image of the robotized man is part of the fun. Beyond pathos, beyond tragedy—but hardly beyond self-irony—Keaton deals superbly with a world in which even domestic life is brutalized by situations "the one best way" is meant to master.[23]

We do not want to say that *even* domestic life is affected by the vagaries of the culture of management. Rather, it is *especially* family living that the ethos of good management wishes to commandeer. The constant cry of reformers intent upon introducing sound management methods to combat social disarray is also "the cry of the children" and fear for "the undermining of family life." Whether it is Jacob Riis, Theodore Roosevelt, Upton Sinclair, and Booker T. Washington, or Melusina Fay Peirce, Jane Addams, Charlotte Perkins Gilman, and Christine Frederick, reformers of various political permutations conceptualize their melodramas of disorder in domestic terms. As a result, narratives that propose to show the way out of mismanagements exacerbated by feudalistic patriarchal systems often replace old stories with modern tales about good fathers and mothers trained in the modern paternalistic principles of family management.

Gertrude Stein's *Three Lives* examines what happens to three women when their very personal relations with the culture of management go awry.[24] The Good Anna aspires to be the perfect manager of one

Figure 1. Buster Keaton, "One Week" (1920). Courtesy of the Academy of Motion Picture Arts and Sciences.

household after another, utilizing her skills in domestic science to make life "regular and quiet."[25] In the pleasure and pain she derives from the "arduous and troubled life"—the "bad headaches" and constant "worrying" that come from her attempts to order the disheveled conduct of all who are foolish, careless, helpless, comfortable, and free—Anna is sister to Frederick Winslow Taylor.[26]

Anna's mid-level managerial skills must constantly meet the tests put to them by the employers, staff, and dogs placed under her "strict orders never to be bad one with the other." Although armed with both the "lash" of her perpetual scoldings and the "plum" of keeping her people "warm and full" and "content," Anna finds no relief in her struggle against "the warmth, the slowness" of "the cries of men and animals and birds, and the new life all round about" that "were simply maddening" and "the bad ways of all the thoughtless careless world."

In the end, Anna cannot sustain "the power to control" either Miss Matilda or Dr. Shonjen, her employers or Mrs. Lehntman, "the only romance Anna ever knew." Ultimately, Anna faults on one of the main principles of good management theory: she becomes "too weary with the changes to do more than she just had to, to keep on living," and thus "the good Anna with her strong, strained, worn-out body died." But then, all of Stein's women die in this tripartite narrative, bruised by their inability to make a truce with an ethos that (thriving as it does on binary oppositions) prefers regularity to carelessness, habits to nature, predictability to mystery, decent conduct to romance, and rational principles to wild facts—oppositions that Stein herself liked to play with in her writing and to live with in her loving.

Business Fictions

The masculine-feminine question is sometimes hidden, sometimes exposed, in the narrative productions of the culture of management, but it is always there. Males are expected to bring rational practices to an industrialized, mechanized, business-oriented society while females are designated as one major source of that potentially uncontrollable energy surge subsumed under the all-purpose term "the human element." It was wayward "womanness" that social scientists were called upon to analyze, merchandisers and advertisers to entice, and women functioning as home management experts to instruct. The intriguing question for us is: under what conditions would narratives ever take the woman's side? The answers are often surprising.

The 1920s saw the heralding of a narrative form that proclaimed itself as belonging entirely to the modern moment. As *System: The Magazine of Business* defined it, "business fiction" has "a practical appeal" in that it is devoted to presenting in narrative terms the thrilling story of "how the general manager discovered a basic principle of modern business management." According to the mind-set of this entirely male enterprise, the Nineteenth Amendment was never passed. The female voice is eliminated, and the only mention of the other sex is that of "the competent young women" adept at supplying secretarial information to the boss "before his cigar was an inch shorter."[27]

Business fiction celebrates men caught up in "the 'work and battle and play' of this big thing called 'Business.'" Recall Ernest Hemingway's tales of male bonding in times of war—as well as the "Rotarian" in his nature, which Gertrude Stein detected—and you will find similarities to business fiction narratives of "team-work," which stress the "old spirit" of "solidarity." Don't, however, think of Hemingway the modernist aesthetician or the cosmic pessimist (or of any of the "classic dodos and Us cultured folks")[28] when considering this aggressively antigenteel, assertively optimistic genre written of and by a business elite made up of "real men." Above all, recognize that "selfish, sordid, grasping, gross, material though [business fiction] be, it has, thank heaven, no such tales of woe to put into verse, drama, history, and essay as one finds on every page of the chronicles of war, politics, and religion."[29]

But even here, located definitively in the midst of the managers, business fiction reveals its reliance on the traditions of the domestic romance and the family melodrama. (I will demonstrate this reliance in chapter 6 with an analysis of a novel in which the good son becomes the good mother.) The modern boss-hero is concerned about "his executive-family." He worries over his responsibilities as the strong father who must rid his world of earlier mores that set his boys "at each others' throats."[30] In turn, the "Chief" learns about the newest business morality from the bright youngsters under his guiding hand. Within the happy world of business fiction, quick profits become secondary to protecting the "kiddies" of the larger community. One's management energies are redirected to the designing of an efficient, caring society over which the "warm sun" shines like "a halo" in "the morning of a new and busy day."[31] But it might not have room for the special needs of Ike or Booker, Buster or Anna, even though it does very well at absorbing them into the general instrumental abstraction.

Corporate Relations

Acts of writing are acts of production and consumption. Walter Benjamin has noticed this, but he is not the only one. Lionel Grossman puts the matter bluntly in reviewing the stages through which writers' work has moved over the past two centuries. With the coming of industrial capitalism, literature was allowed "to appear as essentially different from all other products of labor in the degraded world of industry and the market, but in order to do so, it foregrounded, indeed fetishized the product, concealing or mystifying the processes of its production."[32]

Taylored Lives does not address directly the making of literature as a physical commercial product (a matter currently under examination by other scholars, to the enhancement of our knowledge of the way writers interact with "the degraded world of industry and the market"). Instead, it concentrates upon the nature of narrative products, the design models that shaped them for public consumption, the audiences they aimed to satisfy, and the motives that placed them in the market in the first place—especially the motives, difficult as they may be to trace, given all the "concealing or mystifying" that went into the process. Underlying all else is the touch of the invisible hands, hands that guided what we may call the corporate relations between management practice and theory, and the practice and theory of the narrative act.

The urge to define the nature of Taylorism in particular and to professionalize efficiency systems in general compelled the making of many narratives. As Bruce Robbins recognizes, "A story of the professionalization of narrative—how narrative is refitted as a knowledge base—is also a narrative of professionalization."[33] Narratives were *told to* employers who wanted more productivity at less cost for the sake of greater profits as well as to workers caught up in management's experiments with quality control, which shaped both the making of products and laborers' lives. Just as compulsively, narratives were *told by* managers and workers alike in order to persuade or to dissuade, to justify or to condemn.

Under pressure to tell everybody's autobiography of the various cultures of management, narrative language went every which way. If "social Darwinism," "work," and "science" were being appropriated by any ideology that found them useful, dizzying use was also being made of tropes for "waste" (the foe) and "efficiency" (the good means to good ends).[34] But the central question remains: whose language is it and whose story? the narrativizing of the managers or of the rest of us?[35] We must ask not only *Whose language is it?* but *Who is speaking?* Foucault made these his leading questions, but so have others, adding yet another query, *Who is listening to the telling?* This act of telling necessarily involves both the manager-author and the worker-reader.[36]

Narratologists, such as Thomas Docherty, distinguish the realistic novel from the postmodern novel by designating the former as that story initiated by the rationalist, autonomous novelist-as-god, whose monologue denies the audience the freedom "to enter subjectively into dialogue concerning the 'truth' of the authorial pronouncements," and by designating the latter as the story in which "authority becomes corporate . . . rather than individual and proprietorial."[37]

Docherty's distinctions suggest that the narratives countenanced by the Taylors and the Fords are part of the realist mode, which literary historians have identified as the dominant mode during the years in which Taylor and Ford were honing their management methods. If so, counternarratives proposed by those who see themselves opposing authoritarian control systems can be taken as anticipating the postmodern dialogic act. A great deal, however, hangs on our realization that Docherty's personal preference for the narrative form in which "authority becomes corporate" reflects the position held by the turn-of-the-century community of radicalized storytellers who advocated industrial democracy. Unless we recognize several possible meanings of "corporate action," postmodernism starts to sound like what it is intended to save us from: that modernist culture toward which the realist narratives of Taylorism and Fordism point.

If we are not careful in negotiating the traffic jam caused by the convergence of these *isms,* we get caught up in the endeavors shared by modernist management practices and narrative productions. Hayden White calls the modernist text the text that "narrates"—discourse that reports from the vantage point of the individual ego. He warns us that we are better off staying with the looser postmodernist relationships that arise from the text that "narratizes"—discourse "that feigns to make the world speak for itself . . . *as a story.*"[38]

In any event, no matter which labeling system we choose to define their primary function, authoritative texts come in various guises. Even when they state their intention to speak on behalf of those *from below,* they report *from on high.*[39] Consider, for instance, the 1927 book *What the Employer Thinks.* It significantly devotes the final paragraph of its final chapter to a vision of a future of accord between labor and management, a vision handed over to the author by an aged, work-wasted miner. He requests, " 'tell employers everywhere that belief in men, and some plan to make that belief work, will bring what all of us want—real justice!' "[40]

Once managers are invited to make pronouncements for "the others," their visions are apt to slide into prophecy, a move that does strange things to acts of narrating. Gérard Genette observes that true "narrating can only be subsequent to what it tells." In contrast, "predictive narrative" lays down the ways things will be; by nature, it becomes complicitous with the managerial style it is meant to interrogate.[41]

Narratives of management or reform often define themselves as active reshapers of social structures (especially when they treat management methods *as* reform technique), yet they seek "a state of equilibrium which can signal the end of the narrative." In contrast, radical texts are in the hands of a narrator who "must recreate a state of tension . . . new obstacles or . . . potential dangers temporarily dormant" that point to the continuation of "the degradation process."[42] When narrativization is employed as a radical act, its stories *must go somewhere:* they are obliged to go beyond prolonged stasis and/or endless tensions, else they fail to escape both aesthetic boredom and political paralysis.

One way of *going somewhere* is to make narratives that attempt a general overview, what John Dewey had in mind when he spoke of the urgency to "state things as interconnected parts of a mechanism."[43] The "grand design" gained by viewing the earth from on high is not merely an aesthetic matter.[44] Whether attempted by the narratologist, scientist, social scientist, or political analyst, the successful overview furnishes vital "informational content" about socially inscribed networks, one way in which management control is made effective, but also the way in which the wish to control the controllers is encouraged. "Distance creates clarity and transforms the single image into a symbol, into an accusation here, a hymn of praise there, a manifesto everywhere."[45]

This mix of mathematical precision and mystical vision makes practical advocates of social change just as nervous as it does radical theorists. If management practices are responsible for the elaborate "webs" thrown across the face of society, stories that challenge these practices often turn out to employ the same devices and reveal the same webbed intermixtures. If it is true that "there is no transcendent, privileged cultural space on which to stand that is outside capitalist reification," it is also likely that, in the stories historians tell, there is "no outside of stories, no point at which they stop being stories and abut on hard particles of 'facts.' "[46]

The insistence that there is *no there outside here* could commit one to a despairing sense of abjectness, but it need not. It can press one toward a shrewd awareness of the "corporate relations" between what the creators of management theories do when producing fictive (not false) models of order and what the writers of histories do in logging fictive (not untrue) accounts of change. It can point literature away from the trivial lack of truth it shares with reification; it can turn history toward a particular kind of storytelling capable of becoming a "signifying history of humanity."[47]

Victor Turner speaks to an analogous situation in his essay "Social Dramas and Stories about Them." He distinguishes among *ritual* (both the old-time "flat view" and the definition more recently applied by functionalist anthropologists, who view it as "a set of mechanisms for promoting a gross group solidarity"); *ceremony* ("an impressive institutionalized performance of indicative, normatively structured social reality"); and (Turner's preference) *ritual liminality* (a "many-leveled" and "creative" force that simultaneously serves as a "model for" change and a "model of" order). Because of its complex structure, ritual liminality fully takes into account form; indeterminacy, which provides the field of action for form; and the merger that joins the child's "as if" world of wish with the adult's "as is" world of facts.[48]

Frederick Winslow Taylor consciously dealt in "as is" because of his anxiety about a society run by the childlike who lack managers to "narrate" the facts. Yet how powerfully the "as if" dimension of "narratizing" wish entered into Taylor's arguments for the validity of his "best way" and into the impulses that lay behind them. Embedded within these texts are narratives that follow the tradition of the Bildungsroman, in which the hero approaches truth gradually through empirical means, but also the tradition exemplified by Augustine's *Confessions,* in which Absolute Truth rushes in to overwhelm the protagonist.[49] The narrowness of the Taylorist vision constantly appears to deny "the human element," yet Taylorism is also the product of "the constructive imagination," which aspires to contain human needs within a grand design possessing the capacity to "envisage the whole significance of industrial management," from "the art of cutting metals" to "all its results in human lives."[50]

The hubristic aspiration to know all things great and small is amply demonstrated, since hubris was a ruling trait of the professional elites and technocrats produced in the mass during the age of Taylor, Veblen, and Ford. Think what this means to those who cannot even see *where* they are, caught as they are within programs designed by managers who believe they see everything.

Take Max Weber's description of the assembly-line process he witnessed in the Chicago stockyards the same year Upton Sinclair completed research for *The Jungle.* Which, we ask, is the narrative subject and which is the object: the steer swinging on synchronized machinery on its way to dismemberment or the "ever-new workers who eviscerate and skin it, etc., [who] are always (in the rhythm of work) tied to the machine that pulls the animal past them."[51]

And what of the Ford assembly line—"the whole room, with its interminable aisles, its whirling shafts and wheels, its forest of roof-supporting posts and flapping, flying, leather belting, its endless rows of writhing machinery, its shrieking [*sic*], hammering, and clatter, its smell of oil, its autumn haze of smoke"—where the "one complete lucid spot" is located at the end of the line? Only from this privileged point might the purpose of the Ford method become clear. To the worker dispossessed of an overview, robbed of the privileged theory that explains the reason for the system, life on the Ford line is "the simple life." But its simplicity comes at a cost, because it transforms the would-be narrator into "the special spasm" stripped of "a single thought or emotion."[52]

Many of our current theories about storytelling come from self-appointed tribal bards—the technocrats of contemporary narratology. Revisionists though they often claim to be, our favorite narratologists have much in common with the theorizers who brought legitimation to the new fields of the physical and mathematical sciences, the social sciences, history, literature, business, industry, and politics in the years straddling the nineteenth and twentieth centuries. Then and now, there was a common aim: to make stories that order disorderly facts (even though, ironically, our contemporaries' "ordering" focuses upon proud acts of disruption of the interpretive status quo). Nevertheless, there are differences (nuances, rather) that (potentially) situate the postmodern narratological enterprise in opposition to the craze to regulate that drove the original making of management theory.

(1) Narratology is indeed capable of admitting "the power of the marginal, the supplementary, the exception," not merely the predictable, the centrist, the normative statement. When the theorist takes care to include *particularizing details* that mediate totalizing typologies, he or she resists Taylorizing, "an 'encirclement' of narrative," which puts narratives "into boxes or behind grids" out of fear for what seems absurd.[53] (2) Narratology can, of course, underline *the dualities of purpose* that keep what is being told lively and the act of telling (reasonably) honest.[54] (3) Narratology often finds affinities with the liberalizing practices of industrial democracy when it instills trust among fiction, science, and history, when it lends support to the mutual assertions that "economic relations are finally a guise assumed by social relations" and that "social relations are the source of what stories can and cannot be told."[55] For who desires either narratological or managerial theories that run mad with classifications? That is the way workers and plots get limited to "functional units" defined as binarisms, and the way the scientific model manages to retain its privileged status as the CEO in command.

Not that narratology can ever free itself completely from systems-making, no more than any of our efforts to break loose can. The very trust it places in links with fiction, science, and history, as well as with the economic and the social, is the source of the betrayals and the mergers, large and small, to which it and we are ever susceptible.

"I could tell you true stories that are more interesting than fiction, but not now," Samuel S. Marquis observed in 1916, compiling his "Memo on the Ford Profit Sharing Plan" as director of the Ford Motor Company Sociological Department. He was still at that point in his relations with Ford when he believed in the antimonies of theory and experience it was his task to resolve.

> We are gathering data that we think will be of use in encouraging others to work along lines similar to those we are following. Later on as a result of a work we believe we will have something to give that will be more than theory. It will have back of it the test of experience.[56]

Marquis is timid here about admitting that fluid relations exist between "story" and the act of "narrating," and between showing-representation-mimesis and telling-diegesis,[57] but he expresses the aspiration of ambitious tale-tellers, whatever their relations to the corporate structure. Those involved in productive corporate acts of narrativization like to think they are telling "true stories" that are "more than theory" and "more interesting than fiction"—stories supported by both heartfelt experience and statistical data, stories that somewhat meet the "truth" criteria demanded of the wild facts of history ("the unexpected, the uncontrollable, the unsystematic change") and of fiction, which shares with science a taste for "the ordered, the coherent, the general or universal."[58] Such acts of narrativization rest upon assumptions that are "correct" in that (but, of course!) such stories involve just such conglomerations of material; they are also "wrong" insofar as they have categorized these stuffs as being somehow different in kind.

Not that everyone agrees that all discrepancies have undergone a final, fatal loss of distinct edges. According to Hayden White, *history* is unlike either *science* (since historical texts follow no universal laws or conceptual rigor) or *literature* (texts with less interest in the "actual" than in the "possible"). Narratives have "cognitive authority" only insofar as they instruct us "about the irreducible moralism of a life lived under the conditions of culture rather than nature." If they were merely cognitive ("scientific"), they would teach us how to be machines, but no one learns "to be more efficient" by reading other people's tales.[59]

Even keeping White's dissent in mind, we find more that brings these narratives together than separates them. The stimulating cross-purposes that link the narrative enterprise with the goals of scientists, sociologists, anthropologists, and the systems-makers of the industrial process are suggested by Peter Brooks and Gérard Genette, with an assist from Roland Barthes. Brooks argues that "narrative demarcates, encloses, establishes limits, orders" by means of plotting that displays the authoritative design characteristic of Western societies, whose "need for an explanatory narrative" is insatiable. In an age when "providential plots" are replaced by stories of persons, societies, and institutions, and in which "evolution, progress, genealogy" are the dominant terms of value, it is *plot* that possesses "the instrumental logic" that provides a form of thinking, a way of reasoning. Rather than fooling around with outmoded factors such as character, being, or ethics, plot gives "intentional structures, goal-oriented and forward-moving," filled with notions of conduct, action, praxis.[60]

In order to prevent the managerial narrative from absorbing everything in its path (at least for the sake of extending the argument past a premature closure), we must avoid stopping short with the idea of plot-making/systems-making, an idea that will take us straight into Taylor's territory. "The combinatorial principles" are Genette's way past that territory. He favors "the constellations" bred by nature and by culture over against the straight, the narrow, the single-minded narrative; he backs healthy "monsters" rather than Taylorist tales that insist upon one pure-bred voice having the final say.[61] Barthes also encourages the hybrid nature of narrative, three voices working in fruitful collaboration: the "Voice of the Empirical" (the proairetic code of action), the "Voice of Truth" (the hermeneutic code of enigmas), and the "Voice of Science" (referential cultural codes).[62] Narratives created, as it were, out of high-level labor-management disputes among diverse elements resist Taylorist impositions of centralized authority—a resistance that is possible since narrative "figures at once as an agency that produces skepticism and as an object that requires skepticism."[63]

Happy agreements reached around the corporate boardroom table were, however, seldom in evidence during the age of Taylor, Veblen, and Ford. Too much was at stake politically, just as it is today.

Most stories written into and across the culture of management are overtly political, even when unconscious about their motives. How could they not be? These are, after all, tales about workers, managers, and employers; about native-born Americans and newly arriving immigrants set to labor to produce and to consume; about the racial and ethnic groups in charge, and those racial and ethnic elements the bosses hope to transform from inefficient ne'er-do-wells into productive workers; about women in factory, office, and home guided by masculinist principles of management; about politicians, business leaders, and military men seemingly intent upon turning the nation's institutions into extensions of the well-managed assembly line.

The "writing" of narratives, like the utilization of management principles, is contradictory by nature. There is immense value in discovering texts that go against their own grain, with "tell-tale slips" revealing the "subconscious personality," the "deep self," of their authors. Of course, we always seem to unearth the reactionary impulse in these "slips." Yet, on occasion, we find that scratching the textual surface exposes a disguised radicalism—an act of storytelling more daring than the author's public consciousness might suggest.[64] But if inquiries into motives behind narratives quickly lead to questions about whether they are reactionary, reformist, or revolutionary, we need to ask why it is important to make such distinctions.

One narratologist argues that all traditional narrative structures act to inhibit "individual human growth and significant social change." Since "narrativity itself, as we have known it, must be seen as an opiate," it is the theorist's duty to expose its fraudulence as "a necessary prelude to any improvement in the human situation."[65] This makes good sense, certainly, when dealing with narratives that, in following the opiate impulse, view art as an instrumentalist science, not as a revelatory religion.

Narratives function as opiates when evolution, not revolution, dictates their sense of the passage of time. Floyd Dell made this charge when addressing Theodore Dreiser as a "dodo." Dreiser's fiction is art as Darwinistic science, which "froze the blood of revolution." Like all Progressive literature, it "justifies mid-nineteenth century pessimism."[66] Confronting Dreiser with the rhetorical question, "why do you not write the American novel of rebellion?" Dell supplies the answer: "We can have any kind of bloody world we bloody want."[67]

Dell's question and answer, addressed to writers both in and out of the Progressivist camp, is echoed when we ask, what is the purpose of making systems when the theories only lead to the interpretation of problems? Cannot the problems brought about by the transformative power of suspect systems be transformed into something sound?[68]

The reform mode stands in awkward relation to both reactionary narratives and revolutionary texts, to both the business enterprise and the political left. This awkwardness prompts an examination of the ways in which allegedly opposed ideologies make use of sentimentality and melodrama. In turn, the genres of the sentimental and the melodrama point toward the tonalities of the tragic, the pathetic, and the ironic—setting up interrelations among genre, tone, and ideology that affect the writing and living of economic, social, and political lives.

Sentimentality immediately calls up images of the conservative evasion of direct confrontations with social injustice, but it can just as surely color the practices of would-be radicals. "This is a fighting age," cries Mother Jones to Colorado miners on strike in 1916. "You are too sentimental." Labor historian Lawrence T. McDonnell repeats this charge today, leveling it against labor historians and labor movements alike.[69] He challenges the worth of stories told in praise of workers' psychological and cultural capacity for struggle and survival, tales that too often disregard the harsh fact that it was, after all, the employers who won the economic victories.

Sentimentality toward the labor force eased the consciences of those on top, the "invisible government" whose empty talk simultaneously placated guilt and "undercut radical rhetoric."[70] Sentimentality used by reformers was even more damaging if it only served to stir up middle-class emotions and reinforce social gradualism. The sentimentality that workers held toward themselves could be the most harmful of all, especially if it meant resignation to an existence of perpetual victimization. Yet what of the attacks against sentimentalism made, then and now, not by the radical left but by the entrenched policymakers and businessmen?

"There is no place for sentiment in trade or politics as public interests," William Graham Sumner states in his 1883 defense of "the forgotten man," the hero of Sumner's allegory of a society gone rotten with sentimentality. The virtues of efficiency and diligence are devalued when the public eye is turned upon "the shiftless, the imprudent, the negligent, the impractical, and the inefficient, or . . . the idle, the intemperate, the extravagant, and the vicious."[71] In 1903 a supporter of the National Association of Manufacturers asserted, "All this talk about love in business is rot. The only way to carry on business is . . . with all sentiment eliminated."[72] *Nation's Business,* the house organ of the U.S. Chamber of Commerce, put it just as bluntly in 1926: "The John D. Rockefeller who gives away millions is not a hero, but the Rockefeller who made a billion dollars out of oil is a hero. . . . [The] Carnegie who gave medals to heroes and built libraries was just a sweet old lady."[73]

Which is the most brutal side of the cultural of management, which the worst-case stories to be told about the indignities it imposes? Does the antisentimentalism preached by the U.S. Chamber of Commerce furnish our best example? Or is our main candidate for social brutalism the rhetoric of sentimentality voiced by Judge Elbert Gary when he declared that the bad old coda "The public be damned" must go, lest labor strife accelerate?[74] Or is "the Speculative Type" the hero of the day (see figure 2): that man with the face so famous he needs no identification; that man whose Sunday school lessons and fistfuls of dimes perfectly image the intertangling nature of the times with the brutality of the sentimental?[75]

Any transformations we abet between static information and active thought (or information on the move and thought that stays stagnant) involve us in political acts. This means making selections among possible narrative modes, but heaven forbid that they be as simplistic as the choices just cited. Why duplicate the error of making binary distinctions, say, between pessimism and optimism? The muckrakers charged the genteel intellectual set with pessimism; Progressivist reformers accused muckrakers of negativism; businessmen rebuked reformers for their lack of hope; conservatives tarred socialists with the brush of despair while socialists got back at the conservatives on the same count.

Floyd Dell criticized *Sister Carrie* for "the stark grandeur" of its "philosophical pessimism," and Kay Sloan speaks of film melodramas that gave "a certain grandeur to suffering."[76] These are not compliments. Nor was the comment by Edward Ross, the Progressivist sociologist, that the sen-

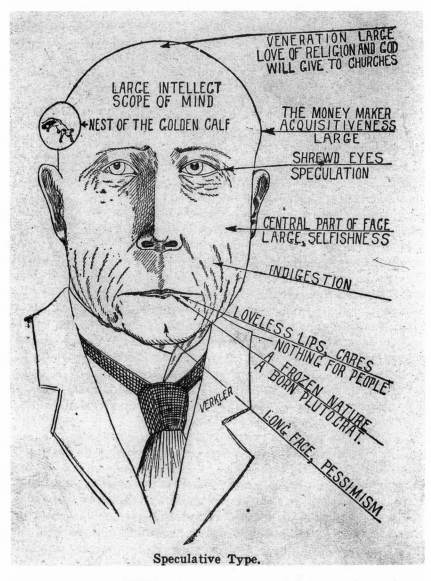

Figure 2. "Speculative Type." From V. G. Rocine, *Heads, Faces, Types, Races* (1910).

timental pleas made by big business can be compared to the melodramas
of pessimism written by the muckrakers who attacked the business interests.[77] Yet the tight fit between sentimentality and melodrama became the
muckrakers' keenest weapon, leagued with hard-edged reportage.

Writers for whom "the front page merged with the fairy tale,"[78]
muckrakers were "control engineers." Using the techniques of journalism, they brought the melodramatic mode into combination with methods of instruction learned from science—statistics, charts, notebooks
filled with persuasive facts. Through their efforts numbers are converted
into crises of feeling. The muckrakers liked to think that their narratives
of injustice spoke in the name of scientific objectivity while calling up the
wild facts of the heart. These narratives, however, sometimes verged on
the tragic and the pathetic—those literary forms that are traditionally
adept at representing the victimized because they deny the possibility of
overturning bad old habits. Melodrama, as we shall see, does not necessarily share in perpetuating this criminal possibility.[79]

One alternative to narratives of suffering, which record the wrongs
done by those in power to those under their control, are the counterstories
that have become valorized because of a belief that special powers are be-
stowed upon those who get to tell their own stories. We seek relief when
faced with texts that "narrate," texts like those produced by Henry Ford
and Theodore Roosevelt, which instruct good Americans how to conduct
themselves within an ever-expanding industrial society. Still, alternatives
to questionable tales may themselves be questionable. Tales of self-reliant
action can lack authentic self-mastery; they may merely replace pessimism
with depressing forms of optimism; they might simply substitute their
own authoritarianism for that of another.

We take alarm at the unrelenting exactions placed upon the individual
will by latter-day rhetoricians of "the strenuous life" and "the frontier
thesis" when they renounce "mushy sentimentalism" and "professional
charity."[80] But what about the strong voice of a woman who calls for an
end to the "making" of women by anyone other than themselves? What is
more appealing than the rhetoric of self-determination spoken by the
woman who has won acclaim as one of the earliest and most articulate
theorizers of modern management?

In *Co-Operative Housekeeping: How Not to Do It and How to Do It,*
Melusina Fay Peirce dismisses the notion that women must be tragic victims, pathetic man-made products of a society fated to suffer ironic gaps
between the promised idea and the experienced circumstance. In her
vision of a "Republic for 'Co-operative Housekeeping,'" women manage
their own lives. Neither melodrama nor sentimentality, nor tragedy, nor
pathos, nor irony have any part in the history she insists that these select

women are capable of writing for themselves. But according to Peirce's antivictimization plots, only native-born "pioneer housekeepers" have a role to play. All others—racial and ethnic groups like the Irish and "the ship-loads of miserable Chinese"—are incapable of anything more than being "posed and paraded as victims."[81] They have no stories acceptable for containment within Peirce's exclusionist historiography.

As we listen to self-assertive narratives by Peirce, Roosevelt, Ford, and others of their persuasion, we should also hear the stories told by victims and about victims, in addition to the few (too few) stories that project the actions of persons who rise to the creative possibilities latent within this highly charged culture.

When liberals and nonliberals alike look to stability, order, and the preservation of what they believe to be basic human values, *conservative* is the label most in evidence.[82] When the favored talisman term is engineering (the professional skill associated with the successful attainment of control, that is, efficiency),[83] we are tempted to use the word *hegemonic*. But we shouldn't. That would be too simple, too monolithic, too predetermining a conception, albeit a tempting one when we take into account the high stakes involved.

High Stakes

The Guiding Hand

Over the past two hundred years we have moved from the invisible hand of market forces "left almost out of sight," which Adam Smith depicted in his 1776 *Wealth of Nations,* to the visible hand "kept always in sight," the hand wielded by the management of industrial and business enterprises. This visible hand rode the crest from the late nineteenth century through the first two decades of the twentieth century, when Taylor's ideas gained widespread public attention; it was altered in those later stages, when the social engineering being introduced into all phases of public and private life laid its lash and offered its plum with hand signals that now you see, now you don't.[84]

The Conduct of Life

In the 1840s Marx and Engels formulated principles of social and ethical behavior based on the only moral absolute they believed the fire storm of historical change would leave unchanged: "Thou Shalt Not Steal."[85] By the close of the nineteenth century, industry, business, and government not only had developed innovative ways to "steal," but also new definitions for proper conduct and how to instill it by teaching, guiding, and aiding the populace at large through "organized morality."[86]

Taylorism and its progeny quickly became synonyms for systems of control. Samuel S. Marquis, director of the Ford Motor Company Sociological Department between 1917 and 1921, wrote that "the Ford idea is to increase a man's capacity for happiness and at the same time to increase his efficiency, his earning capacity, his worth in society, so that he may have access to the things he has been taught to enjoy."[87] Five interconnected capacities are placed on view here: (1) personal happiness, (2) earning power, (3) social worth, (4) consumer access to (5) what one has "been taught to enjoy." These connections are neither simple nor innocent, but the Ford Idea webs everything together, including ties between management control and social conduct, into "that spiritual saturnalia necessary to entire obsolete reform."[88]

The entangled relations between reform movements and the business enterprise permeated every sector of American public life in the years stretching from the 1880s through the Ford Plan and the Bull Moose campaign to the Depression years—decades marked by the efforts of Christian Socialists, adherents of the Social Gospel, muckrakers of every denomination, and the diverse entourage grouped around the National Progressive Party prior to the deletion of the "I" from "Ideal" in the formulation of the New Deal and the decline of intellectual radicalism in the 1940s.[89] The ideological positions available to reformers ranged from the radicalism of revolution to the conservatism of evolution.[90] Debates over management reform on the industrial front ricocheted between the merits of "industrial democracy" (which allowed labor a say in its own betterment) and the updated paternalism of welfare programs (which hoped to keep worker conduct and productivity under control). "Organize, organize!" became the cry of the conservative as well as of the socialist, and many shared the conviction that only an elite should be given the authority to do the organizing of that most unruly element of all.

The Human Element

By the 1910s the level of sophistication brought to bear upon new methods for the financing, production, and distribution of goods had leaped forward at an astonishing rate. At times it seemed there remained only one obstacle to a society perfected through the application of the scientific principles of management: what concerned parties labeled "the human element."

The very presence of *people* on the factory floor is enough to introduce questions of the troublesome relations among reform, conduct, and control. Yet determined efforts were made to close the gap between theories of efficient production and the effect of those practices upon the bodies involved. It was argued that not only would machines and human muscle be as one but that the machine was the great emancipator of mind and soul as well.

> It must be considered that the effect of task and bonus work under the proper conditions tends to greater industry, better discipline, a happier disposition and greater interest in work on the part of the workers. Greater regularity, greater accuracy and neatness must and do have an influence on health and character.[91]

An American scene mapped out in terms of binary divisions between the intelligent who manage and the stupid who obey was further complicated by the pressure of the ever-increasing public presence of women and non-"Americans." Even when contemporary discussions of the machine process were limited to male workers (as they largely were by Taylor, Veblen, and Ford), they created, reflected, and reinforced contrasting attitudes toward whites and blacks, and toward native-stock "Americans" as opposed to the "old" (Irish and Northern European) immigrants and "new" émigrés from Asia and Eastern and Southern Europe. Whatever their racial and ethnic background or class and status, women and children added yet another disordering element to disrupt the hope of installing efficient management systems. Management made its cut between useful workers—phlegmatic by nature and lacking in "rational" powers (not given to strikes and unionizing, for example)—and the wasteful intractability of the "savage" element, which introduced "wild facts" into a situation where the managers feared unmanaged, unpredictable irrationality above all else.

Wild Facts

The culture of management knows who its enemies are, or thinks it does. Some believed Nature was the model the human motor should copy; others saw natural instincts as the main problem. When it came to grading the controllability of the human element, the task was even more difficult. Not only work site issues were at stake. The management of daily behavior was the central concern of the social sciences and related areas of intellectual inquiry. While anonymous men, women, and children were being "jerked" about by speeded-up work processes, and while labor and management were in conflict over the mastery of the factory floor, debates among the academics forced the question of whether the conditions of modern life would result in the rule of the rational or in society's submission to the irrational.[92]

In 1901 William James, the man who delighted in defying easy antinomies, cheekily dramatized the folly that results when the dominant party in a "them versus us" situation acts as though the opposition does not exist. He defined the primary adversaries and located the central arena for the contest in a manner that reminds us of the little "amusette," and its accompanying frisson, that his brother Henry had written three years before. As in *The Turn of the Screw,* there was "the sunlit terrace" of "the classic-academic" mode, where "masculine" rationalism lives out its illusions of perfect control, and the Gothic underbrush of the inquiring "feminine" mind, "where uncouth forms lurk in the shadows."[93]

Once science found itself descending into the realm of the human element, one would think its practitioners would realize the importance of going beyond the divine abstraction of numbers toward the unholy mess James describes with glee as the "menagerie and the madhouse, the nursery, the prison, and the hospital." This is not necessarily the case. Rather than readjusting the idea of applied science and the social sciences to accommodate the presence of the wilder facts, "uncouth forms" were expected to do the adjusting: this includes all nature of men, but especially women, children, blacks, and immigrants—those social elements designated as the irrational forces requiring careful containment.

For William James dogmatism does not enter into either the practice of good science or of sound narrative. The wisest disciples of both enterprises temper their allegiance to intellectual rigor and their faith in reason with sensitivity to the unpredictability of whatever they study, whether the physical universe or human societies. But it is not surprising that less exalted members of the *social sciences,* already defensive about the professional merits of their yet unaccredited activities, valorized rationality to the extreme, felt threatened by the look of the irrational, and gave in to the temptation to be as "excessively determined" as possible.[94]

No wonder that the hard-edged "is" of technology and production got tangled with the amorphous "ought" of moral codes and ethical systems. No wonder that numbers, statistical graphs, blueprints for machine parts, and grids for measuring the physical world were viewed as armatures protecting order and predictability—instruments for bringing into conjunction a universe and a social structure obedient to an interlocking network of general laws.[95] Random stabs into the murk of laissez-faire practices were no longer sufficient in the realm of advanced capitalism. Planning and principles were all.

The One Best Way

Some of those in charge of making things work tried to hold the needle of human nature steady while drawing the thread of control and conduct toward it, but much of the time the reverse technique was applied. Standards, norms, and averages by which the efficacy of production goals and work conduct were judged came first; all else had to bend to them.

There is something about being the person charged with uncovering "the one true theory" that excites the imaginations of the best and the worst of us, notwithstanding differences of historical context that affect the nature of that excitement. Alfred Einstein coupled his belief in the irrationality of the universe with the consuming desire to discover the general law that governs all others. Karl Marx introduced previously untapped complexities into the analysis of social relationships, but he was head over heels in love with tracing the consequences of the great law of historical determinism, just as Charles Darwin and Sigmund Freud labored to develop conceptual schemes that would leave no missing links or excluded middles.

Emerson always shaved the fine line that separates spiritual wildness from the hobgoblin consistency of mental absolutism. "All science," Emerson writes in 1836 (speaking for the generations to come as well as his own), "has one aim, to find a theory of nature." In the self-knowledge that he was as susceptible as the next person to the wish to discover the ultimate explanation, Emerson checks hubris with his proviso, "Its test is, that it will explain all phenomena." [96]

In anticipation of William James, who later itemized what lies beyond the sunlit terrace where many scientists prefer to take tea, Emerson cites the "uncouth forms" that must be covered by any credible theory: "language, sleep, madness, dreams, beasts, sex." Who could be better than these two at intuiting how to get at theories that deflect the tendency to close down on "the everything" out there: Emerson, the poet "without a handle" who wrote brilliantly unsystematic prose; James, the philosopher who never got around to systematizing his own system.

Emerson and James were rarities. It is no surprise that the twentieth-century culture of management was densely populated by intelligent, determined individuals who wished to explain everything that had to be explained in order to achieve an efficient, productive, useful universe and society. No surprise, but there was concern about the consequences of their efforts—particularly when they tried to tidy up those facts they considered wild by forcing them into systems too narrow to accommodate the wildness they themselves let loose.

It was W. E. B. Du Bois who deftly identified the reason for the success of Bookerism, that particular form of systems-making that directly affected his own race: "this very singleness of vision and thorough oneness with his age is a mark of the successful man. It is as though Nature must needs make men narrow in order to give them force." [97]

Abundance Lost and Regained

In addition to its singleness, narrowness, force, and simplicity, the one true theory has the look of having retrieved lost abundance by the elimination of undue waste. The end of waste is the repossession of abundance, which is the primary reason for having the theory in the first place.

It seemed to the European writers of early promotion literature that the North American continent had an excess of everything. Part myth, part reality, and part tall tale, America's natural resources appeared infinite—all those pigeons, cod, and bison. Even after *things* began to vanish, the idea of an endless supply of natural goods continued to inform the imagination.[98] In the early 1890s the streets of "Middletown" blazed day and night with flaming torches of natural gas, even while Frederick Jackson Turner announced the end of free access to the abundance of the land.[99] Afterwards as well, according to the author of a "new-style" Fourth of July oration composed in 1926 for the house organ of the U.S. Chamber of Commerce: "We have no beggars, no meek and lowly, no cow-like women, no starved children. We are rich, fat, arrogant, superior. Why doesn't someone interpret us as we really are." [100]

Well into the 1920s Americans relied on the promise of unlimited prosperity imaged as the "warehouse" mentality—deplored by Emerson, celebrated by Edward Bellamy—which equated the nation's health with its stockpile of consumer goods. Still, general anxiety had begun to set in. The notion that America's abundance has no limits was rapidly being replaced by fears of the consequences of waste. Conservatives, Progressives, and liberals found a common cause in systems-making dedicated to staving off the depletions threatening all sectors of society—industry, business, government, public institutions, private lives, and the universe itself.[101]

While thinkers and policymakers debated whether waste was a matter of physics (thermodynamics), biology (laxity in the screening out of the weak, the ne'er-do-well, and the non-Caucasian), economics (relocation of trading centers), psychology (malaise of body and spirit), or social institutions (loosening of family ties, whether in government or the home), the rest of life went on. The body, the brain, the heart, the soul, and the world had to respond to lash and to plum, urged on by the code words "organize," "system," and (always) "efficiency." Otherwise, the culture of management would be forced to acknowledge the nightmare suggested by the First World War: that history is "unintended action" after all.[102]

Appropriate Actions

The narratives that emerge from the culture of management contain many kinds of endings. Say we wish to consider alternatives to conclusions that enforce stasis within a universe of irregular motions and erratic time shifts. Say we reject endings that inflict unbearable rules of rational order upon an often confused society. Consider, then, Pierre Janet's way as described by William James and the Gramscian way as Stuart Hall outlines it. The first looks like the best method the liberal imagination has for solving bad endings when we are tangled with things as they are; the second is inspired by the radical imagination of things as they might yet become.

Janet's procedure is used to liberate "the poor, passive, trance-personality" that has become "stuck" in a "stagnant dream." Janet's patients, mostly female "hysterics," are locked into "some perverse buried fragment of consciousness" that inhibits "the normal flow of life." Victims of "senseless hallucinations" that are "stereotyped and habitual," their stories stand for all bad stories told of assembly lines that atrophy thought, emotion, and will.[103]

Viewing Janet as a benign narrator-manager, we discern the implications of his curative plot. By means of hypnosis, one by one Janet returns his patients to that original scene during which "the primary self" is overwhelmed by the "stability, monotony, and stupidity" imposed by the "subordinate selves" that take over the management of the patient's life. Janet reaches back to that point in past time where the victim is fixated, both then and now, upon the panic of her faultily or misread story. He then pulls her forward into a present provided with a different future. By viewing life as plot development, he gives her old story "a different *dénouement.*" He substitutes "a comic issue for the old tragical one which had made so deep an impression." The narrator-manager draws forth the submerged story of "the hidden self" and corrects it with a "happy ending," thereby ending the nightmare of a ceaseless repetition of "stability, monotony, and stupidity."[104]

Janet's method has much to offer. It is excellent narrativization except for one thing: the inherent problem raised whenever someone other than ourselves shapes the tale and the telling. Janet's management procedures eliminate wasteful, unproductive conduct but create a managed life all the same. We think it would be nicer (albeit a mere delusion?) if we were able to rewrite personal histories after our own fashion, in terms of our own sense of plot structures and anticipated conclusions.[105]

Gripped by another delusion (as his critics argue), Stuart Hall believes the Gramscian way will enable us to do this by relocating us within narratives of agency. Working from

> Gramsci's recognition that every crisis is also a moment of reconstruction; that there is no destruction which is not also reconstruction; that, historically nothing is dismantled without also attempting to put something new in its place; that every form of power not only excludes but produces something, . . . [we are given] an entirely new conception of crisis—and of power.

Hall argues that we, not others, can seize "the opportunity to reorganise in new ways" the "old economic, social, cultural order"—to "refashion, to modernise and move ahead." In order to make such stories work, we must first recognize (in James's terms as well as Gramsci's) that there is no "block universe," no coherent ideology that predetermines the plots we are given to enact or the conclusions toward which we progress. Instead, society "articulates into a configuration, different subjects, different identities, different projects, different aspirations. It does not reflect, it *constructs,* a 'unity' out of difference."[106]

Throughout *Taylored Lives* we shall find instances of the inspiration of these two "ways" for remaking bad stories into stories that honor the necessities of "the human element." But we also see endings of another kind, drawn from texts that write/manage people's lives according to routines of "stability, monotony, and stupidity" in the name of "the best way." These stories speak of the questionable consequences that occur when reformers try somewhat too officiously, and inefficiently, to substitute good endings for bad. A handful of endings attempt to reach the goal of "industrial democracy"—that American version of radical action in which workers sit down with bosses to write plots agreeable to both. If none of the conclusions found here meets all of the requirements for Gramscian narrativization, this suggests either that (1) the plots were not as wildly revolutionary as total self-telling requires, or (2) faith in the capacity to control one's own narrative is itself a flagrant act of reactionary backpedaling toward the dead old days when selves were thought to be other than well-managed machinery.

Marx and Engels often despaired over the apparent inability of American workers to release their tremendous energy into radical action. They singled out two factors preventing this "irresistible force" from spreading "with the rapidity of a prairie fire": the myth of American exceptionalism and Americans' "Anglo-Saxon contempt for all theory." [107] An additional obstacle to the radicalization of American society came from the Progressives, whose "pluralistic politics" of reform tried to achieve "social justice without socialism," even as they sought to beat back old-line conservatism. [108] Largely overlooked by the politically minded was yet another force William James said ought to be tapped: the ordinary folk who possessed "the Unclassified Residuum"—the "irregular phenomena," "the *"wild* facts . . . which threaten to break up the accepted system." [109]

This is James speaking once again about the need for his contemporaries to reach beyond the notion that "the totality of Truth" is the possession of any one kind of mind, especially that mind cloistered within the academy or fetishized by the elite culture. He opens his 1890 *Scribner's* essay, "The Hidden Self," by reminding his immediate audience—"you, gentle subscriber to this MAGAZINE"—that neither it nor "the scientific-academic mind" is as capable of responding vitally to "the Unclassified Residuum" as is "the general public"—the readers of the "popular press," the possessors of "the feminine-mystical mind." James's conclusion (stated in his inimitably nonconclusive way): "it is the Mystics who have usually proved to be right about the *facts,* while the Scientifics had the better of it in respect to the theories."

However astute Marx and Engels were about America's debilitating "Anglo-Saxon contempt for all theory" systems-making of every kind dominated James's generation, as did the arrogance of those who assume that they have the power "to discern the totality of Truth." Yet there were and are those who believe in spontaneity, whether they are readers of the *Fireside Companion* (James's example) or Oliver Wendell Holmes, Jr., whose book *The Common Law* did a good job of undermining absolutes by focusing upon the facts of "the hidden self." For those, like James, who trace cultural possibilities (members of the Frankfurt School on their off days, those who speak out of the Birmingham School venue on all their days), spontaneity means following facts as well as theories. The two, in tandem, will take us through a world "full of partial stories that run parallel to one another, beginning and ending at odd times, [that] mutually interlace and interfere at points, but [which] we cannot unify . . . completely." [110]

To be assured, spontaneity must be historicized moment by moment; it is just as much a party to "control" factors as any other so-called impulse. [111] But this does not erase the validity it has for many as a possible force of resistance. Note that Adorno believed spontaneity "diminishes" when "administration" takes over from "culture," when "planning" becomes more important than "individual impulse, predetermining this impulse in turn, reducing it to the level of illusion, and no longer tolerating that play of forces which was expected to give rise to a free totality." [112]

Note that spontaneity suggests putting up with the uncertainties and pleasures of "inherent vice"—the chemical process used to describe what happens to the surfaces of paintings undergoing "traction crackle," "varnish slide," "perennial plastic flow." [113] Note as well that spontaneity means innovations that result from the play of "idle curiosity"—the sport for which scientific management withholds its approval, unless it can actively draw such curiosity into serving the needs of its own program. [114] All these sweet dreams of freedom aside, what matters is that spontaneity can provoke crises by causing us to look intently at the lessons the culture of management derived from its own sense of "spontaneous" crisis.

Capitalism is always in process, as is the revolutionary spirit whose leaders must "criticize themselves constantly, interrupt themselves continually." [115] From this point of view, we are encouraged to write narratives more to our liking, "depending on the historian's choice of plot-structure," since "in history what is tragic from one perspective is comic from another." [116] This does not merely mean rewriting what has already taken place. It entails *writing ahead* to alter futures. There is nothing frivolous about valorizing "self-assertive entertainment and self-transcending commitment." "Stories and histories and other narrative or descriptive accounts help us to *escape boredom and indifference*" by the commitment "either to change the world or to change ourselves." [117]

In the early years of this century, George Herbert Meade proclaimed the power to change societies, a power that arises from the "novelty" originating in the interplay of the "me" (the "conventional, habitual individual"), the "I" ("one who reacts to [the] community and in his reaction to it . . . changes it"), and the Others whose status quo is shaken into life by this "interrelationship of energies." [118] Karl Marx, Ralph Waldo Emerson, William James, George Herbert Meade, and many of their female contemporaries believed that we not only should, but could, transform ourselves and our society through interchanges with "the others." This hardly means playing with " 'mere difference' cosily embraced as happy liberal pluralism." [119]

Granted, many of the narratives that lie ahead will disappoint by not going far enough, by failing to be sufficiently "wild" and "idle," by not giving themselves over to transforming forces of "inherent vice" or "mystical" facts, or simply because the wild and the idle have been co-opted by the managers in charge. True, too many reformers "meant well" but accomplished little because of their complicity with "the productivist obsessions" of the business interests they sought to correct, self-deceived as they were by a "positivist belief that scientific knowledge could float in a cloud of neutrality high above the sordid realm of economic and political power." [120]

Still, gains were being made in those heady and anxious years, when it seemed that all of life's ills might be solved through an inspired application of industrial, business, and human engineering. They were not solved; they still are not. The effort, for example, to "rationalize" twelve diverse European nations into one monocratic Common Market administration reminds us that Taylorism in whatever form does not rest at a distance "in a museum case"; it affects the way we live today. Nonetheless, whatever history's propensity for "unintended action," history need not be defined (as it was by Dos Passos's disillusioned young men and women) as a narrative string of "blahblahblahblahs." [121] The stories are much better than that.

ONE

Barbaric Fictions

"Well, hell, here we are!"

NO, THIS IS NOT YOUR AUTHOR starting off by being pretentiously profane. This is Richard Harding Davis, the hugely successful "popular" writer from turn-of-the-century America, quoting from Stephen Crane, one of the major "serious" authors of the same decade. In turn, Crane is creating what an American infantryman said upon gaining the top of San Juan Hill during one of the decisive engagements of the Cuban campaign of 1898, inaugurating America's imperialistic moves, first into the Caribbean, then, the following year, into the Pacific.

This quotation resonates with questions of geographical, temporal, and psychological placement (*here* we are, but *where* is that? and will *now* be different from later on?). Why this is the place to commence *Taylored Lives* will become clear over the course of the next two chapters. The moment alluded to by Davis and Crane, presented in a particular manner, will be linked with other moments in other stylistic modes, all commemorating "whereness." They have been extracted from narratives called "barbaric," because William James and Thorstein Veblen implied in 1899 that this was the best term to use. These examples will demonstrate the uneasy mix of facts, values, and efficiency systems at the center of many turn-of-the-century American texts, including those of James and Veblen as well as the systems they chose to interrogate.[1] In these texts, "facts" indicate the importance assigned to scientific rationalism, "values" underwrite the moral arguments intended to validate imperialistic visions, and "efficiency systems" point up the diverse considerations that men like Frederick Winslow Taylor and Thorstein Veblen (Max Weber, too) brought to their treatment of two major forces of their age: "the business enterprise" and "the machine process." Also intertwined with these narratives of business and machines are stories of war.

Wm. James (social critic); T. Veblen (literary theorist)

It is 1899 and William James goes on the attack in the *Boston Evening Transcript* against the expansion of American force into the Philippines. James mocks the clichés of a national morality that asserts, "We are to be missionaries of civilization, and to bear the white man's burden. . . . We must show our ideals, plant our order, impose our God." But he is even more scathing in his analysis of an imperialist rhetoric that defines "civilization" in terms of the "big" and the "loud."[2]

James's immediate target may be President McKinley, whose recent speech at a Boston banquet is the occasion for James to express his anger, but it could just as well be the voice of Theodore Roosevelt he deplores: "big, hollow, resounding, corrupting, sophisticating, confusing torrent of mere brutal momentum and irrationality." It is not merely "the cold potgrease . . . of cant" used by McKinley, the front man, that James detests. It is the delight that men like Roosevelt take in bigness, in noise, and in "the war fever" while advancing policies of imperialism.[3] "Cold" marks the presence of that ruthless and efficient common sense by which "advanced" societies prefer to be known. "Fever" attests to the lingering traces within such societies of the hotly irrational impulses associated with preindustrial culture, which it is the mission of "cold" countries to obliterate.

In singling out the feverishness of the American bent toward imperialist expansionism, James brilliantly captures the strange amalgam of archaic passions and dispassionate modernist calculation, the mixture Veblen would anatomize that same year in his assessment of the way the modern age simultaneously encapsulates older and newer stages of evolutionary development. James remarks that the imperialists' "state of consciousness"

> is so new, so mixed of primitively human passions and in political circles, of calculations that are anything but primitively human; so at variance, moreover, with their former mental habits; and so empty of definite data and content; that they face various ways at once, and their portraits should be taken with a squint.

It is 1899, and Veblen's *Theory of the Leisure Class* has just been published.[4] His idea of evolution goes like this: (1) the earliest stage is that of the savage—peaceable, easygoing, nonreflective. (2) The next stage is that of the barbarian—predatory, warlike, given to ruthless seizures of life and property. Then come the quasi-predatory, overtly bellicose eras that (3) introduce capitalism and, eventually, (4) late nineteenth-century "pecuniary culture," which redirects the barbarians' brutal energies into the marketplace rather than onto the battlefield, replacing the bludgeon with shrewd calculation.

Veblen's economic and social theories (what David Riesman has described as an "anthropology" that was "a Just So story of stages in a universal unilinear human destiny")[5] insist that vestiges from these earlier times linger into the twentieth century, somewhat after the manner of the "tails" we all possess, thanks to our ape ancestors. As Veblen eyes his own generation, he detects "the conservation of archaic traits" from the savage era, however overlaid they may be with subsequent "barbarian traditions and conventionalities" and "readjustments to the exigencies of civilized life."

In 1899 Veblen is mainly concerned with indicating the clash between the "conserving" traits of the savage type and the acquisitive traits of feudal lords, which are being carried forward into the final days of the barbaric nineteenth-century business enterprise. In order to expose the tensions between an ancient morality of truthfulness, equity, and prideful workmanship, and latter-day extensions of "the methods and animus of barbarian life," he underscores the amoral aggressiveness and sly seizure of "trophies" in both contemporary warfare and business. Such "archaic traits" retard the advance of the truly "modern" man, the one whom Veblen soon will identify as the technologist who commands the efficiency systems seeking to banish irrationality and waste.

But now it is 1906. In his essay "The Place of Science in Modern Civilisation" Veblen reads civilization as a condition directed by the "matter-of-fact" nature of modern science. The coolness of the "technology of the machine industry"—which gives its disciples "an impersonal dispassionate insight into the material facts"—appears to have rendered obsolete the feverish self-interest of the business enterprise that had ruled the American consciousness less than a decade before.[6] Suddenly Veblen stops in the midst of describing the economic effects of the scientific principles being applied by the new elite, the engineering technocrats starting to gain authority within the nation's industrial plants. Unexpectedly, he starts to write as a literary theorist about the difference between narratives told by modern men of science and narratives told by literary types (whether the preindustrial savage or the barbarian of contemporary business culture).

"The ancient human predilection for discovering a dramatic play of passion and intrigue in the phenomena of nature still asserts itself" in the face of modern circumstances that privilege "matter-of-fact knowledge" and the impersonal nature of scientific inquiry. Veblen's poetics implies that modern-day storytellers often write out of their "revulsion . . . against the inhumanly dispassionate sweep of the scientific quest." Because of their "savage need of a spiritual interpretation (dramatisation) of phenomena"—whether "furtively or by an overt break of consistency" with "the truths of that modern science whose dominion they dare not question"—they "still seek comfort" from "their jungle-fed spiritual sensibilities." [7]

"Archaic narratives" appearing by 1900 might all possess vestiges of the "dramatic play of passion and intrigue," but Veblen's comments, together with James's, suggest that distinctions are to be made between narratives formed by the savages and by the barbarians of that day. Savages of the 1890s retain faith in nature and spirit as essential to men's lives. They subscribe to a textual tone that reflects the "smooth and easy," the "sweet and indispensable archaic way of thinking." Their barbaric brethren go in for noise and heat, what William James called the "big, . . . resounding, . . . confusing torrent of mere brutal momentum and irrationality." In contrast both to the savage's gentle fireside tale and the rousing barbaric narrative is that yet-to-be-written story structure intended for the true man of the swiftly approaching technological era—Veblen himself. Placed within that perfected narrative, Veblen would act as "the disinterested observer" who sublimates personal passions to the "morality" of postpredatory cooperative ventures and enlightened efficiency systems. [8]

Like Veblen in the opening years of the twentieth century, Frederick Winslow Taylor envisions the takeover of the machine process by dispassionate engineers, heroic agents of a utopian future in which industrial warfare will no longer exist. But whereas Taylor believed that the perfected future was almost at hand if only wise men would follow his lead, Veblen sized up the situation as being rather more complicated. According to Veblen's 1906 historiography, businessmen are still in control. "Modern warlike policies" still command the political scene as well as the business enterprise. As for *the future there* that might replace the present tense of "Well, hell, here we are!": Veblen could not predict exactly what lay ahead. Perhaps the archaic war culture would remain in ascendance; perhaps the pecuniary culture would continue to dominate for a while longer. Still, Veblen held to his belief in the eventual destruction of an increasingly outmoded business system and the emergence of the engineer—the unsentimental technocrat—as the leader of a reformed industrial age.

Neither Veblen's historiography nor his poetics of barbaric storytelling faced up to the fact that a variation on the modern engineer-manager was currently figuring in an entirely different set of narratives. The passionate patriot engaged in imperialist crusades was not the kind of stiff-collared public hero Herbert Hoover, the ex-engineer, became by the close of World War I. The favored type—charismatic, aggressive, sexy—is represented, straightforwardly, by Robert Clay, the heroic protagonist of Richard Harding Davis's 1897 novel, *Soldiers of Fortune,* and, more obliquely, by Charlotte Stant, who masterminds managerial campaigns so magnificently in Henry James's astute critique of barbaric fictions, *The Golden Bowl* of 1904.

From the 1870s through the close of the nineteenth century, Americans like John Fiske busied themselves in writing hopeful versions of evolutionary theory in which they (like their inspiration Herbert Spencer) called up pictures of social progress that veered from militarism toward peaceful industrialism, thereby transforming the struggle for brute survival into "the continuous weakening of selfishness and the continuous strengthening of sympathy."[9] In actuality, the uses to which Spencerism and its latter-day counterpart, Teddyism, were put meant switching terms for strength and weakness so that the strong might still triumph over the weak.

The virtue of "sympathy" became the vice of "sentimentality" in the view of the advocates of manliness (unaware of the sentimental patriotism to which they themselves were prone), while "selfishness" became "strength" once it was associated with the American Way of predatory business and industry. Theodore Roosevelt never faltered in viewing weakness as proof one had "failed in life." "Failures" were men marred by "misfortune" or "misconduct," with no distinction made between bad behavior and bad luck. Manliness meant being right, lucky, and virile. It meant the American male's power to breed healthy children; it meant being the strong father of the nation's government and the leader of the world's destiny.[10]

Not only politicians marketed the rhetorical style and narrative mode that redefined who was hard and who was soft, a style and mode that was at once "archaic" in its harkening back to feudalistic times and very "modern" in its practices. By the 1910s, Max Weber, student of the "heroic age of capitalism," would comment upon the "formalistic, hard, correct character" of capitalist activities, while V. I. Lenin, leader in the toppling of capitalistic structures, would mandate "the use of compulsion" in the fight against "the practice of a lily-livered proletarian government" standing in the way of productive labor.[11] By the 1920s, enemies of both American reformers and foreign revolutionaries would speak out against "mushy sentimentalism," declaring that "the 100 percent American believes in the doctrine of selfishness."[12] The "place of science in modern civilisation" was far from what Veblen and Taylor had had in mind during the previous two decades. The post-1920 American business model did not fit the Bildungsroman Taylor devised prior to World War I, when he plotted the emergence of the hero of scientific management; nor did that model synchronize with Veblen's exemplary tales about the possibility of evolution toward scientific rationalism. That proverbial miss (which is as much as a mile) separated what Taylor and Veblen wanted to have happen to history and the history that actually happened to them. One reason for the disjunction was the way they underestimated the inefficiency of societies driven by the martial spirit, whether expressed in the factory or on the battlefield.[13]

Efficiency was a primary virtue for both Taylor and Veblen. The former believed that efficiency would bring moral rightness into shop management while raising productivity and profits; the latter believed that efficiency would curb the barbaric sentimentalism underlying purportedly rational economic processes. Perhaps both men should have listened to the stories told by veterans of the War Between the States.

Mismanagement at Chancellorsville (1863)

By the time Veblen wrote of the workings of the early twentieth-century machine process, Weber had detailed the mechanisms of modern bureaucracy and Taylor had touted the common sense of scientific management; the narrative forms complicitous in the advocacy of efficiency systems had taken on a different cast from the efficiency extolled in Transcendentalist fables of cosmic economy and compensation schemes. They were no longer like the stories warning against waste that Emerson told to the Mechanics' Apprentices' Library Association in Boston; they were of necessity different from the classical Marxist recasting of the wastes expended between the reigns of Napoleon I and Louis Napoleon in the 1851 *Eighteenth Brumaire of Louis Bonaparte*. But they were not all *that* different from the scandalous narratives of wartime waste that emerged between the 1860s and the mid-1890s.

Soon narratives taking their contexts from the moves of the United States into the Caribbean and the Pacific would extol efficient wars and rational business enterprises, even while glorifying their own kind of wastefulness of human life. But prior to that bully time when Roosevelt "left Washington and touseled his hair and became a rough Rider,"[14] cautionary tales were being told, tales of the mismanagement and waste that had taken place upon the factory floor of the American battlefields in the 1860s.

Miss Ravenel's Conversion from Secession to Loyalty by John De Forest is by and large a "smooth and easy" romance devoted to reconciliation, compensation, and coming out even in the ledger books. But buried within its expertly executed formula is a disruptive scene, one that suddenly appears from another realm of storytelling. Surgeons in hastily erected hospital facilities at the edge of the battlefield dismember the

Young American whom Emerson, in 1841, had prophesied would find completion as the Whole Man.

> In the centre of this mass of suffering stood several operating tables, each burdened by a grievously wounded man. . . . Underneath were great pools of clotted blood, amidst which lay amputated fingers, hands, arms, feet, and legs, only a little more ghastly in color than the faces of those who waited their turn on the table.[15]

In nightmarish anticipation of the mass production processes and efficient parceling of machine parts later to be perfected by the management team at the Ford Motor Works (and in adumbration of the "dismantling of Lemuel Pitkin" required by the market economy portrayed in Nathanael West's *A Cool Million*) stand the "surgeons, who never ceased their awful labor, . . . daubed with blood to the elbows."

Caught within tragic narratives of waste, surgeons execute their dread efficiency systems at the edges of battlefields. In the midst of action, officers and men enact scenes of comic confusion and ludicrous mismanagement—scenes that would horrify all would-be scientific managers, whether John Quincy Adams, compiler of the 1821 report on standard weights and measures, or Frederick Winslow Taylor, who meticulously pursued "speed" and "feed" studies at Midvale Steel in the mid-1880s.

Take the battle of Chancellorsville, for instance, as it appeared to those who were there on May 2, 1863:

> May I never be a witness to another such scene! On the one hand was a solid column of infantry retreating at double-quick from the face of the enemy, who were already crowding their rear; on the other was a dense mass of beings who had lost their reasoning faculties and were flying from a thousand fancied dangers as well as from the real danger that crowded so close upon them. . . . On the hill were ten thousand of the enemy, pouring their murderous volleys in upon us, yelling and hooting, to increase the alarm and confusion; hundreds of cavalry horses, left riderless . . . were dashing frantically about in all directions; a score of batteries of artillery were thrown into disorder . . . ; battery wagons, ambulances, horses, men, cannon, caissons, all jumbled.
>
> Union Army witness.[16]

> . . . stampeded pack-mules, officers' horses, caissons, with men and horses running for their lives.
>
> Major General Darius N. Couch[17]

In the stampede of the Eleventh Corps, beef cattle, ambulances, mules, artillery, wagons, and horses became stuck in the mud, and others coming on rushed them down, so that when the fight was over the pile of debris in the marsh was many feet high.

Brevet Major General Alfred Pleasonton

There occurred a "jam" of living and dead men, friends and enemies, and horses, and the weight of the rear of our squadron broke us into utter confusion, so that at the moment every man was for himself.

Captain Andrew B. Wells

As he rounded a hillock, he perceived that the roadway was now a crying mass of wagons, teams, and men. From the heaving tangle issued exhortations, commands, imprecations. Fear was sweeping it all along. The cracking whips bit and horses plunged and tugged. The white-topped wagons strained and stumbled in their exertions like white sheep.

Private Henry Fleming[18]

Then the camps of the wounded—O heavens, what scene is this?—is this indeed *humanity*—these butchers' shambles? There are several of them. There they lie, in the largest, in an open space in the woods, from 200 to 300 poor fellows—the groans and screams—the odor of blood, mixed with the fresh scene of the night, the grass, the trees—that slaughter-house! . . . One man is shot by a shell, both in the arm and leg—both are amputated—there lie the rejected members. Some have their legs blown off—some bullets through the breast—some indescribably horrid wounds in the face or head, all mutilated, sickening, torn, gouged out.

Nurse Walt Whitman[19]

The rout at Chancellorsville—which Stephen Crane later would write up as the emblem of war dreams in collision with war practices on the eve of the nation's moves into Cuba and Puerto Rico—largely centered around the Eleventh Corps. This unit, whose "cowardice" was constantly explained in press accounts by the fact that it was made up of non-American, German-speaking "foreigners," was headed by Major General Oliver O. Howard, noted for being a "strictly conscientious" man who led "a pure, holy, and consistent life."[20] Howard was witnessed that day by yet another soldier on the run, as the general stood alone amidst the fleeing men,

his maimed arm embracing a stand of colors that some regiment
had deserted, while with his sound arm he was gesticulating to the
men to make a stand by their flag. With bared head he was plead-
ing with his soldiers, literally weeping as he entreated the unheeding
horde.

Cavalryman John L. Collins[21]

As General Howard stated more than twenty years later in the section
devoted to the Chancellorsville fiasco in *Battles and Leaders of the Civil War,*
"everything, every sort of organization that lay in the path of the mad
current of panic-stricken men, had to give way and be broken into fragments."[22] In May 1863, General Howard—the man who led "a pure, holy,
and consistent life"—was unable to provide a battle plan that held firm
(just as he later was unable to manage effectively the Freedmen's Bureau,
which was placed under his direction in 1865).

Instead, it was another officer (on the opposing side) whose management prowess helped "win" the battle. It was Stonewall Jackson who, in
Howard's words, "in bold planning, in energy of execution, which he had
the power to diffuse, in indefatigable activity and moral ascendency, . . .
stood head and shoulders above his confreres." But alas, in the melee of
combat Jackson was wounded by the fire of one of his own men confused
by the clash of arms, and died. The good manager's carefully controlled
gains were cancelled by the random mismanagement that did him in.
Robert E. Lee was left with no efficiency expert to assist him in pursuing
this barbaric war (an enterprise formed out of a jumble of moral, political,
and business interests) to its swift close. And so the war dragged on, wasting and maiming—a constant symbol of how not to run a war, a business,
or a nation.

What did the battles and leaders of the Civil War contribute to the
narratives called upon to depict the predatory nature of a postwar society
moving away from internal clashes toward wars flung out across the
Caribbean and the Pacific?

Battles and Leaders of the Civil War, published in the late 1880s under
the genteel sanction of *The Century,* was a compilation of reminiscences
and reports that attempted to bring some order to the chaos of the actual
events. It struggled to supply those causal relations that historians find
crucial, whether their studies follow the patterns of Emersonian Transcendentalist historiography, Marxist material history, Veblen's economic
theory, or Weber's science of sociology. The Century Company's four
neat volumes gave the illusion of having arranged the clamor of a war that
in fact never benefited from a cooly efficient administrative program,

which would have made possible a rational understanding of what was taking place.

In the fragments that make up *Specimen Days,* Whitman cries out, where is humanity to be located in the midst of accounts of the slaughterhouse? *Battles and Leaders,* as both publishing venture and business enterprise, is filled with data about "the human element," but human suffering is belittled by data insisting upon scientific notions of reasoned causes, even though they lead to catastrophic results.

The battle of Chancellorsville has no plot, no central protagonists to stay the course (too many are incompetent; the sole hero is killed by mistake), no origins, no endings, no moral, no unifying point of view, no ruling tone for the telling. There are only disparate accounts by a random scattering of officers who describe the confusion taking place in the ranks as their men break and run, bewildered by the lack of a scientific plot to follow or the absence of an ancient bard, who might narrate into being the meaning of the extravagant waste surrounding them.

Thirty-odd years later Stephen Crane wrote a version of the battle of Chancellorsville that divorces itself from the pleasure in barbaric storytelling being reintroduced during the 1890s.[23] Crane's tale of May 1863 is set down by an author in 1895 who moves beyond the margins of narratives finding public favor at mid-decade. The stories against which Crane reacts were told for the edification of the citizens of a nation being readied to bring the concept of "good" and well-managed American wars into line with the amoral facts of political developments, which, in turn, invited the telling of such narratives. But from where Crane positions himself within the boundaries of his own postfeudal poetics, he launches a story about his decade's reabsorption in the ethos of feudalism—a feudalism (as Veblen began to point out in 1899) already in ironic collision with the machine processes of turn-of-the-century industrialism.

To point up but one example, Crane's inclusion of both beast and mechanistic imagery in his representation of the Civil War battle scene of 1863 is a cool comment upon the feverish synthesis of waste and efficiency, barbaric impulse and modern rationality, amoral acts and moralistic intentions that made up the cultural myths of 1895. The only moments of order and peace Crane's soldiers experience come as they create interludes of "the domestic romance" for themselves, carrying out, as it were, the practical advice of Henry Fleming's mother—keep your socks dry. But as we shall see, mother wisdom will be taken out of the hands of the boys and given over to the managers in charge of domesticating the machines of business and war.

The War of 1812 and the Birth of Teddyism

By 1898 Theodore Roosevelt would be making history on his own in quasi-predatory terms,[24] whereas Henry Adams, who had long since despaired of ever becoming a major figure in American narratives of power, remained out of sight, reformulating a scientific historiography. But by looking back one decade into the 1880s, we find both Roosevelt and Adams in the act of commenting as historians upon the relations between American wars and American reforms, and upon the relations among war, reform, and efficiency systems. Roosevelt in his twenties and Adams in his fifties were writing, respectively, of the Naval War of 1812 and of the administrations of Jefferson and Madison (a chronicle that treats the management of the 1812 war).

Emerson remarked that history is biography. Rear Admiral William S. Sims, in his preface to Theodore Roosevelt's tour de force of 1882, *The Naval War of 1812* (composed at high speed in a matter of months when Roosevelt was but twenty-four), makes clear that a history book like Roosevelt's is itself biographical.[25] Roosevelt's assessment of why the United States Navy defeated the British at the same time as the nation's army fared so wretchedly on land focuses upon the dashing efficiency of the navy on the seas and the appalling inadequacies of the government back home.[26] But Roosevelt's account is also, in Sims's words, "a document which helps us to appreciate his character and understand his career. 'By their works shall ye know them' applies to historical works as well as to works of another sort" (7:ix).

In 1882 the future assistant secretary of the U.S. Navy and the future president of the United States is already revealing his ability to dig out hard facts, to apply "habits of accuracy and thoroughness," to manifest his delight in "the ideas and acts of those men who have made [this] nation great," and to display "his painstaking industry and versatility" (7:ix). But above all, what makes Roosevelt's critique of military success at sea and failure in administrative procedures what it is—and what *he* is—is his "intense patriotism" (7:ix). Roosevelt is an accomplished historian precisely *because* he is the patriot desirous, as he informed the American Historical Association in 1912, of telling the "exact truth" of "our disasters and shortcomings just as well as our triumphs" (7:xiii). *Because* he is the vigorous patriot, still others declared that Roosevelt's historian's pen exposes the falsehood and ignorance of narratives created out of "mere offensive braggadocio." In contrast to the inadequacy of previous accounts, he expounds a "true history" based on Rooseveltian principles of character: "the noble idea of the gentleman as opposed on the one hand to the practices of the bully, and on the other hand to the creed of the coward and weakling" (7:xvi).

Post-Veblenesque historical accounts would be more ironically aware than Roosevelt's narrative was that "manliness" and "weakness" are terms all too appropriate for the quasi-predatory members of barbaric societies. Newer histories written after the 1890s, concerned with such matters as whether naval ships are well designed and capably administered, might well model themselves upon the language of the later reports compiled by scientific management teams—language inspired by the principles Taylor was developing in the 1880s, at the same time Roosevelt and Adams were engaged in their historiographic projects.

Truly "accurate" histories would include, for example, calculations of the amount of metal discharged by the guns on each side. Indeed Roosevelt includes such data: pages of it in such detail that within four years regulations required every U.S. naval vessel to possess a copy.[27] But Roosevelt keeps introducing other matters indicative of his particular brand of history-as-biography. While stating that "heavy metal is not the only factor to be considered," he will insist that the ships' personnel be measured in light of its "Americanness"—that special quality (as Sims paraphrases it) possessed by men of a free nation that encourages "self-reliance" through a "life of adventure and hardship" (7:xx).

Roosevelt stated that "courage united with skill" enabled the U.S. Navy to triumph on the seas in 1812 (7:xxi). In contrast, land battles resulted in defeat because of the "triumph of imbecility" that characterized the administration of James Madison (7:xxii). As the nation's top executive, Madison was responsible for the country's faltering fortunes. Because of him the United States "drifted helplessly into a conflict in which only the navy prepared by the Federalists twelve years before, and weakened rather than strengthened during the intervening time, saved us from complete and shameful defeat" (7:xxii).

Roosevelt's preface to the third edition (1883) slammed home who was most at fault in retarding the navy's eventual victory. Madison's mismanagement of military affairs exposed the legacy of "criminal folly" he inherited, "the ludicrous and painful folly and stupidity" of "the government founded by Jefferson" (7:xxxi).[28] Such a botched state of affairs was exactly what Roosevelt would not allow once he stopped writing history and began to insert himself into history as the acting secretary of the United States Navy in 1897 and as president in 1901.

Efficiency experts who hew to the seemingly scientific impersonality of Veblen's historiography or who work according to Taylor's apparently dispassionate principles of scientific management do not stoop to ad hominem arguments about who is great and who is small. Strength and weakness of character and the moral quality of individual conduct would not, one might think, enter in. Yet as we shall see in the following chapters, the case is otherwise. This certainly was the case in regard to Roosevelt. The efficiency-expert-cum-happy-barbarian felt free to think in terms of the great man he knew he would become and the helpless weaklings he scorned to emulate.[29]

Roosevelt adhered to the barbaric custom of viewing wars as moral contests between manliness and weakness. This required him to insinuate melodramas of right and wrong behavior into his historical accounts of battle fire. When describing the management practices of the War of 1812 in his dual role as accurate historian and passionate patriot, Roosevelt included biographies of Jefferson and Madison as ineffectual administrators, men lacking in character, leaders without courage. These biographies of failure are rehearsals of the autobiographies of success Roosevelt soon will write about his own prowess at the time of his own wars.

The War of 1812 and the Growth of Adamsian Doubts

As a historian of the events bracketing either side of the War of 1812, Henry Adams did not attempt to write his own autobiography. The nine volumes upon which he labored throughout the 1880s (overlapping the demonic spurt of Roosevelt's compositions in 1882) concern the actions of notable men. At that stage in his career, Adams still held to the belief, however qualified, that whoever had achieved a high place is part of the story of how the new republic fared after 1800, the date he chose as his point of entry. The presences of Jefferson and Madison in Adams's telling, however, hardly bear out the Emersonian doctrine of history as the shadow of great men. The "dramatic view of history" called out for heroes, with "war as the chief field of heroic action," but "history as a science" (*his* view of science, that is) might involve "lack of motive, intelligence, and morality, the helplessness characteristic of many long periods in the face of crushing problems, and the futility of human efforts to escape from difficulties religious, political, and social."[30]

Adams's most ambitious attempts to formulate historical writing according to the principles of scientific inquiry lay ahead. They would culminate in the 1900s, the same decade in which Thorstein Veblen and Lester Ward would apply similar principles to the writing of economics and sociology. But even in the 1880s Adams's work was at odds with Rooseveltian readings of history, which barbarized Emerson's earlier gentle-savage treatment of Representative Men. Adams's research did not yield unassailable truths and pugnacious assurances derived from merging technical skill with bully-boy strength. He did not linger over images of courageous American fighting men who convert history-as-science into barbaric fictions of adventure, romance, and sentimentality. Rather, Adams preferred to stay with subjects of interest "for the man of science rather than for dramatists or poets" (1334). Whereas Roosevelt wrote history filled with "the archaic traits" that Veblen assigned to turn-of-the-century predators, Adams aspired to write history as Veblen argued that the truly modern mind conceives of it.

Like Roosevelt, Adams records the victories America's naval forces won at sea. He also notes the effective skills of America's craftsmen, who designed good, fast ships, and of its seamen, who manned the gunnery works that were often swift, accurate, and deadly. But he places his emphasis elsewhere: first, upon the "new and scientific character" of warfare that had been introduced by "the sudden development of scientific engineering" at West Point ten years before (1341); second, upon the fact of British inflexibility that (notwithstanding the superior experience of the Royal Navy) led to the enemy's inability to learn the same lessons the United States Navy shrewdly extracted from speedily assimilated empirical data about the making and sailing of ships. It is neither manliness pitted against weakness nor courage over cowardice that makes the historical difference in the fighting of wars. It is the suppleness of that mind kept open to scientific innovation that will master minds closed down by conventionality; it is the young nation's seizure of the newest methods of efficient combat that will lead to victories at sea over tired old seadogs.

Adams is especially alert to the dramatic moral contest taking place between two different mind-sets, conflicting tensions within Adams himself. Along one side are ranged the traits governing the British navy ("savage," conservative); to the other side is the flaunting of tradition carried out by the captains of the American privateers ("barbaric," progressive—traits pointing toward the practices of modern science, business, and industry). The British navy is not defeated according to patriotic clichés that pit the manly self-reliance of Yankee seamen against monarchical tyrants. The British lose because, as when they captured the American schooner *Wave,* they rebuilt this fast, light, beautiful, effective fighting craft to fit traditional notions of the proper nature of ships. The result of their mental regressiveness was "a clumsy, dish-shaped Dutch dogger" with masts "taut and stiff as church-steeples" (843).

It was the British who tried to justify their defeat by translating the Yankee victories into moral terms. The privateers fought unfairly; unlike gentlemen, they failed to adhere to decorum.

> Americans instantly made improvements which gave superiority, and which Europeans were unable immediately to imitate even after

seeing them. Not only were American vessels better in model, faster in sailing, easier and quicker in handling, and more economical in working them than the European, but they were also better equipped. The English complained as a grievance that the American adopted new and unwarranted devices in naval warfare; that their vessels were heavier and better constructed, and their missiles of unusual shape and improper use. The Americans resorted to expedients that had not been tried before, and excited a mixture of irritation and respect in the English service, until Yankee smartness became a national misdemeanor. (1337)

Theodore Roosevelt equated honesty with physical and moral manliness, duplicity with bodily and emotional weakness. Adams allied efficient action with intelligence and the "acuteness . . . or smartness" needed to get done the things that needed doing in the new republic. True, "much doubt remained whether the intelligence belonged to a high order, or proved a high morality," but the charge that Yankee "shrewdness was associated with unscrupulousness" was a charge that "could neither be proved nor disproved" (1342); nor did this charge much matter to the Yankees in the face of victory.

No wonder that Adams (the self-styled "conservative Christian anarchist," the American counterpart of Leo Tolstoy in the 1880s) was caught between the horns of dilemma. Does the successful man hew to principles or to facts, to transcendent laws that dwell within and guide moral conduct or to historical events that leave troubling tracks across the face of things, which a person can only try to interpret, knowing full well he is unable to be as "scientific" as science requires him to be. In 1841 when Emerson describes the conservative type in contrast to the reformer in his essay "The Conservative," he separates the man of habit bound to the past from the man of innovation alert to the future. There Emerson demands that Americans make a choice between the two modes of action, lest they become like the man who rides two horses at once to his destruction. Adams, however, was unable to make the final choice. He was fated to care deeply about the fact that the values of the Enlightenment could be annihilated permanently, even when he realized that the retention of such values led to defeat in the modern age. Besides, he always showed his (somewhat grudging) admiration for the success coming to the man who adjusts to the times by making up the rules as he goes along.[31]

Roosevelt's historical narratives of the American wars of 1812 and 1898 have relatively simple dramas to relate: heroes are men who go into combat—the manly men who act bravely far outnumbering the poltroons who cower and run in the face of risk; villains are the inept (read "cowardly") administrators grouped behind the lines, whether generals or statesmen or presidents. By extension, the best (the most efficient) leaders are men whose histories are biographies. Well-told accounts of past lives warn the populace of the current mismanagement of the nation's affairs, or inspire the nation's citizenry through the history of heroic deeds in battle. Roosevelt's history-as-biography achieves these things, and therein lies the cause of much of his fame. What his war writings seldom stop to do in their headlong, manly rush into the noise and dust of the fray (military or administrative) is to provide a science of history activated by a meticulous, keen-edged mind, a mind prepared to pause en route in order to analyze, and to cast Adamsian doubts upon, what is happening.

Roosevelt fills his history of the War of 1812 with impressive technical details about the shrewdly intelligent tactical maneuvers executed by well-trained seamen on smartly designed fighting craft. Adams's account has all this, too, but also something more important, both for the storyteller and for the analyst of efficiency systems: that is, the study of the changes taking place within the American mind from the inception of the American republic through the early 1800s.

Adams does not write history-as-biography from the point of view of historian-as-patriot. His writings are closer in kind to Emerson's essays. (Consider "The Conduct of Life," "The Young American," "The Conservative," "The Reformer," and "The Natural History of the Intellect.") Roosevelt gives us updated war reports that incisively highlight those actions that win on the spot. Adams provides the long overview; he cares about the material and economic causes (however untidy their consequences) that hover behind our response to historical events. Roosevelt's literary predecessors are the work manuals compiled by marine engineers, James Fenimore Cooper's sea tales, national romances, boys' adventure stories, and tales of exploration and expansionism. The immediate writerly references one thinks of for Adams are Karl Marx and Ralph Waldo Emerson, and, looking ahead to the near future, Thorstein Veblen, Max Weber, and William and Henry James: Marx, Veblen, and Weber for Adams's attention to the economics and sociology of the mind; Emerson and the two Jameses for the way Adams incessantly returns to questions of the American character and social behavior.

Taking a Fix on Jefferson (1889)

Adams opens the first volume of his history of Jefferson's administration by itemizing everything that was *absent* in the United States in 1800—the negations out of which Jefferson had to shape something commensurate with the high-sounding principles laid down by the Constitution in 1787. Without progressive transportation and communication systems, the nation was "under constant peril of losing her political union." [32] This was the same situation that had perturbed George Washington and that would obsess John Quincy Adams when he took office in 1825. For Jefferson in 1801, the nation's economy was perilously lacking in rational modes of efficiency.

> The machinery of production showed no radical difference from that familiar to ages long past. The Saxon farmer of the eighth century enjoyed most of the comforts known to Saxon farmers of the eighteenth. (15)

But even Jefferson—

> the inventor of the first scientific plough, the importer of the first threshing-machine known in Virginia, the experimenter with a new drilling-machine, the owner of one hundred and fifty slaves and ten thousand acres of land, whose negroes were trained in carpentry, cabinet-making, house-building, weaving, tailoring, shoe-making,—claimed to get from his land no more than six or eight bushels of wheat to an acre. (25)

In chapter 2, Adams moves on to the study of "the formation of men's minds" in the symbolic year 1800 (as symbolic to him as 1900 was when he experienced the power of the dynamo over the human mind). Resistant to change, the "conservative habit of mind"

> was more harmful in America than in other communities, because Americans needed more than older societies the activity which could alone partly compensate for the relative feebleness of their means compared with the magnitude of their task. (47)

As a result of the hidebound nature of American thought in 1800, the startling inventions of Robert Fulton and John Fitch were ignored by their countrymen, who also had dismissed the fact that James Watt's steam engine had been "causing a revolution in industry" in England for ten years already (47). Chapter 2 closes with this warning: "A world which assumed that what had been must be, could not be scientific; yet in order to make the Americans a successful people, they must be roused to feel the necessity of scientific training" (53).

At this juncture, Adams places his finger on the one thing that can be counted upon to stir people from their habits of mental inefficiency: *money.*

> Until they were satisfied that knowledge was money, they would
> not insist upon higher education; until they saw with their own eyes
> stones turned to gold, and vapor into cattle and corn, they would
> not learn the meaning of science. (53)

In the America of 1800, progressive thought opens the way to ad-
vancements in the area of applied science. The drive toward progress
comes only when the American mind equates scientific training with
profit. Where does public morality fit into this scheme, particularly when
"science" is defined either as (1) the rational formulation of efficiency systems committed to "facts" that bring in money, or as (2) disinterested
thought and action practiced "ethically" for the sake of reason itself? Was
the typical American of 1800 starting the train of events by which the
country's affairs would head in several directions, depending upon
whether it was hard facts or soft ethics that mattered most? Would the turn
toward scientific thought find future satisfaction with the democratic reforms proposed by gentle Emersonian savages or would it choose to
plunge into the jungles of barbaric and quasi-predatory action led by
America's Rough Riders? Or would the consequences be marvelous in
their mixture of both strains—concluding with what a later commentator
on the American scene called "the brutality of the conflict," which the
scientific management of lives simultaneously mitigates and accelerates?

In Adams's narrative—the one that most satisfied the imagination of
this child of New England—he compares the "intellectual and moral
character" of each of the thirteen states as they existed in 1800. He finds
that New York

> left much to be desired; but on the other hand, had society adhered
> stiffly to what New England thought strict morals, the difficulties in
> the path of national development would have been increased. Inno-
> vation was the most useful purpose which New York could serve in
> human interests, and never was a city better fitted for its work. (78)

Inevitably, according to the popular myth (one Adams did much to refine)
that gives Massachusetts, New York, and Virginia distinctively different
moral characters,[33] problems of principled social behavior arise when "the
metaphysical subtleties of Massachusetts and Virginia" come into contact
with New York's moral indifference, its commercial acumen, and its
scientific innovativeness.

By this point in his opening volume, Adams has separated out at least
three strands that make us aware of the way his reading of the conditions
of 1800 foreshadows those he found falling into place by 1900, conditions
that would bear upon turn-of-the-century barbaric fictions: (1) the intel-

lectually sluggish, who hold to a belief "in a society so simple that purity should suffer no danger, and corruption gain no foothold" (79); (2) the "average American," whose type, "becoming every year still more active-minded," reaches an apotheosis in the triumphs of Franklin, Fitch, Whitney, and Fulton, men whose "inventions transmitted the democratic instinct into a practical and tangible shape" (123); (3) an innovative society like New York, which "pledged itself to principles of no kind" in order to be in on the main chance whenever "progress" promises the getting of money.

Captains of Industry (1895–96)

Eventually the inventor, the manager, and the technocrat—systematizers represented by Thomas Edison, Henry Ford, and Herbert Hoover—would become cultural heroes, displacing military leaders and old-time entrepreneurs, men more appropriate to cruder times when Americans still honored "the archaic traits" of overtly predatory methods. The spell the new-style barbarians cast over the imagination even by the mid-1890s influenced the assessments being made of the nation's business enterprise.

Paul Bourget, the well-known French author, devoted a chapter of his 1895 book about his visit to the United States, *Outre-Mer: Impressions of America,* to "Business Men and Business Scenes." In his analysis of railroad practices and the running of Chicago's meat-packing industries, Bourget concluded that it took a "colossal effort of the imagination on the one hand, and, on the other, at the service of the imagination, a clear and carefully estimated understanding of the encompassing reality" to determine the crucial factor that procures material success in America.

The "full-panoplied modern warfare" that won the victory for the Union Army and the continuing contests of modern business competition are the result, Bourget states, "of that essentially American turn of mind,—the constant use of new methods." "The entire absence of routine, the daily habit of letting the fact determine the action, of following it fearlessly to the end" stand opposed to that "extreme clearness, perspicuity of administrative order [that] always spring from an *a priori* theory."

> All societies and all enterprises in which realism, rather than system, rules are constructed by juxtaposition, by series of facts accepted as they arise. But how should the people here have leisure to concern themselves with those small, fine points of administrative order with which our Latin peoples are so much in love. Competition is too strong, too ferocious, almost. There is all of warfare and its breathless audacity back of the enterprises of this country.[34]

As we know, Frederick Winslow Taylor helped create the new managerial type—the man devoted to the "extreme clearness, perspicuity of
administrative order [that] always spring from an *a priori* theory." He
understood well the old business type he hoped to replace, and in 1909 he
described both the new and the old when he came to the Harvard School
of Business to speak on "Workmen and Their Management." In a narrative intended to inspire his listeners to elevate the American manager to
his rightful role as the nation's cultural model, Taylor made no less of an
effort than Emerson did in his 1837 Phi Beta Kappa oration at Harvard,
which launched the value-loaded figure of the American scholar upon the
scene.

In order to extol the "able, competent, and well-trained" mover of
contemporary business enterprises, Taylor feels the need to include a narrative flashback to the physical and mental type that still commanded the
scene a decade before his principles of scientific management began to
turn this type into an anachronism. As Taylor describes them, the businessmen of the late nineteenth century have many of the attributes of
Theodore Roosevelt himself.

> The great captains of industry were usually physically large and
> powerful. They were big-hearted, kindly, humorous, lovable men,
> democratic, truly fond of their workmen, and yet courageous,
> brainy and shrewd; with not the slightest vestige of anything soft or
> sentimental about them. Ready at any minute to damn up and down
> hill the men who needed it, or to lay violent hands on any workmen
> who defied them, and throw them over the fence.[35]

Before 1900 there was still a place for Theodore Roosevelt. There
were still "hot" stories to be related about war and patriotism, money and
efficiency, predatory outreachings beyond the nation's rim and moral pronouncements: stories with the mixed elements of "primitively human
passions" and "calculations that are anything but primitively human," of
imperialistic feverishness and "the cold pot-grease of cant" of which William James wrote in scorn in 1899. But a new kind of man was on the way,
a man capable of managing imperialist enterprises in ways that would
emphasize "perspicuity of administrative order" while cutting back on
"breathless audacity."

Once World War I was over, "the bully amateur's world" was annihilated, but the figure of the Rough Rider (and his brothers-in-arms, the
captains of industry) was on the way out even in 1909. This was ironic
since Taylor, who promoted the new and better American-as-
professional-manager, believed until his death in 1915 that he, like the

Roosevelt Dos Passos describes here, upheld the "Strenuous Life, Realizable Ideals, Just Government."[36]

Contained in an appendix to the 1896 report submitted to the fifty-fourth Congress urging the Senate to recognize Cuban independence are remarks made in 1859 by John Slidell, senator from Louisiana, who advocated the annexation of Cuba by means of negotiation and purchase. Slidell's mid-century desire to allow the imperialistic impulse (likened to the "law" of organic growth) free play is Darwinism converted into government policy with lightning speed—an appropriation taking place in the same year as Darwin published *On the Origins of the Species According to Natural Selection.*

> The law of our national existence is growth. We can not, if we would, disobey it. While we should do nothing to stimulate it unnaturally, we should be careful not to impose upon ourselves a regimen so strict as to prevent its healthful development. The tendency of the age is the expansion of the great powers of the world.[37]

Henry Adams authored the 1896 Senate report, although it was sent forward in the name of Senator Donald Cameron of Pennsylvania. Well past his own Darwinian phase, Adams mounts an argument based on the legality of "precedents." He chronicles past incidents in which groups have claimed independence through revolution. He details James Monroe's creation of "the American system" to resist European intervention. But the phrases Adams incorporates into his 1896 report are even more significant, for he surrounds his depiction of the United States—a nation identified as one of "the great powers"—with an aura of benevolence and sweet reasonableness.

In Adams's language we see the United States taking an "active and serious interest" in Cuba's well-being, but always in the manner of an individual of good character representing an advanced state of civilized behavior: "friendly offices," "our good offices," "friendly arrangement," "patient delay," "none but the friendliest feelings," "anxious wish to avoid even the appearance of an unfriendliness." Whatever happens, this expansionist nation will forego the "almost invariably harsh and oppressive" practices employed by European nations when they (barbarically) intervene. Says Adams, "The practice of the United States has been almost invariably mild and forbearing."

Nonetheless, by 1898 Roosevelt's war discourse finds its best expression in the "primitively human passions" of men excited by power moves. Buried within the line of argument of the assistant secretary of the U.S. Navy-become-Rough Rider may be "the cold pot-grease of cant": he maintains that the United States desires nothing but good for Cuba and for Spain, yet the heat of battle fever races along the ridges of his prose. Roosevelt's barbaric narratives of strong brothers pouring onto Cuban shores to save the sibling weaklings of the Western hemisphere echo what Paul Bourget observed about the American businessman in 1895 and what Frederick Winslow Taylor, reminiscing in 1909, said about the late nineteenth-century captain of industry. In contrast, Adams's discourse of 1896 is still poised at the edge of the next stage of development, looking toward the modern manager of men and nations. As chapters 3 and 4 will show, it shares a great deal with the "friendly offices" described in Taylor's self-explanatory narratives, narratives arguing for the good that would come to all people if they would but live according to the principles of scientific management.

Soldiers of Fortune

THE FIRST WORLD WAR may have brought, as Dos Passos maintained, an end to "the bully amateur's world," but amateur hour was already closing down as American soldiers straggled up San Juan Hill. Three books written between 1897 and 1899 are flashes that streaked the sky at the moment "the boy culture" of volunteers was displaced (and absorbed) by the "dirtywork" of regulars committed to the culture of management.[1]

Theodore Roosevelt's *The Rough Riders* was the last of the three to reach the waiting American public, following fast upon Richard Harding Davis's romance, *Soldiers of Fortune,* and his journalistic coverage of the Spanish-American War, *The Cuban and Porto Rican Campaigns.* Roosevelt's account of the rush of events—the landing of American forces in Cuba on June 14, 1898; the march into Santiago on July 17; and the departure of his Rough Riders, decimated by malarial fever, for the mainland on August 8—is a "campaign biography" in several senses: the dramatic narration of his exploits as the leader of brave men in a brief but glory-making military campaign, and the selling of his capabilities as a leader for whatever political campaigns might lie ahead. But it is something else as well. Together with Davis's two books, *The Rough Riders* represents the transition between old and new ways of managing the chaos of war. It extols planning and professionalism while celebrating free play and manly games. It calls for a cool administrative head and a heated heart. In fact, it "squints" in two directions—just as William James claimed all imperialists did when caught between desire for rational accomplishments and need for irrational excitements.

Cuba and the Manly Arts

In 1882 Theodore Roosevelt was elected New York state assemblyman and wrote *The Naval War of 1812*. Within the corridors of the Albany state capitol and the pages of his history, Roosevelt carried out militant assaults against every kind of mismanagement "on the business and administrative side" of government. In 1897, as assistant secretary of the navy, he continued to attack any practice that might imperil "the fighting edge" of Americans at the front, inefficiencies that "would have been comic if [they] had not possessed such tragic possibilities."[2] Then he was off to Cuba in 1898, heading his own band of feisty volunteers, quickly to return and quickly to write up his experiences in *The Rough Riders*.

A sequel of sorts to *The Naval War of 1812*, *The Rough Riders* lambastes the bureaucratic ineptness that negates the energies of the self-reliant American male, who is plunged into the excitements of a war that ought to be "the best moment" of his life.[3] Not that Roosevelt wants the United States to ape Old World traditions of robotized efficiency. Over in Europe the soldier is "trained to complete suppression of individual will, while his faculties become atrophied in consequence of his being merely a cog in a vast and perfectly ordered machine." Such regimentation need not be the case in the New World, at least not for the fighting unit's commanding officer; he can charge "into and out of the meshes of red-tape" by the exercise of "every pound of resource, inventiveness, and audacity he possess" (13:37).[4]

The American combatants' enemy in the Cuban campaign was not Spain. It was the ineptitude of Captain Sigsbee, commander of the sunken *Maine*, who was found to have been completely unfamiliar with his ship and its routine; it was "the sense that no one was in control" when the American troops debarked from their transports; it was the panic experienced by the New York Seventy-first Volunteers (as embarrassing as the route suffered by Howard's Eleventh Corps at Chancellorsville), caused by botched orders from on high; it was the indecisiveness of Brigadier General William Rufus Shafter, whose bloated three-hundred-pound bulk became "a metaphor for the campaign as a whole."[5]

Roosevelt's book wishes to lay bare all these faults in a cool appraisal of what goes wrong when stupid fumbling replaces intelligent planning. But *The Rough Riders* squints in other directions as well. It rewrites Veblen's machine process as adventure, Weber's bureaucracy as the triumph of charismatic will, and Emerson's self-reliance as a boy's romp. The excitement over the thrill of combat felt by the book's central figure, Lieutenant Colonel Roosevelt, is heir to the dance of joy executed by the officer on horseback in Stephen Crane's *Red Badge of Courage*.

Roosevelt might figure as a character *within* a war narrative as told by Crane, but in his own account of martial exploits Roosevelt rejects Crane's aesthetics.[6] Upon hearing a group of wounded men spontaneously take up the chorus of "My Country 'Tis of Thee," Roosevelt declares with scorn, "I did not see any sign . . . of the very complicated emotions assigned to their kind by some of the realistic modern novelists who have written about battle" (13:81).

Rooseveltian narratology is in league with romantic premodern fictions of war. It is one more example of that cohabitation of the "archaic" and the "modern" about which Veblen and James were so perceptive. Brashly up-to-date in his ideas about the scientific management of military campaigns, yet tenaciously old guard in regard to the narratives he sanctioned for portraying a fighting man's experiences in battle, Roosevelt was the consummate amateur who wishes to enjoy the thrill of authority possessed by the new-style professional. But wanting it both ways is the sign of Teddyism and the cause of its eventual demise.[7]

Feelings and Efficiency

The Cuban and Porto Rican Campaigns first appeared as a series of communiqués that Richard Harding Davis sent to the *New York World,* one of the papers that "created" the war in the first place. Davis's reputation as a war correspondent who possessed both archaic dash and modern journalistic skills contributed to the public's avid interest in the escapades of the Rough Riders, which he placed at the center of his reports from the front. As will be evident when we look next at Davis's *Soldiers of Fortune,* published the year before he arrived in Cuba, he was well prepared to write up the Teddyism of the charismatic efficiency expert. *Soldiers of Fortune* is a splendid example of the nonrealistic, nonmodern "barbaric narrative." It points the way toward Roosevelt's and Davis's campaign accounts, which similarly define war as romance and as business enterprise.

Like Roosevelt, Davis possessed the personal style fitting to a man who engages directly in the martial narratives of the 1890s. Contemporary photographs shot in Key West prior to debarkation, and in Cuba during lulls in action, capture the insouciant dress and manner affected by Davis and Roosevelt as war correspondent and rough rider respectively. Style was all important to the males embodying "the barbaric variant" in "the modern man" of whom Veblen speaks in *The Theory of the Leisure Class,* a book that appeared a year after Davis's report and the same year as Roosevelt's.

On the other hand, Davis's *writing* style avoids the lush imprecision twitted by Mark Twain in his parodies of Cooper and of the serialized

romances beloved by his generation. It also stays clear of the language of
the Homeric tale and medieval epic mocked by Stephen Crane. The writing style used by Davis and Roosevelt alike is sturdy, journalistic prose—
strong on details, swift off the mark, constantly propelled forward along
a straight sequence of events leading to big scenes. What matters most is
that their style is *manly,* for what *was* war at the service of national expansionism but the chance to become the ultimate American male?

Manliness as prose style eschews the "complicated emotions" to
which "modern" authors—with their weak wills, damaging doubts, and
"feminine" sensibilities—succumb. Still, the manly narrative of "the barbaric variant" has its own modes for being steeped in feeling. Davis
handles emotion differently in his journalistic reports than in his novels,
but it is there nonetheless.

Emotions are crucial to the telling of war stories, whether they are
composed by newspaper men or by presidents in the making, especially
those who believe in the imperialistic mission. But the tellers take great
care to displace unmanly emotions away from the American males, who
now must signify sensible self-reliance, efficiency, and shrewd managerial
skills while continuing to represent the nation's heroic, self-sacrificing
spirit.

Three passages from *The Cuban and Porto Rican Campaigns* demonstrate different ways to structure a narrative that equates national destiny
with American manliness, a unique quality said to balance both feelings
and efficiency. First, there is the sequence that focuses upon the futuristic
perfection of the utopian machine process to which strong men submit
their wills and emotions. Second, there is a passage that encodes the kind
of modern realism Davis saw fit to include within an essentially barbaric
narrative. Third, there is the climactic scene of exuberant sentimentality
released at the moment of America's victory, a scene that is an amalgam of
hardheaded practicality and visionary fantasies of power.

The departure of the American invasion fleet from Key West is heightened by the newsman's awareness "that bulletin-boards were blocking the
streets of lower New York with people eager for news, and that men and
women from Seattle to Boston were awake with anxiety and unrest."[8]
Where better to locate messy, potentially weakening emotions than in the
collective heart of the American civilian population. Let America cling
expectantly to the news supplied by Davis and his fellow correspondents,
who bravely accompany brave men into the combat area, their own emotions firmly controlled by their professionalism.

In contrast to the edgy sleeplessness of noncombatants back home,
the transport vessels standing off Florida's coast stay awake "all through
that night," talking with one another "in a language of signs," calmly in

control, "their rows of lanterns winking red and white against the night
. . . carrying messages of command to men many miles at sea" (6). But
are the men packed into those ships feeling "complicated emotions"?[9] One
cannot tell from Davis's description. He expends his words entirely upon
"the leaden-painted war-ships [moving] heavily in two great columns"
and "the torpedo-boats [that] rolled and tossed like porpoises at play" (7).

Davis's narrative about the projection of American military power
upon the Caribbean opens by carefully deflecting attention away from the
men crowded onto the transports. His strategy of depersonalization emphasizes the efficiency of the "modern war-ship" as "the perfection of organization." Frederick Winslow Taylor, already on his way to becoming
the Father of Scientific Management in 1898, would have been pleased to
read that the "discipline of the New York was rigid, intelligent, and unremitting, and each of the five hundred men on this floating monastery
moved in his little groove with the perfect mechanism of one of the eight-
inch guns" (16). The crews of the warships that Theodore Roosevelt, as
acting secretary of the navy, had hastened into readiness for the war he
hoped would take place will not participate in the freewheeling, bully-boy
fun that Lieutenant Colonel Roosevelt of the Rough Riders experienced.
Nonetheless, the aura Davis casts over his depiction of shipboard activity
is not one of menace. Only the ships get to frolic like happy porpoises.
However, the caretakers of the "floating monastery" supposedly are content to function in ascetic obedience to the manly, spirit-sustaining rules
of the war machine, initiated the previous year by Roosevelt's managerial
efforts.

Concurring with Roosevelt's critique of the appalling mismanagement of the island campaign under the inept hand of Brigadier General
William Shafter, Davis excoriates the absence of "a strong man in command of the expedition." Like Roosevelt, he assails the breakdown in the
provision of needed supplies, which cripples the progress of the war from
Washington, D.C. to Key West and across the waters to Cuba.[10] The call
for scientifically managed, efficient organization becomes a major thread
in the turn-of-the-century narratives. Creating heroic drama means telling of strong men endangered by the moral and technical incompetence
of weaklings and fools. War is the occasion for testing correct feelings of
bravery and patriotism; business is the occasion for deciding who has a
good head for planning. The two must go together. American military
enterprises of the late 1890s are simply variations of the American business enterprise. Both must evolve together toward the perfected level of
technology that Veblen and Taylor were about to articulate in theory and
practice.

But once the action shifts from the floating monasteries of the U.S.

transport ships to the men storming Spanish positions in Cuban jungles, Davis as war correspondent appears to put his management narratives aside. He is now seemingly free to recount tales of brave men by means of literary formulas hallowed by tradition. Yet the new-style connections between men's behavior in war and the management of war remain.

The marks of tradition are strong. Davis, like Roosevelt, discounts the possibility that the ordinary American military man could ever behave dishonorably; his actions will continue to incarnate the patriotic orations stirring the American mainland.[11] Overall, Davis's account of men in combat cleaves more closely to Roosevelt's unproblematized rendering of the neoromantic hero than to the modern realism represented by Stephen Crane's incessant exposure of doubt and unmanly feelings. It is true that although *The Rough Riders* refuses to mention Crane's presence at San Juan, Davis willingly singles Crane out as the best of the lot of war correspondents in the field.[12] Like Crane, Davis is sharp of tongue about the "series of military blunders" from on high that have brought "seven thousand American soldiers into a chute of death" (214).[13] However, like Roosevelt, Davis prefers to expose the kinds of mistakes that good management would rectify. He does not join in Crane's assault upon the general mismanagement of the universe.

The real test of Davis's capacity for *more than Teddyism* comes when he writes up the winning of San Juan Hill, the second of the three scenes I have tapped here for analysis. Davis reaches for standard phrases in defining the battle as "a miracle of self-sacrifice, a triumph of bull-dog courage, which one watched breathless with wonder" (22), but he goes on to insist upon the clearheaded accuracy of his account. He sets his updated approach in opposition to the romanticism and sentimentality of the stories routinely worked up by the picture papers. While the tabloids accentuate invincible military might, Davis stirs pity for the vulnerability of brave men.

> I have seen many illustrations and pictures of this charge on the San Juan hills, but none of them seem to show it just as I remember it. In the picture-papers the men are running up hill swiftly and gallantly, in regular formation, rank after rank, with flags flying, their eyes aflame, and their hair streaming, their bayonets fixed, in long, brilliant lines, an invincible, overpowering weight of numbers. It was not that way at all: . . . I think the thing which impressed one the most, when our men started from cover, was that they were so few. It seemed as if someone had made an awful and terrible mistake. . . . You felt that someone had blundered and that these few men were blindly following out some madman's mad order. It was

not heroic then, it seemed merely terribly pathetic. The pity of
it, the folly of such a sacrifice was what held you. They had no glittering bayonets, they were not massed in regular array. There
were a few men in advance, bunched together, and creeping up a
steep, sunny hill, the tops of which roared and flashed with flame.
(218–19)

When it is all over, and the few of the few to survive have reached
the top,

their own point of view and sense of relief and surprise were thus
best expressed in the words of Stephen Crane's trooper, who sank
upon the crest of the hill, panting, bleeding, and sweating, and cried:
"Well, hell, here we are!" (227)[14]

Where are we exactly at the moment Davis takes us to the top of San
Juan Hill? We are thrust into a realistic narrative about men whose heroism is measured by blood and sweat, a "modern" narrative that offers its
challenge to that outmoded pictorial romanticism where men win gloriously, immune to the letting of their own blood.

But does the inclusion of this passage, fixed firmly in the present moment of human experience, indicate that Davis has committed himself to
a sustained critique of the barbaric costs of war? Is he actually going to
offer a text for modern times that captures the needs both of the savage
imagination and of the rational man of science, needs that have moved
beyond merely barbaric impulses? Will Davis provide a text that, without
embarrassment, includes the realism of Crane's trooper, a man who tells
us *this is all there is:* the present *here,* a fragment whose whole can never be
grasped, an "episode of war" stripped of any teleological hope since it is
confined to the raw responses of men whose only triumph consists in having survived?

No, not really. However much Davis's narrative qualifies itself at certain points, it partakes of the same imperialist tradition that controls *The
Rough Riders*. But there is more to it. To state that Davis's report from
Cuba is part of an ongoing literary treatment of manly exploits tinctured
by archaic traits in the cause of romantic quasi-predatory American imperialism *is the same as saying* that it is committed to a quasi-realism whose
methods of sharp observation match those being introduced by contemporary journalism; *it is also the same as saying* that Davis's work is quasi-
modernistic in the sense proposed by Veblen, Weber, and Taylor, when
they refer to the way dispassionate scientific calculation and impersonal
efficiency systems have infiltrated everyday life. Davis's record of the campaign of the summer of 1898 is both realistic and archaic; therefore, it is

"modern"—that unsettling mixture of "calculations" and "primitively human passions" to which William James called irate attention in 1899.

The Cuban and Porto Rican Campaigns launches its story with a celebration of the perfect organization of great warships. It pauses midway to honor the handful of human survivors who make it to the top of San Juan Hill. But if it is to be truly effective as an imperialist narrative, it must conclude with an apotheosis that goes beyond either the cool impersonal power of warships or the warm pity expressed for brave but battered men.

An impartial account of the altered conditions, both historical and narrative, under which the Caribbean campaign was brought to a close would result in a severe drop in dramatic intensity. As long as Davis focuses upon scenes of combat, his incorporation of the cruel details of the unnecessary waste of men's bodies advances his purpose of pointing up American heroism thwarted in its noble effort to bring democracy to an oppressed people. Creating pity for the men's ordeals elevates their manliness. Realism serves romanticism; facts support sentimentalism. Efficiency, or the lack thereof, is central to the tale of the value of expansionist emotions. In contrast, the riot of emotions Davis lets loose in his description of the troops marching into Puerto Rico seems markedly different because it is so patently romantic—the epitome of boy culture on a holiday in "the bully amateur's world."

Because rumors of peace encouraged the Spanish troops to lay down their arms, and because for once the competency of the American general in charge made this phase of the Caribbean campaign "an affair of letting blood so amusing" to the army, the men regarded the final stages of the campaign as "a picnic" (300). *The Cuban and Porto Rican Campaigns* moves from the technical perfection of invulnerable machines to pity for vulnerable men to picnic time for the boys, from impersonal generalization to collective waves of feeling to easygoing comedy. Such abrupt narrative shifts might have resulted in anticlimax, a consequence to be avoided at all costs by neoromantic, neorealist, neoimperialist narratives of 1898. Yet anticlimax is precisely what Davis's narrative does not allow. His story ends with the triumphant entry—orchestrated to "the jubilant swing of a Sousa march"—of American troops into Coamo, Puerto Rico, whose citizens ran "to greet their new masters, who had been masters for only the last three hours" (353).

There is a final twist, however. This is not a scene of innocent boy culture after all (as though boy culture were ever innocent). In the final lines Davis suddenly drops into a rhetorical mode better suited to an allegory of a proud and powerful nation on the threshold of its global destiny.

Fifty-seven years before, in his essay "The Young American," Emerson had tried to lessen anxieties about the nation's future by identifying that future with a glorious imperialism of the spirit. But in 1898 Davis does not shrink from literalizing the imagination of a New World empire in ascent.[15] Land masses, not merely noble thoughts, are seized by the young American.

> The son and heir was coming fast, blue-shirted, sunburned, girded with glistening cartridges. He was sweeping before him the last traces of a fallen Empire; the sons of the young Republic were tearing down the royal crowns and the double castles over the city halls, opening the iron doors of the city jails and raising the flag of the new Empire over the land of the sugar-cane and the palm. (353)

To force home his point, Davis places a map of the new territories now under American control across the page from his closing words. Puerto Ricans bless the American flag "which must never leave the island" since *theirs* is an island that "will bring *us* nothing but what is for good" (353; my emphasis). One may gasp at the candor (or naïveté, if you wish) with which Davis wraps (as one would the flag) his quasi-predatory romantic vision around a core of practical business realism, a vision inspired by the moral imperatives of empire. What the Caribbean campaign brings "for good" includes the "good" that accrues to the American sugar interests once "the flag of the new Empire" flies "over the land of the sugar-cane."[16]

The moral pretensions of the expansionist tale sanctioned by Roosevelt are inevitably tied to the business enterprise as described by Veblen. War, morality, and business are determined by, to use Davis's phrase, the needs of a "course of empire [that] to-day takes its way to all points of the compass" (360).[17]

Davis welcomes the thought that Puerto Rico "came to us willingly with open arms." He hopes that any future forays the United States makes beyond its borders might "move always as smoothly, as honorably, and as victoriously as it did in Porto Rico." If this were the case, the nation's military and its civilians "need ask for no higher measure of success." Yet he shows no qualms in exposing the allegiance of his "barbaric narrative" to "the business enterprise" that lies behind all political considerations. "Had it been otherwise" than a smooth, honorable, glorious victory greeted "with open arms" by the natives, the island still "would have come to us" (360).

This, then, is the point at which the three passages from *The Cuban and Porto Rican Campaigns* come together to demonstrate that a new narrative mode is in the process of coming into being. We have before us the tale of adventure told about an ideal democratic society, a tale that provides at once (1) the human realism of the "complicated emotions" voiced by Crane's trooper on San Juan Hill, (2) "the perfection of organization" represented by the modern warship, and (3) the archaic barbarism of imperialistic exploits. There are tales committed to journalistic reportage of manly exploits abroad; tales filled with the glitter of cartridges, sparkling in the sun of islands near and far; tales that prize sentimentality, pity for the suffering of brave men; tales with comedic touches of boys engaged in picniclike war games; tales that repress the tragic conclusion or the ironic critique; tales that roll up a tangled skein of traditional genre traditions and rhetorical styles into a composite narrative form keyed to the imaginative needs and strategic devices of the newly accredited age of acquisition.

The Sexuality of War

What are the implications embedded in Davis's meld of the realism of "this is where we are" with the visionary imperialism of "this is where we must go"? We need to know, since this hybrid constitutes that narrative form one may name either turn-of-the-century neoromanticism or "transmuted" (Veblen's term) modern barbarism. Three novels written between 1897 and 1904 by Richard Harding Davis and Henry James suggest useful answers to these questions. But first, let the following remarks by Henry Demarest Lloyd, Thorstein Veblen, and Max Weber provide testing points for the fictional narratives Davis and James provide.

In 1901 Henry Demarest Lloyd writes with exuberance about the destinies of the United States, fresh from its successes in the Caribbean and the Philippines, and the Russian empire, still stinging over defeats at the hands of the Japanese navy. Lloyd predicts that both nations will "achieve unity brutally, to the great grief of those professors of love who have made a private luxury of brotherhood." The necessary brutalism of the present will progress through "the unity of brutality" to the future "unity of the peace of the people." Be of good cheer, for "imperialism will build the roads on which will travel the new gospel that will destroy imperialism."[18]

Two years earlier Thorstein Veblen was in the process of describing the barbarians in command of the world of affairs. He pauses to refer to the workers whose labor supports the "collective interests" of "the modern community" centered upon "industrial efficiency"—a comment that reminds one of the little people who populate the realistic novels of William Dean Howells. The workers possess the solid stuff of

> honesty, diligence, peacefulness, good-will, an absence of self-seeking, and an habitual recognition and apprehension of causal sequence, without admixture of animistic belief and without a sense

of dependence on any preternatural intervention in the course of events.[19]

Such people harbor none of the manly energies of the barbarian hero, nor do they have "the idle curiosity" that arouses both the savage imagination and the inventive powers of the modern technologist. These people are good Howellsians; they are also the good workers of whom Max Weber spoke, people whose "proletarian rationalism" has led to their complete indifference to "the influence of magic or providence"—people with "a consciousness of dependence on purely social factors" and their "own achievements."[20]

"Proletarian rationalism" has nothing to offer barbaric readers who long for excitement and efficiency. The uselessness of such a stance is summed up by Veblen's comment about its "prosy human nature." There is "little ground for enthusiasm for the manner of collective life that would result from the prevalence of these traits in unmitigated dominance." In contrast, Lloyd's juxtaposition of "the unity of peace" with "the unity of brutality" has everything to do with imperialistic fictions, as do the unprosy people destined to bring about this future bliss.

With these remarks of 1899 and 1901 in mind, we can approach those fictive characters who, by their "unmitigated dominance," control the centers of *Soldiers of Fortune, The Wings of the Dove,* and *The Golden Bowl* while avidly pursuing the gospel of imperialism. Now we realize this gospel can go in different directions. Imperialism can take the straight path to power; imperialism can turn itself inside out by finding "the moral equivalent to war" (as William James would wish); imperialism can inadvertently destroy itself or it can do this by design (as Lloyd maintains).[21] The same divergences obtain in the fictional portrayal of the sexuality of imperialistically managed wars—a sexuality of possession with the capacity both to consume and to create, to sustain and to demolish all it stands for.

Davis's 1897 romance novel maps out an archaic narrative that is thoroughly modern in terms of the diverse but hardly contradictory strains that make up the hero's character and conduct. *Soldiers of Fortune* is no *Nostromo,* Joseph Conrad's 1904 novel that also centers upon a South American setting, foreign mining interests, and intrigues of greed and power. For this very reason, the lesser stature of Davis's novel reveals the relative transparency of the surface of popular texts, notwithstanding the haste such fictions take to conceal their fear of the horrors of modern life—imaged as "the other" race, class, or gender—which threaten to overwhelm the imperialist enterprise if ever the Anglo-Saxon, male, capitalistic vision that supports it gives way.

Soldiers of Fortune presents us with an imperialistic fiction in full flush.

Its "agents of hegemony" are masterfully at home in an archaic, thoroughly modern narrative.[22] Precisely *because of* the anachronistic traits that Robert Clay, the hero, shares with his barbaric contemporaries; *because of* the managerial authority he wields as an engineer immersed in turn-of-the-century imperialist enterprises;[23] *because of* his practical common sense, his commitment to his "vocation," his rationalism and efficiency, his charisma, the "sexuality" of his patriotic sentimentalism, and the boy's delight he takes in manly exploits—*because of* all these qualities, Robert Clay embodies what Veblen, William James, and Roosevelt, too, believed was shaping the modern modes of science, business, and war.

However entangled, the plot of *Soldiers of Fortune* is quickly told.[24] The American millionaire, Andrew Langham, arrives in the small South American republic of Olancho with his two daughters. He has come to see how affairs are going at his iron mine, which is being managed by Robert Clay, a young American engineer. Clay had previously fallen in love with a photograph of the eldest Miss Langham, but she is a jaded woman of the negatively modern sort. Closed both to barbaric daring and to practical common sense, she is overly susceptible to "the complicated emotions" Roosevelt distrusted. Eventually Clay shifts his devotion to Hope Langham, the sister who is everything the up-to-date American girl should be. Davis and his illustrator, Charles Dana Gibson, who worked together on this publication for Scribner's, clearly project the "masculine" and "feminine" norms expected of that decade's heroes and heroines.[25]

When Olancho's president is assassinated by the villain Mendoza, who aspires to become dictator, Clay takes over the local counterrevolution, backed by his loyal band of engineers and a motley crew of "rough riders" (Negroes and wild Irishmen brought from the States). The Americans succeed gloriously and restore titular power to Rojas, the vice-president. During the fray, Clay's life is saved by Hope (who is the plucky pal as well as the dream woman), thereby proving that she is as "manly" as she is beautiful, virtuous, and true. Consequently, the two tall, brave, young Americans will wed and, it is assumed, breed the sound, healthy children that Theodore Roosevelt declared would rule America's new empire in the name of managerial efficiency and adventurous moral righteousness.

The formula for the love story Davis uses is old and roomy enough to adapt itself to any number of retellings. It is the imperialist ramifications, however, that are important here. They are the primary focus for this novel and the provocation for Davis's incorporation of other American motifs: the self-made man, the race hero, the barbarian boy's adventures, the sentimental sexuality of patriotism, and the loss of male freedom once success in both political and business enterprises has been achieved.

The details of Clay's life since he left his Colorado ranch home as a sixteen-year-old orphan read like a short list of primary works from the American literary canon: tales of adolescents shipping out before the mast told by Richard Henry Dana and Herman Melville, of cowboys on the range by Theodore Roosevelt, and of rough life along the Mexican border by Bret Harte. Clay has also lived through an anthology of international adventure narratives: a soldier in the Nile campaign, sapper in the French foreign legion, president of an international congress of engineers, the best poker player in Spain, a baron of the German empire (a title awarded for his having designed a fort on the Baltic), and the builder of "thousands of miles of railroad," "the highest bridge in Peru," and "a fort in the harbor of Rio de Janeiro during a revolution" (125). However fantastic the stories may be, they are written "big" by Davis in the imperialist tradition begun by Walt Whitman's globe-spanning Soul on its millennialist "passage to India."

Clay has fought and built and torn down mountains under the flags of many nations, but he is an American patriot through and through: the fabled Yankee jack-of-all-trades, Mark Twain's Hank Morgan reinserted into modern times as the engineer from the West.[26] He is the manly man skilled in practical crafts, a man whom a New York millionaire can post to the jungle with confidence that his man will put a stop to "laziness and mismanagement and incompetency" (37). Doing "the work of five men and five different kinds of work, not only without grumbling, but apparently with the keenest pleasure," Clay is a man his workers "could not long resist." Realizing "that the iron mine had its social as well as its political side," he "conciliated the rich coffee planters who owned the land which he wanted for the freight road" and made a gift of precious ore "to the wife of the Minister of the Interior in a cluster of diamonds" (39).[27]

Most important, Clay is no "soldier of fortune" in the degraded sense assigned to the figure of Burke, the mercenary who sells armaments to anyone planning a coup d'état. " 'As long as you've no sentiment,' " Clay says in scorn to Burke, " 'you might as well fight on the side that will pay best' " (208). But this advice does not apply to Clay himself, for he is the engineer as soldier and patriot,[28] the man who is, as we shall see (and necessarily so for such narratives), a rank sentimentalist.

In all ways, therefore, Robert Clay is worthy of being the leading man in Davis's imperialist narrative: first, his head for business does not mean business affairs preclude patriotic sentiment; second, he embodies the "calling" for science that commits him to the Protestant ethic Taylor and Weber were about to mandate as the essence of modern capitalism; third, his driving sense of vocation is precisely what allows him to commit himself to his own ideas, his employer, and the United States of America.

Happily, Clay's interests, Langham's interests, the interests of America, and the interests of Olancho are identical. Good business sense is the same as sound moral sense. From the rationalistic point of view of the American engineer, this means becoming a soldier in the cause of his nation's fortunes.

Clay tells the natives of Olancho that if their leaders ever drive out the American business interests, they will face a future as slave laborers in the mines. Working for Americans continues to assure them of good wages and the benefits of democracy. But just in case they ever see fit to act irrationally against their own interests, Clay will act to uphold the concession "made by one Government to a body of honest, decent businessmen, with a Government of their own back of them"—by force if necessary. He says he would, without hesitation, instruct Langham to call in a man-of-war "to blow you and your little republic back up here into the mountains" (63).[29]

Practicality defines Clay's every decision, and he acts decisively both as an engineer and as a military commander. Not limited to being the conventional gentleman hero, Clay is as ruthless as any businessman in his dealings with the enemy. But once he brings off his military assault at the head of his men, Clay "laughed like a boy as he swung himself into the saddle." Now it is Teddy time: the time for the sheer enjoyment of one's success as a manly patriot. He passes "between massed rows of his countrymen with their muskets held rigidly toward him. The housetops rocked again at the sight, and as he rode out into the brilliant sunshine, his eyes were wet and winking" (352).

Taylor and Veblen believed that the role of the efficiency expert was not to excite passion, since passions were precisely what the rationalism of Veblen's economics and Taylor's management practices were intended to eradicate. But this is precisely where the archaic traits about which Veblen was so knowledgeable (and William James so incensed) break through the thin veil of rationalism overlaying the modern imperialist narrative. Most archaic of all is that sentimental, nationalistic pride essential to the telling of manly exploits in the modern age.

Old-style sentiment is amply evident in *Soldiers of Fortune*. It appears in the love story, when the hero discovers the worthiness of the pert young girl at his side—a girl he ignores until he learns to look away from the wrong woman. Conventions also insure that Clay will be gentle toward all white women (that is, true American girls), even while on the rough in foreign lands.[30] There is nothing surprising about the intense affection expended upon Clay by the men who worship him, or the homoerotic quality of one of the novel's most emotional scenes: when young Stuart is shot down before Clay's eyes by a murderous mob of natives. At this point

Davis's prose and Gibson's illustrations provide a tableau of tenderness in which Clay gathers Stuart up in his arms before laying him out as an effigy of the fallen warrior, sword at his side. It may be a bit surprising, however, to read that Stuart's wound flames in contrast to skin as milk white and soft as a girl's, and to experience this voyeuristic glimpse at the violated body over which Clay kneels in mourning. As the novel's designated heroine, Hope Langham may be lively, brave, and beautiful, but Davis never lets her reveal milk-white flesh for men to yearn over. It is the heroic males—the engineers, soldiers, and patriots with sunburned faces—who get to have voluptuously pale torsos eroticized by the blood-red wounds they win fighting for the cause of American business interests and national honor.

But above and beyond the uses Davis makes of prior literary conventions (the old-style avoidance of sexuality between male and female; the old-style inclusion of male "love stories"), what makes *Soldiers of Fortune* most modern in its sentiment—what makes it succeed as an authentic imperialist narrative for the 1890s—springs to the fore in its scenes of triumphant patriotism. When the soldiers of fortune cheer their engineer-manager-warrior-hero, and when the sunburned Americans (nothing more glamorous than the effect of tropical sun upon firm Caucasian flesh) ride by, tall in their saddles, their weapons glittering in the South American sun, this is high emotion, this is sexiness, this is the imperial moment.[31]

To think that Robert Clay must give all this up: the glory and the sexuality of war, the passionate sense of calling, the conviction of his personal worth as an engineer capable of destroying whole mountains and as a soldier leading his rough riders into battle against duplicitous Spaniards for the good of the natives. He has won everything he has fought for: the Olancho mines, the security of the republic, and Hope Langham, but it is this last victory that defeats him—thereby squelching the hope expressed by Henry Demarest Lloyd that brutality is the means to happy peace and that good imperialism will end imperialism's evils.

As one of his adoring associates tells him, Clay must now "graduate from the position of manager-director and become the engineering expert."

> "What will you be to-morrow? To-morrow you will be Andrew Langham's son-in-law. . . . Andrew Langham's son-in-law cannot ask his wife to live in such a hole as this, so—Good-bye, Mr. Clay."
> (353)

The vision of the future that lies ahead for the erstwhile world-wandering engineer-hero of many talents and no boundaries is a sad one.

Once married to the conventionalities of the business enterprise as well as to Hope, he will be slotted into the next stage of Veblen's historiographic trajectory, fixed in place as the technocrat-specialist. When Davis inserts this jarring note of psychological realism, he creates a scene analogous to the glimpse he gives us at the summit of San Juan Hill, when he called up the shock of recognition voiced by Crane's trooper. "Well, hell, here we are!"

Of course, Davis dare not let this sadness and this shock overwhelm the purpose of his novel. In order to write a best-selling barbaric fiction, he must suppress the anxieties that threaten all popular narratives. Besides, his novel ought not give away the fact that it is thoroughly "modern" in the Veblenesque sense, that is, a retrograde amalgam of realistic details with romantic ideals. Whether consciously or unconsciously, in his final pages Davis muffles the fright of what it means for Clay to be the hero of an imperialist fiction that barely masks its ruthlessness. The last paragraph of *Soldiers of Fortune* places Clay and Hope, a matched pair of perfect American types, at the rail of the yacht bearing them back to the States. This works well for Davis's purposes, but not completely. It does not erase the words Clay's best friend speaks as Greek chorus in the penultimate chapter:

> "You will grow fat, Clay, and live on Fifth Avenue and wear a high silk hat, and some day when you are sitting in your club . . . this will all come back to you,—this heat, and the palms, and the fever . . . and you'll want to chuck your gun under your chin and shoot into a line of men, and the policemen won't let you, and your wife won't let you. That's what you're giving up. There it is. Take a good look at it. You'll never see it again." (353–54)

The "Well, Hell" of Where We Are

"We shall never be again as we were!" heralds the conclusion of yet another turn-of-the-century narrative about the Pyrrhic victories that come to scientific managers who are too successful at winning to be victorious in the final account.

The Wings of the Dove (1902) and *The Golden Bowl* (1904) are narratives about imperialist moves and the contested effectiveness of conflicting efficiency systems. They are brilliant critiques of unacceptable situations. True, James, unlike his writer colleagues Stephen Crane and Joseph Conrad, never wrote about war campaigns or South American mining interests. True, James was explicitly singled out by Theodore Roosevelt as the epitome of wasteful unmanliness.[32] True, James has often been belabored for being incapable of dealing forthrightly with the business preoccupations of the American males of his generation. These charges are accurate enough, but James *was* able to incorporate into his novels of 1902 and 1904 astute accounts of the grave problems (problems that make his a "modern" world) caused by the squinting mixture to which his brother William called attention in 1899: the unholy alliance of barbarous instincts of acquisition and rationalistic managerial practices. Where Richard Harding Davis says yes, yes, yes! and thereby succeeds in writing a best-seller, James says maybe and no, and gives us literary masterpieces.

With Kate Croy's pronouncement to her lover Merton Densher, "We shall never be again as we were!" *The Wings of the Dove* concludes with one of the most shattering lines in our literature, nearly equal in its tragic finality to Lear's final words, "Thou'lt come no more. Never, never, never, never, never!"[33] What has led up to this moment reveals the obverse side of the stories of triumph that others were telling about good engineers and soldiers of fortune, men who win empires of power, romantic love, and moral ascendancy by means of their merger of efficiency systems and codes of manly courage.

Central to *The Wings of the Dove* is the decision of Britannia (represented by the massive form of Maud Lowder) to recolonize America by "making good use" of Milly Theale, the heiress and emblem of the nation currently perfecting its skills at making use of the rest of the world. Maud Lowder also attempts to extend her authority *within* the British empire by appropriating Lord Mark's title through her adroit management of her niece Kate Croy's magnificence.

Note that it is the women, Maud and Kate, who assume the role of efficiency experts and modern managers. The manner in which Aunt Maud as the head boss "drives" Kate to do her bidding would have won the approval of Frederick Winslow Taylor as he prepared to deliver his seminal address on "Shop Management" before the American Society of Mechanical Engineers in 1903. But Kate, with her "cool controlled facility," also shows she could have matched Robert Clay in any contest of wills and wiles (20:131). The tension mounts when Kate introduces managerial countermoves against her aunt and, simultaneously, against Milly as the most effective means of taking plunder in the name of "the good" of the vanquished.

Still, taking *The Wings of the Dove* as a paradigm for imperialistic management techniques is limited by the fact that James's tropes are allied not with business enterprises per se, but with the world of the theater in which stage managers rigorously enforce principles of performance for the sake of the fine show offered the spectators seated in the boxes (20:34–35). It is James's next novel, *The Golden Bowl,* that takes us directly into the midst of the modern world, the machine process ruled by the complex motives and methods of advanced capitalism. It is here that James reflects most profoundly upon the cultural space he shares with Veblen, Weber, Taylor, and Roosevelt.

The Golden Bowl receives a great deal of attention these days in regard to whether it is a critique of turn-of-the-century capitalistic practices or is complicit with them. Marxist analyses assess the role played by the American business tycoon, Adam Verver, and reflect upon James's incessant use of the discourse of commodities and exchange. It has become almost obligatory to cite *The Theory of the Leisure Class* in considering the idle lives of the Ververs, whose conspicuous consumption centers on the two most magnificent objects in their art collection, Prince Amerigo and Charlotte Stant. However, too little has been said about the canny use to which James's "translation" puts the language and themes connecting scientific management to imperialism, or about the striking way his narrative mimes the calculations of efficiency systems that aspire to end all waste.[34]

Bring to mind certain essentials about the marriage contracted between Maggie Verver and her Roman prince, itemized in a labor-management document meticulously worked out by the lawyer-mediators on both sides of this major business merger. Maggie will bring American money and security to the prince. He has a title to offer; even more important, he has the kind of "history" that newly born Americans have yet to accumulate. The prince is named after the man who mapped a continent during the era when Europeans were trying to expand their commercial interests into the New World. He brings the Ververs a heritage of Old World barbarism, the kind upon which Veblen would have been glad to expound. The prince's family has a public history of exploits in battle, ruthless crimes, marriages of alliance, flamboyant follies, and the immense waste of blood and money. But this barbaric heritage, which constitutes much of Amerigo's charm to Maggie's "savage" imagination, is only half of who he is. The other half Maggie has yet to discover, and to use wisely. For if the hidden, personal quality he holds within is left idly unproductive because it is poorly managed, the marriage process the Ververs set in motion at such high cost will be broken upon the factory floor of Eaton Place.

Prince Amerigo has sincere hopes that his unused self will receive proper handling by his new employers, Maggie and her father. In words whose correctness Taylor would acknowledge, the Prince considers that he "was allying himself to science, for what was science but the absence of prejudice backed by the presence of money."[35] Perhaps that public part of Amerigo's life—the superstitious barbarity of his ancestors—might be redeemed by good management. If so, his "life would be full of machinery, which was the antidote to superstition" (23:17).

The novel commences, therefore, with a crucial management problem. On the one hand, a valuable collector's piece can be saved by applying the paramount attribute of modern capitalism Max Weber defined the same year *The Golden Bowl* was published: "so far as the transactions are rational, calculation underlies every single action of the partners." [36] On the other hand, the consequences will be dire if the Ververs prove to be modern barbarians more wasteful in their ineptitude than any of the prince's feudal ancestors.

Enter Charlotte Stant, the female efficiency expert. Like Kate Croy in *The Wings of the Dove,* Charlotte will attempt to outmaneuver the unproductive measures resulting from the irrational management practices put into effect by those who hold power over her life and the life of the prince. Both Charlotte and her exlover have been manipulated into becoming part of the machine process of the Verver ménage; both feel that others have been put in charge; both realize the Ververs have failed to use their *sposi* to the satisfaction of every person contained within this bizarre partnership (one that is simultaneously marital, commercial, and imperialistic). Since James makes it clear almost immediately that women perform while men, waiting, receive whatever the women produce, it is inevitable that the prince will turn for succor to Charlotte's "perfect, . . . brilliant efficiency" (23:318).

The remainder of James's inordinately complex narrative is devoted to the war campaigns waged, as it were, across the terrain of the Verver empire. For a while it is Charlotte who manages the bosses, who, unwittingly, have forfeited their authority to manage. It is Charlotte who, refusing to have passion wasted, calculates ingenuous ways to make the highest productive use of the time-motion studies into which she plunges. Witness the full sexual use to which she and the prince put their hours together at Gloucester.

At the moment when Charlotte attains the peak of her managerial powers, however, Maggie chances to detect the waste surrounding her marriage. Once Maggie "sees," the story becomes a battle between the consciousnesses of two exceptionally capable executive wills. In the end, Maggie defeats Charlotte, but why? And does she really?

Perhaps Maggie wins because Charlotte never completely controls her passionate response to the prince's sexuality, or to the prejudicial anger she bears toward her employers. In contrast, Maggie (stifling cries of pain over her physical desire for the prince) directs all her efforts to the use of the scientific method, the process that Amerigo earlier defined as "the absence of prejudice backed by the presence of money" and as the presence of a life "full of machinery, which was the antidote to superstition." Or perhaps it is because Maggie draws upon that special source of strength that comes to all good little American imperialists: her sincere belief that whatever she does, however ruthless her practices, is for the benefit of the natives, once she extends the moral authority of the nation she represents as its leading "daughter and heir."

The actual nature of Maggie's triumph in this war over who will succeed in managing and who must submit to being managed is as problematic as the victory achieved by Robert Clay. Holding the golden leash that ties Charlotte to his side, Adam Verver has departed, leading Charlotte back to American City, her rebellion against her employer stifled. Alone with Amerigo, Maggie faces that moment when she will be paid the reward for what she has produced by successfully employing the most sophisticated techniques of modern management. But suddenly she feels that "instant of terror" that "always precedes, on the part of the creature to be paid, the certification of the amount" (24:367). As Amerigo holds "the money-bag for her to come and take" (24:368), she is suddenly no longer the manager; she is an employee caught in dread suspense about the amount and kind of wages allowed her by the person with the power to determine the worth of her services.

There is a further bit of exchange Maggie has to negotiate with her employer before she can accept sexual ecstasy—an ecstasy that, in one form or another, pervades imperialist narratives at that moment when it appears as though Americans are reinforcing their power over the people (like the prince) they have colonized by means of their New World money and morality. But Maggie finds she cannot seize sexual joy at the expense of the memory of Charlotte, "before whose mastery of the greater style she had just been standing dazzled" (ibid.).

Maggie's situation approximates that of Merton Densher at the end of *The Wings of the Dove.* Kate Croy stands before Densher, ready to pay him sexual coinage if he will only efface from his mind the image of Milly Theale. But Milly, the dead American heiress, wins the war because Densher cannot forget that she was the woman with the "mastery of the greater style," which she had wielded in the face of Kate's own magnificent managerial skills. Because the little American imperialist is victorious even in death, Densher turns away from Kate, who realizes that they can never be again what they were.

In the final paragraph of *The Golden Bowl,* Maggie Verver silently acknowledges the power of Charlotte Stant. Charlotte was the one who had utilized (to use Weber's words) the "calculation" that had underlaid "every single action of their lives." Even now, the memory of Charlotte's role affects how Maggie will take what the prince "gives" her—payment for successful work that confirms our sense that Maggie, as manager and employee, having won, can only lose.

As Maggie disappears into the prince's embrace, "his whole act enclosing her," we experience the final "pity and dread" of the narrative (24:369). Like Kate and Densher, Maggie and the prince can never be again what they were before the deadly battle of competing interests began.[37] The folly of Maggie's hope that she might revert to her original state as the innocent, gentle American savage is exposed. The "unity of brutality"—the imperialism of her pursuit of the Old World prince—did not lead to the "unity of peace" and the destruction of imperialism. She has merely evolved into an American barbarian of the "transmuted" modern kind, a creature vanquished more by her own use of the calculations of turn-of-the-century New World expansionism than by the superstitious barbarities of Old World feudalism.

The hidden qualities of the prince that might have saved both himself and Maggie are never developed scientifically because of the contradictions of shrewdness and ineptitude built into the Ververs' managerial methods. The only payment Maggie now can receive is the profound stillness of her sexual vanquishing by the prince. The only power the prince retains is the stasis of his archaism, fated by the ironic fact that his wife's modern business enterprises (like those of Robert Clay) have succeeded all too well. James foregoes the "big" climax offered at the close of Richard Harding Davis's account of the Cuban and Puerto Rican campaigns, with its promise of a triumphant future for the young American heir of all the ages. Instead, James leaves Maggie and the prince with the terrible reality of *where* they are—the "well, hell" of the present moment.

THREE

Brutality and Betterment

IT IS 1929, and Henry Adams is eleven years in his grave at Rock Creek Cemetery, one hopes at rest, under the shadow of the silent, seated figure sculpted by Augustus Saint-Gaudens. It is February, and Wall Street will not crash until October, in the panic that once again will expose the inefficiency riddling the nation's economic and governmental systems. It is February 1929, and men have gathered under the aegis of the Taylor Society to discuss once again the plaguing question of the effect of new management systems upon industrial workers. One of the men, F. A. Silcox, union leader and future New Deal official, is disgusted by the conciliatory stance union representatives were taking when faced with the force of Frederick Winslow Taylor's "rationalizing" principles, laid down in the early 1900s during the same years in which Henry Adams was attempting to apply the principles of scientific history to his study of the laws of force held over us all.

Silcox's ironic characterization of the code of conduct ruling twentieth-century American industry is strikingly similar to Adams's earlier ironic analysis of the rifts between facts and values rending American government, commerce, and industry, as well as the "begonia" life of that grandson of presidents.

> The acquisition of power is the primary thing that counts. . . . With a favorable balance of power there is only one workable course of action and that is to take all the traffic will bear when the taking is good. . . . The ethical moralizing with oughts, shouldn'ts and don'ts is an effort to mitigate in some manner the brutality of the conflict used mostly by those who do not possess sufficient power to enforce their own will.[1]

When Silcox focuses upon the unholy balance of power that manage-ment holds over labor, he takes no account of the fact that Taylor origi-nally justified his scientism as a program of ethics. Taylor contended that production procedures become moral acts through the agency of science and the engineers in charge of the machine process. Taylor may have been lying through his teeth, but his promise stands: the evils of waste and the chaos of class tensions will cease in the society governed by his principles; worker and manager will be joined together as the lion lies down with the lamb on the factory floor.

Thorstein Veblen was always skeptical of such prophecies, although aware they might carry an absurd truth of their own. From where he stood at the threshold of modern management in 1904, he foretold what Silcox would proclaim in 1929: "the business enterprise" seeks to define itself by "charging what the traffic will bear." In theory at least, business is rewarded through its shrewd employment of impersonal processes, whereby it achieves a "sagacious calculation of profit and loss, untroubled by sentimental considerations of human kindness or irritation or of hon-esty."[2]

In practice, however, there were "obstacles in the way" to success, to use words of Lewis Mumford, who, like Veblen, traces the unsettling ef-fects of vestiges from the past upon a world of "technics." Because of the "deep gap between the paleotechnic and neotechnic phases," there are "habits of mind" that clog the easy passage between the old order and the new.[3] For example, the wish to placate stirrings of archaic conscience in the midst of modern conditions might result in bad business and a weak society besotted by sentimentality. Neither businessmen nor their Pro-gressivist critics could remain "untroubled" by "the brutality of the con-flict," nor by the potentially harmful consequences of acting entirely out of altruism. Since efficiency, rationality, and science set contemporary standards for "the best way" to the best society, the question was whether these reified concepts were in league with love, or whether love was the sham that intelligent leaders must expose.[4]

If it was more sensible to follow motives of self-interest, was self-interest served more effectively by the brutalization or the betterment of the working class? But wasn't what some called brutality actually better-ment? What meaning could "betterment" have in the midst of the culture of management other than controlled conduct? Surely, gaining "one's own good" set in motion a process in which strict supervision is maintained over the workers, but also strict self-discipline on the part of the em-ployer?

Nowhere was the confusion more apparent than in the language used by management and labor alike. Neither American capitalism nor American democracy claimed a distinctive discourse that defined ideological boundaries with precision. A complex set of rhetorical and narrative forms grew up around the business enterprise amidst the apparent separation of the power of *facts* (that point forcefully to the way things are) from the powerlessness of *values* (weakly represented by such words as "ought," "shouldn't," and "don't"). Analysts struggled to make new facts out of evolving values in an age that drew back from the language of men like J. P. Morgan and C. T. Yerkes, who once had dared anyone to deny old-style tycoons the right to say, "the public be damned."

Divided Texts

After J. David Houser completed investigations funded in 1927 by the Jacob Wertheim Research Fellowship for the Betterment of Industrial Relations, he put together a book-length report, *What the Employer Thinks: Executives' Attitudes toward Employees*. Houser's numerous interviews with heads of major manufacturing and business concerns led him to question "the widespread use of phrases" used by executives in their daily dealings with labor, in which they attempt to "imitate" the "abstract idealism" the American public expects of them.[5]

Like the bosses F. A. Silcox bitterly describes two years later, the executives Houser approached were not readily susceptible to "sentimental considerations." On the other hand, their "desire for social approval or the fear of social disapproval" created an awkward situation. The language of goodwill they directed toward both employees and public was "very prone to conflict with inner urges, predispositions or emotional bias."

Businessmen at odds with themselves are hardly free to seize nonchalantly upon the opportunity "to take all the traffic will bear." Deeply involved in "the brutality of the conflict," they realize a "favorable balance" depends upon their retention of "sufficient power to enforce their own will." Nevertheless, Houser believes they experience the debilitating "phenomenon of 'rationalization' "—a term currently being used "to explain the mental process of attempting to conceal a bias or inner urge not in conformity with personal ideals or social standards." What an odd situation we find here. Pressed into certain business practices by adherence to what their grandfathers and fathers had valorized as "rational" behavior, these men are victims of "rationalizations" that cloud logical thought.

Businessmen shaving the line between workaday brutality and lofty social reforms catch at phrases that are "clearly substitutes for thought"— phrases "charged with so much emotion that they resemble shibboleths." " 'Management's responsibility,' 'the desire to be fair,' 'employees' ingrat-

itude,' 'decent treatment,' 'paternalism—prying into men's affairs,' 'it pays
in dollars and cents' ": these are words business uses to fight "free from
any intellectual process." "There is apparent," Houser comments,

> a strong, naive tendency in the executive to grasp at formulae and
> single devices as panaceas. Are not these blind prescriptions, these
> unthinking gestures, often testimonies to inadequate preparation
> and inability to confront problems?

The very nature of Houser's 1927 study—the fact that it is sanctioned
by institutional funding and publication, and that it is structured largely
by interviews with executives who need to tell stories with "a 'good' reason, rather than the 'real' reason for conduct"—makes the book complicitous with the conditions Houser wishes to analyze. Naturally we question the questioner, adept at his task as he may be. For example, we ask
just how true is the "truth," when Houser finds that by the late 1920s the
nation's "social attitudes" were "more and more sharply set against greed
or power at the expense of the workers." On the other hand, although it is
unlikely that the great American public was in full cry for social reform
on the eve of the Depression, there are advantages to working through the
fertile implications of Houser's contention that the "individual conflicts
and rationalizations" agitating the minds of "self-sufficient and self-
expressive personalities" prompt the "need for cloaking these unworthy
desires."

Words were at odds, yet in league. They were used both for thinking
and for the avoidance of thought about labor-management relations. Language that "imitated" the ideals purportedly upheld by public opinion did
not stay put on the printed page. People in power had to deal "not only in
words but also in actions." The will of the business enterprise was enforced, and sometimes enfeebled, by confusing words, confused actions.
Moral imperatives were implicated in "the brutality of the conflict" at the
same time those "oughts" tried "to mitigate in some manner" that same
brutality, a method others said could only assure failure.

Paternalistic welfare programs urged upon management were "sometimes a type of organized industrial hypocrisy," but the alternative discourse offered by the advocates of industrial democracy was also at odds
with the goal of attaining betterment for the entire work force. Because of
dissension within the workers' ranks that brought "the brutality of the
conflict" into the shop, the language of the democratic ideal was frequently displaced by expressions of divisive fears over matters of race and
ethnicity, of hierarchies of skills disturbed by the new technology, and of
gender-conditioned relations among home, family, and work. Little wonder that the words of workers and employers echo the same confusions

that divided (and bound together) reform theories and workaday practices.

The following three issues were obsessively placed on public view: (1) the conduct of life best suited to a business enterprise devoted to getting "all the traffic will bear," but also to gaining the approval of the public at large; (2) the need to dissociate welfare plans from sentimentality by underscoring the general "good" gained through the scientific management of men and machinery; (3) the justification of the embarrassing drift toward reform measures by identifying reform as the most practical way to fend off social upheavals.

That these were matters of acknowledged concern came as the consequence of the following four factors: (1) the social and economic conditions resulting from accelerations in the machine process; (2) the transfer of authority away from shop bosses into the hands of a new managerial class; (3) the pressures of centralization, which decentralized what any one person (factory worker, manager, or employer) might "know" about the business enterprise and the machine process; (4) the influx of a new labor force, increasingly comprised of immigrants, migrating blacks from the rural South, and women who continued to assert the need to work outside the home. But these concerns all seemed to come down to the single, seemingly unsolvable problem of how to get effective machine productivity in the face of having to accommodate "the human element."

Subsequent samplings of contending (and complicitous) narratives concerning what is and what ought to be are only a portion of the immense flow of words expended upon the subject. Most come from the magazines, pamphlets, books, newspaper articles, and speeches that provided the public forum for the managerial class, but we can probe these texts for our own purposes. They are particularly valuable once we realize that none of these statements stands alone; each is in a relationship. Only when read together do they suggest the "event" they unfold before our eyes.

"Thou Shalt Not Steal"

In the late 1870s Karl Marx and Friedrich Engels attacked the moralistic codes still in place long after changes effected by the newest machine processes came into play. In 1879 Marx denounced the German Social Democrats for trying to lead workers toward "good taste" and "good form" in their wish to cleanse the masses of "coarse proletarian passions" and "disreputable behavior." Ever alert to the capitalists' conflation of conduct and economics, Marx understood that this effort to impose "a thoroughly respectable 'bourgeois behaviour' " was tantamount to reinforcing immoral economic conditions. These acts were made even more outrageous when glossed with words like " 'true love of humanity' and empty phraseology about 'justice.' "[6] In 1878, while in the process of writing *Anti-Duhring*, Engels also rejected the attempt of bourgeois moralists

> to impose on us any moral dogma whatsoever as an eternal, ultimate and forever immutable ethical law on the pretext that the moral world, too, has its permanent principles which stand above history and the differences between nations.[7]

Within the next two decades, William James and John Dewey would propose codes of social conduct appropriate to the new century and American democratic ideals. In their dismissal of outmoded codes based on moral absolutes, neither James nor Dewey called for "the proletarian morality" urged by classical Marxism, a morality "derived from the practical relations on which their class position is based—from the economic relations in which they carry on production and exchange." Although the social theories of the two Americans might verge upon the detested position of the German Social Democrats or the vagaries of the American Progressive Party, James and Dewey concurred with the Marxist belief that social ethics comes down to the single commandment, "Thou Shalt Not Steal."[8]

The narrative mode favored by classical Marxism requires the imperative voice as well as the future tense. It is not enough to argue the obligation to bring about a perfected society in which justice slashes free from the corruption and tyranny of earlier institutions. Arguments leaning upon language limited to "ought" and "should" are as ineffectual as the kind relied upon by socialist sentimentalism and liberal Christian reform. In contrast, "Thou Shalt Not" calls upon the rhetoric of the Lord of Might handing down instructions to Moses, his earthly manager. All further conduct is prescribed by the imperative voice, whose demands may not be disobeyed since history (Providence, in the Judeo-Christian version; historical materialism in Marxist nomenclature) brooks no disobedience.

Unfortunately, the aftermath of the meeting on Mount Sinai reveals "bad" history. The status quo remains intact. The children of Israel continue to dance in worship before the golden calf, and Moses suffers the fate of all who speak with voices less powerful than that of Yahweh. Mediating mortal languages can only attempt (as did the words of Marx and Engels) to bridge the chasm between the clarity of the real and the distorted rhetoric of society's fondest fantasies.

When the Adams manikin (mock-hero of *The Education of Henry Adams*) lies broken-necked upon the threshold of the twentieth century at the base of the dynamo on display at the Paris Exposition, he does not try

to imitate Moses, who at least commanded a radical new society to leap
into being. Adams moves through time and space only when he experiences the fall into a new kind of history. Therein lies his hope of offering
an effective critique of a society that, whether through ignorance or fear,
refuses to confront the facts of modern force.

By calculation, *The Education of Henry Adams* is a story about helplessness and impotence, as traditional moral principles of "ought" and
"shouldn't" are dashed, one by one, to the ground by the impersonal,
amoral force of "what is." Adams's representation of the dynamo universe
(anarchical, impersonal—that golden calf before whose shrine such terms
as "justice" and "mercy" have no meaning) is reinforced by its considered
contrast to an earlier feudal universe. Once upon a time there was the force
of the Virgin, that powerfully irrational, whimsical, personal presence
who promised a mercy that mitigated the stern justice, if not the brutality,
of the Father and the Son. Adams recognizes that American minds have
no recollection of this tale of the Virgin. Without ownership of an imaginative precedent for the strong sentiments of Marian mercy, they rely
upon misguided, erratic, enfeebled impulses toward Protestant charity.
The welfare programs about to be stitched onto the business enterprise in
the name of scientifically efficient management principles simply replace
the Bonifacius of late eighteenth-century philanthropy and the evangelical
modes of the nineteenth century, still caught in the cleft between outmoded ideals and dynamo facts.

Veblen steps in where Adams fears to tread. He points to the imperatives of "shalt not" that have superseded those once voiced on Sinai by
Original Force. Both men treat a situation in which the assumed contradictions between the facts and values tied to the business enterprise throw
society and its languages into a series of misalignments. But whereas
Adams tells a *story* of what it is like to feel "what is" during the dynamo
age, Veblen advances the *theory* of the machine process as it "ought to be."

Veblen's 1904 *Theory of Business Enterprise* confirms what Adams experienced at the Paris Gallery of Machines in 1900. Contemptuous of
those who need soothing, Veblen acidly conveys what happens to an
American economic system when notions of social equality bear little reference to the surge to get "all the traffic will bear." The sentimental language of businessmen aspires to lessen life's brutality, but not if it requires
a radicalized change of habits or institutions. Narratives of betterment enacted with too much fervor in the shops would prevent the bosses from
achieving their true goal: the making of money and the continuation of
the status quo.

Businessmen argue that their moral function is to coordinate the machine process with "heightened serviceability."[9] Veblen acknowledges that a certain "value" accrues to such talk if it gains the businessmen self-approval and the approval of the nonbusiness community. He even allows there may be "a modicum of truth in it as an account of facts." After all, the businessman can be "moved by ideals of serviceability and an aspiration to make the way of life easier for his fellows."

With a certain sardonic glee, Veblen warns of the dangers of talk about ideals. Having lived through a story of financial success, the businessman's taste for the pursuit of service is weakened; besides, service itself can be weakening. Shrewd enough to see that "motives of this kind detract from business efficiency," he will decide that moral considerations are for less able men—the weaklings in the marketplace (or, by implication, spectators like Henry Adams). Whereas the strong stay powerful, the weak get weaker because of their allegiance to notions of "equity, fair dealing, and workmanlike integrity." On rare occasions, the "genial" employer who puts aside "exacting the last concession that a ruthless business strategy might entitle him to" will arrive at "a speedier conclusion and a smoother working of the large coalitions than would follow from the unmitigated sway of business principles." But even this temporary burst of "sentimentalism" stays "within the range of business principles, not in contravention of them."

The maxim "caveat emptor" stays intact and patterns of capitalistic ruthlessness remain in place as long as business limits its moral view to "a conventional abrogation" of immoral practices. Canonized narratives are not overturned by introducing revisionist "history" or radical "story" into the factory. These are businessmen after all. Their ledgers must stay balanced; narrative texts written for or about them must remain static. "The moral need of balance" between service to society and pecuniary gain works only if acts of altruism result in an equilibrium manifested in *money* terms. Anything less than profits stemming from business efficiency and the unimpeded machine process becomes, in Veblen's theory, the sentimental sacrifice of power.

The rhetoric of dealing justly with others' labor is, however, free coinage. It can be, and is, traded in by anyone once it is perceived as containing its own kind of power and profit. The rhetorical strategy of classical Marxism seeks to reveal the historical reality of every worker's ownership of his or her own labor, but what is one to do with Henry Ford's appropriation of what *sounds like* the same argument? What is one to do with Ford's statement that the "moral fundamental"—the "reality" according to which he runs his automotive empire—rests upon the admonition, "Thou shalt not steal" from any man his right to his own labor?[10]

Or how should one respond to Ford's incorporation of the mythic phrases sacred to American moral lore, "self-reliance and self-sufficiency," or to his vision of "a world in which everybody has all that he wants"?[11]

What we *could* do is subsume Ford's use of the language of altruism within the schema Veblen defines as having as its sole aim the making of money. We could immediately discount Ford's words that echo Emersonian natural law: "what we call moral . . . is natural; it represents the way that life must go if it is to go at all. . . . Morality is a part of good management . . . —the plain, practical development of life according to its nature." We can dismiss the onward rolling clauses of the jeremiadlike sentence, which forcefully itemize what *cannot be* in a good world: "no man can survive, no industry can survive, no government can survive, no system of civilization can survive which does not continually give service to the greatest possible number."

Let us go, however, with the suggestion made by Reinhard Bendix, who, in the process of analyzing the bureaucratization of American business practices, observes that it is "more illuminating to examine the strategy of argument than to insist that the argument is selfish."[12] The practice of examining strategies does not guarantee that texts will disclose their "intentions." Nevertheless, without disappearing into the philosophical sinkholes of indeterminacy and intentionality, we can think in terms of *degrees* of awareness and *gradations* of apparent intent when approaching texts of the Fordian persuasion.

In considering the effects that the actions of men like Ford had on industry, Veblen applied "theory," not "philosophy"—abstractions that tend toward messianic hopes rather than realistic earthly achievements. Ford, however, dismissed Veblen's focus upon present practicalities when he titled the opening chapter of *My Philosophy of Industry*, "Machinery, the New Messiah." Ford also rejects the Adamsian mode. The ironic stance of the doubter has no place in Ford's merger of machine with the Christ who comes to save society from itself.

There are evident differences between Ford's phrasing and the tonalities introduced by Veblen and Adams. What of the likenesses between Ford's wording and Emerson's sanctification of self-generating energy? Consider the pitch of the following statements in which Ford outlines crucial difference between "being *statically* 'good' and being *dynamically* good."[13]

Once we get past crudities of phrasing that would have been distasteful to Emerson as a Harvard graduate, ex-Unitarian minister, and Concord intellectual, Ford's speech patterns bring us close to the notions of holism, compensation, and efficient use of personal force found in Emerson's 1860 essay, "The Conduct of Life."

Our motive cannot be the attainment of some kind of goodness which is apart from life itself, but the attainment of inherent rightness, physically, mentally, spiritually, so that this complex instrument which we call society may efficiently function. The *right* way is the only *way*. . . . Rightness in mechanics, rightness in morals are basically the same thing and cannot rest apart.

Fordian morality is in line with Emerson's "great man" theory of history, with faith in universal law, with the equalizing power of "correspondence," and with the merger of matter and spirit in the "larger" and "longer" view. Ford concurs with Emerson in affirming that leaders of "morality in progress"—those men unchallenged by external pressures of change—control circumstances for the service of all.

Ford's language partakes of the verbal flatness of Rotary Club moralism (as well as its parochial patriotism) when he claims that other nations "are feeling the benefit of American progress, our American right thinking," but it also possesses the sweeping line of the Transcendentalists' prose style in phrases such as "the reign, the rule, the law of the highest relations," or "the right way" that gives one "the world . . . without poverty, without injustice, without need." What gives Fordian rhetoric away as a strategy appropriate for its own age, not Emerson's, is the way the twentieth-century positivist does without the upper reaches of the transcendent.

Ford refers to the Sermon on the Mount when speaking of men's need to seek God's kingdom of righteousness, but he immediately relocates that kingdom by qualifying what his rhetoric has just intimated. Moral qualities are equated with a well-run world, where "clean living, square dealing" make life "successful . . . , smooth-running and helpful to everyone." Factory, home, and society alike are clean, efficient, and in fine equilibrium. We know where we are once Ford tells us that although his comment "sounds religious," it is "just a plain statement of facts." God is the business enterprise, God's kingdom is Highland Park, and the Ford Motor Company's assembly line is the new messiah, which is exactly what his "philosophy" has "intended" all along.

Friedrich Engels appropriates Old Testament texts for new purposes, but he never loses faith in a reality lying outside the mental narrows of the profit motive. In the same way, the language Emerson used to put forward a dynamic concept of the conduct of life *trusts* itself. Classic Marxist and Transcendentalist discourses struggle to keep from descending to the petty level of a world bounded by a businessman's notion of "what is," a notion sharing embarrassed space with "should" but never with "shalt."

"We need more facts," the Ford philosophy states, "but they must be universal facts." [14] This sounds like Emerson, and so do the sentences that follows: "We never go forward on known facts: we learn the facts afterward. The world is the fundamental fact." Once again the giveaway comes when Ford declares that the business mind controls the world's facts, and that only this mind possesses the ability to endow the world with value. Value derives from an equivalence between life's worth and products of quality. In the end, Fordian goodness is hardly distinguishable from making a good deal on a well-made Ford car.

Is this, then, all we can expect from the texts to come? Writings sanctioned by early twentieth-century capitalism, which make easy use of devices filched from the strong rhetoric of more radical utterances? Language that proclaims itself free of lies and sentimentalism because it takes as its model the rationality of science and the common sense of business? Language that works to justify its moral claims, only to give away its game at last? Texts bound by the iron necessity of ideological oscillations, which make everyone's prose "sound alike" as far as *meaning* goes?

Does not this statement sound like Thorstein Veblen or Karl Marx in the urgency with which it calls upon clear-eyed analysts to exact stern critiques of contemporary social circumstances?

> The analyst takes the situation apart and lays the facts bare. Then comes the power of criticism, which means the weighing of values, the rating of all facts according to universal standards. Faultfinding is emotional, analysis is intellectual, criticism is moral. [15]

Granted, Marx and Veblen would make clear that "universal standards" applied to the ever-changing laws of historical materialism have nothing to do with the so-called absolutes of philosophers. But they would not deny the importance of advancing effectively scientific dissections of society. Alas for our sense of the rightness of things! Reactionary reformers together with Bolshevists are the faultfinders impugned here, and the critic on the attack is Henry Ford.

Part of our difficulty comes from texts that reflect the essential weakness of the moralists of "ought" and "should," those who compromise their attempts to correct imbalances within society by upholding the pretense that they stand outside the problem. Still other texts actively recruit the very forces they wish to destroy, only to subject them to a violence of language that, like a surgeon's knife, cuts out the bad and leaves the good. The latter type of text is exemplified nicely by Lenin's 1918 essay, "Raising the Productivity of Labour." He states that Soviets "must raise the question of applying much of what is scientific and progressive in the Taylor system." That system,

> the last word of capitalism in this aspect [learning how best to work], like all capitalist progress, is a combination of the refined brutality of bourgeois exploitation and a number of the greatest scientific achievements in the field of analyzing mechanical motions during work, the elimination of superfluous and awkward motions, the elaboration of correct methods of work, the introduction of the best system of accounting and control, etc.[16]

Lenin's strategy for placing mutually antagonistic elements under his control would be Veblen's, too, if he could make it so. Whereas Lenin speaks confidently of the gains *that will be had* once the "good science" of Taylorism is stripped away from the corrupt flesh of capitalism, Veblen speaks with agitation about the consequences if faulty practices ever were to throw off the steadying hand of scientific theory.

The Theory of Business Enterprise opens with language that seeks neutrality through its pose of scientific objectivity. Veblen removes the human element entirely from his description of the "productive mechanism," as in his sentence: "By virtue of this concatenation of processes the modern industrial system at large bears the character of a comprehensive, balanced mechanical process."[17] But then Veblen (even Veblen!) introduces the charged imagery of bodily and mental disease. He warns what may befall this careful balance if any "degree of maladjustment in the interstitial coordination of this industrial process at large in some degree hinders its working."

> A disturbance at any point, whereby any given branch of industry fails to do its share in the work of the system at large, immediately affects the neighboring or related branches which come before or after in the sequence, and is transmitted through their derangement to the remoter portions of the system.

Through recurrent use of the words "disturbance," "derangement," "maladjustment," and "disabling," Veblen reinforces his warning:

> the keeping of the balance in the comprehensive machine process of industry is a matter of the gravest urgency if the productive mechanism is to proceed with its work in the efficient manner, *so as to avoid idleness, waste, and hardship.*" (my emphasis)

Veblen's uncharacteristically nervous description, extending over two pages of printed text, likens a nonhuman system to one dangerously susceptible to organic ailments. By the close of the cautionary sentence above, he has singled out three consequences of "maladjustment" in the industrial plant (itself a word suggestive of living, growing things subject to decay), couched in terms familiar to any moralist: idleness, waste, and hardship.

What is the cause of the "disturbance" that agitates Veblen, usually the coolest of writers? Not the workers; not the engineers. Disturbance is introduced by the unpredictable nature of the businessman who "comes into the industrial process as a decisive factor." Like Taylor and Lenin, Veblen wishes to place his faith in an unvarying, finely adjusted machine process predicated on strictly scientific principles. But introduce *the outsider,* the meddling men from the main office who have the power "to make or mar the running adjustments of industry," and the perfect text-as-theory becomes an animistic melodrama of derangement and decay. According to Lenin's plan, the outsider can be controlled by the central will of the party; theory and practice will be one. In Veblen's society—an awkward imbalance of capitalism and democracy (each one characterized by an imbalance of theories and practices)—no such guarantees are possible.

In the many narratives (fictive and "straight") of this period that center around industrial procedures, the hero is frequently the engineer as manager.[18] Villains are of several breeds: in Veblen's telling, the business enterprise that works counter to scientific principles; in Lenin's case, uncontrolled remnants of bourgeois capitalistic practices; in Taylor's arguments, troublemakers include both ignorant owners at the top and misguided workers on the bottom. The engineer is the hero because he alone abides by the laws of the machine process. Through obedience to its principles, he places himself on the side of the higher morality of rationalism and efficiency.

Whether the texts are owned by a capitalist, a Marxist, or a democratic technocrat, the true enemy is identified as "the human element": the corrupting force of private will and public expectations threatens mechchanistic perfection. Alternately imaged as the individual (worker, manager, owner) or the collective entity (class, race, gender, ethnic type), whatever is *not* the machine has the power to throw the metaphoric sabot that disrupts workplace and society. Under such narrative pressures, morality must be fully adjusted to the machine process; immorality is the uncontrolled intrusion of any human being who has yet to be converted into the machine. In either case, "is" becomes the operative word, not "ought" or even "shalt." This, however, does not stop the telling of stories that proclaim the happy union of body and machine, if only we follow "the one best way."

Managers and the Moral Revolution

In the 1880s and 1890s Frederick Winslow Taylor devoted himself to bringing efficiency to the production line. By the early 1900s he had another, potentially self-contradictory goal: to bring contentment into the lives of workers and owners alike. If Taylorism failed at its mission, the misguided would introduce welfare programs into the factories. Since Taylor detested any program imposed from outside his own system—especially those that undermined his scientism with sentimentality—he took it upon himself to argue that Taylorism was "the one best way" to meet all eventualities.

Language was a powerful agent in Taylor's efforts to justify and promote his notions about the scientific regulation of management practices and worker conduct. He set out on his own to provide rhetoric that persuaded, soothed, agitated, and controlled; narratives that dramatized strengths and errors; phrases that defined new concepts and defined old mistakes; layered, loaded words that imported the look of home truths into the workplace. Take the word "union" for example.

In 1903, at the annual meeting of the American Society of Mechanical Engineers, Taylor delivered his lecture "Shop Management," one of the key documents shaping the affairs of modern industrialization. During the discussion period, a Mr. F. F. DuBrut rose to urge his colleagues to "take into account a very important factor": "the factor of Unionism."[19] Although it is hardly surprising to hear an industrialist of that period characterize the Machinists' Union as socialist, it is instructive to hear De-Brut's depiction of the specter "Unionism" as a tyrant force let loose to enslave both worker and owner.

> How many employers know that the vast majority of workmen are forced into the Unions against their wishes, this being particularly true of *good men*. Being in the Union, being subject to its laws and regulations without any hope of freeing themselves from the tyranny of the Walking Delegate and the Strike Boss, such men are unable to do what they would like to do, and what they should be encouraged to do, in the way of bettering their wages and increasing their output. (my emphasis)[20]

Tempering DuBrut's display of raw anger against outside agitators who harm "good men," Taylor treats the "moral" question of unionism in his own way. In plants run according to his methods, the union becomes a banding together of "first-class men" joined

> to secure the extra high wages, which belong to them by right and which in this case are begrudged them by none, and which will be

theirs through dull times as well as periods of activity. Such a union commands the unqualified admiration and respect of all classes of the community; the respect equally of workmen, employers, political economists, and philanthropists. (1363–64)

Taylor deplores the fact that the words " 'labor union' " are "closely associated in the minds of most people with the idea of disagreement and strife between the employers and men." Accept his practices, and management and labor will alter that language through the establishment of "the ideal labor union."

DuBrut characterized unions as immoral out of hand. Taylor does not. He contrasts the sacred with the profane and the American with the un-American in phrases as central to his statements about the morality of his system as the technical discourse to which he resorts when analyzing its mechanics.[21]

Union labor is sacred just so long as its acts are fair and good, and it is damnable just as soon as its acts are bad. . . . The boycott, the use of force or intimidation, and the oppression of non-union workmen by labor unions are damnable; these acts of tyranny are thoroughly un-American and will not be tolerated by the American people. (1451–52)

Immediately afterward, Taylor speaks of the need for "discipline"— an American trait quite different from "un-American" union "tyranny." He bases his argument on assumptions currently undergoing a discursive transfer from theological precedents to the secularized discourse of the social sciences. His belief in what men are "naturally" is the logic behind his practice of slotting laborers into different categories according to their work functions—a process once left solely in the hands of God (angry or otherwise), who determined the elect according to the functionality of their souls. Attentive to an individual's innate capacities, Taylor assigns to each an appropriate regime of "correct conduct and good morals."

Only the elect few "require no discipline." They are men (always men) "so sensitive, conscientious and desirous of doing just what is right that a suggestion, a few words of explanation, or at most a brotherly admonition is all that they require." For most workers, however, words of moral weight have little effect on those who "are both thick-skinned and coarse-grained" (metaphors Taylor constantly used to connect physical composition with moral character).

The remedies Taylor proposes for dealing with the brutalized, unredeemed mass of the labor force place no reliance upon the vagaries of welfare programs or the interference of welfare secretaries (more often than not, sentimental women). Through scientific management, the worker's conduct can be closely monitored and corrected: through lowering his wages, laying him off for a period, or fining him when he receives "bad marks." But it is through language that Taylorism exerts an important mode of control.

"Shop Management" is not your usual conference paper, especially if we assume that mechanical engineers are essentially nonverbal and non-literary. Directed by his own desire for personal efficiency and self-control, as well as for dictating the shape of an industrial system of his own making, Taylor refers to himself as "the writer" throughout his 143-page text.[22]

Taylor's use of the third person looks like the distancing strategy Adams uses in *The Education of Henry Adams* to emphasize his lack of power in the face of circumstance and to highlight the theoretical nature of his experiences. There are major differences, however. Taylor is not in the business of powerlessness, and he closes that distance by constantly reminding his audience that "the writer" is a man who has tested the principles of shop management in the workplace where theories alone cannot survive. When Taylor tells of his early days at Midvale Steel and Bethlehem Steel, he gives no indication that he has been "betrayed by history," as Adams felt he was.[23] Taylor is not the nervous historian who blunders through a series of educations only to have his ignorance confirmed by an irrational universe of supersensual force. The persona of the engineer stands firm as one whose numerous "educations" let him control a rational world defined in terms of the machine process.

Taylor does not share Adams's agenda as cryptoanarchist and recorder of Marxist disruptions. Still, the engineer's narrative must do more than inform the industrial community of certain useful techniques devised by clever mechanics. *The Principles of Scientific Management* would not appear until 1911, but in Taylor's 1903 paper there is already a sharp sense of his conviction that the widespread adoption of his ideas will lead to the triumph of the scientific rationality in all things, large and small, and the making of a better, less brutal world.[24]

Capital letters highlight "THE OBJECT OF ADVOCATING HIGH WAGES AND LOW LABOR COST" (1343). Using typographical tactics to intensify and explain new concepts is standard practice in the preparation of business reports, but Taylor's inventiveness extends much farther. He uses the parable tradition, extracted from the Scriptures, to tell the story of two men, Smart and Honest. One of them "soldiers" on the job for four hours; the other produces the same amount of goods in one and a half hours but receives no reward for his speed, as he would if he were working for the Good Manager (1355). Taylor also tells beast fables, for example, of the contractor who, like any trade union boss, foolishly misuses "fine dray horses" by setting them to tasks donkeys handle just as well (1450). We are to learn from these tales that Honest will be better served by Taylorism, and that the first-class man who performs like a fine dray horse must not be harnessed, because of absurd union regulations, together with "a slow or inferior workman"—a donkey—"under the cloak of the expression 'a fair day's work' " (1450).[25]

Taylor does not overlook the chance to entertain his audience, as when he drops in an "amusing instance" to explain how to instruct children working in factories in "the value of task work,"[26] but the moral tone dominates once he sets out to present his plan whereby management links high wages, low cost, and efficient production. Profit is always the motive, hidden or not, as Veblen knew. Yet Taylor—the man who devalued welfare programs and disdained reformers[27]—speaks continually about fairness as the means to the end of bringing about the great capitalistic revolution: "fairness" for the sake of terminating the harshness of the old system that pitted worker against employer; "fairness" that will cause a "complete revolution in [the workers'] mental attitude toward their employers and their work" (1411).[28]

Taylor bases his system upon his belief that production processes and human character are analogous—analogous but not equally important since the demands of the machine process come first. Because he is persuaded that he alone knows how to bring the workers' animal energies into line with the mechanical energies of the machines they service, he deploys every possible narrative strategy to convince employers that once they learn how best to force the human element to adjust to the bipartisan "fairness" of the machine process, society as a whole will benefit from this happy, brutal change.

Human nature (male nature, at that) is clearly defined by Taylor's paper: (1) workers are valuable for the individual acts of labor they perform, not for the individuality of their thought; (2) workers must be led by the few uncommon leaders, "men of unusual energy, vitality and ambition," the "first-class men," the "better men"; (3) most workers are like children; their discontent results from the universal cast of mind and has no relation to the particular conditions under which they labor; they "naturally" loaf even when not consciously indulging in "systematic soldiering"; (4) good wages and material gain are the only spur to which workers respond (1349, 1353, 1372, 1418).[29]

In his 1860 essay "The Conduct of Life," Emerson urged all men to become "large" and "whole." This challenge was appropriate in Emerson's day, that early industrial phase when the average workman with a wide range of skills might work closely with the head mechanic in charge of an entire production process.[30] Forty years later Taylor argues that the "good manners, education" and the "special training and skill" Emerson liked to think his true American mechanic possessed have become obsolete. Such qualities now "count for less" than "grit, determination and bulldog endurance and tenacity that knows no defeat" (1417–18). Whereas the Emersonian mechanic, like the Emersonian poet, was a whole man, Taylor maintains that no one worker can be "well rounded." Today no one commands "the variety of special information and the different mental and moral qualities necessary to perform all of the duties demanded"— duties of "Brains, Education, Special or technical knowledge; manual dexterity or strength, Tact, Energy, Grit, Honesty, Judgment or common sense, and Good health" (1388–89).

Since "the new process" precludes wholeness, "all possible brain work should be removed from the shop and centred [*sic*] in the planning or laying-out department" (1390). In "functional management," each workman fits into "eight different groups according to the particular functional boss he happens to be working under at the time" (1391). Brains (and authority) are located in the planning office; muscle (and obedience) are relegated to the shop floor.

Modern industrial fragmentation goes even further in creating the basic divisiveness of human action abhorred by Marx and Emerson alike. Taylorism assumes that even foremen and gang bosses are incapable of possessing the "nine qualities" of the ideal manager, Taylor's justification for cutting back drastically upon their traditional supervisory powers. The goal "will not have been realized until almost all of the machines in the shop are run by men who are of *smaller* calibre and attainments, and who are therefore *cheaper* than those required under the old system" (1395; my emphasis).

Taylor's system of high wages/high productivity/low cost/small worker denies the ideals of personal redemption once held as a workable spiritual truth, but his language often says otherwise. In speaking of the slow stages through which shop workmen rise to increased levels of efficiency, he urges employers to focus upon his system at "a few points, leaving the ninety and nine under the care of their former shepherds" (1414). Through this allusion to the popular Protestant hymn "There Were Ninety and Nine," he seals his mission to "save" his men, one by one. This redemptive task must be carried out, however long it takes and however much it costs him emotionally and employers financially, so that management and morality alike may become "scientific."[31]

Despite Jackson Lears's belief that Taylor was "the tough-minded cynic" who made "no claims about transcending class issues and promoting social harmony," Taylor's stories continually return to his intention to

advance his workers' moral well-being by means of the morality of efficiency.[32] Taylor argues "that for their own good it is as important that
workmen should not be very much over-paid, as it is that they should not
be under-paid." If overpaid, many will work irregularly and tend to become

> more or less shiftless, extravagant, and dissipated. It does not do for
> most men to get rich too fast. The writer's observation, however,
> would lead him to the conclusion that most men tend to become
> more instead of less thrifty when they receive the proper increase for
> an extra hard day's work. . . . They live rather better, begin to save
> money, become more sober, and work more steadily. (1346)

No wonder Taylor finds the piecework system objectionable. It encourages "soldiering"—that natural tendency of all men to loaf when left
unguided by a rational system administered under close managerial discipline. Soldiering damages a man's moral fiber, since it "involves a delib-
erate attempt to mislead and deceive his employer, and thus upright and
straight-forward workmen are compelled to become more or less hypo-
critical" (1351). Furthermore, the workers "grow lazy, spend much of
their time pitying themselves and are less able to compete with other
men" (1450).[33]

The care Taylor pays to the words he uses to persuade men in power
to adopt his plan is not to be wasted on the workingmen. "Let no one
imagine . . . that this great change in the mental attitudes of the men and
the increase in their activity can be brought about by merely talking to
them" (1412).[34] The audience for his discourse consists of men of his own
class. They may require tutoring in what he already knows, but at least he
can talk with them as near equals. Talk expended upon workingmen is
kept to the level of lessons in the way things work. But no matter whom
he addresses, no matter which device he uses, Taylor relies upon the imperative voice. His is a commandment, the reformer's call for a life dedicated to "shalt." If any of his auditors fail to listen and to obey, that person
must take full responsibility for the loss of company profit, factory productivity, and the worker's soul.

There was no place at the Paris Exposition of 1900 for Henry Adams
to make a leisurely, thereby wasteful, contemplation of ethical principles.
Adams had had many earlier occasions to sit and ponder the jagged edges
between events and morality: as the child-animal who experienced the imbalance between individual rights and imposed authority the day his
grandfather marched him off to school in silence; as his father's secretary
growing up fast but confused in the London of Palmerston; as the begonia
who witnessed the dinosaur inertia of President Grant and the dizzying

pace of an age gilded by goldbugs. As long as the Adams manikin wore clothes of an older era, albeit in a state of increasing tatters, reflections upon moral issues infiltrated the "specific structures" of those "specific histories." But the new century and the new men created after 1900 appeared to exist in a moral void. Some said everyone was simply too busy hanging on to give much thought to what was right or wrong, but this was not the case—even though moral concerns often led to dealing in the unreality of "ought" rather than in the hard facts of "is."

In 1903 Taylor as mechanic-engineer-manager placed morality exactly where he felt it belonged: in the factories, the site where, if anywhere, an ethics of accuracy, efficiency, and obedience would structure daily life. Guided by his principles, the evils of waste would be defeated and the chaos of class tensions would be resolved into social harmony.

In 1904 Veblen's *Theory of Business Enterprise* testified to what Taylor saw in 1903, but it did much more. Antonio Gramsci, locked away in an Italian prison between 1929 and 1935, had even more to observe than Adams, Taylor, or Veblen about "the contradictory conditions of modern society, which must create complications, absurd positions, and moral and economic crises often tending toward catastrophe."[35] Gramsci's notes concerning "Americanism and Fordism" is his meditation on the years when Taylor's theories were translated into the language of Ford's practices. The result of this shift created "a new way of life," a "new culture," "new methods of work," "a new sexual ethic," "a new type of worker and of man," and "a specific mode of living and of thinking and of feeling life."

Gramsci disavows the notion that the new conditions he cites are part of a properly defined new order. Reconstruction and freedom will not automatically come about through the peculiar necessity to which "Americanism" condemns a society, but Gramsci considers the possibility that Taylorism and Fordism are the essential stages by means of which a weary European culture will close down its feudalistic past. The human passage through history, marked by the patterns of Taylorism and Fordism, is

> an uninterrupted, often painful and bloody process of subjugating natural (i.e. animal and primitive) instincts to new, more complex and rigid norms and habits of order, exactitude and precision which can make possible the increasingly complex forms of collective life.

Each in his own way, Taylor, Veblen, and Lenin, too, agreed about the suppression of "the element of 'animality'."[36] Each in his way concurred that it would take the brutality of "rigid norms and habits of order" to achieve the final betterment they sought.

If Taylor the engineer paid more attention to moral issues than might be expected, albeit to those conducive to heightened productivity, the

winning of the efficient life was also the primary concern of the new generation of philosophers and sociologists. Through the pressure to redefine
the nature of their professions, they probed the "twofold aspect of life and
conduct" (as William James put it), "the social aspect of conscience"
(Charles Cooley's phrasing), and "the socialization of achievement" (the
crucial "problem" singled out by Lester Ward).[37] James, Cooley, Ward,
and John Dewey and James Tufts concluded that the following elements
simultaneously defined the problematic nature of the new age and suggested the means to make living bearable in such an age:

(1) "The actually possible in this world is vastly narrower than all that
is demanded; and there is always a *pinch* between the ideal and the actual
which can only be got through by leaving part of the ideal behind"
(James).

(2) "To violate conscience is to act under the control of an incomplete
and fragmentary state of mind; and so to become less a person, to begin
to disintegrate and go to pieces" (Cooley).

(3) "Most philanthropy is also mere temporary patchwork which has
to be done over and over again. . . . It is static, not dynamic. The new
ethics, on the contrary, goes to the root and deals with the conditions and
causes of evil. . . . It is dynamic. As already said, it is applied sociology"
(Ward).

(4) "The old honesty could assume that goods belonged to their makers, and then consider exchanges and contracts. The new honesty will first
have to face a prior question, *Who owns what is collectively produced,* and are
the present 'rules of the game' distributing the returns honestly and
fairly?" (Dewey and Tufts).[38]

Living in a pinch between ideal and actuality, between the static and
the dynamic, between individualist theories and collectivist facts, the new
self suffers the constant threat of fragmentation—the same derangement
of vital parts Veblen warned might destroy the machine process itself. Philosophers and sociologists called for a new ethics devoted to the "question
of organization," an ethics that might allow citizens of the new age to
achieve "never a state of rest, but an *equilibrium mobile.*"[39]

The philosopher, "qua philosopher," James wrote, "sees somewhat
better than most men what the question always is." Such a mind

> knows that he must vote always for the richer universe, for the good
> which seems most organizable, most fit to enter into complex com-
> binations, most apt to be a member of a more inclusive whole. But
> which particular universe this is, he cannot know for certain in ad-
> vance, he only knows that if he makes a bad mistake the cries of the
> wounded will soon inform him of the fact.[40]

Although he had been trained as a scientist, James realized the limitations of the scientific method. He thought it wishful thinking to expect
that the new ethics could counter the hurts caused by scientific principles
of the kind that backed Taylor's management theories or powered Ford's
assembly line. He acted on the hunch that brought his views into line with
what later thinkers like Gramsci could argue: that the scientific methods
of the new ethics were part and parcel of the scientific principles of the
industrial brutality they tried to mitigate. Whichever way they fell, their
mistakes would be cried to the world by the wounded.

Saving the "Foreigners"

In 1901 two leading industrialists, Charles J. Harrah and John H. Patterson, made statements about the principles that dictated their dealings with
their employees. Harrah, president of the Midvale Steel Company in Philadelphia, testified before the United States Congressional Industrial Commission that "we try to make the place attractive to the men, because it is
for a very selfish reason."

> There is no philanthropy in it. We invest a great deal of capital in the
> education of a man. . . . After you have a man thoroughly educated
> you can not afford to lose him. It is not because you love the man; it
> is not because you want to be a philanthropist, it is from pure com-
> mon business sense; that is all there is in it. [41]

Harrah speaks with the economy of a man who believes that simple
answers are best, but, as the series of "it is not" clauses suggests, he thinks
it important to clarify what his company abjures. The rhetoric of negation
frequently results from a person's inability to define with precision what
he *is* doing. In Harrah's case, the string of "nots" comes from his belief in
"pure" and "common" business sense. Is it not practical for him, during
the verbal give-and-take of a hearing, to clear the ground of such impuri-
ties as sentimentalism before explaining a quality so "common" as to be
taken for granted and so "pure" as to be transparent as a motive?
Harrah's blunt pragmatism stands in contrast to the example set by
John H. Patterson, head of the National Cash Register Company of Day-
ton, Ohio, who was frequently cited as one of the saints of old-school
business paternalism. [42] By 1901, however, his is a benevolence that is very
conscious of its marginality. Patterson remarks of an essay written for *The
Engineering Magazine* that he hopes it "may not be out of place in this
magazine." [43] As Harrah's contemporary, he dares not present himself as a
mere philanthropist or a vague theorist. The proper use of "altruism and
sympathy" means money, he agrees; it "will pay the great employer many

fold more to have . . . thoughtfulness for the hundreds or thousands in his employ." "Thoughtfulness" is Patterson's operative word; it joins an employer's sympathy with his practical intelligence.

Patterson's advocacy of welfare programs rests on the thoughtful premise that the laborer should be recognized "as a man with human aspirations, often with keen sensibilities and with love of home and comfort . . . and that poverty, lack of education, and narrow views are not necessarily evidence of a lower form of life." His insistence on this essential fact—that laborers are human—reminds one of the care Jacob Riis lavished in 1890 to persuade his middle-class audiences that the filthy, degraded objects representing "the other half" were, after all, sentient members of the human race. It was the same argument that the abolitionists worked for all it was worth in antebellum days, and that muckrakers and the Progressives currently were repeating in the popular press.

Despite the precedents set by reform-minded individuals in projecting this ever-novel notion of a common humanity, Patterson has to remind readers of *The Engineering Magazine* of its basic truth before he can detail what he is doing for his employees: a dining room for the workers' lunch period; facilities for weekly baths on company time; elevators for the women; stools with backs and footrests; a ten-minute morning and afternoon recess for the women, as well as a rest room where they may withdraw "in case of illness or weakness"; an employees' club for educational lectures; entertainments with stereopticon shows; cooperative arrangements with community clubs for providing libraries, kindergartens, and neighborhood beautification projects; facilities for "practical instruction in the true ideas of moral life." Patterson must provide the business logic for "thoughtful" things, lest he be perceived as throwing money away on a mass of ignorant, ungrateful animals.

As long as the workers in question were native born, most men in business and industry were willing to accept the idea that employees were material maleable enough to benefit from improved working and living conditions; in turn, this meant they would reward the company with a day's hard work. The proliferating presence of the possibly unredeemable foreigner was considered the major obstacle placed in the path of scientific management principles (intended to increase efficient production) and of effective welfare programs (meant to reinforce the innate moral fiber of "real" American workers).[44]

Immigrants pouring into the United States, blacks moving north into industrial areas, and new surges of women entering the work force all came upon the labor-management scene in the midst of the debate over the nature of "the good laborer," male or female. Did the worker need brains to work with full efficiency (that is, as "rationally" as a machine)?

Must he or she consciously strive to assimilate, to acquire American moral intelligence? Or should "the foreigners" stay as they were—cheaply maintained, docile work animals, drilled into effective performance through force of habit, through isolation from dangerous unionizers, and through throwaway gestures of benevolence at the shop?

Native-born workingmen often felt threatened by the immigrants' willingness to do the hardest work for the least money. They feared that once the new machinery began to accomplish what only master mechanics had previously had the brains, training, and experience to do, and once Taylorism's drilled patterns of behavior set the standard for productive labor, foreigners might be used to replace skilled workers altogether. But it was the employers' opinions that counted, not those of the workers in the shops.

Whenever there was a debate over the amount of attention that employers should pay to worker welfare, the terms differed according to whether they were considering the native-born worker or the immigrant. But relations among social conduct, intelligence, and work efficiency came under scrutiny in all cases.[45] Support for welfare programs increased whenever it appeared that a clear exchange was taking place among these three elements. Why else reward respectable behavior unless it served as a guarantee for productive labor? For many employers, the fact that a worker got drunk on Saturday or beat his wife on Sunday mattered only if such actions affected his work skills on Monday.

When the foreigners lined up at the factory gates, employers were caught between their desire for low-cost brawn and their distaste for the problems caused by racial inferiors without either "Yankee" intelligence or "American" morals. They had to consider whether welfare programs (like the naturalization procedures introduced in the 1910s) would enable them to increase the efficiency of this welter of cheap labor by containing its unruly social conduct. Such consideration was sharpened through the telling of tales about the redemption of uncouth strangers.

In the narrative that Lawrence Lewis laid before his readers in *The World's Work* in 1905, verb tenses and "before and after" plot structures point the blame and apportion the praise. The bad "before" was the result of the bestial "environment the workmen *made for* their children, the dwellings they *provided for* themselves, the manner in which they *handled* the liquor problem, and the way they *amused* themselves when left to their own devices." Good endings come "after" the aliens "were led" away from "conditions of drunkenness and dirt to well-ordered living" once "the managers of the company 'interfered' by beginning a systematic effort for their social betterment."[46]

In Lewis's "Uplifting 17,000 Employees," the middle-class readers of

The World's Work hear the praise of John C. Osgood and Julian A. Kebler of the Colorado Fuel and Iron Company, the men credited with creating the firm's Sociological Department in 1901. In order to show what it was like before Osgood and Kebler extended the meaning of "scientific management" into the area of "social betterment work," Lewis includes a series of sordid narratives presented in language made familiar by the sensationalist fiction of the day.

> One fine evening a few years ago, an Italian dragged his wife by the hair from their hovel in Starkville, Col. . . . and in the presence of fellow coalmen, and a large group of the neighbors' children, calmly cut her throat with a razor. A few days later, two intoxicated Mexican "coke-pullers" in the same camp, surrounded by the same young boys and girls and babies just able to toddle, fought with knives until one, stabbed to the heart, fell in his tracks. The other, after staggering a few hundred feet, died in his blood midst the coaldust and dirt, bottles, tin cans and filth of the "street." (5939)

Osgood's and Kebler's impressive management skills are placed in contrast to this material and moral foulness. Together they organized thirty company towns in Colorado, Wyoming, New Mexico, and Utah, adding 178 miles of railway and 1,835 miles of telegraph, and thereby gained control over "600 square miles of the finest coal". In addition, they upgraded the Laramie rolling mills until they ranked "among the largest in the West." They turned the steel plant in Pueblo into "the largest in the world" (5940). In their hands, "the machine process" linking the Colorado Fuel and Iron Company's sixty-five properties was an unqualified success. But the potentially disastrous situation created by "the human element" remained.

Seventeen thousand workers represented between twenty and thirty nationalities; with their families, they made up a population of seventy or eighty thousand individuals sharing deep race hatreds and few languages. Clearly "the difficulties of social betterment work among such a population are overwhelming" (5942).

"Uplifting 17,000 Employees" outlines what Osgood and Kebler accomplished. "Purely paternal methods were discarded; nothing has been forced upon any community" (5941). Miners were offered illustrated talks about travels in Italy; a weekly magazine was established; school teachers were hired through the local school boards and kindergartens were begun; stereopticon lectures brought home "the necessity of proper sanitation"; night classes, reading rooms, traveling libraries, circulating art collections, and cooking classes were introduced to the mining communities (5942).

   While enumerating the activities of the Sociological Department, Lewis cleaves to the journalist's faith in itemization, but he drops back into the narrative mode in approaching material that lends itself to little dramas of corrupted children and the evils of drink.

>   While the doctor was driving past a school one day, two of the little girls asked for a ride.
>   "Where are you going?" he asked.
>   "Home."
>   "You have a nice home, haven't you?"
>   "Yes, when papa's not drunk," answered the older, who was not more than eight.
>   "Does he get drunk often?"
>   "Pretty near every Saturday and Sunday. One day he made me drink a big glass of beer and then some whiskey. I didn't know nothing for the rest of that day and for two days more."
>   "You won't drink any more beer and whiskey, will you?"
>   "Well," answered the little girl, "I likes beer first rate, and drinks it when I get a chance, but they gets no more whiskey down me if I can run." (5946)

After this Dickensian scene, certain to rouse horror in the minds of many of his readers, Lewis supplies a happy ending by pointing to the company's success in running a regulated saloon, a restricted club, a soft drinks club, and an open reform saloon.[47]

   This narrative of failed lives redeemed by successful management practices is supplemented by photographs. One sees a band concert, kindergarten children hoeing a garden, the hospital, the camp children's Christmas tree, cooking and sewing classes for the wives, and a miners' reading room. The article concludes with the announcement, "Conditions such as were illustrated by the incidents described at the beginning of this article no longer exist" (5940).

   All well and good, but an odd statement intrudes. Embedded early in the text is this observation, both oblique and straightforward in the information it offers.

>   This work, which still goes on, despite a change in the control of the company [in 1903] from their hands to those of Mr. John D. Rockefeller and Mr. George J. Gould, and despite a long, costly and bitterly contested strike, is the work of Messrs. Osgood and Kebler, the two . . . to whom is due, also, credit *for whatever Colorado is now* as a great producer of coal and as a manufactory of iron and steel products. (5940)[48]

Readers not devoted to the complacent uplift of *The World's Work* might well respond negatively to the ambiguity of the phrase "for whatever Colorado is now." Within the context of this article, what Colorado *is* is the success accorded "a great producer" of goods under the laws of the business enterprise, but it is also a company in which the human element remains essentially untamed, for it continues to draw workers from the inhuman, bottom layer of immigrant labor.

Why, then, did Lewis disclose the fact that the workers of Colorado Fuel and Iron are out on strike? True, he could hardly omit mentioning it altogether since the press was actively covering its troubles. What is unusual is that he refers to the strike near the start of his glowing review of the accomplishments of the company's Sociological Department. So placed, it can only serve to throw a pall over the subsequent narration.

Lewis's telltale sentence is significant in its use of the word "despite" to point out two ruptures in the success narrative of Osgood and Kebler, *until recently* chairman of the board of directors and general manager, respectively. This construction forces the question as to why they no longer control the company, why the welfare work "still goes on," and why the strike (whose "long, costly and bitterly contested" nature is not concealed) came about in the first place. This single sentence undercuts the story of "well-ordered" living the article wishes to celebrate. Perhaps the strike represents the release of the same ignorant, brute force expressed in the narratives of violence and blood with which the account opens—a brutalism no welfare program could overcome. Or perhaps it comes back to the warning signaled on the first page with the word "interfered"— a suggestion that the strike is the workers' response to precisely those welfare programs that have robbed them of the right to have "made," "provided," "handled," and "amused" themselves on their own terms. This was the situation with no easy answers that confronted the managers trying to negotiate between brutality and betterment.

Male managers conducting welfare programs had problems from the start; female welfare secretaries had an even harder time. In 1904 Gertrude Beeks, secretary of the newly formed Welfare Department of the National Civic Federation (NCF), attempted to define and justify her work to the manufacturers whose interests the NCF represented from its inception.[49] She attempted to define, to justify, and to persuade. She needed to convince clients that bringing John Patterson's "thoughtfulness" into the factory would not hurt company productivity, and that supervising workers' welfare hours need not undercut the management of their factory lives.[50] And she had to do this as a woman, not as one of the men in charge.

Beeks's treatment of issues concerning the management of employee welfare programs coincides with the principles determining sound shop management Taylor detailed the previous year. A "steady, an equitable wage, and reasonable hours of labor" are essential to shop and welfare planning alike. Both Taylor and Beeks call upon the manager's "patience to endure the slow realization of his plans"; both require "tact, executive ability, common sense, acquaintance with local jealousies and sometimes with racial prejudices"; both insist they avoid "condescension." The big difference comes when the authority of the women in welfare work is placed over against the power of final decision held by the male managers.[51]

Beeks's use of the masculine pronoun in her outline of the limitations placed upon any person heading a company's welfare department only masks the gender tensions caused when women tried to prescribe management policies.

> He must recognize and in no way interfere with the authority of the superintendents, who are responsible for the successful operation of their departments, the administration of labor, and the maintaining of discipline. He must gain in advance their full approval of each effort, and use every proper method to enlist their full co-operation.

What never lets up is the conflict between the ends of welfare (women's work) and the means of shop management (men's concerns). The welfare department wants to provide "physical comfort wherever labor is performed," but Taylorism has the power to negate this goal through its acceleration and routinization of the workers' movements. On the other hand, many managers did not consider pertinent welfare work's attention to conditions that affect the laborer's life off the line—matters of recreation, education, and decent housing. Welfare secretaries had a world of convincing to do from below.

Beeks takes her first go at persuading the bosses in an essay for the inaugural issue of the *National Civic Federation Monthly Review.* She places in the title the question she must answer, "What Is Welfare Work?" but she also has to deal with the issues raised by her subtitle, "conditions of success and causes of failure." She itemizes her achievements, making full use of the journalist's format of short paragraphs and boldfaced leads: free laundries, bathing facilities, ventilation, rest periods. She just as quickly states:

> Yet these very things, simple as they seem, are of the utmost practical value to the employer. The one provision for cleanliness alone, for example, improves the spirit of every worker as well as the health, and raises the moral tone of the force, even improving discipline.

Regulating conditions in factories employing women is a particularly touchy matter. Beeks closes out what had begun as a moral issue—the going and coming of men and women on different shifts separated by five minutes—with a reminder of the practical benefits gained by employers.

> This simple precaution for the protection of the feminine element among the employees of any large establishment has the effect of preserving respect for womanhood. Experience shows that, where this system prevails, the establishments soon acquire a higher tone. . . . When the general morale of a factory is not in good repute, it is difficult for the employer to induce desirable working-women to accept employment.[52]

However sincerely conceived in the name of aiding the worker, betterment programs must offer the assurance that they will not foster radical ideas, such as the notion that employees should have more say in their own affairs. Beeks promises that decisions affecting the workplace will always come from above.

> But any effort at welfare work may be regarded as more or less paternalistic. A resort to direct paternalism, however, is necessary or desirable only for recent immigrants who in their native lands have been accustomed to the guardianship of superior authority. Going to the other extreme, in the so-called democratic idea, is also to be avoided. When their confidence has been gained, employes [sic] will generally prefer to entrust the direction of welfare work to the employer.

The general audience for "Uplifting 17,000 Employees" heard tales about the subhuman living conditions and conduct the foreigners "made" for themselves, a situation that means they must be "led" toward betterment. Gertrude Beeks's manufacturer-clients are also told about the problems signally created by those aliens who, unlike the American worker, require "the guardianship of superior authority." In the reckonings of Lewis and Beeks, "being human" is limited to managers and welfare secretaries. This is a consequence of their class, their status as native-born Americans, and the burdens they shoulder because of the disturbing presence of immigrant labor—that obstacle to the smooth running of the business enterprise and the establishment of high moral tone.

Graham Taylor, head of the Department of Christian Theology at the University of Chicago and active member of the Social Gospel movement, had something else in mind when he contributed a short piece to the *Chicago Daily News* in 1906, titled "The Policy of Being Human in

Business." Taylor's article concerns a series of informal gatherings Chicago business and industrial leaders held to discuss just such problems. A different voice suddenly intrudes, distinguishing itself from those that dominate the rest of the article. It belongs to an outsider attending an evening devoted to "Foreign Immigrants in American Industry." In "a burst of indignant self-respect" he declared: " 'I refuse to be considered "a problem." I am a problem to no one but myself. I and my people have created the industry by which we not only make our own living, but have enriched the lives of everyone else in America.' "[53]

Such voices were rarely given space within the narratives of brutality and betterment the business enterprise provided during the first decade of the twentieth century. Take, for example, a booklet, subtitled "Some Deplorable Conditions," that reports the 1908–9 findings of a group the NCF Welfare Department authorized to inspect workplaces hiring women for the New York City garment industry.[54] The team moves systematically through the factories, looking and evaluating; in several instances flagging abuses by adding red tags marked "Unclean," on occasion calling in the state labor department to close down the machines temporarily.

The NCF report carefully itemizes the good and bad working conditions at each plant in "the matter-of-fact" manner Veblen defined in his 1906 essay, "The Place of Science in Modern Civilisation," as the prevailing style of the times. Brief, random descriptions that "read" the factories as indices of the immigrant women workers' character stand out against the background of the generally utilitarian prose. These descriptions confuse the logic of the main argument by questioning strict cause-and-effect relations between environmental conditions and worker conduct.

Toilets are in a bad state, but "nothing more could be expected from the careless class of people employed." A tidier working area is found in another factory with "the same type of employees," which suggests that better conditions "may [be] attain[ed] with proper supervision, discipline, and good janitor service." In some shops, "employees have a seedy appearance, with hair unkempt," but elsewhere "unsatisfactory conditions were reflected in the type and deportment of the employees, with whom the committee felt sincere sympathy."

The investigators draw no conclusions from their cursory, conflicting reflections on the connection between physical environment and moral behavior. Are the women slovenly because their workplaces are filthy or is this disarray the result of the immigrants' inability to learn "habits of decency"? What the NCF investigators *are* sure about is that these people—who are *less* than Americans because they have no traditions of liberty and self-reliance—will make good employees if proper supervision and discipline can be imposed.

The factory workers and bosses "are foreign, Russian Jews and Italians mostly," people to whom it is "difficult to teach . . . habits of decency." But the bosses have at least one great merit: they have "great respect for the majesty of the law. They obey more readily than the same class of Americans." The NCF appears to have discovered that inferior foreign material is more dependable than superior American types possessed of a strong spirit of individualism.

It was up to the men in scientific management to bring discipline into shop practices; it was up to the feminized welfare programs to introduce moral discipline into the workers' lives (although Taylor believed that the practice of his male principles was morality enough). Women in welfare work had to teach their lessons differently than the engineers did. These differences in approach come across vividly in a piece presented in praise of Gertrude Beeks.

Written by one woman in admiration of another, "A Woman of Achievement: Miss Gertrude Beeks" appears in *The World's Work* in 1913. The prose style used by its author, Sarah Comstock, is noticeably more self-confident than the style Lawrence Lewis used in the same journal in 1905. Lewis wrote when welfare practices were just beginning to be applied to factories; his audiences had much to learn about the conditions regulated by the owners of the Colorado Fuel and Iron Company, and about the need for management "interference" in furthering the "uplifting" of the immigrant labor force. Lewis found it necessary to intersperse factual data with sensationalized tales of the violent ways of uncouth workers, who had to be led into the American industrial process by Messrs. Osgood and Kebler. Comstock, in contrast, recounts the highlights of Beeks's success as a consultant-troubleshooter in an ebullient, almost breezy manner.

Welfare programs flourish because of dedicated people like Beeks. By 1913 this is a certainty, not merely a hope. The human material with which Beeks works on a daily basis does not appear to involve drunken louts who razor slash their women or collapse in pools of blood at the feet of dirty-faced children. It is entertaining to recount Beeks's accomplishments. Since readers now understand the purpose of pairing welfare work with scientific systems of work management, it is unnecessary to run readers through a course of instruction in the moral and pecuniary merits of Beeks's work.

Comstock's descriptions of Beeks's achievements differ from Beeks's own earnest, somewhat nervous explanations back in 1904, when she was just starting her career. But Comstock—like Beeks in 1904, Lewis in

1905, and the NCF pamphlet of 1908–9—agrees that "the problem" comes from the bottom: from the men and women of the immigrant class who must be dragged upward toward the light.

Comstock's piece dispenses with the literary devices of Lawrence Lewis's melodrama, whose heroes were the strong-willed managers of Colorado Fuel and Iron. Hers is a lighthearted girls' book account in the tradition of Jo March sallying forth to take broth and cheer to poor Irish families. At the heart of Comstock's piece is the story of how Gertrude Beeks brings assurance to a worried industrialist, Cyrus H. McCormick of the International Harvester Company.[55]

McCormick and his managers have failed at bringing "system" to the management of his workers' personal habits. He turns to the plucky Miss Beeks and says, "'See what you can do to make the three hundred girls and five thousand men who work for us like to work for us.'" In the formula favored by writers of adolescent adventure tales, our heroine does not "get her breath back for a few seconds. Then, 'I'll begin on the girls,' she said."[56]

Beeks enters the new Harvester twine mill where "the girls" worked. "'She's a missionary,' they whispered, as she walked through the mill. She was not one of them, they did not know her purpose, and they did not want her."

> But she continued, making close observations and laying her plans quietly. She saw strange Lithuanian sausages, slabs of dark Slovak bread, and uncouth Polack pickles emerging every noon from lunch-baskets. The first thing these girls needed was a hot, wholesome lunch. But Miss Beeks realized that the mere announcement of the opening of a lunch-room would meet with no response from girls not at all interested in their own welfare *as the trained mind sees it*. (my emphasis)

Beeks supplies "dinner and entertainment," including a piano, and weans the reluctant girls away from their "uncouth Polack pickles," replacing their diet with the virtues (described in words that make American wholesomeness almost palpable) of "hot soups, good stews, baked apples, and well-made gingerbread." The lunchroom is a success, and the Harvester managers "also made a discovery: *Efficiency was being increased*." Next she "screwed her courage to the point of tackling the five thousand men."

> She was the first woman who had ever entered that vast shop, and the men resented her even more than the girls had. She tried in vain for awhile to reach these murky, child-like natures. It was a queer

little incident that turned the tide. She overheard, in the midst of foreign gabble, a remark that her rose was pretty. Instantly she took it from her buttonhole and handed it to the man. The human note was struck. She had their friendship.

In Comstock's telling, a woman and a rose lessen the risk that the machine process might undergo "derangement" by "these murky, child-like natures." With this anecdote, it seems possible that the American business enterprise can advance with confidence toward the demands soon to be placed upon it by the nation's entry into World War I. But not before Frederick Winslow Taylor is called before Congress to justify the principles of his "one best way."

Testimonies

It is back to the shop and into the planning office as Frederick Winslow Taylor takes command of the debate over the benefits or liabilities of scientific management. It cannot be left to female welfare secretaries, with their scientism of sentiment, to argue the cause of this most male-oriented of procedures. The profit motive was only one compelling factor in Taylor's lifelong effort to impose shop management principles; his need to eliminate immoral waste motion in the workplace and to replace dissonance with harmony in society at large was just as powerful.

Taylor was a man with great anxieties. He was neurotically obsessed with imposing strict order and discipline over his every action.[1] Yet to return to Taylor's words is to be in the presence of a man whose language admits neither doubt nor hesitation—an even better reason to examine the ways in which Taylor's public pronouncements attempted to instill confidence in machine rationality as the happy solution to the errors and irrationalities of the uncontrolled "human element."

The Management of Language

In his defense of scientific work principles, Taylor confronts one obstacle after another—obstacles placed in his way by management ("your plan costs too much and takes too long to put into effect"), by labor organizations ("your plan turns men into cogs of machinery"), and by fellow engineers ("your system is not the supreme 'one best way' "). Sometimes he maneuvers quickly around whatever impedes his will; sometimes he meets objections head-on. His tone is usually confident, cheerful, unhurried, man to man. His critics' anger or recalcitrance is childish stubbornness, which the Father of Scientific Management will overcome by means of impartiality and common sense.

Taylor counters every criticism of his system with facts shaped in the form of a story, drawn—as he unwearyingly reminds his listeners—from his wide experience in factory management. His language is masculine, muscular, placed like a bull in one's path, but the bullying tone is generally absent. The mind is powerful, notwithstanding (or perhaps as the result of) its narrow focus upon machine processes; it appears to encompass the needs of all modern industry. Taylor's ideas are most often wrong in what they state or imply about the relationships binding laborers and machines. This does not detract from the force of the methods he uses to insist (genially, but unrelentingly) that he is completely right.

Prior to 1911—when Taylor's big book, *The Principles of Scientific Management,* was published—Louis Brandeis, noted reform attorney from Massachusetts, was credited with inaugurating the idea and name of scientific management. In the court case he leveled against the railroad interests in 1910, Brandeis had argued that American consumers should not be charged the high prices attached to rail-transported goods as the result of increased freight rates. If railroad owners would apply the newest efficiency methods, daily shaving one million dollars from the cost of running the trains, the public would no longer be the scapegoat.[2] Headlines bannered the million-dollar savings, and a nationwide craze for efficiency systems absorbed the collective fancy. But once Taylor's book appeared in 1911, an increasing number of people in the United States and abroad recognized what the profession had known since Taylor delivered his 1903 paper before the ASME: that Taylor, not Brandeis, was the true prophet of scientific management.

The general public took little interest in sophisticated details about drills, gears, and measurement gauges, but a single anecdote extracted from Taylor's book struck a popular note: the story of Schmidt, the pig-iron handler—the stupid little Pennsylvania Dutchman to whom Taylor taught the basic law of efficient time-motion labor. This anecdote vividly fixed four of Taylor's most important principles in the public imagination: *selection* (tapping the right man for the level of physical and mental skill any particular task requires); *repetition* (getting the worker to do that job over and over until it becomes an ingrained habit); *obedience* (making the man follow orders without question); and *reward* (spurring the worker on with the only thing he responds to—money).

No such person as Schmidt existed to be taught "the science of shoveling" pig iron. Taylor made up his story based on a very different kind of worker, one Henry Noll, but the imaginary Schmidt furthered Taylor's thesis: getting the right man "to handle 47 tons of pig iron per day and making him glad to do it." A mix of pleasantries and tough talk accomplishes what *the boss* wants (more goods produced at lower costs) and what *the worker* wants (higher wages).[3]

January 1912 provides Taylor with his supreme moment as raconteur and publicist. He is called before a Congressional committee investigating the effect of Taylorism upon the workers who have to implement its methods. In order to head off critics and win converts, Taylor comes armed not only with the tale of stupid but efficient little Schmidt but with his "Pat and Mike" stories, and with a full string of rhetorical strategies and narratological devices.

"Gentlemen," says Taylor, as he addresses the committee chaired by William B. Wilson. This is not like addressing the American Society of Mechanical Engineers. "Gentlemen," he says as he faces a hostile audience largely comprised of labor representatives, few of whom belong to the upper class that is his social niche by birth. He insists that what others might say against his ideas only reflects their misguided acceptance of the old system with its irrationalities and inefficiencies. He intends to bring his listeners around to the same trust in the system of rationality and efficiency he believes his own workers have accepted.

Taylor is openly pleased with his talent for getting "almost any workingman to talking with [him] intimately and saying exactly what he believes and feels without reserve."[4] He sees no reason not to create the same rapport with the union members gathered in Washington, D.C. This is no time for him to suggest they might be stupid or tainted by political radicalism. He declares he has "much sympathy with the workingmen who have testified before your committee because I feel that they firmly believe that it would not be for their best interests to turn in a larger output." More in sadness than anger, he suggests that "these men are honestly mistaken just as the rest of the world has been honestly mistaken in many other instances." (30).

Taylor's role before the Congressional committee is that of the man of tact, experience, and common sense, one willing to explain patiently why an all-pervading ignorance blocks the path to "the one best way." He reiterates the honesty of the laborer's innate fear of efficiency management: "it is no fake view; there is no hypocrisy about it" (9). Even labor leaders (who might be expected to know better) are blameless in their blindness. He looks upon men of this "class"—a term Taylor digresses to explain means any group "with somewhat similar aims in life, and not at all with the 'upper and lower class' distinctions usually associated with the word"—"as strictly honest, upright, straightforward men" (11).

Taylor makes a daring move at this point. In order to reinforce the generosity of his refusal to ridicule the ignorance of the public (the Congressmen and managers who balk at his system; the labor leaders lined up against him), he rehearses the history of the emergence of the power loom in the British textile industry after 1790 and the Manchester weavers's violent reaction to its use in the 1840s. Once he equates the anger of the weavers against the "labor-saving device" of the looms with the resentment held against his own system, he states that "even after that exhibition of fearful violence, gentlemen, I do not hesitate to say that I do not feel very bitterly toward those men. I believe that they were misguided" (15).

But if Taylor cleverly places himself on the workers' side, he also protects himself from the employers' anger. "I do not want to be misquoted in this. These men did murder, violence, and arson." *That* he does "not endorse for one moment—but I cannot help but feel a certain sympathy for the men who believe, with absolute certainty, that their means of livelihood is being taken away from them" (15).

Most men are ignorant, not evil. All they require is training by experts in the practice of scientific management. The workers cannot be blamed for not knowing what is best for them, nor can they be blamed for being "naturally and very properly suspicious of their employers." (Taylor keeps remarking that the men's distrust of poor management is based on genuine causes, whereas their suspicion of the excellencies of Taylorism comes from misinformation.) "Now, again, gentlemen, I do not wish to be quoted as saying that all employers are tricky, but I do wish to say that, in my judgment, employers are just as tricky as workmen are tricky, neither more nor less so" (38).

It is still early in his testimony, but Taylor likes to think he has established his credentials as a man of practical wisdom and total trustworthiness. Surely his next remarks about the nature of scientific management will be taken at their full value. Ready to explain (and to defend) his system, he denies flat out the standard charges made against Taylorism: that it consists of a series of suspect devices for (1) speeding up the mechanistic production process at the cost of inflicting an ever-accelerating rate of labor upon the workers; (2) dividing the job process into work units so small that traditional notions of the wholeness of each laborer's contributions are discarded; (3) passing control from the shop floor into the hands of management; (4) enforcing total obedience to the bosses in defiance of whatever vestiges of the American ideal of self-reliance remain.

Taylor reviews these slanders, "the devices the average man calls to mind when scientific management is spoken of":

> Scientific management is *not* any efficiency device, *not* a device of any kind for securing efficiency, *nor* is it any bunch or group of effi-

ciency devices. It is *not* a new system of figuring costs; it is *not* a new scheme of paying men; *it is not . . . ; it is not . . . ; it is not . . .* (26; my emphasis)

Taylor is involved in more than the immediate need to respond to Wilson's Congressional committee. By seizing this semipublic moment, he will negate whatever "the average man" (employee, owner, Congressman, layperson outside the business enterprise) mistakenly thinks of Taylorism. He not only shakes his system loose from the particular elements to which his critics tenaciously attach their attention; he disengages himself from imitators whose flawed systems give his policies a bad name. With missionary fervor, he announces the true "essence" of his own system, one that transcends all other industrial processes. Scientific management is nothing less than

a complete mental revolution on the part of the workingman . . . as to their duties toward their work, toward their fellow men, and toward their employers. And it involves the equally complete mental evolution on the part of those on the management's side—the foreman, the superintendent, the owner of the business, the board of directors. (27)

Ever sensitive to skepticism, Taylor anticipates the audience's reaction. "I know that perhaps it sounds to you like nothing but bluff—like buncombe—but I am going to try to make clear to you just what this great mental revolution involves" (27). Before any man there can respond in disbelief to the statement that Taylorism is *not* about time-motion studies or bonus wages, Taylor introduces yet another surprise. In that glad day when scientific management commands the future, there will be a better world in which "this new idea of cooperation and peace has been substituted for the old idea of discord and war" (30–31). This mental revolution (the overthrow of the dark, satanic mills once heralded by William Blake) will result in

substitution of peace for war, the substitution of hearty brotherly cooperation for contention and strife; of both pulling hard in the same direction instead of pulling apart; of replacing suspicious watchfulness with mutual confidence; of becoming friends instead of enemies. (30)

This is already heady stuff, but Taylor presses on, calling upon the age-old rhetorical devices used to announce the means and ends of true religions, language that promises the coming of a new heaven and new earth of brotherhood and peace. Although his vision relies upon the "sub-

stitution of exact scientific investigation and knowledge for the old individual judgment or opinion," he allows himself to speak of the yearning
of men of science toward that utopia Taylorism will bring to pass. (31).

Not everyone listening finds redemption. Once the discussion period
opens, Chairman Wilson, Congressman from Pennsylvania and former
secretary of the United Mine Workers, wonders aloud whether Taylor's
belief in the workman's full cooperation with management will not "be
very much like the lion and the lamb lying down together with the lamb
inside" (152; my emphasis). But the time has not yet come when Taylor
must deal directly with his skeptics' counterarguments. He is still in command of the floor, still adroitly making use of a strikingly diverse set of
techniques for explanation and defense.

One pattern of discourse Taylor returns to repeatedly is statement
then illustration, assertion then proffered proof, using analogies to commonplace events from his and (he believes) others' shared experiences.[5]
But he clearly relishes going farther afield by telling little story-dramas,
complete with pungent working-class dialogue in which he enacts all the
parts.

Taylor slides quickly into the first of his Pat and Mike stories. He
recreates a scene in which "you" call a workman over to ask, "See here,
Pat, how much ought you to take on at one shovel load?"

> These men were then talked to in about this way, "See here, Pat and
> Mike, you fellows understand your job allright [*sic*]; both of you fel-
> lows are first-class men; you know what we think of you; you are
> allright [*sic*] now; but we want to pay you fellows double wages. We
> are going to ask you to do a lot of damn fool things, and when
> you are doing them there is going to be some one out along side of
> you all the time, a young chap with a piece of paper and a stop watch
> and pencil, and all day long he will tell you to do these fool things,
> and he will be writing down what you are doing and snapping a
> watch on you and all that sort of business. Now, we just want to
> know whether you fellows want to go into that bargain or not? If
> you want double wages while that is going on allright [*sic*], we will
> pay you double; if you don't allright [*sic*], you needn't take the job
> unless you want to; we just called you in to see whether you want to
> work this way or not. (51)

Could Theodore Dreiser do better, or Upton Sinclair, or John Dos
Passos in the decade to come, at capturing the language of the boss at
work, "driving" his men with the honeyed words of shop lingo, not having to tell them why he is doing what he is doing (too scientific for their
comprehension anyway) but ever exuding the "atmosphere" of friendly

cooperation? In his version of the proletarian scene, it is a happy shop Taylor portrays.

The snippet Taylor inserts soon after this drama also reflects the atmosphere of comradely give-and-take. It demonstrates the good relations his system creates between the "teacher" sent down from the main office and the worker instructed in the new efficiency system.

> The workman, instead of hating the teacher who came to him—instead of looking askance at him and saying to himself, "Here comes one of those damn nigger drivers to drive me to work"—looked upon him as one of the best friends he had around there. He knew that he came out there to help him, not to nigger drive him. Now, let me show you what happens. The teacher comes, in every case, not to bulldoze the man, not to drive him to harder work than he can do, but to try in a friendly, brotherly way to help him, so he says "Now, Pat, something has gone wrong with you. You know no worker who is not a high-priced workman can stay on this gang, and you will have to get off of it if we can't find out what is the matter with you. I believe you have forgotten how to shovel right. I think that's all there is the matter with you. Go ahead and let me watch you awhile. I want to see if you know how to do the damn thing, anyway." (60–61)

With the little drama between Pat and the manager fixed into place, Taylor sums up the case: "Now, gentlemen . . . this is not nigger driving; this is kindness; this is teaching; this is doing what I would like mighty well to have done to me if I were a boy trying to learn how to do something" (61). The fact that Taylor's workers, Pat and Mike, forever will remain "boys" ("niggers"), jollied into complying with the manager's instructions, is clouded over by his shrewd reference to "the old way"—when there was no talk between manager and worker, only brusque directives and cussing out on the part of the boss: " 'You are no good; we have given you a fair chance; get out of this,' and the workman is pretty lucky if it isn't 'get to hell out of this' " (62).

For all Taylor's self-satisfied revelations of a New Jerusalem with lion and lamb in amiable cooperation, there is another, sharper story he has to tell: the time of "hard fighting" he went through in the early years at Midvale Steel, when he tried to convince the workmen of the sweet reasonableness of his methods.

> I was a young man in years, but I give you my word I was a great deal older than I am now with worry, meanness, and contemptibleness of the whole damn thing. It is a horrid life for any man to live,

not to be able to look any workman in the face all day long without
seeing hostility there and feeling that every man around is his virtual
enemy. (83)

Taylor confesses the loneliness and isolation he felt because of "the
stone wall" erected by the words "tyrant" and "nigger driver," words
thrown at him by his men. This confession is a necessary part of the special testimony he makes to himself: in reiterating the principles by which
he "drives" himself, he goes far beyond what the Congressional committee requires. Management of language is central to the personal witness he
makes regarding the amount of efficiency and rationality he has had to
bring to his entire life.

Henry Ford said machinery is the new messiah, but Taylor's sense of
messianic mission both validates his public confidence and nourishes the
concealed anxieties that continually force him to explain and persuade. In
his mature years, he feels compelled to tell stories that center on the mar-
tyrdom he endured in his youthful days, when he was bitterly scorned for
the truths he selflessly continues to place before employers and workers
alike.

The battle is not wholly won even now. As Taylor informed his engineering colleagues in 1903, scientific management will not be "true" until
its truth abides everywhere. In 1912 he is still repeating the story of his
years of pain and persecution, still hoping to convince those sitting in
judgment to do unto him as he insists he has always done for the good of
Pat, Mike, and poor little Schmidt.

Linguistic Gauntlets

Chairman Wilson opens the question period and Taylor forthwith loses
the source of his greatest strength: the ability to control the direction in
which his arguments flow and to present without interruption the dramatic illustrations with which he supports his more abstract statements—
bringing to them the illusion of the human element that acts to mitigate
the impersonality of the machine process. Chairman Wilson is skeptical,
tough, unrelenting in his pursuit of the weaknesses he finds in Taylor's
testimony. Taylor continues to do well for himself, but the artifice of the
seeming plausibility of his argument begins to be exposed. In particular,
his habit of speaking *as if for* the workers under his supervision, and the
tight equivalences he draws between his own experiences and those of
"the average man," are more readily exposed as verbal manipulations. It is
not that Taylor's testimony collapses at this point, or that his language

signals desperation in reaction to his stern inquisitor, but Wilson is capable of making rifts appear where previously Taylor's control over his narrative allowed him to sustain the look of a seamless whole.[6]

One by one, Taylor's favorite rhetorical methods are challenged. First, there is Taylor's self-portrait as a man who worked his way up through the ranks, learning every step of the industrial process shoulder to shoulder with the laborers whose best interests he insists he wishes to protect. Wilson's questions expose the information that Taylor's rapid upward movement as a mechanic's apprentice was made possible because his father "had some means," thereby freeing the eighteen-year-old Taylor from distracting, debilitating anxieties over the necessity of holding down a job (112). Wilson wants to shake Taylor's claim that he speaks directly for the worker. He pushes this point when Taylor states he "was perfectly contented" and "did not feel driven" when the pace of his own line work was accelerated. "Would not the fact," Wilson asks, "that your people were in better financial circumstances than the average workingman remove from your mind the same fear of ultimate exhaustion that would be continually in the mind of the workman who was dependent entirely upon his day's wages for his living?" (123–24). Wilson presses, presses to widen the spaces between what Taylor thinks about working conditions, what Taylor says he "believes" the men think and feel, and what (Wilson insists) the men's actual reactions might be.

Second, Wilson challenges Taylor's recurring use of beast fables to illustrate the grades of labor he expects to get out of his workers and the amount of intelligence (very little) he believes most people bring to their assigned tasks. Taylor has been elaborating upon one of his favorite analogies (a variation of the one he used in the 1903 paper): the difference between "the first-class" trotting horse and the animal (here described as a dray horse) who does the heavy labor natural to a "second-class man." Taylor suggests that the dray horse is strong, but lazy, stupid, and hard to bring up to the level of efficiency required by his scientific methods. Wilson asks, "Scientific management has no place for such men?" Taylor replies, "Scientific management has no place for a bird that can sing and won't sing." Wilson: "I am not speaking about birds at all." When Taylor continues to refer to "work for the dray horse and work for the trotting horse" as his way of contrasting good with poor workers, Wilson remarks with asperity:

> We are not in this particular investigation dealing with horses nor singing birds, but we are dealing with men who are a part of society and for whose benefit society is organized; and what I wanted to get

at is whether or not your scientific management had any place whatever for a man who was not able to meet your own definition of
what constitutes a "first-class" workman. (175–76)

Taylor stubbornly refuses to back down, but he drops the beast analogies in replying, "There is no place for a man who can work and won't
work." Wilson is equally adamant. He continues to press Taylor to admit
that scientific management discards so-called "second-class men" without.
a thought for their futures. In doing so he exposes yet another flaw in
Taylor's self-portrait as a man dedicated to meticulous attention to fact.

Taylor, temper rising: There is always a job somewhere for any physically fit man. *Wilson:* Are you aware of the figures on permanent unem-
ployment, which show three to four million workmen out of work at all
times, men "who are willing to work but unable to secure it?" *Taylor,*
admitting his unfamiliarity with these statistics: "it is merely an impression on my part, and from the difficulty I have had personally in getting
men I would say that it was not true" (177). To think of this "impression-
ism" coming from the man who prides himself on the accuracy of his
measurement of steel gauges and the precision of his investigations into
work patterns!

Finally, Wilson challenges Taylor's proclivity for shifting from personal opinions to generalizing statements that dismiss problems taking
place outside his immediate ken. He holds Taylor's habit up to scrutiny as
well as Taylor's assumption that he knows what goes on in other men's
minds. In the absence of the real Pat and Mike, Wilson cannot contest the
tales Taylor told about their type, but when Taylor tells the chairman what
he himself is thinking, Wilson pulls him up short. "You have a wrong
concept of what is running in my mind, and I want to set you right" (180).
This is no minor quibble. As long as Taylor and men like him claim that
their ideas about "the one best way" are the ideas shared by those under
their authority, any chance of initiating democratic procedures is negated
by the autocrats of the business enterprise.

By 1912 blatant disregard of the needs and beliefs of everyone other
than the man in charge (summed up by the motto "The Public Be
Damned") has been displaced by the myth that bosses and workers must
act together as a matter of course. Not everyone believes in this myth.
Taylor's testimony and Wilson's critique exemplify the linguistically based
social struggles taking place just prior to World War I. Sometimes at odds
with each other, sometimes in league, were publicly sanctioned language
patterns that supported class harmony and goodwill yet were entangled
with the Janus-faced, squint-eyed discourse of scientific systems—a dis-

course that directed a capitalistic society in an advanced state of rationalized industrialization toward both betterment and brutality.

What Wilson *does* have on his mind is whether Taylor's insistence
upon the worker's obedience to management's orders indicates his opposition to collective bargaining and the other means by which labor resists
being told how much physical exertion is good for it. Taylor twists and
turns in his responses to this issue. It is unwise for him bluntly to deny
what Wilson cites as every worker's "right to determine" the nature of a
fair day's work. He refrains from directly opposing the idea of democratic
process in the workplace. Instead, he tries another of his talk-stories. This
time he tells of the surgeon who blithely tells his untrained, inexperienced
young interns to chop away on a patient's leg with a hatchet, axe, or any
instrument of their choosing. Surely, Taylor declares, anyone would recognize the folly of permitting such uncontrolled initiative on the part
of one's underlings. At this point, Taylor is relieved by the calling of a
five-o'clock recess, but during the evening session Wilson will have one
last go.

Taylor starts off on the terms that best favor his style. He makes a
statement of the kind preferred by ideologues backed into tight places.
Momentarily escaping from one-on-one questions that confront him with
the cold actualities of labor-management tensions and high unemploy-
ment rates, Taylor proposes a vision heated by his enthusiasm. Scientific
management will soon enhance the already splendid reputation of American workingmen throughout the industrial world.

> I am looking forward to the day when the working people of our
> country will live as well and have the same luxuries, the same oppor-
> tunities for leisure, for culture, and for education as are now pos-
> sessed by the average business man of this country, and this condi-
> tion can only come through a great increase in the average
> productivity for the individuals of this country. That is the road we
> shall have to travel. (209)

Taylor may have thought he was safe once he lifted his eyes to the
rhetorical mountainside in praise of American labor and in prophecy of
the good things to come to all "first-class men," but Wilson will not let
Taylor go free so easily. "If the American workman is already more productive than any other workman, and by systematizing the work you can
still further increase his productivity, then what necessity is there for adding to the discomfort of the workman by requiring the expenditure of
more energy on his part?" asks Wilson (209). Taylor cannot answer; his
vision is predicated on the saved energy that accrues to the machine pro-

cess itself, not on any energy given back to the workers at the machines.
A glorious future for the dynamo; cloudy times for those lying at its base,
their historical necks broken.

The closing moments of the testimony bring Taylor and Wilson into
close contention over what it means to say "to add to the comfort and
well-being of mankind" (211). Once more, Wilson tries to force Taylor to
stop substituting his own words for those of the workers. Wilson presses;
Taylor equivocates. There is no clear victory in what has been from first
to last a battle over the facticity of language, but Taylor continues to fight.

Taylor picks up on a line of argument employed by other managers at
the time, one Henry Ford would use continually in the decade to come.
Laborers who do not like the way Taylorism sets their work pace are free
to quit their jobs. (Taylor's tone throughout is not sarcasm but astonish-
ment that anyone could imply that members of the American work force
are trapped within any form of legalized slavery denying them full choice
in how and where they work.) Further, Taylor asserts, employers suffer
far more than the workers when they refuse to accept the scientific management system, for it is they who are penalized by losing workers to
rapid turnover.

Wilson counterattacks: "But if the workman leaves, quits his employment, would he not be placed to a greater disadvantage by virtue of his
quitting his employment than the employer would be by virtue of the
workman quitting?" Taylor: "I think it is almost impossible to generalize
on that" (214).

Taylor's response is noticeably weak if one is, like Wilson, convinced
of the essential wrongness of Taylor's position. It is sufficiently persuasive,
however, if one is convinced from the start that the positions taken by
management and ownership are de facto correct. But then this has been
the case all along.

In the final accounting, Taylor's arguments neither stand nor fall
based on whether he is good at telling beast fables, Pat and Mike talk-
stories, glib analogues, prophetic visions, or other techniques for playing
to his audience. His testimony works for those who want to hear what he
says, as long as it gives proof of the power that bears out the powerlessness
(in F. A. Silcox's words) of those who try to, but cannot, overcome "the
brutality of the conflict."

We see Taylor's testimony constantly sliding away from the bedrock
of scientific inquiry that he insists validates the truth of everything he says.
This slippage is not necessarily exposed simply because Chairman Wilson
is present, relentlessly weighing Taylor's every word. In the long run, neither Taylor's usually agile use of expressive forms nor Wilson's refusal to
be taken in by them (and his own use of language to attack what he views

as the weakness of Taylor's logic) can be said to make or break Taylor's case before the House committee.[7] Embedded beliefs create the conditions under which language works to reinforce those beliefs. Still, beliefs— as in the rightness of efficiency systems—have a history; they can change. As Taylor and Wilson use them, words and the material facts they simultaneously embody and obscure are crucial to the making of those histories.

Cussing Back

"We are not the problem." It was not easy for words like these to be heard when members of the American labor force were speaking them. They seldom penetrated the din of statements advanced in the print media by the managers and owners. Too often, as in the case of the worker who spoke out before the gathering of Chicago industrialists noted by Graham Taylor, declarations of the contributions made by immigrant labor to the American business economy are placed on a back page of the city newspaper, easily overlooked, quickly forgotten. Too often, as the testimony Frederick Winslow Taylor gave before the House committee shows, self-justifying fictions represented as gospel truths asserted that workers favor the patterns of life and labor under which they are obliged to exist.

An established tradition of reform literature supporting the cause of the working class was, of course, in place by 1912, and workers themselves vigorously advanced their views in their own newspapers and journals.[8] In the first instance, no matter how much of an impact they had upon middle-class audiences, reformers like Jacob Riis and Upton Sinclair could only offer representations of lives of struggle at a remove from the source. In the latter case, the self-representations marginal groups issued in print were read largely by their own kind. Converting those who had already seen the light (and experienced the dark), these accounts seldom extended their influence beyond their indigenous boundaries. It was an event of great rarity and some importance when members of the laboring classes had a chance to dictate some of the terms of confrontation, when their stories could be heard where the business enterprise ran its own often wayward course.

Such an occasion occurred in January 1911, exactly one year before Taylor appeared at the Congressional hearing, when the welfare workers division of the National Civic Federation met for its eleventh annual conference. (A photograph shows men and women in evening attire grouped around tables after the banquet in New York's Hotel Astor.) Members of the NCF executive council included Samuel Gompers, the vice-president. In addition there were participants from the three main subcommittees:

(1) "on the part of the public" (William Taft, president of the United States, Senator Elihu Root of New York, and Andrew Carnegie); (2) "on the part of the employers"; (3) "on the part of the wage earners" (Gompers and Daniel Tobin of the Teamsters are among those listed).[9]

There was a full agenda, and a steady stream of eminent guest speakers addressed the main topic of the evening, "Scientific Management—Efficiency." Harrington Emerson and H. L. Gantt headed the list, but not because the audience expected them to talk about the ideas Taylor was to advance later that year in *The Principles of Scientific Management.* They were featured because of the public interest the Brandeis Eastern Rate case had raised the previous years. But after Emerson and Gantt spoke of the wisdom of "waste not, want not" (the catchy phrase with which Emerson opened his updated Franklinian economic theory), two men who opposed management's position came forward to speak: first was Warren S. Stone, head of the International Brotherhood of Locomotive Engineers, then John Mitchell, president of the United Mine Workers from 1899 to 1908 and current chair of the NCF Trade Agreement Department.

Mitchell uses a no-nonsense approach in his talk. Equipped with charts to establish the "undisguised" facts lying behind the falsehoods promoted by contemporary industrial theories, Mitchell states he will prove that the newly acclaimed production system is simply the hated old "piece-work system under a new name." From the heart of the audience (an incident written into the record of the proceedings) comes the challenge: "A Voice: *No,*" but Mitchell continues undeterred. In concluding he broaches the touchy issue of who has the right to speak for the workers, the ones most affected by the introduction of the new efficiency measures.

> I am not speaking for the railroad companies; they are abundantly able to speak for themselves. . . . But I do speak with reasonable authority for the wage-earners. . . . The working people will reserve to themselves the right of having something to say in determining what conditions of industry are good for them; and we suggest that the advantages of the new theory of efficiency be presented, not in the name of the wage-earners, but in the name of the manufacturers, because the system is not acceptable to the wage-earners, and should not be put forward as their friend.[10]

Warren S. Stone, who preceded Mitchell, provides an even sharper example of what a labor union man can do in presenting his constituents' case: saying "no" louder than any "no" raised from the dress circle at the Hotel Astor. Stone begins with a nice gambit. Harrington Emerson had opened his address by informing the audience that he was ready to distribute printed copies, "so that you can see definitely what I am saying and why I am saying it." Stone says, "I have no prepared speech printed for distribution like the gentlemen who preceded me. I am a graduate of the school of hard knocks—twenty-three years of my life have been spent in the cab of a locomotive, and I at least think I know whereof I speak."[11] The forte of the man of the people is the spoken word, delivered in its dramatic immediacy, not printed words got up by one of the bosses to be looked over at leisure.

The early moments of Stone's talk (a presentation far longer than Mitchell attempted) announce his opposition to the bonus system supposedly favored by Taylorism. They are enlivened by the irate interjections of H. L. Gantt ("I beg pardon. That is exactly wrong—"), until Stone turns to the program chairman to protest. "I have come a thousand miles to talk twenty minutes, and I hope I will not be interrupted again." He refuses to be denied his full time on stage, particularly since he wishes to recount a vivid narrative of the hair-raising dangers the intrepid locomotive engineer encounters on every run. This engineer is hampered by lazy, inept mechanics back at the yard, men whose careless maintenance work the bonus system encourages.

> Picture that engineer out on the road . . . every nerve keyed up to the highest possible level, every sense alert, the one cool, keen-eyed, wide-awake man in the cab pitting his skill and watchfulness against the dangers that confront him in his everyday struggle to bring the limited train in on time. A joint on steam chest or cylinder gives way, or the packing on a valve-stem or piston blows out. At once he is riding in a cloud of steam that blows back and forth, windows are instantly coated over, and, with his head out of the window, and the wind cutting like a knife, he is trying to distinguish the signals. A failure on his part . . . spells the difference between safety and disaster to the hundreds of passengers sleeping in safety behind; the danger to all has been increased a hundred-fold.

The story unfolds; more suspense builds as Stone describes other runs made under bad conditions, until the terrible day when a wreck takes place, headlined "by the paper next morning, 'Many People Killed and Injured on Account of an Engineer Disregarding Signal Displayed.' " This is an outrage, for the brave engineer is dead "and cannot explain that his life was sacrificed on account of the bonus system."

Stone needs no charts for his presentation. His strength is his tale, a tale that—like the cliff-hangers being filmed by the new moving picture industry—portrays trains rushing down the tracks toward disaster. Stone closes his talk (perhaps not wisely) with a comic poem he clipped from a

Boston paper, which satirizes Brandeis's argument. Melodrama serves
Stone's argument better than labored humor, but, either way, Stone does
not waste his allotted time as he speaks in the name of all graduates of the
school of hard knocks.

It was difficult for anyone to introduce alternative narratives, given
the rhetoric of self-justification crowding the business and industrial scene
with much noise and some confusion. When the men and women directly
affected by the machine process were blocked from doing this on their
own, their champions tested various expressive means to do it for them.
One of the most arresting attempts was made by Josephine Goldmark. It
was arresting not so much for the evidence she brought against the cult of
scientific efficiency as for the manner in which she waged her attack.

In 1912, under the auspices of the Russell Sage Foundation, Goldmark
published *Fatigue and Efficiency: A Study in Industry*.[12] It is clear from her
opening statement that her approach will be different from that of Warren
Stone, who used melodrama to depict the courageous locomotive engineer sent racing to his death because of inefficient work encouraged in the
name of efficiency. Nor will she overtly play upon the terror and pity
evoked by reform narratives such as *How the Other Half Lives* and *The
Jungle*. Goldmark instead chooses to fight fire with fire.

Fatigue and Efficiency constantly alternates between compilations of
scientific data and the presentation of overburdened bodies driven to a
state of depression. A struggle is taking place, however, as Goldmark
strives to find the best way to appropriate methods of scientific inquiry, so
that she can correct the threat technology and management systems pose
to human bodies. She can never quite settle upon the perfect balance between the "new" and "old" modes of language. The following example
stands for the many such tensions that run throughout her text.

Goldmark points the way to "a scientific basis of legislation" based
"upon the scientific study of fatigue—one of the most modern inquiries
of physiological, chemical, and psychological science."[13] Indeed,

> such scientific authority is precisely what is most needed today for a
> more rational progress in the future than in the past; something
> more exact and demonstrable than the appeal to pity, less subject to
> temporary variation. . . . Just because the more cruel, dramatic ex-
> ploitation of workers is in the main a thing of the past, exact scien-
> tific proof is needed of the more subtle injuries of modern industry,
> its practically illimitable speed and strain.

Yet when it comes to cases, and when Goldmark has to drive home
"the basic principle which has emerged from our study of fatigue—*that
rest must adequately balance exertion,*" she shifts from the scientific language

she uses to describe mathematical qualities to the more "familiar" discourse applied to the science of bodily functions.

Goldmark cites a technical passage from Taylor's *Principles of Scientific Management*. Filled with pounds and percentages, this passage is based upon mathematical studies "in which each element of the work was graphically represented by plotting curves, to give a bird's eye view of the data and records accumulated." Then she breaks this train of argument, the particular tonality associated "the most modern inquiries": "But to explain the formula thus evolved, we must revert again to the familiar language and conceptions of physiology."

Goldmark here adds *blood* to mathematical abstractions, just as she introduces *spirit* in her chapter devoted to "The Bad Effect of Fatigue upon Morals." We can appreciate how difficult it was for Goldmark's generation to excise completely flesh, blood, and spirit from "the most modern inquiries of physiological, chemical, and psychological science."

Goldmark founds her study on a solid moral base. Considerations of the relation between fatigue and efficiency must not be restricted to discussions about ways to increase commodity production or to gain greater profits through more rational use of smoothly running machines and carefully controlled workers. The inner life within the human bodily mechanism is constantly in view. Tales of moral derangement extracted from copious documentation, meticulously compiled according to the best new statistical methods, demand a hearing alongside testimonies of derangements affecting nonhuman industrial processes.[14]

> Among the higher functions of certain brain tracts is that of inhibition. . . . The effect of fatigue on these centres is seen very quickly in any prolonged effort. . . . In general, self-control is lost, and the lower, the baser, and the more selfish faculties of our nature run riot.

> Dulled senses demand powerful stimuli; exhaustion of the vital forces leads to a desire for crude, for violent excitation. . . . In such circumstances, culture of hand or brain seems unattainable, and the sharing of our general heritage a remote dream. A consideration of even more immediate importance is that such circumstances impel undisciplined girls toward unsocial action, toward vicious or criminal behavior.

> There is such a thing as the moralization of time in reference to its effects upon personal character. The worker who formerly toiled long hours from morning till night and six days in the week, left idle on the seventh day, was under great temptation to make a brute of himself on that day. Too tired to do anything, jaded body, starved

brain, brutalized soul, there could be no Sunday rest for such; there was nothing left to do but get drunk as the natural result of a tired and brutalized body and soul.[15]

Three years later, Robert Franklin Hoxie would introduce his own plea for the workers' cause. The Hoxie Report of 1915, the result of the hearings on scientific management conducted by yet another Congressional commission assigned to investigate troubled industrial relations, was perhaps the most important public statement organized labor had made against Taylorism up to that moment.[16]

The Hoxie Report does not marshal a forceful display of narrative techniques and rhetorical strategies. Its prose does not offer itself to the lambent analysis of the fascinating dialectical (and, at times, dialogical) movements taking place between the scientific discourses allied to discussions of the early twentieth-century machine process and the diverse means utilized to tell the stories of the people implicated in that process. Its significance lies in the discursive space it gives to accusations of linguistic impropriety leveled against its foes. The Hoxie Report states repeatedly that, in the name of pure science, men of management concoct deeply flawed arguments from non-"scientific" phrases in order to dominate in their relations with labor. The purpose of the report, therefore, is to make the following charges about the ways in which language is used rightly or wrongly.

(1) Organized labor objects to "systems of *the so-called 'scientific management' cult.*"[17]

(2) The "controversial literature" of scientific management, contributed by both advocates and critics, should be judged by "what it is in fact, *and not what the ideals or theories of its advocates or opponents would have it be*" (2, 5).

(3) In cases where management procedures "generally lay emphasis on so-called welfare work, or, in general, eliminate the spirit and the means for the expression of democracy, then welfare work must be considered a part of scientific management, and the absence of democracy a feature of it, though the former be excluded from the theoretical exposition of its leaders, and *democracy be declared by them to be the essence of scientific management*" (5).

(4) Expose the fact that "*there is a good deal of nonsense talked about* the close touch which exists between the managers and the men. *From recent magazine articles, one might be led to believe* that the 'front office' is the habitual resort of workmen in trouble or with suggestions to make. This has not been the experience of the investigator" (94).

(5) "*The whole gospel of scientific management to the worker is to the individual, telling him* how, by special efficiency, he can cut loose from the mass, and rise in wages or position to a man of consequence" (106).

(6) "The only way, then, by which *the voice of the workers* can reach the management fully and clearly is through group organization." (109).

(7) Among the "certain potent causes of present evil" is the "persistent attempt on the part of experts and managers to apply scientific management and its methods outside their natural sphere." Such evil comes when men "*speak of* modern industry as though it were all of one piece" (113). Some of these men are "fakirs," but most are engineers and employers whose subjectivity develops unformed economic and social theories "*almost wholly on the basis of their own experience*," or on the basis of "narrow, absolutistic assumptions" that bear "the marks of the naivete of early scientific beginnings" (117, 119).[18]

The Hoxie Report concludes with a particularly telling statement:

> because of [scientific management's] youth and the necessary application of its principles to a competitive state of industry, it is, in many respects, crude, *many of its devices are contradictory of its announced principles,* and it is inadequately scientific. *Nevertheless, it is to date the latest word* in the sheer mechanics of production and inherently in line with the march of events. (137)

Taylorism, in taking credit for principles that prepare for a finer future, ought to possess a utopian language. But it does not. What it does have are the present facts of the brutality of its practices and the language of "the sheer mechanics of production," which provides "the latest word."

One final note. In appendix V (the Hoxie Report contains all of the apparatus appropriate to scientific documents), trade union members list their own objections to "the alleged general character and spirit" of their adversaries. Once again, their objections center on the issue of flawed nomenclature.

> Organized labor makes a clear distinction between "scientific management" . . . and "science in management." It does not oppose savings of waste and increase of output resulting from improved machinery and truly efficient management. It stands, therefore, definitely committed to "science in management," and its objections are directed solely against systems devised by the so-called "scientific management" cult. (169)

On both sides of the ideological gap there is an intense awareness of the primary importance of "true" words set over against "so-called" definitions. The trade unionist can support one phrase but reject the implications of another while management stands firm on the rightness of language confirming the scientific rationality of its decisions.

"Industrial democracy" is another loaded term. It forces the issue of whether the lamb of labor and the lion of management can exist harmoniously within the same world of words. One contributor to the May 1916 issue of *The Annals of the American Academy of Political and Social Science* defines industrial democracy as "the power of employes [*sic*] to think, to act, to be heard on individual matters."[19] Yet in the same issue another writer not only reverses his colleague's definition but challenges the way all language is being misused in the discussion. First, there is misuse by people within industry:

> It is an especially grave misfortune in industry if one party to a contention clothes its thoughts in words that misinterpret these thoughts to the other. But this is a danger to which industrial disputes are peculiarly susceptible, and much would be gained if we could get the language in which these should be argued reduced to certain forms which should have a common meaning to all.[20]

Second, reformers and dilettantes given to "philosophizing about the claims of society and the common good" introduce errors.

> Perhaps it is because so many have been writers that we have now in common parlance certain dignified phrases of meritorious sound which convey as many different shades of meaning as there are people voicing them. It is at any rate a fact that too many of the reforming guild are literary stylists first of all, and most zealously. Euphony and mellifluous diction go extraordinarily far with us as a people, and phraseology too often wins a widespread approval that would not be given to the logic which it implies if it had not been verbally sweetened. It consequently becomes essential for us, not too infrequently, to analyze the catch-words of our political, religious, or social language to determine whether we are using words primarily to bespeak thought or because they have a certain rhythm to their jingle. (58–59)

Whether one is for or against industrial democracy in its various definitions, for or against the dialectics of the "necessarily" disruptive effect of socialism upon established social structures, it is apparent that warped language wounds and good words might heal.

On the one side, "industrial democracy" is defined as that which upholds the best of American society. On the other side, this phrase encourages a "period of destructive agitation which [tears] down necessarily as a prerequisite to clearing the ground for upbuilding," thereby creating dangerous shifts in institutional structures (59). Still others wholeheartedly welcome what the latter analyst condemns: workers seizing authority— "tearing down necessarily" as the prelude to "clearing the ground for upbuilding."

Writing in *The Masses,* Charles Edward Russell blasted the National Association of Manufacturers for the "lying and hypocrisy and slimy fraud" of "their pretenses about 'freedom of contract' and 'law and order.'" He roundly cursed the "grand company of foolish, prating, mouthing incompetents called optimists [who go] to and fro in this country uttering stale old stuff about the sacredness of the Constitution and the glory of our institutions." [21] James Harvey Robinson, Columbia University professor of history and author of the prestigious book, *The New History,* published in 1912, also assailed the fact that our language "is cluttered up with meaningless words and phrases. . . . We must criticize and perfect our tools of thought; we must shape language to fit our task." [22]

But "fit our task" by means of *which* language? In a society where scientific management has become the standard that defines effective discourse, how many workers and their supporters can find means of their own to "perfect [their] tools of thought" for the attainment of greater social and political efficiency? Was any language, written or spoken, capable of affecting sweeping, "necessarily" radical, changes within a system that was bounded in one way or another by the narratives of Taylorism?

Turn back to the testimony Taylor gave before the 1912 House committee. Hear what he had to say about the efficacy of language and its power to form the nature of the workers' lives. Taylor's verbal combat with Wilson is coming to an end. Once again Wilson asks what kind of controls scientific management expects to impose to achieve its goals of high productivity and low costs. In response, Taylor speaks of those methods of "persuasion" and "discipline" that he believes will encourage democracy in the workplace. [23]

> Under scientific management the discipline is at the very minimum, but out of kindness to the workman, out of personal kindness to him, in my judgment, it is the duty of those who are in management to use all the arts of persuasion first to get the workman to conform to the rules, and after that has been done, *then to gradually increase the severity of the language* until practically, before you are thru, *the powers of the English language have been exhausted in an effort to make the man do what he ought to do.* And if that fails, then in the interest of the workman, some more severe type of discipline should be resorted to. (my emphasis)

Wilson immediately corners Taylor, demanding that he expand upon the notion that swearing is one way to achieve industrial democracy.

> The Chairman: Is it part of scientific management that the workman shall cuss the higher up when the man higher up violates his own formulas? Mr. Taylor: It is part of the democratic feeling that exists between all hands that under scientific management they should talk to each other very freely and very frankly. And I think it is safe to say that if I, for instance, were to swear at one of these fellows here (pointing to some of the workmen who were present at the hearing) he would swear right back at me without the slightest hesitation. . . . I have not seen any great distinction between the two when it comes to swearing.

For a brief moment it appears as though the man in the ranks can achieve "industrial democracy," if he invokes his inalienable right to "cuss the man higher up." But this glimpsed utopia, based on the equal opportunity of all men (all males, that is) to use language to talk back, is overturned by Taylor's next observation: once "the powers of the English language have been exhausted in an effort to make the man do what he ought to do," unilateral authority rests with management to impose "some more severe type of discipline," discipline that exceeds the power of language.

What do we have now? We have language for cussing out the bosses and for being hollered at by irate managers; language for making up stories about people who cannot speak for themselves, and for narratives told by those who find their own words to attack the conditions under which they work; language that uses strategies drawn from generations of storytelling, pretending to speak for Pat and Mike or exposing the fallaciousness of such tales. We also have language used by managers, who blurt out that the machine process and the business enterprise are all that really matter; language used to cloak brutal purposes under the guise of sentimental betterment; language used in the sincere attempt to work through the most radical implications of industrial democracy; language that begins and ends within the masculine work/world vision Taylorism imposes, until others come along to wrench it open.[24]

We loop back to where we began at the start of chapter 3, to F. A. Silcox in 1929 and his anatomization of the languages of power and powerlessness. We heard him state that realism means accepting "the brutality of the conflict" that promises power to those who stay with "is," while idealism tries to mitigate (not end) brutality with "oughts," "shouldn'ts," and "don'ts"—a language of betterment whose users are the more enfeebled constituents of the business enterprise. But Silcox's own words must be placed more fully within their context.

A participant at the 1929 Taylor Society conference titled "Workers' Participation in Management," Silcox has been preceded at the podium by two men: the head of the Full Fashioned Hosiery Workers of Philadelphia and a professor of economics from Antioch College. On hand to represent the New York Employing Printers' Association, Silcox breaks past the earlier speakers' promises that labor and management will learn to act out of mutual respect. "Naïve" he calls them. They depend upon mere "phrases carrying with them certain moral implications of what workers' organizations ought to do." [25] Once these statements are "stripped of their verbiage," little remains but for the workers to use whatever leverage they gain in a way that "least challenges the established power" and avoids "exciting" the employers' "antagonism." Silcox's retort is angry. Why "waste many words" in "a naïve ignoring of the implications of that power or a fond idealistic hope that in spite of the play for power" there awaits "a millennium of co-operation as a substitute for competition"?

"The brutality of the conflict" is the context for Silcox's demand that those who speak for betterment test their words "realistically" by facing up to the following facts: (1) "the acquisition of power is the primary thing that counts"; (2) "every group . . . must of necessity play for power"; (3) "the purpose of the accumulation of power is . . . to acquire more power"; (4) power plays keep things "in motion; therefore conflict and competition are desirable as vital agents in the promotion of progress"; (5) "power will be used with subtle refinements, as with differential calculus or, crudely, as with a butcher cleaver"; (6) during rare moments when opposing groups come into "periods of near equilibrium," then, and only then, both can "take all the traffic will bear when the taking is good"; (7) "ethical moralizing with oughts, shouldn'ts and don'ts" is a waste of time and words: inefficiency and unproductivity writ large.

This is Silcox's conclusion: we should use the facticity of language and direct it toward lives that are run efficiently, scientifically, and realistically. Only on these terms can workers gain power to offset management systems and betterment programs that run their lives for them wastefully, irrationally, fantastically.

We have come back full circle to Taylor and *his* arguments. We have come back to Adams as well, felled to the floor of the twentieth century, yet up on his feet again. Both men are still speaking at odds and in league with the conditions they attempt to describe and to alter.

Women Workers: New Era, New Force, Old Narratives

SCIENTIFIC MANAGEMENT marks the "new era": Sue Ainslie Clark of the National Consumers League states this in a 1911 editorial in *Life and Labor*. The woman who attempts to consolidate the entry she made into the workplace during World War I is "the new force let loose in industry": so Ida Tarbell announces in the first of her series of articles for *Industrial Management* during 1920 and 1921.[1]

Claims of newness, then as now, are considered good journalism if not always good history. The question that always needs asking is: to what purpose are narratives about newness put? Agreed that scientific management creates "a new epoch" in the monitoring of work, agreed that women were entering industry (however temporarily) "on a new basis" stemming from wartime manpower shortages, but what *kinds* of stories were being told about the convergence of these two, perhaps alien, forces—Taylorism and working women?

Did the spate of stories about women in the workplace fall within the boundaries of the realist, naturalist, or romantic mode? What precise emotions were exploited when, on the one hand, editors demanded that their staff supply "a thrilling series of articles" about conventional victims; or, on the other hand, when women workers themselves called for stories that "tell of struggle" and of "people who want justice passionately"?[2] To make a narratological metaphor of one of Taylor's favorite terms, what "functional work" was assigned to the women placed within these narratives? Did this particular type of woman's work effect positive social change, or were narrativized women rendered ineffectual as a political and social presence to the extent that their stories were complicitous in thwarting their emergence as a genuine new force?

Thematically speaking, what impact did the portrayal of lives exposed to Taylorism in the workplace have upon various sectors of the reading public? Did Taylorism supply the dramatic conditions that allowed women who had entered the male world of industry to assume the narrative role of the heroine?

These questions and others demand as many answers as there are narrative examples, but one thing is clear: there was an active industry among legislators, journalists, reformers, and champions of the causes of labor and of management in crafting the narratives and counternarratives that put women (actual and fictive) to work in order to argue the social consequences (dire or beneficial) of the incorporation of this new force into the complex patterns of the machine process.

The More Cruel, the More Subtle

Sue Ainslie Clark and Ida Tarbell did more than herald the coming of a new era and a new force. Their writings saw to it that the interlocked subjects of woman's labor and scientific management stood as testimony either to social advances or to troublesome problems for women and men alike. Tarbell's articles for *Industrial Management* are resolutely cheery in the reassurances they give that all is well in the world of the men in charge of managing the influx of women into the work force.[3] The managerial class to which Tarbell directs her reports can rest easy. Through soothing anecdotes, she confirms her belief in women's contentment with their lot and the heightened productivity the bosses can count on if they make shrewd use of both Taylorism and efficient female labor.

Clark is far more guarded than Tarbell in what she tells her readers (male and female). The country buzzes with the words "efficiency" and "scientific management," but while some are convinced that Taylorism "standardizes machines and materials [and] raises to the highest degree the efficiency of plant and worker," others call it "Scientific Slavery."[4] Yes, scientific management has brought in a "new era." Yes, it is no longer "a theory, it is a fact." Yes, it has gained favor with many employers, but what of the workers? In particular, what does it mean for the woman toiling at the machine?

Women experience greater efficiency of production, but also "the menace of greater monotony." They receive an increase in take-home pay, but what guarantees are there that any woman will receive "a fair proportion" for all she does? Bonuses abound for workers who keep to a certain level of efficient performance, but at what risk of unbearable bodily strain caused by "the speeding method"? Are not the opportunities given to the "best" workers gained at the cost of excessive layoffs of the average worker?

By the 1910s scientific management had acquired two faces—good and evil. (The actual situation was hardly that simple, but sophisticated nuances disappeared in the midst of oppositional polemics.) Those who backed the new systems evisioned excellent benefits: higher wages, fewer work hours, improved working conditions, defused labor unrest. Those on the attack viewed the touted "transformations" as reworkings of the same old story—management's exploitation of labor, disguised in newly deceitful ways.

Tarbell is quick to reassure management that it need not fear that the presence of women will lead to unrest on the shop floor or a rise in unionization. Women are no threat. Because of the essentially conservative nature of their temperament, they hate the destructiveness and idleness of strikes brought about by unruly men.[5] Hire women and maintain a tranquil shop.

For her part, Clark calls upon women to organize when faced with the questionable benefits of the newest efficiency systems. Clark reminds them that their sex was "caught unaware" in the early 1800s when industry was first revolutionized by brain applied to mechanical force.[6] Unorganized then, women "were chained to machines." In 1911, in the "new era" of scientifically managed industry, she asks, "Are women to be caught unawares as all were a century ago?"

Tarbell writes male success stories that feature the manager as hero. Women workers are given a minor role, one all too familiar at that. The traditional angel in the household is transferred to the factory. Women uplift brutish males by their presence and provide attentive nurturing to the great machines placed under their tender care. Clark's women workers appear in oft-told tales, too, but not those that recall domestic idylls smoothly relocated into the workplace. The familiar narrative tradition upon which Clark draws is that of the melodrama, featuring violated bodies and threatened virtue.

Tarbell and Clark devote themselves to representing the coming of "a new era" and a "new force"—what Tarbell describes as the "transformation of a shop from more or less rule of thumb methods to the highly specialized form of scientific management." But Tarbell celebrates the "pull upward of the body of industrial women" working "under modern management" while Clark exposes the terrible new strains that pull down the bodies of individual workers.[7] The former specializes in happy tales told to male bosses about the productive body of the female work force; the latter addresses unhappy tales told to the general public about the bodies of working women laid low by fatigue.

Neither Tarbell nor Clark, however, could rely entirely upon the narrative structures and discourse systems already in place. The changes taking place as nineteenth-century factory methods gave way to the industrial processes in place by World War I saw to that. Josephine Goldmark succinctly stated the consequences of these shifts in *Fatigue and Efficiency*. In 1912 she wrote that "the more cruel dramatic exploitation of workers" has been replaced by "the more subtle injuries of modern industry, its practically illimitable speed and strain."[8] According to Goldmark's implied narratology, the cruelly dramatic narratives of the past relocated villainy out in the open, where common sense could discover its vile intentions and offer remedies through reform legislation and welfare programs. The new-style subtlety of injuries inflicted on the powerless—introduced by means of covert deceit and disguised irrationality—can be exposed only if up-to-date tales incorporate the current tools of scientific analysis and make shrewd use of scientific discourse.[9]

But would writings that focus upon "the more subtle injuries of modern industry" have the same impact as narratives that rely upon long-tested patterns for portraying "the more cruel dramatic exploitation of workers"? Can cooly rational "modern" discourse sufficiently engross, entertain, and move the common reader to action, or might the passionate advocate have to revert to narrative appeals that successfully appropriate familiar formulas to thrill, stir, and arouse?

Melodramas of Failure

A number of discursive methods were available to shape the true-life drama centering upon the working woman in modern industry, but an even more basic issue had yet to be resolved: should women be in the workplace at all?[10] The answers writers and readers gave to this question often determined the kinds of stories that would be told about the woman bending over her machine. Whether or not women should work is a socioeconomic consideration with numerous political ramifications, but so are questions about the nature of the narratives to which working women lend themselves. The ideological nature of the responses writers bring to various literary genres and narrative devices is made clear by Flora MacDonald Thompson's highly charged 1904 essay for *The North American Review*.

Thompson's "The Truth about Woman in Industry" is a no-holds-barred attack against any woman who strays beyond her allotted sphere. She who enters the man's world is "an economic pervert," "a social menace," "a frightful failure," and "an element as abnormal as convict labor."[11] What is arresting is Thompson's choice of the melodramatic form to back her economic conclusions. The plot she unravels leads to mass suicide; the dark force is the working woman; the victims are the American male and the American nation.

Thompson unerringly puts her finger upon the importance of the
kinds of stories shaped around women who are "both costly and hopeless"
because of their "impaired physical ability to perform the maternal function" (756).[12] Wrongheaded though she may be, the implications of her
observations cannot be overlooked, for think of the consequences if her
warnings were heeded. Because narratives compiled by male economists
and businessmen portray women as objects of charity and victims of modern modes of production, Thompson cautions that their storytelling results in waste and inefficiency (read "death") for the nation as a whole and
for male workers in particular.[13]

Male statisticians write "in the spirit of pity and benevolence—a spirit
of gallantry and compassion aroused by a spectacle of woman's misfor-
tunes" (751).[14] These "eminently philosophical reports breathe the tender
concern of good men for frail women." Data from stories told about men
at work concentrates upon volume of production, cost, profit, and loss.
But when it comes to women at work, these misguided statisticians
"dwell only upon whether [this] work is proper, pleasant, profitable or
otherwise in relation to her sex—always in relation to her sex" (752).

Business accounts inspired by the tradition of literary melodrama
might pass for "official information," but their conclusions are determined by the man who "never forgets that he is dealing with ladies in
production, and, like a true gentleman, he assembles facts accordingly."
Tenderhearted tale-tellers work up charts devoted not to production figures but to matters of morality. They attempt to calibrate whether male
workers swear in the presence of women and whether the sexes are in
contact during working hours. Under the spell of the melodramatic
mood, true scientific accounting goes by the board. So-called business
data is transformed into narratives about fragile womankind adrift outside
the protective shelter of the home, cast into the cruelly masculine world.

Thompson declares that such male narratives are fraudulent at their
core. They ignore "the law of the business world" that has nothing to do
with the Golden Rule. Sounding as though she has just put down the
complete writings of Thorstein Veblen, Thompson asserts, "Strictly
speaking, business has absolutely nothing to do with the humanities—
absolutely nothing to do with the individual save as a contribution to the
wealth of the nation" (752).

Gentlemen who view working women as eternal victims are victimized by their own sentimentality. What is worse, they do grave damage to
the economic health of the nation. In writing up business reports that read
like sentimental novels, they encourage "business suicide" and race suicide as well (752). They encourage silly, idle club women to swallow tales
that advocate a woman's equal right to engage in men's work. They aid in

the "overthrow of the family, the destruction of humanity" (758). So who is the true victim of the authentic tragedy? It is the working man, he who, "manly pride gone, home and children neglected, walks the street in despair." Thompson's diatribe against sentimental tales about victimized women concludes with a melodrama of her own concoction: "it is better even for the family to suffer want than to entail upon the man the degradation of character imposed upon him when he becomes dependent upon a woman's earnings for support" (760).

Thompson's socioliterary critique received its rebuttal almost at once. Within three months Elizabeth Carpenter had placed an essay in *The North American Review,* questioning Thompson's gender-driven pessimism and, by implication, her theory of the way genre affects gender issues. Carpenter goes through Thompson's assertions one by one, breaking their backs with her counterarguments. She is particularly sharp about Thompson's notion that women's entry into the workplace leads inevitably to the writing of two types of melodramas: (1) false and sentimental ones about women placed in the victim's role; (2) true and tragic ones about men forced into despair by women's folly. But Carpenter writes her own sentimental fiction. Note the moves she makes. She progresses from a denunciation of Thompson's thesis toward an argument that finally duplicates the traits of the kind of narrative she says she disavows.

First, Carpenter allows that economists and businessmen make much of their concern about the conditions under which women work, but she sees this as a beneficial change in attitude by the business community. These men's words are proof of the "steady progress of the general world towards broader, gentler, more Christian actualities, in the very heart of the business centres of to-day." [15]

Second, Carpenter denies Thompson's notion of the factory as the stage upon which the male imagination scripts its brutal melodramas. "Business men are not 'ravening beasts,' that delicate or even sickly women need quake with terror when the stern necessities of life force them into office, store, factory or mill" (222). Just the opposite. The activities of laboring women inscribe themselves, as it were, upon the pages of *the realist novel,* which presents a clear-sighted representation of the evolution of everyday affairs in a nation dedicated to what William Dean Howells had called the "smiling aspects of life."

Third, race suicide does not result when women go to work. Quite the opposite. If men attempt to keep women at home in a harem atmosphere, males will become as decadent as Oriental potentates. When one realizes that housework is "among the most trying, enervating and exhausting strains to which the feminine physique can be subjected," how can anyone argue that factory jobs cause more bodily harm? As for

Thompson's commiseration with men whose manly role is usurped by working wives, Carpenter upends the situation. The woman with a needy family would never sacrifice her children in order "to sustain the feeble manhood of her husband." Instead, she goes resolutely into the workplace in order to guarantee that her offspring "are properly trained to atone, by developed energies, in a new decade, for their fathers' incapacity in this" (224).

But for all Carpenter's arguments in favor of forward-looking, optimistic narratives whose pragmatic plots counter the reactionary pessimism of Thompson's grimly sentimental melodramas, she concludes her article by reverting to literary conventions that enshrine notions of woman's sphere. She lists the types of heroines she repudiates: the "Amazonian virago, clamoring for 'woman's right'"; the "swaggering hoyden, aping men's modes and manners"; and the "too-ambitious worker insisting upon an equal race for power, within purely masculine limits" (224).[16]

Carpenter's socioliterary choice of the realistic narrative genre leads to women's narratives being kept apart from men's, equal but separate. The difference between male "realism" and female "realism" rests upon the fact that a woman's tale must center upon "her basic values as a reproductive factor" (224). It is 1904, and Carpenter's narrative by necessity extends into new settings beyond the hearthside. But wherever she locates her story—in office, factory, or home—the woman still figures as "the eternal feminine," whose finest role is that of the "Mother of all the living" (226).[17]

Edith Abbott's April 1905 article for *Harper's Weekly* was a vastly different kind of rebuke to Flora Thompson than Elizabeth Carpenter's article. Her remarks also offer an alternative to the sentimental melodrama or the realist novel. Abbott poses her question in her title, "Are Women Business Failures?" She answers resolutely, No, they are not. Abbott briskly goes down the list of Thompson's fallacious assertions, "proof" of the other woman's errors of logic. Abbott's statistics are not those used by charitably inclined gentlemen filled with mawkish pity toward helpless women, nor is her data the kind that irate women like Thompson use to demonstrate that the nation's males are being victimized. The most significant aspect of Abbott's counterattack, however, is what she suggests about *the kind of writing* women workers deserve.

> The question of women in industry is one for scientific investigation rather than for emotional generalization from a limited field of observation. The time has gone by for hysterical denunciation of the "horror of wage-earning women."[18]

Shape up, demands Abbott in 1905, just as Josephine Goldmark will in 1912; change your writing habits. Modern industrial life requires the creation of appropriate narrative structures, expressive forms as "scientific" as the conditions they set out to represent. The scientific account, neither melodrama nor the realist novel, is the proper genre for the times. Twentieth-century women may be harmed by "the new era" in industry, but this is no excuse for portraying them as nineteenth-century victims embedded within nineteenth-century narrative forms.

Rest assured, scientific objectivity has its own kind of emotional appeal. Edith Abbott and other muckrakers were out to realign their readers' feelings. Whatever look of "truth" their ever-present charts and statistics gave to their reports, nothing went into print without the full weight of feelings. Using a drily impartial approach, reformers could deflate the feverish figures used by the Flora MacDonald Thompsons of the opposition, but no one committed to winning the debate flaming over the place of women at work could do without emotion altogether. What the machine world was doing to the modern mind was important; just as important as foci for effective "scientific" narratives were *body, heart,* and *soul.*

Scientific Narratives and Mentshlekhe Bahandlung

Julius Henry Cohen was responsible for the text of the Protocol of Peace that resulted from the New York City garment workers' strike of 1912. Cohen's document was praised at the time because it redefined the political and economic ramifications of the terms "efficiency" and "inefficiency"— and because "its clarity and brevity" was a "joy." [19] Through his attention to style, Cohen not only aided in establishing *mentshlekhe bahandlung* (humane treatment),[20] he provided a discourse that "has not been designed only for LL.D.'s or students of that mazy and abstructive masculine achievement labelled logic, anyone, even the little girls who work in the trade, will be able to understand it."

Josephine Goldmark published *Fatigue and Efficiency* the same year that the Protocol of Peace was formulated. Like Cohen, she exposed the bodily hardships brought about by the fatigues underwritten by the new industrial system. Like Cohen, she replaced the legalisms of the courts with medical language in order to define the effects of inefficiency as a disease that afflicts human bodies. (Examined "scientifically," inefficiency is a pathological state, not a criminal one.) Like Cohen, she was praised for a writing style that merged the life-language of the working woman with the language used by the male labor analyst. As one reviewer put it, Goldmark "has interpreted to us the language of the scientist and physiologist" in ways that make clear that the "girl in the factory and the man of science . . . have reached the same conclusion" about the effect of scientific management.[21]

Unlike Cohen, Goldmark has two very special, very difficult problems to meet, the one steming from the other. First, she has to alert the public about the advent of a new kind of narrative. Once there had been "*the more cruel dramatic exploitation* of workers [that] is in the main a thing of the past." Now there lurks the presence of "*the more subtle injuries* of modern industry."[22] Since narratives about "subtle injuries" result from applying science to management and labor practices, and since detecting these "injuries" relies upon "exact scientific proof," she must take care not to play into the hands of the enemy. Her own heartfelt scientific narratives must not commit the sins of scientific callousness.

In 1904, people like Flora Thompson did not want to read sad tales about young women standing for weary hours over machines that demanded more than female bodies or minds could accommodate, but this is precisely the reason why, in 1912, Goldmark felt compelled to "aid in the practical problem of reducing the long working day in industry"(3). Going beyond what she conceives of as weak tools—"the purely economic" motive and the legalisms of the language common to politicians, employers, trade unions, judges, and philanthropic agencies[23]—she wants to provide a vivid sense of the unhappy conditions of modern industrialism while deflecting attention from the mawkish stories Thompson scorned and others consumed greedily.

Goldmark decides that the "pathological" cases she uncovers in her research into the realm of "the broadly physiological" are best served by the narrative voice of "scientific authority." She wishes to elicit not ineffectual tears but "a more rational progress." She believes in means to her ends that are "more exact and demonstrable than the appeal to pity" (3).

First Goldmark has to overcome the sad fact that her model, the man of science, in his self-isolation from the practical concerns of the workplace, has become the person for whom "the industrial world has been an undiscovered country" (10). Yet the engineers are no help, since human distress in the shop results from their inadequate understanding of the effects of physical movement. She must to do better than either the man of pure science or the practical engineer; she must provide an analysis more "exact and demonstrable" than either man can. In her hands, the language of science must become the language of the woman who grafts the strong, pure discourse of the laboratory onto the knowledge of the world gained through the social sciences.

Developments within various branches of science, emerging writing styles, and innovations in narrative technique had been bound together since (to fix a convenient point in time) the 1880s. Émile Zola and the French naturalists began forays into the unmapped territory where human lives exist as pathological (noncriminal) cases. By the 1890s the language of scientism infused the fictions of Frank Norris, Jack London, and Theodore Dreiser. By 1912 it was hardly surprising that Josephine Goldmark, chair of the National Consumers League committee on the legal defense of labor laws, would draw upon the "physiological" narrative mode in order to promote effectively "the scientific study of fatigue—one of the most modern influences of physiological, chemical, and psychological sciences" (3).

But many narratological problems remained as a result of this choice, just as they had for her predecessors in authorship. Pathology and the physiology, chemistry, and psychology of fatigue lead inevitably to a focus upon the minds and bodies of the workers. The minds, bodies, and souls of exploited women had long been the inspiration for narratives of sentimental and melodramatic victimization. Goldmark's approach might be scientific, yet the inherent piteousness of her subject still left it open to the scorn of reactionaries like Flora Thompson, and to the handwringing of Progressive reformers. A further difficulty appeared, too. Although she had not declared herself in opposition to Taylorism, would her "objective" data provide what Taylor's critics needed in order to expose him as the covert enemy of the ideal of *mentshlekhe bahandlung?*

Goldmark's text is filled with tension over how she ought to address the question of whom and what to blame for past, present, and future disjunctions between the machine process and the human element. Similar tensions marked the assessments made by other women activists committed to finding out whether or not "the employers' application of scientific laws" benefited the workers' health once it replaced the "haphazard" ways of the shop mechanics' old-style methods. The evidence was inconclusive either way, since it appeared that Taylorism had helped some women in certain ways and had harmed others. They also had to weigh in their perception that a working woman's fate may depend less upon Taylorism per se than on "the entire equity and candor shown by the [male] management" in its diverse use of that loosely defined term.[24] Just such questions of interpretation made the analysts more determined. No one tried harder than Josephine Goldmark; no one discloses more clearly the way a text both succeeds and fails at its task.

Fatigue and Efficiency carefully incorporates statistics, charts, and case studies about the effects the "speeding up and pact-making" processes had upon all workers, but Goldmark's particular interest in women is flagged in the section titled "Dangers of the New System." She takes as her example the women bobbin-winders in cotton mills, whose traditional bur-

den has been heightened by the speed rate of Taylorism. Performing one
task is hard; multiplying the number of times a routine must be repeated
increases the suffering many times over. But in all this, Goldmark holds
back from either exonerating or condemning scientific management
in her attempt to evaluate "scientifically" the stress placed on women's
bodies.

There is, however, a breakdown in Goldmark's concerted effort to
keep the pros and cons in balance and her subjective evaluations in check.
This breakdown comes in the appendix that brings the volume to its close,
perhaps the most arresting aspect of *Fatigue and Efficiency,* from a narratological point of view. Although Goldmark chose to incorporate it into her
book, the fact that she does so gives it the privilege of a final say. And that
"say" is a story told by a man in the same sentimental mode Flora Thompson previously had attacked in her attempt to send working women back
home.

The appendix reproduces the words of the Oregon Supreme Court
decision delivered on February 24, 1908 in *Muller v. State of Oregon.* The
judge's words return us to the world of legalisms, where a learned and
sentimental gentleman tells of that type of helpless woman whose body
must be protected by husbands and brothers, "not merely [for the sake
of] her own health, but [for] the well-being of the race" (562).

There is the further fact that Goldmark does not simply include the
Oregon judge's narrative, haunted as it is by the specter of race suicide,
but that she helped to make this narrative possible. Behind the court's
decision to forbid women to work more than ten hours a day lay the combined efforts of Goldmark the pathologist and her brother-in-law, Louis
Brandeis the lawyer. The result is a melodrama, that nineteenth-century
mode whose moralism is supposedly at odds with Goldmark's declared
allegiance to the objective morality of twentieth-century scientific narratives.

The judge centers his decision upon the argument that since "healthy
mothers are essential to vigorous offspring, the physical well-being of
woman becomes an object of public interest and care in order to preserve
the strength and vigor of the race" (562). His claim that the present conditions experienced by any particular woman matter less than the unending chain that binds a woman's body to the future of sound American
progeny is exactly the argument women activists had rejected when
trying to stop the enactment of the "protective" laws they viewed as restricting a woman's work life.

The harm done to women forced to work at the killing pace sanctioned by Taylor's time-motion studies might be less than the harm done
to their right to work whenever and however they chose. This greater

harm was supported by stories such as the Oregon court had to tell, a story that the broader narrative of *Fatigue and Efficiency* does not appear to support. Yet here it stands at the end, in possible betrayal of the signification of Goldmark's preceding argument, with its counter argument "that woman has always been dependent upon man" and that, like other "minors," "she has been looked upon in the courts as needing especial care" in order to "protect her from the greed as well as the passion of man" (562).

Fatigue and Efficiency can be said to serve the enemy it sought to defy so that women might find their own place in the work force. For all its impassioned commitment to the ideal of scientific rationality as inspiration for its discourse, the discursive space it gives to the Oregon Supreme Court decision throws the text back upon an older narrative tradition— so-called feminized emotionality, which lies in wait to be snapped up by those in the 1910s who fear race suicide, prize the blessings of maternal duties away from the factory floor, and assign the men the duty of being the legal protectors of frail bodies.

Because of the tension her inclusion of this appendix occasions, the effort Goldmark makes in the body of her text to create a newer, more effective way of presenting an accurate record of (so as to correct) "the more subtle injuries" prevalent in the modern world is called into question. She may have wished to better women's working conditions; instead, it sounds as if women must be kept at a safe distance from modern times altogether. In any case, in both narratives (text and appendix), the part played by Taylorism—as the villain or benefactor of the story, as enslaver or liberator—remains undecided. Only one thing is clear: Entirely new plots have yet to be written, new literary strategies have yet to be devised. "Scientific" writing alone will not do the trick.

The Power of Sentimentality

The strains caused by the speeding-up process were characteristic of modern life in general and of the industrial system in particular. These tensions affected the way labor was viewed in terms of both class and gender.[25] It took a while, however, for storytellers to find effective means of representing the impact accelerating pace and repetition had upon the female body without allowing this data to argue for the exclusion of women from the workplace. In addition, writers faced the need to secure woman's presence on the scene, lest she vanish from view.

In 1904 Henry James and Max Weber both witnessed the crash and power of the great mechanism of New York's harbor.[26] In 1906 Upton Sinclair's *The Jungle* supplied the famous description of Chicago's packinghouses, whose "cruelly dramatic" words assault the mind, conveying the pounding pace that makes victims both of the men on the "killing floors" and of the hogs they slaughter according to the latest Taylorist principles of "speed, speed, speed!"[27] In contrast, women beset by the pressures inaugurated under "the new systems" seldom were accorded the same narrative treatment as male workers. Glimpses of women in the workplace usually confined them within forms of sentimental fiction left over from the previous century.

To borrow Henry Adams's inimitable phrase, as every schoolboy knows, the early years of the new century were a period of transition. This was true not only in terms of the volatile economic situation caused by the increased entry of women into the work force, but also in terms of literary forms caught between old and new eras, old and new forces. The predilection for nineteenth-century sentimental fiction, with its privitizing force, lingered on in the portrayal of working women. The dangers of relying on this form were evident: to Flora Thompson, who referred to them in her attack against women at work; to Josephine Goldmark, who struggled to replace emotive with scientific discourse in order to advance the cause of working women. Still, the potential power of sentimental narrative was acknowledged then and should be now.

The rhetoric of romanticism and sentimental sensationalism vividly set out the conditions under which women toiled. Working women passionately involved in unionizing campaigns and strike action knew the value of those hyperbolic cries when they used them to demand relief from their daily pain. Further, the act of uttering those cries for justice transformed their perception of their own existence. No longer were they merely society's victims; they were romantic heroines in a historic drama.[28] Still, stories of victimization were powerful in their own way. Middle-class women advocates of better working conditions learned to manipulate this discourse to jolt the public out of its lethargy.[29] But the sentimental tradition was mainly the most effective weapon the woman journalist possessed to rake up the muck caused by an industrial process that left women's bodies at the mercies of men and machines. What mattered was that the seemingly sentimental (a soft, fantasy form) be revealed as the ultimate realism (strong, brutal, true).

Rheta Childe Dorr's 1907 article for *Harper's Weekly* makes unblushing use of cruelly dramatic terms. Five years later Goldmark would "scientifically" analyze the subtle injuries characterizing modern industry, but Dorr's title determines her own tone of approach: "Bullying the Woman-Worker: How Female Labor in the Shops and Factories Is Obtained by Means of Ruthless Oppression and Violation of the Law on the Part of Unscrupulous Employers."[30]

Dorr urges full enforcement of the New York laws banning women's night work, laws regularly broken by department stores, millinery trades, big factories, and printing and book bindery shops. Her own treatment of what "violation of the law" does to women makes male lawbreaking equivalent to the violation of breaking of a woman's body.

Simply stating the facts about the lack of enforcement of necessary laws hardly does the job, as any reform journalist realizes.[31] She must also project the emotions experienced by women forced to be abroad during the night after the workday is over. So Dorr moves directly from title to first sentence with words that immediately place her readers within a narrative of terror and menace.

> At half-past three o'clock on a winter morning, a year ago, two young women hurried through dark streets in the neighborhood of Brooklyn Bridge—streets deserted for night prowlers and an occasional policeman who looked suspiciously after the girls as they passed. (458)

Because the women do not "dare walk the final mile home," because of the infrequency of street cars and ferry crossings over the river,[32] and because they are denied shelter by the man in charge of the ferry house, the women must crouch in a cold hallway "in silent terror" until a car finally arrives, which will get them home at dawn.

Dorr concludes this vignette with the taunting question: "Am I writing a melodrama? Not at all. I am relating a commonplace incident in the lives of respectable working women in New York city" (458). Dorr makes her "literary critique" as important as the social critique she advances by its means. It is misleading to read Dorr's narrative as sentimental melodrama, even though it has that look and feel. The grim fact is that the narrative form she uses here conforms to the stark realism of the everyday. It may look as though she is complying with her editors' request to work up "what the city-room called a sob story," but, she insists, "It was a new kind of story."[33]

As early as the 1880s, William Dean Howells, Mark Twain, Mary Wilkins Freeman, and Sarah Orne Jewett were among those attempting to overturn the narrative models they viewed as mindless sentimentalism, escapist romances, and silly melodramas. Their efforts led to the literary innovations of Frank Norris, Stephen Crane, and Theodore Dreiser in the 1890s. But these changes contained certain contradictions: the realism of the commonplace fed on melodramatic extremes (as in Crane's *Maggie: A Girl of the Streets*), and journalistic attention to the anomalies of modern life was self-consciously the new romanticism (as voiced by Norris's famous "plea"). How could the proud new literary form of realism condone such seeming self-betrayals?

Very easily, as Dorr declares when she first asks whether she writes melodrama in the debased sense and then denies that she does. Her tale-in-a-paragraph is realism by means of, not in spite of, sentiment and melodrama. How else could she convey the fright experienced by two women imperiled by the "unscrupulous" and "ruthless" actions of male bosses in the workplace, and the fears of what "night prowlers" may do to them when forced upon the streets to make their way home? Dorr's realism exposes the terrible truth: that no one is ready to protect women for whom "the night has its own special aspect"—neither the man at the ferry stop, nor the policeman on the beat, nor the judges who disregard laws made to protect women from exploitation.[34]

Night menaces cast women upon empty streets; machines geared up to the "speeding" rate sanctioned by Taylorism menace them in the shop. Women are particularly vulnerable when wearied by the extra hours the bosses exact, yet they cannot object for fear they might lose their jobs. Look at Catherine: she works at a bindery, "all night long feeding magazines to a great hungry steel and iron mouth." Then comes the shift when she is fatigued from long hours facing "the jaws of the monster."[35] "The great jaws snapped at her hand. She shrieked—and shrieked. They stopped the machine, but not before the jaws had devoured her arm just below the shoulder".[36] Night is a terrible time: it is the time when heavy metal monsters violate women's flesh in the shop and the time when "the night itself menaces women as it does not menace men" (459).

What results from Dorr's choice of anecdotal narrative, whether we call it realism disguised as sentimental fiction or sentimentalism cloaked as realism?[37] Its carefully manipulated devices have the power to stir fundamental fears, convincing readers like Flora Thompson that women should stay out of the workplace altogether. It also has the power to translate reform measures into laws that mitigate some of the brutality of the conflict within the shop. But does it have the power to present authentic power to the women themselves?

Thompson would view Dorr's argument, and the narrative methods by which she pleads for the enforcement of protective laws, as a perfect example of what she called "the complete failure" of the sex once it removes itself from the shelter of the home. Dorr does admit that "women are timid, they are weak, they are unorganized." But while Thompson argues that women workers are of no value to anyone, Dorr's ironic point is that it is precisely the fact that women are helpless that makes hiring them profitable. "This is what the manufacturers mean when they say they employ women because women are more easily handled than men" (458). And so the argument continues, with Dorr and Thompson trading stories, as it were, over the inert bodies of weak women.

Are there more effective narratives than those that transmit the chilling "shriek" of Catherine the bindery worker? We would like to think that if Catherine only could have shrieked for *herself,* the powers of the sentimental mode would have accrued to her.

We wish to distinguish the voice of "the outsider" (whether it is that of the bullying boss or the reform-minded champion) from the voice of the person who exists *within* the experience itself, though we "know" how easily narratives are "devoured" by the jaws of the machine process, no matter who does the speaking. But we are prone to be fools in regard to the myth of agency, which promotes self-telling as self-mastery. We may even be wise fools, insofar as we pay close attention to what self-telling meant to the women who aspired to relate their own personal melodramas, giving them endings that seemed to remove the menacing shadows cast by manager or machine.

Speaking Out or Being Spoken For

Taylor had opined that cussing back was the right of the free worker, another instance of an idea having no relation to practical reality. Cussing out is ineffectual against either the greater authority of managerial power, which needs no words to effect its will, or the dynamo, whose presence is disclosed only by its almost inaudible hum. Still, it was hoped, at least, that any man has a right to curse. Women, however, were not supposed to use cuss words. They were not even encouraged in that act of "talking back" that takes the form of telling one's own story. It was the common fate of women to be enfolded within narratives of sentiment or melodramas of pathos, with an occasional curse in their honor thrown in by their self-appointed narrator.

We ache for exceptions to this rule of silence. We think we find one in the story of Teresa, a fifteen-year-old Italian girl working at a silk mill in Paterson, New Jersey. Teresa's tale initiates a break past the melodrama that strives to assign her the unending role of victim. Unlike the "unorganized" women Dorr portrays, Teresa finds her champion in the union. Should that protector prove to be yet another male guardian liable to betray the hapless heroine, however, Teresa has her own words to say. Yet we cannot overlook the fact that Teresa's voice is edited by two women who, however sympathetically they may listen and record, appropriate what she has to tell for the purposes of the journal they represent: *The Masses,* the socialist journal whose self-appointed task was to cuss out all corrupt and unjust practices.

"As told by her to Inis Weed and Louise Carey," the story opens as "Teresa led us through a narrow passage into an inviting little garden"—

proof to readers of the "definite contributions from these Italians to the civic life of Paterson."[38] Once enclosed within the "garden" of its narrative structure, we realize how much Teresa's story draws upon those literary turns familiar to readers of nineteenth-century fictions about brave but victimized young girls.

Teresa shakes "her pretty head" to deny that America is as beautiful as Italy. Her command of vocabulary and grammar, borrowed from Weed and Carey, approaches that of Oliver Twist—the prototypical waif of upper-class lineage whose exquisite diction and syntax belies the harsh conditions under which waifs generally labor. Teresa pauses "broodingly" when telling of her sainted mother's death of consumption after years of brutal toil at the mills ("I am so tired. I am so tired."). Even the plot line of Teresa's life follows accepted narrative patterns of victimization. Forced from refuge with her kind grandfather in Caserta, she is returned to Patterson and to an unsympathetic fairy-tale stepmother, who demands that thirteen-year-old Teresa start earning wages as a winder.

Working conditions at the silk mill are sordid: the windows are sealed shut in the summer; in the winter the girls' fingers "get so stiff they can't work fast" since there is no heat. The mill is full of rats, dirt, and bad air. The work is "one long record of 'speeding up'" with constant abuse from the bosses. ("The bosses they holler and curse at you so. The superintendent and forelady, they aren't so bad, but they *have to holler* when the bosses come round.") Then comes the accident when a large wheel falls on Teresa's head. ("No. they didn't call in a doctor—not on your life. They had fear of a damage suit.") But she must go back to work because there is "no escape from the contract" her father made with the mill because of anxiety for his own job.

As told here, Teresa's tale has a good ending. The Paterson mills go out on strike, and Teresa is happy at last. Making "an unconscious gesture toward her heart," she proudly declares, "We are all together. We stand solid. My father he says there will always be bosses. I say, 'Yes? Then we shall be the bosses.'" The strike is a success.[39] Teresa receives a 25 percent wage increase; children no longer do mill work; no more contract system; a labor inspector enforces safety measures; whitewash spruces up the walls. "Nor do they holler at us so."

> "Will this last, do you think?" we asked.
> "I don't know. If it don't, we strike again."

Teresa has a voice in *The Masses*. And she has the I.W.W. as well. "I like I.W.W. better than God. God, he don't talk for me like I.W.W.," she says. But actual events overpower the amelioration the I.W.W. had aggressively sought for Teresa and her fellow workers. *What happened* (the strikers lost) denied full narrativizing autonomy to Teresa, to Bill Haywood, and to John Reed's Paterson pageant. Teresa's need to speak for herself should not be dismissed, nor should the modicum of self-assertion it demonstrates. We must recognize, however, not only the serious affront "history" made to the enfeebled power plays of personal narrative but also the diminishment that results when that story is turned over to recording angels (whether to *The Masses,* God, or the I. W. W.). The risk is ever present that the would-be teller will be repositioned as one of the voiceless and victimized.

One is a victim indeed when, like Catherine at the bindery described by Rheta Dorr, the only "word" uttered is a shriek of pain and terror as the monster's jaws clamp over one's arm. It is even more unfortunate when women are erased from the page altogether—not only silenced but rendered invisible, as in the account William C. Redfield gave in 1916 to an audience of upper-class women concerning conditions in a plant employing one thousand females: "The conditions of employment are such that *the ladies here might wear their white dresses* going through the factory, without danger of soiling them. I took my wife there to see it" (my emphasis).[40]

Other "violations" are made upon the body of a woman's story when it is appropriated by someone like Bessie (Mrs. John) Van Vorst. Van Vorst and her sister-in-law Marie presented their observations on the workplace first as a serialized account in *Everybody's Magazine* during 1902, then as a book published the following year under the title *The Woman Who Toils: Being the Experience of Two Gentlewomen as Factory Girls.*[41]

The Van Vorsts decided to live among "this class" of working women in order to "discover and adopt their point of view, put ourselves in their surroundings, assume their burdens, unite with them in their daily effort." "My desire," Mrs. Van Vorst announces, "is to act as a mouthpiece for the woman labourer and to place my intellect and sympathy in contact as a medium between the working girl who wants help and the more fortunately situated who wish to help her."[42]

We should not disparage accounts written by those who choose to be temporarily "down and out" in London, Paris, New York, Chicago, or Pittsburgh.[43] Likewise, we should not damn out of hand the exploratory investigations initiated by upper-class reform-minded women. During the Progressive era, information from "above" but garnered from "below" helped promote ameliorative measures (however inadequate or conservative) and also nudged slumbering social consciences. The Van Vorsts' project, however, reveals this tradition at its worst.

Before the Van Vorsts start to *speak for* the women they meet in the workplaces they visit, they allow their own voices to be preempted by the

letter from President Theodore Roosevelt they include in their preface.
Roosevelt indicates that the only thing that disturbs him about the Van
Vorsts' account of the women's working conditions in 1902 is the threat of
"race suicide," criminally caused by any woman who ventures outside her
home.

Even before Roosevelt's letter, two markers betray the suspect nature
of the Van Vorsts' project: (1) the photograph of the authors in the "disguises" they wore in order to look like the women they were not; (2) the
title page, which bears the words "The *woman* who toils, being the experience of two *gentlewomen* as *factory girls.*" Many of the workers *were*
"girls" in terms of their age, but the indiscriminate, patronizing use of
that word by those on high makes "girls" seem determinedly inferior. The
Van Vorsts' description of themselves as "gentlewomen" further reinforces class distinctions. There is, after all, no such word as "gentlegirls."

The Van Vorsts' self-appointed task as "gentlewomen" is to speak for
the plight of "woman" (generic), because they have shared some work
space and time with the "girls." And speak the Van Vorsts must, since the
"girls'" conversations is "vulgar and prosaic." As Bessie Van Vorst remarks, "There is nothing in the language they use that suggests an ideal
or any conception of the abstract. . . . In all they say there is not a word
of value" (38).[44]

When Anzia Yezierska thunders, "As one of the dumb, voiceless ones
I speak," we *hear* her voice and, through her, the voices of others uttering
"words of value."[45] When Yezierska recounts her attendance at a lecture
given by a welfare director on the subject of "The Happy Worker and His
Work"—a sleek man who announces that "efficiency is the new religion
of business" and who rambles on "in educated language that was over my
head"—we understand why official declarations can never serve as a substitute for Yezierska's own story. It was very hard, though, for most
women to get the words out.

> I would like to write a poem
> But I have no words.
> My grammar was ladies waists
> And my schooling skirts.[46]

There is, however, a 1911 book, *Making Both Ends Meet,* that brings
together a number of significant threads: (1) investigative reporting, gathering data—both economic and physiological—according to the model of
scientific inquiry Goldmark would make famous in *Fatigue and Efficiency*
the following year; (2) assessments of how scientific management alters
women's work lives for better or worse; (3) attempts on the part of upper-

class women to keep their mediation of working women's stories to a minimum. But *Making Both Ends Meet* also demonstrates what happens to the dominant narrative line when the authors allow Frederick Winslow Taylor's vision of the future to overpower their final pages.

Sue Ainslie Clark and Edith Wyatt of the National Consumers League are not the sole "authors" of *Making Both Ends Meet,* an investigation of women's earnings and outlay in the New York area. The preface states that "to record rightly any little corner of contemporary history is a communal rather than an individual piece of work." This record must evolve "as the product of numerous human intelligences and responsibilities," becoming a "synthesis of facts" that flows "from many authors, many authentic sources." [47]

Unquestionably, elements of this composite tale are contributed from "above"—by college women from Bryn Mawr, Smith, and Wellesley; by Florence Kelley, Pauline and Josephine Goldmark, Louis Brandeis, and Willa Cather; and by learned informants from Europe—but the book emphasizes its incorporation of "the word-of-mouth tale" of Anna Flodin, of Elena and Gerda Nikov, and of Natalya Perovskaya. These women's words are considered to be of great value, despite what Mrs. Van Vorst might think. Their lives do not portend the suicide of the race, as the nightmare concocted by Theodore Roosevelt would have it. Nor is the city where these women struggle daily "the New York best known to the country at large"; it is "a new and different New York—the New York of the city's great working population" (ix).

We have here a new setting and new voices, new working conditions as well. Clark and Wyatt do more than record the economics of working life. Their concerns, like Goldmark's are physiological; they deal in stories that represent the effect of scientific management upon women's bodies.

European informants supply important data: from Switzerland—"the unremitting, tense concentration of watching the machine" "fatigues the worker"; from England—the machine "pursues its relentless course," placing the worker in "a competition of sensitive human nerve and muscle against insensitive iron"; from Germany—facts substantiate "the absence of spontaneity or joy in work"; from Italy—machine work engages but "one brain-centre" at a time, endangering "the entire organism" (119–20).

These testimonies from the authorities are impressive, but they are not at the heart of *Making Both Ends Meet.* Anna Flodin's story appears to be. This seamstress in a corset factory speaks with "an almost ambassadorial dignity, which was inexpressively touching" (130). "The voice of [her] chronicle [was] distinctively thrilling."

She told her experience in her work with great clearness, sitting in a
little dark, clean room in a tenement, looking out on a filthy, ill-
smelling inner court. The only brightening of her grave, young face
throughout her story and our questions was her smile when she
spoke of her one visit to the theatre, and another change of expression when she spoke of the other girls in the shop, in connection
with the strike about thread. (131)

The "spontaneity and joy" that reformers wanted to bring to the act
of labor appear only fleetingly upon Anna's face. Only the "good" intens-
ities portrayed upon the stage or experienced at the shop lift weary body
and tired mind above the antidrama of the machine process.[48] But even
here it is not Anna herself who speaks. Her story is told for her by those
who, having listened, edit out her actual words and substitute the embel-
lishments of their own, supposedly more expressive, style. Soon Anna
Flodin and her fellow workers disappear from sight and sound altogether.
    The preface of *Making Both Ends Meet* announces that the first six
chapters provide information about the "unstandardized conditions in
women's work," which cause women great hardships. Chapter 7, titled
"Scientific Management as Applied to Women's Work," will judge—
scientifically, unsentimentally, without bias—whether Taylor's highly
standardized work patterns reduce or heighten the strain in the workplace,
that is, whether Taylorism replaces old problems (clumsy work habits,
low wages) with new problems (work patterns tied to stressful accelerations of pace and tedious repetitions).
    Taylorism has indeed cut back on hours and helped to raise wages, but
doubts remain in the minds of Clark and Wyatt about the impact the
bonus-plan and speeding-up methods have had on women's minds and
bodies. They take care to include Taylor's arguments for the merits of his
system: it "differs radically from former business management" because it
insures that "machine power and human energy can at once be most productively and continuously employed" (232). They also take care that
their readers recognize that women's bodies are undergoing "a muscular
[and] a nervous strain," the likes of which they had not experienced prior
to the inception of the modern machine process.
    Clark and Wyatt make up a credit-debit ledger. On the credit side
they place stories of women who find "refuge and protection" in workplaces run under the Taylor system. These women find escape from
"wrong and oppressive maltreatment at home" in factories guided by the
orderly, rational principles of scientific management (268). On the debit
side is the story of Lucia, employed at a New Jersey cotton mill, who
"used to run wildly from one end of the frame to the other, and in the

summer-time fainted several times at her work from exhaustion" (255). The managers set the machines at a slower speed, as much to correct the poor quality of piecework as its effect on "the excitable little spool winder." Quality improves, and Lucia says "she was so much less tired" (255), but the other women are disheartened since the slower work pace means a cut in wages.

Fair enough. Circumstances *do* differ at each plant, both in the inherent difficulty of the work and in the varying attitudes management and labor hold toward the new system. But the final pages of *Making Both Ends Meet* give away the kind of narrative to which Clark and Wyatt have committed themselves from the start. The meticulously scientific neutrality they have maintained to this point is replaced by a fervent sense of mission.

Up to now Clark and Wyatt have held back on their final assessment, yet they always placed their faith in Taylor's promise to bring "prosperity" to employers and workers alike, insofar as prosperity means that the individual gains "the best use of the highest powers" (232).[49] They describe Taylor as "the widely reverenced author" of a system that "makes an art of all work. It gives the most primitive manual task its right dignity, and turns knowledge, science, and the powers of direction from the position of tyrants of labor to its servitors" (224). Because Clark and Wyatt are true believers in Taylorism, they view its failures as resulting from the misapplication of its procedures. But "scientific" reports are *not supposed to want anything in advance.*

Now we have it: Anna Flodin's voice is allowed to express the tragedy of a life held down by the crushing weight of "unstandardized conditions." Little Lucia gets to express her double-edged dismay at being worn out by speeding up and at being denied the money she can make from a bonus plan that causes her "to run wildly from one end of the frame to the other." Yet despite the fact that this book defines itself as a "communal narrative," it ends with the "dream hope" imposed by Clark and Wyatt and borrowed from Taylor. The pure "tendencies" proposed by the "reverenced" authority of Taylorism shine forth at last. Wish fulfillment supersedes scientific method. Taylor as hero displaces Anna and Lucia as heroines.

"Tendency" (that word beloved of Emerson and other American reformers who envisioned the push of history toward a better tomorrow) is the word that betrays *Making Both Ends Meet*. It pulls this report away from its primary stress upon the right of working women to live in dignity and in health. "Tendency" converts an investigative study into a narrative of passionate hope about the mission Taylor's followers must be given the chance to fulfill. On the side of the enemy is "the imperfect installation" and the "incomplete adoption" of Taylorism by men "not in general sympathy with Scientific Management." On the side of the good is Taylorism's "whole tendency . . . toward truth about industry, toward justice, toward a clear personal record of work, established without fear or favor" (263–64, 268, 269).[50]

The closing pages do not stop with this lesson. Notwithstanding the authors' faith that Taylorism ought to prevail, the text admits that final authority lies in the hands of the men in charge of America's business enterprise. Neither Clark nor Wyatt, neither Anna nor Lucia, not even Taylor himself, can assure that true virtue, on its own, will command the future. Visionaries can only propose; it is up to the managers to dispose "its magnificent dream." Everything depends upon chance: upon the hope that "greatness of spirit and the executive genius" will activate the employers and engineers (270).

We are skeptical about the greatness of the bosses' spirit and genius. We wonder whether workers like Anna and Lucia have the power or desire to bring about this "finer dream" in a society that continues to disregard their dream of "industrial democracy." But before *Making Both Ends Meet* is dismissed out of hand, exposed as a highly flawed piece of "science fiction" whose futuristic vision of social good is entirely dependent upon the goodwill of male managers and engineers, take a look at the scene Clark and Wyatt present on the penultimate page.

This scene arises from *the present moment.* It possesses the same sense of modern immediacy that Henry James and Max Weber cast over New York's harbor and that Upton Sinclair endowed upon Chicago's packinghouses. Not only is this scene located in the "industrial civilization" that affects "in some measure every life in this country to-day," it singles out *women at work.* At the least, it grants them dignity by acknowledging what it is that they *do:*

> the hundred operations of human hands and muscles required for placing a single yard of cotton cloth on the market, the thousand threads spinning and twisting, the thousand shuttles flying, the manifold folding and refolding and wrapping and tying, the innumerable girls working, standing, walking by these whirling wheels and twisting threads and high piled folding tables. (269)

Making Both Ends Meet is saved to the extent that it includes this scene upon the factory floor where women, not just men, are placed totally *within the modern world.* They are potential victims, yet are granted the feel of a strong story, a modern story—a story, however, still being *told for them.*

Strangers to the Public Good

Anyone wishing to improve the economic, physiological, and cultural lives of working women becomes discouraged by the prevalence of social narratives focusing on process rather than progress. Simply to have things change—new machine technology, new patterns of industrial management, new corners of the workplace opened up to women (all that Tarbell and her contemporaries called signs of "the new era" and "the new force")—does not give us radically new narratives. In the early 1900s it would appear that tales of woe about "Nellie, the Beautiful Cloak Model" were the best contributions working women could make to management or labor interests. Only in that form were they viewed as effective producers of goods marketable to the general public.[51] For those who cared, the question was how to move past salable tales of dependency toward the production of equally appealing narratives of self-authorization, that is, toward the inclusion of true heroines.

Now, the *heroine* type is not the *victim* type. Second, the heroine is a *woman,* not a *girl* and not a *boy.* Third, the heroine must be recognizable as an authentic part of "the *human* element." She cannot be some allegorical essence, nor a subhuman force for change, nor fragments torn from the whole being—a body under stress or a tangle of nerves. Fourth, she must occupy *this time and place*—exist credibly within history.[52] She must not hover in the fantasy realm of Charlotte Perkins Gilman's utopian novel *Herland,* where dreams of female power have already come true. Last, to be made acceptable to a wide audience, the new heroine needs to be *attractively powerful*—neither an insignificant other nor a threatening destroyer. For the woman to be granted this new status in the new narratives, it seemed as though human nature itself had to be redefined. Only then would members of the female sex avoid being singled out as "strangers to the public good."

Mary Van Kleeck ("a founding sister of management science") located the main problem of effective change outside as well as inside the shop.[53] Society at large was the culprit because it was incapable of realizing the necessity of applying "the art of management" to solve "the present disastrous results of industrial organization."[54] Too often this failure of vision arose from the intensely masculine notion that "human nature is *human nature.* . . . You can't change a man's ways in a day, and nobody has yet been able to remold a woman's mind in a lifetime, so 'What's the use trying?' "[55] Here is the classic double bind. According to entrenched male notions, the male nature is difficult to change while female nature is unalterable.

A paradoxical flash of hope came once the managers decided that human nature was perhaps more female than male, that is, more intuitive than rational, more social in its needs than self-absorbed. In the early decades of the twentieth century, managers believed that the rationalistic practices of Taylorism—including appeals to self-interest and wage-incentive plans—could be used to restore the human race to its rightful heritage of male common sense. But before long, even the strongest advocates of scientific management learned that controlling the workplace meant more than putting up with the occasional annoyances of stupid little Schmidts or silly females. First they needed to recognize that most human behavior is irrational; second, they needed to convert hot impulses into cooly effective productivity; third, they had to admit that management personnel as well as workers react unscientifically.

Elton Mayo confirmed the changing views management held toward human nature in his analysis of the work patterns of women who made telephone assemblies at Westinghouse's Hawthorne plant. Mayo's tests overturned the central Taylorist belief that workers respond largely to the logic of self-interest. The managers learned of the importance of chumminess on the job and the pleasures of team behavior. Mayo's industrial psychology provided "a new vocabulary of motivation," which implied the possibility of different narrative patterns. Thereafter, stories would center on the worker "as a creature of sentiments and nonlogical thinking, whose one overriding motive was the desire to stand well with his or her fellows." [56]

The 1920s shift from the scientism of material factors to the scientism of social behavior smoothed the way for narratives that coupled "feminized" motives with the "public good." Once it was allowed that working women were not complete "strangers" to that public good, heroines might command stories constructed under these new conditions. In the 1910s, however, Elton Mayo's industrial psychology still lay in the offing. Managers still held as a precious, although steadily eroding, truth that the men in charge of the machine process were as rational as the machines themselves.

Even before Elton Mayo, there were the Gilbreths. Frank and Lillian Gilbreth, leading innovators of scientific motion studies, wrote worker individuality into a program that broke human action into discrete, systematized steps for the sake of greater cooperative effort. They were elated by the possibility that workers could be taught techniques of efficiency that translated isolated movements into good citizenship, whether in factory production or municipal affairs. [57] Willing self-subordination would come about by persuading workers to give themselves over to "being interested" and "being interesting."

"Interesting" is the operative word in the Gilbreths' essay, "The Effect of Motion Study upon the Workers." Studying motion is interesting for the analysts; eliminating bad work habits enables the worker to be interested.[58] Once the true and ever interesting import of the words *to do well* is widely accepted, a reformed individualism emerges that is eager *to do the public good.* "Being interested" no longer means being absorbed in self-interest (getting higher wages); "being interested" *"makes 'to do' mean 'to be interested,' and to be interested means to be more efficient, more prosperous, and more happy."*

Once again we are asked to envision a better society—a society made up of happy, prosperous selves released from bad old habits by the principles of scientific management. But this vision of hope depends upon each and every person being equally interested in the work at hand. Was any credence given to the notion that the women who worked would be so "interested"?

Wiseacres of the period constantly pointed out that women were not, and never could be, as truly interested in shop work as men were. Some women expressed pride in their work,[59] but, on the whole, beaux and cheap amusements ruled the talk of the unmarried. For wives and mothers, worries about troubling conditions at home denied them the kind of joyful interest the Gilbreths celebrated. For still others, all that mattered was getting through another deadening day of bodily strain and emotional tension. Yet if a woman ever *did* become interested enough to aspire to rise within the workplace, the men in charge took fright. This kind of interest indicated ambition on the women's part; it meant they had forgotten that "the public good" required that they stay home in order to stave off race suicide, or, if they must go out to work, that they remain "domesticated" in the factory.

The male management system was roughly equivalent to "society" in general. Women not under the protective eye of father or husband at home were expected to continue in the role of dutiful daughter or wife during their hours in the shop. New industrial needs allowed women to move into mid-level positions (from forewomen to welfare directors), but management did not go out of its way to urge women to be "interested" in more, certainly not in *much more.*

Whether it is Ida Tarbell speaking directly to management in 1921 or C. E. Knoeppel addressing himself to labor organizers in 1914, what those who wrote about working women emphasized is that *men need not be afraid.*[60] Both before and after the war, they continued to stress the docility of working women, the single virtue that helped to counter women's inherent emotionality and physical fraility. For those frightened by rumors about the uncontrolled new energies abroad in the land, these were soothing things to hear. Heaven forbid that new narratives would center upon women audacious enough to speak of themselves as heroines—heroines who take interest in their work, thereby *coming inside* where authority lies.

As one writer states it prettily, women workers remain "strangers" and "apprentices" in the world of industry, dissociated from the concerns of men.[61] By the close of World War I, fewer victims fill the pages of the narratives managed by employers, labor unionizers, and the reform press. Taking their place are more and more strangers, but seldom a heroine. Taking this place are more "boys" than "girls," but never a "woman." Taking their place, too, are useful "female materials," not thinking human entities.

In 1904 Flora Thompson declared, "The woman's choice of occupation should be legally restricted," lest woman ruin the universal economy that mandates her true function as being a producer of the maternal, reproductive kind.[62] In 1906 O. M. Becker assured management that giving forewomen supervisory authority over women workers did not imply that forewomen would ever supervise male workers or prove independent of the general foreman.[63] But Ida Tarbell put it best (however chillingly) in an essay—one of five that appeared during 1920–21 in *Industrial Management*—aptly titled "The Manager Must Know His Material."

Tarbell discusses the utilization of women as personnel by referring to the utilization of new industrial materials. While she agrees there is "no sex in industry," there certainly is sex in the worker. As a result, managers must keep the material of the female worker in the place proper to its "sex."

> It is quite as unscientific to attempt to handle the women in industry without knowledge of her physical nature, her temperament and her social and economic experience, as it is to attempt to handle a metal without knowledge of its properties, its reactions to heat and cold and strain, and of the established processes for its treatment.[64]

It is for "the public good" that women are pliable material, ductile and docile, efficient, unthreatening. All in all, they are quite a good bargain if scientifically managed. But even when journalists and reformers, male and female, set out to write cheerful stories that urged management and labor not to fear the strangers coming into their midst, it was not uncommon for them to itemize the anxieties working women caused.

Sex in the worker, indeed! Managers suffer headaches because women get "headaches and crying spells," have the vapors, and go hysterical. Like metals (hot and cold), women suffer from "fatigue" at the most inopportune moments. Women have to be provided with cots because they tend to "feel indisposed" as men do not. Concerned welfare directors must furnish "resting rooms," and also changing rooms where women can switch from street garb to work clothes in privacy—another nicety, along with separate, sanitary toilets, that your average shopman does not require.

Then there is the constant worry over morality. Enlightened employers are sensitive to the fact that factories drawing a certain type of female employee suffer the reputation of being no better than a brothel. Overseeing female virtue means the expense of hiring matrons and women personnel directors, and of having to provide separate entrances, divided work spaces, and staggered work shifts. Class snobbery is another "female" problem. Women clerks disdain to sit with the factory women at lunchtime. Women in "better" work areas do not care to associate with women doing "inferior" tasks elsewhere in the plant. Black women and Polish women are shunted out of sight of the group while "nice," American-born women prefer not to have contact with "loud" and "coarse" Italians and Jews.[65]

Were it not for the fact that women are cheap to employ, docile, and adept at the traditional feminine skills of "neatness, accuracy, precision, and dexterity," the disadvantages of this particular "material" clearly would outweigh the gains.[66] To make an even stronger case for hiring women, these texts promote the advantages by portraying them as characters in animal fables, boys' adventures, and the myths and histories of charming primitives. Strangers all, but useful for the public good.

An *Atlantic Monthly* essay published in 1912 demonstrates why the female sex is more desirable than the male. Based on the division of labor ruling the animal world, "the stallion, bull, or ram is too katabolic, too much of a consuming, disturbing, destroying force, to be very valuable in the daily routine of agriculture or commerce." Males are kept "only for breeding purposes," but the female of the species—"quiet, easily enslaved"—does excellent work for its masters.[67] This analogy stands the "race suicide" argument on its head: males are the breeders, undomesticated brutes to be kept at home in the field or stall; females are sent out to do the world's work yet must remain as "domestics" at the side of great machines.

The public good is also served by the "girl" capable of doing "a boy's work" without the expectation of ever arriving at "man's estate." This is the way Ida Tarbell puts it in her essay, "The New Place for Women in Industry."[68] Actual boys cause problems in the shop: they are cheeky to superiors, idling at their work or ducking out for smokes, their flirtatious ways aggravating the matrons who try to keep a "respectable" work area. By contrast, women workers as "boys" take care with their tasks; they do what they are told and do it well.[69]

What does it mean in real terms when women are made to play the "boys" in the workplace, to compete with young males employed at the same plant? Differing pay and work benefits, for one. One manager said, "We consider girls superior to boys but inferior to men, and cheaper than either."[70] Another difference is that women are cut off from "the vocabulary of the shop." Without the "knowledge" that the "man unconsciously acquires from boyhood," women are limited to their primitive tongue, unable to deal advantageously with either the language or materiality of the machine process.[71] But the greatest difference lies in denying the women a sense of future time.

Real boys are perceived as having ambition. They possess a future history into which they evolve as they pass from one stage of growth to the next. As one of the bosses tells Tarbell, boys have an interest in mechanical matters that propels them onward, whereas the women he supervises are in "the phase now in machine work that I went through as a boy." Before female "boys" can ever become "competitive like men," they have a long way to go up the evolutionary ladder. It is strongly implied that they are at an historical impasse; no advancement is in sight.[72]

Importing terms from Veblen's theory of human history, it can be said that women are gentle savages left over from the earliest phase of evolution. They lag behind the aggressive, predatory males of the barbaric age who, however anachronistic their behavior has become in modern times, are at least capable of making a place for themselves in a still brutalized mechanistic world. Words connected with phases of male growth—"boyhood," "youth," "manhood"—are not applicable to women. Without these words, women have no parallel vocabulary with which to recount a story of sustained evolutionary progress. Measured against the men they can never become, women are frozen at the intermediate stage of "the boy."

On the one hand, managers formulated a historiography that applies a different time scheme to men's and women's advancement. Having reduced the notion of progress to a matter of evolution, they question whether women so fixed in time can ever be freed to become something new. On the other hand, Progressives like Ida Tarbell and Harrington Emerson scorned the tradition-bound manufacturers, who hesitated to give women workers responsibility because their motto is "never has been."[73] In contrast, up-and-coming enthusiasts of scientific management discard the practice of "keeping records" in favor of establishing "standards." "Records grope in the past, standards reach into the future, ultimate standards are always ahead of what has ever been." Good efficiency systems—those that manage workers in the best ways—are concerned with "what *ought to be*," not "what *has been*."[74] All this sounds nice, but

Tarbell's and Emerson's sense of the future still presents problems in terms of the kinds of narratives a working woman might be able to tell.

Tarbell believes that companies that "are adopting the modern scientific organization" are more open to women being assigned to supervisory duties than are plants run along old-style lines. Women can rise from the ranks if they have merit and if there is "a willingness on the part of the management to recognize ability."[75] Once again we are confronted by the time gap between *where a woman is* (possessing talent, with ambition) and *where management is* (perhaps willing, perhaps not, to recognize that talent and ambition). The plane upon which evolution, progress, and "tendencies" function to the advantage of men and machines is clearly different from the plane upon which women exist.

Harrington Emerson takes pleasure in the opportunities scientific management practices offer for historical progress, but his stories of hope are like Tarbell's: although they negotiate between past (what has been) and future (what ought to be), they do not allow women to take a central part in, or even to share, the same sphere of history accorded to men. In Emerson's eyes women remain *essentially* feminine. They have little or no social sensibility or talent for organizing group efforts; they are intuitive, maternal, traditional, held captive by the minutiae of the moment. As proof of the world of difference these eternal qualities make in the ways they work, he takes the example of the building of the Suez and the Panama Canals. Peasant women in Egypt worked hard but ineffectually in the construction of the Suez Canal. Like their female ancestors through the millennia, these women laboriously scooped up sand in baskets and laboriously carried their burdens up and down the deep defiles banking the canal. Was this diligence? Yes. Inefficiency? Oh yes. In contrast, men effectively completed the task of building the Panama Canal with their sophisticated use of advanced technology and techniques of group organization.

Emerson ends this sequence with another little lesson, teased forth from myth, not history. Men work wonders as long as they go it alone. If ever they get entangled in the behavior of the other sex, the result is bad management.

> It was Eve who ate the apple, but Noah who made the ark; it was Rebecca who deceived Isaac, Rachel who robbed her father, but it was Joseph with Pharaoh who organized the first trust to control the food supply and who ran the first corner in grain.[76]

Tarbell's "new force" of women are positioned within narratives about the "new era" in factory employment (however dim their chances for advancement). Emerson's women figure only in Old Testament tales and "primitive" histories of endangerment and inefficiency. It is just as Sue

Ainslie Clark, Edith Wyatt, Josephine Goldmark, and others keep repeating: scientific management and the new technology is already a part of the future, that future which it is "men's estate" to possess as soon as possible. Working women are "boys" who will never be granted the status of "men." The "attitudes" of too many members of society, both men and women, remain *back there,* somewhere between "never has been" and "what has been," between the far past of the gentle savage and the recent past/present of the predatory barbarian. When would "attitudes" catch up with the times? Would women ever get to tell modern stories about being modern heroines, not victims, not domesticated cows, not boys?

Heroines and the Law
of Averages

"I FEEL IT'S EFFICIENCY for Americans to find out what's in me so different," cries Anzia Yezierska, "so I could give it out by my work." This plea for an efficiency system that would replace the dead power of objectified work with living labor and use value extends to all who share Yezierska's sex, class, and status as a recent arrival on American shores. "Here you see us burning up with something different, and America turns her head away from us."

Unfortunately, the immediate audience for Yezierska's impassioned appeal is the young college woman presiding over the personnel office of the factory where the frustrated Yezierska must turn out goods according to a rationalized routine, a routine that opposes individualistic deviations from the dulling norm. The counselor (first puzzled, then exasperated by the Yezierska's demands) rebukes her: "First you must become efficient in earning a living before you can indulge in your poetic dreams." This restrictive causal sequence receives the caustic response it deserves. Yezierska points to the immoral waste inflicted upon workers and nation alike by a system of "averages" that substitutes "making" for "doing and being."

> All about me I see so many with my longings, my burning eagerness, to do and to be, wasting their days in drudgery they hate, merely to buy bread and pay rent. And America is losing all that richness of the soul.[1]

America also loses its chance to have true heroines. When women are held at arm's length as strangers to the public good, things are bad enough. When they are absorbed into the workplace according to the law of averages, things are even worse. "Difference" is not acknowledged as a positive contribution in either case. Until the managers stop viewing female difference as a "new force" that must be contained by total leveling or excluded altogether, they deny the entrance of "richness" into the realm of the public good and deny the creation of heroines for the "new era."

Making Exceptions

Throughout 1920 and 1921 Ida Tarbell addresses herself to an audience of bosses. Tarbell takes a far more sanguine view than Yezierska of the economic and moral exchanges taking place between labor and management, particularly where women workers were concerned. In the midst of her other happy narratives about women who hew to the expected law of averages, she offers a short, happy narrative about female exceptions.

Tarbell's series of articles on "The New Place of Women in Industry" reassures the bosses that "girls" perform tasks more effectively (because more predictably) than adolescent males, whose obstreperous conduct disrupts the even routine exacted by the principles of scientific management. In her final article, however, Tarbell inserts the tale of two women who rise above the mean to function as heroines of their own narratives. It demonstrates her notion of the good that comes from occasional exceptions to the rule of averages and from the stabilizing routine that controls the nonnormative.

There is a industrial plant that is administered by the widow of the former owner. It has functioned with great efficiency ever since she decided that production and profits would increase only if the plant were "put on a scientific basis."[2] Tarbell's "illustrative case" is twofold. There is another exceptional woman at the same plant, a woman who has not inherited property and power. Beginning as a common worker at the age of eighteen, this woman had risen "from the bench, under the old system to a foremanship." Now, because she is efficiently utilized in the new system of management instituted by the woman at the top, the former forewoman has moved up to the post of assistant superintendent.

Tarbell's two heroines elate her. Not only can she celebrate their specialness; she can also generalize their achievements into *an average of success* for any woman who has "followed the normal, logical path for advancement in any trade or profession." Encompassed by the nineteenth-century narrative mode brought to perfection by Horatio Alger, these decent, hard-working, twentieth-century Everywomen have overcome the anonymity of most businessmen's widows and women on the factory floor. Success comes to those who had "begun at the bottom, stayed by their task, struggled for improvement, and when the opportunity came, had seized it."

Tarbell does not question her inherited narrative formula or its operative notion that success results from merit rewarded. She leaves untouched the suspicion that upward mobility has not been the "average"
history for any woman, or man, upon the American scene. Tarbell takes
no notice that two women hardily constitute a statistical average. She does
not pause to wonder whether the exforewoman's rise to the position of
assistant superintendent will ever be followed by an appointment to full
executive capacity. Yet Tarbell extrapolates a glowing generalization: "Indeed, the factory as a whole is a brilliant example of the capacity of
women to fill all the positions of an industrial establishment from the
bench to the presidency."

But should managers be apprehensive about exceptions to the everyday routine of the postwar American economy? They need not be, since
Tarbell shows how securely her heroines are contained by the norms they
are used to reinforce. The woman who "is getting her chance in the scientific upbuilding of industry" advances only if she marshals two distinct
forces: "her initiative and determination" and "the attitude of mind of
management."

These two demands jolt loose any aspiration to voluntarism that Tarbell's telling of her tale might initially invite. First, the burden of proof
falls upon the average woman: she must produce a greater amount of "initiative and determination" than the average man. Second, having freed
herself of the function of "the girl" (endlessly doing the tasks of "boys" in
order to become an exception), her future as a worker still depends upon
"the attitude" of male management—the authority still determined to
write the law of averages into most of the tales told at the time the Nineteenth Amendment came into being.

The Go-Betweens

Did the women who entered white-collar office work in increasing numbers have a significantly better chance at achieving a life of doing and
being, the life Anzia Yezierska dreamed of, in which one releases "difference" as part of the everyday labor exchange? Hardly. The literature written specifically about this "upward" move from factory into office reveals
the same purposeful contradictions that keep the basic formula found in
Tarbell's tales of averages and exceptions poised awkwardly at the edge of
disruption.

The Girl and the Job, from 1919, is a catalogue of the different work
areas into which a young woman might venture after the close of World
War I. Special sections on "The Business Field" and "Office Workers"

highlight the belief of authors Helen Hoerle and Florence Saltzberg that "the business world offers the broadest field of work for *the average girl* who does not or cannot go to college for highly specialized training."[3]

"The average girl" can start out at age fourteen to sixteen being "generally useful" as an "office girl," a niche once occupied by boys.[4] The question remains: how far can she go in competing with men for promotion? *The Girl and the Job* insists that advancement is possible as long as the working woman does not view success in terms that involve sexuality. Not only must she "work harder and longer" than men do in order to receive the same notice, she must use her self-controlled conduct to overturn the stories the general public wants to hear. She must undo the plots featuring lustful males who take advantage of the authority they have over women in their employ. She must not strike bargains that equate moving up with sexual compliance. At this point, the authors rush in with their own readings and their gospel for the modern office, which goes like this:

Businessmen are too busy for office seductions. Since they only harass those women who call attention to themselves, it is up to "the average girl" to control the sexual situation through her choice of dress and behavior, and to control the gender situation through her choice of work activities. The girl is fully responsible for her success; she is doubly at fault if she fails. It is imperative that she choose the correct stories to tell about herself. Under the rules laid down by Hoerle and Saltzberg, she is denied access to two outmoded narrative traditions: the plot of the victimized girl given no chance to get ahead and the plot of the innocent woman seduced by her employer. She is also instructed to reject two "modern" narratives of failure: first, the work narrative that traces what happens when "girls" choose not to perform like men; second, the sex melodrama in which "females" indulge in self-destructive misconduct.

In the place of these "bad" stories, old and new, *The Girl and the Job* offers "the average girl" tales of free will retold as stories of exceptions to the rule. First, she must exceed *the averageness of her sex as a worker* (since she will be viewed as inferior to males unless her efforts are markedly "productive"). Second, she must exceed *the norm of her role as an attracting sexual force*. That is, the average girl must always exceed the average male—surpassing the work norms expected of him, and suppressing the sexual image he expects of her according to public fiat.

Hoerle and Saltzberg's call for young women to make their way by creating new narratives of so-called empowerment circumscribes them just as the old tales of victimization did. It does nothing to help women become authentic heroines of business dramas. Is any ground gained by looking into accounts men of business wrote for other men of business about the facts of office productivity?

In his 1920 essay for *Industrial Management,* "Getting the Office Work Done," Wallace Clark betrays no innate talent for storytelling.[5] The carefully regulated surface of Clark's report on the installation of centralized stenographic systems for maximum efficiency in "the average office," however, is disrupted by yet another of those gender-driven melodramas from which the business enterprise was never fully able to free itself.

The prose of Clark's "efficiency report" has not yet slipped over the line into the bureaucratic sludge that characterizes the later writings of managers and engineers. In its control over efficient syntactical means and linguistic ends, its mundane clarity and effective forcefulness, it is scientific management as writing process. Nevertheless, it gives away the game played by all members of the business enterprise.

Even though not in the same league as the Father of Scientific Management, with his audacious manipulation of narrative patterns, men like Clark are forever *telling stories.* This is especially evident when their reports analyze work efficiency according to gendered functions. Placing women within job categories other than those held by men means locating women within distinctive narrative categories.

"Getting the Office Work Done" lays out four principles that dictate the kinds of narratives "the average young woman" can inhabit in the world of *Industrial Management:* (1) Business school training (analogous to study at a woman's college) does not prepare her to meet the standards exacted by scientifically run offices (analogous to the real world run by men). "The necessity for doing accurate work is not brought home [in the schools] to the average young woman until her daily bread depends on it" (116). (2) She must contend with status hierarchies among the female office staff. Clerks do clerical work, stenographers type, but the latter believe that what they do is "more interesting and more important."[6] (3) "Accuracy of work" is not solely a matter of the stenographer's ability to type without factual errors. "Character," not mere empirical data, is at stake. A typed document reflects "the character of the management" and must make "a good effect on the man to whom it is sent" (121). (4) Stenographers are not to be located "at desks next to men who [have] thinking jobs" (117). The clatter of typewriters must not be allowed to impede the effective masculine production of ideas. The "silent woman" honored by tradition has become a fixture in the modern office as well as in the home.

Clark's "efficiency report" clearly lays out the relationships and rankings that order sex-determined work in the modern office world. At the top of the hierarchical structure is the thinking man; the exceptional quality of his ideas is what moves his firm ahead of the competition. Next is the stenographer, positioned above the clerks because of her machine skills and her understanding of the need for accuracy. Last, at the same level as the man in charge of the original office, there is the thinking man in another office across town or in another city. He is the one who, upon receiving the letter in which the first man's thoughts are reproduced by the stenographer's machine, will decide what business to send their way.

All goes well along this interconnected chain of production when each unit in the process knows its place. By 1920 "the average young woman" is a business necessity in the properly managed office. Her career (if so dignified a term can be applied to what remains a "job") is severely limited by the averageness expected of her sex, yet it is the very predictability of her classification as an "average" operator of an office machine that frees the thinking man. Thanks to her, his work, not hers, is taken to be exceptional.

This is the way things are run within the walls of Wallace Clark's scientifically managed office. This is why when we encounter Miss Hammond later in this chapter, she is carefully placed as the eternal go-between linking John Rowntree and Hustus Lockhart, the "Captains in Conflict" of Robert Updegraff's "business fiction" of the same name. This is why no 1930s or 1940s movie filmed in a business setting can do without a faithful female located in the front office. Whether in Hollywood films or in novels of the time, whether blonde or brunette, "the girl in business" is always there at her typewriter, by the telephone, ready with a stenographic pad to take down the hero's dictation and speed him on his way to success.

Later the literary and movie type becomes more sassy and agreeably sexy, once she begins to serve as the go-between for men like Sam Spade. It will take time to move "the average girl" into another story line entirely. Only when she refuses to figure merely as the loyal go-between—only when she seizes the center of erotic attention as "the other woman" or as "the boss" herself in mannish Crawford suits—will the narrative structures enforced by Hoerle, Saltzberg, and Clark break down, to be reformed into different configurations.

Unduly Expensive Individuals

In 1870 2.5 percent of all clerical jobs were held by women; by 1930 the figure had jumped to 53 percent.[7] Twentieth-century technology and scientific management practices opened up the nation's offices to a massive infiltration of women workers, but they offered women no access to executive authority. Statistics, which bear out the fact that by the 1920s the average office task was in the hands of the average women, are inadequate to suggest that woman's financial status, her little victories over habits of mind (both male and female) that limited the nature of her achievements, or her work competency. There had certainly been changes, among them the common practice of naming women to special task forces to study the performance level of other women employees.[8] But since these performance reports were used to determine the production standards enforced by male management, they did nothing to place women at the center of a scientifically managed world. The pieces patterning the job market had been rearranged, but men still "dictated" the work to be done and the telling of stories without heroines. The woman continued to be singled out as "an unduly expensive individual" in the midst of the business enterprise.

From the very start, back in the 1880s when the young Frederick Winslow Taylor began his experiments at the Midvale Steel plant, the point of scientific management had been to eliminate "unduly expensive" persons from the work process. At that time and later on, all the slow little Schmidts and all the idle, gossiping girls remained unalterably *average* in the eyes of their supervisors. Even when made over as units of work energy to achieve higher levels of productivity, the ingrained inefficiency of their personal character remained unchanged. As private individuals, they were fixed in place, forever hovering around the mean. Only during work hours could they overcome their averageness in meeting the demands of the ever-perfected machine process; only on the shop floor might they make exceptions to their ordinariness.

The "civilized" mechanisms of scientific management follow laws of nature that inspire males of the managerial class to do better, to be more productive, and to say stop to the expensiveness that pulls inferiors (women, children, and lesser races) back into the past. The future has no room for average performance from average individuals, therefore the need to prod with "plum" and "lash." Since the average woman employee is even more average than the average man on shop floor or in the office, she must be placed within carefully managed situations that demand she be efficient at all costs. But how is "efficiency" to be defined? Helen Bennett asks this question in 1917 in her book *Women and Work*.

> Here is one of those words that suddenly for no apparent reason overrides a generation. It is swamping us just as "environment," "culture," and "strenuous" have at various times rolled up over the beach of the everyday vocabulary.[9]

Bennett recognizes the potent attraction of the word during the decade when "the efficiency craze" was at its peak, but she takes the fact that it is still "dominant" in common discourse to be "thoroughly obnoxious."

When an intelligent man cites as his ideal of an efficient workroom one where one hundred girls at one hundred typewriters sit working without lifting their eyes from their copy, without exchanging a word for an entire afternoon . . . one may well wonder if efficiency is not a thing to be sent back speedily to its parent in the lower regions. (19)

This is a hellish scene, not the setting for a story with heroines. As a melodrama for its times, it reappears two years later in the form of a five-stanza verse from the pages of the *Bulletin of the Taylor Society,* the journal that helped to sanctify the dead master's efficiency system. These awkward lines utter the plea of "Miss Ten-A-Week" against "the System" and its practices. "Fearful Dangers lurk" not in the principles of the system but in what goes into "making the System work." Upon "the shoulders of poor little clerks, / Like Johnny and Mary and Kate," rests "the working-out of the System."

> So, to the Men who are Higher up
> This is a meek little prayer;
> When the Conference Light is burning,
> And the mighty are gathered there,
> And they think of a WONDERFUL SYSTEM
> That is manifold, intricate, neat—
> (and full of unparalleled terrors
> for little Miss Ten-A-Week's Feet)
> May the Merciful Spirit that softens
> The lot of the Little in Pay
> Be given a Voice and Substance.[10]

The system "in the hands of the Great" has the power to tell "the little" and "the average," who earn ten dollars per week, that they are too "expensive" to employ in the name of "Efficiency"—a word, as Bennett points out, not found in any New Testament inspired by "the Merciful Spirit" that listens to the pleas of the meek of the earth.

Bennett wants efficiency that repudiates its link with "a barren science which wreaks [*sic*] of machinery rather than of men, having for its real object the advance of capital at the expense of labor's individuality." She believes that if efficiency is to be "immediately valuable and productive to society," it must not be "limited to laboratory technics or a knowledge of figures and statistical tables . . . [but] may be expressed through action, being, or even a state of being" (20).

"State of being" and "individuality" as the means to the ends of efforts that are "immediately valuable and productive to society": these are not terms that leaped to the minds of managers when determining how best to cut back on the expense of the human element, especially the costliness of women. Managers who urged that "industries must be humanized" realized this meant making them "fit for women."[11] And doing what was "best" for women workers could lead to the lowering of production standards in an intensely masculine system, a system that dared not risk being "humanized" downward in quantity.

The average woman was considered inferior in terms of productivity. She was efficient—that is, "exceptional"—only when segregated into certain work areas and set to doing certain tasks. It was unlikely that the average woman would ever reach beyond "the state of being" allotted to boys in a man's world. Cheaper in the short run in terms of wages, she was too expensive in the long run ever to warrant the rewards of a progressive business economy. Viewed as being of limited use, she was kept to the limits of her job, exceptions grudgingly admitted. Once more, the search for a heroine for the "new era" was thwarted, since *within limits* is hardly the place to find her.

Statistics as Stories

The decision to tell a story about a unique instance as opposed to a typical case is an important choice, whether the teller is a novelist, journalist, literary theorist, social scientist, or businessman. Material about "the human element" can be read both ways: as personalized representation and as data in the service of generalizations. Even so, one or the other of these poles tends to receive the greater emphasis. When the data in question deals with "scientifically" regulated women's work, the narrators' aspiration to be "scientific" in their handling of material frequently leads to the suppression of individualizing particularities.

Journalists introduced literary devices when reporting on factory or office procedures; novelists infused the feel of the new sociology into their fictions. Either way, scientific discourse set the standard for accuracy and effectiveness. One way to assure that one's text would not be dismissed as a random, isolated, and thus trivial, instance falling outside the bell-curve of probability was to surround that text with the prestige of scientific verification. This was the case in *How The Other Half Lives,* where Jacob Riis includes charts and statistical listings with the greatest of passion.

The new psychology, the new social sciences, the new economics, the new physiology, and the new fictional narratives modeled in their image made use of recent advances in statistics to analyze the effects "the new era" of industry had upon "the new force" of women's labor. Just as the term "efficiency" spread itself thin across the popular vocabulary, impervious to the more rigorous definitions called for by the *Transactions of the American Society of Mechanical Engineers* or the *Bulletin of the Taylor Society,* "average" was common parlance. The precise (though ever-changing) meanings professional statisticians attached to the term when tracking "the logic of measurement" were usually overlooked in material directed at the general public.[12] Phrases such as "the average woman" or "the average office job" were read as signifying *what is typically the case,* references clear enough to audiences comprised of "the average businessman" or "the common reader."

The word "standard" also could not be pinned down precisely. In his 1917 examination of office procedures, Walter D. Fuller defines "standard" as the level of performance managers consider "acceptable"—the "100 per cent figure of efficiency" that stretches above the "actual" performance of which workers are capable.[13] Fuller has to close in upon a predictable "unit of measurement" if he wants to achieve "a successful application of scientific principles" that will remedy present inadequacies. But the hard part remains. How is the management consultant to apply this theoretical standard of 100 percent efficiency—one that starts out by posing an impossibility—to "the average office"?

In the shift repeatedly made by twentieth-century Taylorites and technocrats, midway through his report Fuller stops writing as a man devoted to the exact science of office management and picks up the manner of the practical visionary. Whether we call the impulse behind his attempt at definition evolution, amelioration, millennialism, or utopianism, Fuller's "unit of measurement" is an ideal that disappears off all charts committed to hard facts. Since he can only grasp at its nature as an "unmeasurable quality," he ends up calling his standard of absolute perfection "a psychological something." He can but hope that by having such a Platonic idea hovering over the office, "the high average worker" will aspire to what only a truly exceptional worker might, in theory, achieve.

Scandalously vague when used by the man dedicated to the scientific, "a psychological something" is not so shocking a phrase for the visionary. Fuller, however, continues to struggle to pin down the way this "something" can be applied to the profitable "standardization of office work." He identifies two attributes of this motivating force when he describes how performance charts can be used as a concrete form of the "psychological something." First, this "something" "costs nothing," yet it produces results. Workers will go beyond the typical in order to reach "the high average," to experience the "bonus" of pride when blue stars appear by their names. Second, the charts make the standardizing procedure "easier," "quicker," and "pleasanter" for "manager, standardization man and employee"—although not for that "average girl" who, condemned by the scarlet star affixed to her name, must suffer the "psychological some-thing" of public humiliation.[14]

Averages, Tendencies, and Good Futures

In 1912 Patrick Geddes and J. Arthur Thomson reiterated their vision of the good society that lay ahead. In analyzing "sexual dimorphism," they discovered the joys of sexual difference. As the race ascends, "the essential functions of the males and females become more and more different," but ugly strife need not be the result of these inequalities.[15] Even earlier, Geddes and Thomson had foretold that through the sexual union of male and female, "complementarity"—that excellent interdependence—would replace "difference." " 'Creation's final law' is not struggle but love."

Josiah Royce came to much the same conclusion. In 1914 he convened a group of Harvard professors, mostly scientists, to listen to his paper, "The Mechanical, the Historical, and the Statistical," which concerned those "tendencies" leading the race toward a better future. Shortly we shall ask how Royce's notions apply to the narratives about the destiny of the woman worker formulated by writers like Ida Tarbell and Harrington Emerson, and to the stories about Marija Bercynskas, Carrie Meeber, and Una Golden related by Upton Sinclair, Theodore Dreiser, and Sinclair Lewis. But first we need to consider the role "tendencies" play in the worlds of the mechanical, the historical, and the statistical, particularly in regard to the way each discipline looks to mathematical probabilities as a requirement for the pursuit of individual destiny or the collective fate.

Taylor hoped to make his principles of management comply with the rigorous exactions of scientific thought. This comes from a mechanical engineer with no direct entry into the sacred circle of late nineteenth-century science. Others who practiced variations on the new social sciences also wished to break into that circle, whose members' pride was their ability to trace universal acts unmoved by the whims of the individual case.

It was understood that accidents and uncertainties lurk at the core of physics and mathematics, not to mention the oddities of biological fortunes and the vagaries of the human mind. Still, managers continued to aspire toward predictability. The statistical methods that developed during the nineteenth century increasingly informed many ambitious, and somewhat wishful, projects. Statistical measurement would aid in sorting out the relations (if relations there were) between evolution and progress; probability curves could mediate reconciliations between chance gestures and teleonomical systems.[16]

Little Schmidt's movements, routinized by Taylor's factory flowcharts, helped to map quantitative predictions for shoving pig iron around. William James's and William Graham Sumner's assessment of re-current patterns of behavior extended interest in probabilities into every-day affairs and internalized life. But it was statistical charts, with their record of "tendencies," that offered the most sweeping predictions for the race and the future of society, notwithstanding the fact that their teleolog-ical narratives could not promise the absolutes or the drama offered by Saint John's Book of Revelation.[17]

Prior to Taylor and the new breed of late nineteenth-century social scientists, Ralph Waldo Emerson had enfolded "tendency" into his vocab-ulary of American hope. For Emerson, the word referred to the actions of the individual who makes history his mere shadow. For Karl Marx "ten-dency" meant otherwise: the foreshadowing of collective movements of aggregate societies working themselves out through history. But when it came time for Emerson to elaborate upon our answerability to the "iron laws" of heredity, he, too, admitted that the autonomous individual might be absorbed by the sheer numbers of the aggregate. He announced that the precious idiosyncrasies of the American self might bend under the pressure of racial destiny (this in 1860, on the eve of the war whose statis-tics would measure hundreds of thousands of unnatural, random, prema-ture deaths).

Emerson's statement:

> One more fagot of these adamantine bandages is the new science of Statistics. It is a rule that the most casual and extraordinary events, if the basis of population is broad enough, become matter of final calculation. It would not be safe to say when a captain like Bona-parte, a singer like Jenny Lind, or a navigator like Bowditch would be born in Boston; but, on a population of twenty or two hundred millions, something like accuracy may be had.

Emerson drops in a stony footnote that fixes unrelentingly upon the fatality of this statement. He cites Adolphe Quételet, the man credited with raising statistical theory to the level of sophistication increasingly exacted by mid-century scientific thought.

> Everything which pertains to the human species, considered as a whole, belongs to the order of physical facts. The greater the num-ber of individuals, the more does the influence of the individual dis-appear, leaving predominance to a series of general facts dependent on causes by which society exists, and is preserved.[18]

Recent scholarly accounts of mid-nineteenth-century statistical theory, such as those by Stephen Stigler, Theodore Porter, Ian Hacking,

Raymond Boudon, and François Bourricaud, focus upon what happens when "tendency" (the power of numerical measurement applied to the realm of mathematics) gets transferred to the realm of the social sciences, which is already beset by "the interactive variables" of individuals. Faith in the predictable is shaken by the introduction of uncertainties. "Statistical tendency"—another phrase for "correlation"—"tempts" the sociologist to extrapolate rock-solid theories, but "tendency" is a conditional term, and therefore correlation theories must remain conditional.[19] Warnings about the waywardness of statistical data put a crimp in the writings of nineteenth-century visionaries, who were inspired by the possibility of revolution and/or social progress.

The contending figures in the Marxist/capitalist drama are *homo oeconomicus* and *homo sociologicus*. The former stands for "interchangeable individuals gifted with an identical rationality" governed by the will to match means with ends; the latter has "the social characteristics of the actor" and a rationality that leads him to pursue "not his interests but his preferences" (287). Suspense mounts. The outcome of this plot depends upon who will be the claimant of the new heaven and the new earth: the collective entity or the utilitarian "I."

By the 1890s Herbert Spencer realized it was impossible to declare that society is measured either in terms of innumerable individuals (interchangeable or not) or by the aggregation defined by Quételet, which subsumes the single solitary soul within the qualitative pressures of the mass. By the close of his life, this former absolutist came to believe that "laws" of sociology were only "tendencies." He submitted to the wisdom of speaking of "ideal models" in lieu of drawing decisive, causal conclusions from statistical correlations (370). Generalizations risk nominalism, even when blandly called "typical." It was more sensible to stress process, specifics, and the unplanned consequences of "the aggregation of many actions" (371).

An aging Spencer—concerned with the delicate balance among evolution, tendencies, and uncertainties—came to sound more like William James in his denial of the block universe (the kingdom over which Taylor would have ruled if he could) than the younger Spencer, whom James had taken on in his opposition to philosophical determinism.[20] And to sound like William James on the vagaries of the human condition usually means *not* sounding like Josiah Royce.

When Royce spoke out boldly as a philosopher to a captive gathering of scientists in 1914, he posed a most practical question: what value is there in attempting a comparative study of highly diverse disciplines in the hope of eliciting cooperative efforts? He offered his own answer: in order to meet the imperative need to resolve methodological divisions that separate the philosopher from the scientist, take statistics as the means by which men of serious thought and good intentions can share cognitive procedures and act to aid humankind in its evolution toward a better day.

Royce parses the title of his talk, "The Mechanical, the Historical, and the Statistical," in order to define the limitations and the possibilities of each term. "The mechanical" refers to invariant universal laws, "the historical" is the record of individual events, and "the statistical" is the study of averages.

> In brief, *the object of historical knowledge* is the single event, occurring in the ideally simple case, to the individual thing. A free-will act or an observed eclipse serves as an example. *The object of mechanical knowledge* is the unchanging natural law. . . . *The object of statistical knowledge* is not the single event and is not the invariant law but is the relatively uniform behavior of some average constitution, belonging to an aggregate of things and events.[21]

Statistical method discloses nature's "unconscious teleology." This in turn delineates a future where the human community is ruled, as it were, by both *homo oeconomicus* and *homo sociologicus* in an orderly merger of "interests" and "preferences." The purposiveness of statistics is humanity's hope. It grants more hope, certainly, than history does, marked as it is by random, single, free-will events. It promises more hope than the impersonal force of mechanical law does. There is hope because statistical method is grounded upon "tendency," and "tendency" for Royce is a good. "Tendency" is not the state of conditionality that alarms those with logical minds.

The mechanistic side of our endeavors (*things*) is "rigid." History (single *events*) is "disorder." What falls within the realm of the statistically definable are *averages*: "habits which nature gathers as she matures" (perhaps, at last, our "average woman" as heroine) (2:732).

> Life, although it has its history, has also its statistics. And averages cease to be dry when they are averages that express the unities and the mutual assimilation in which the common ideals and interests, the common hopes and destinies of the men, of the social orders, of the deeds—yes, and perhaps of the stars and of all the spiritual world are bound and are expressed. (2:733)

As a philosophical idealist, Royce was viewed by his professional colleagues (not to mention members of the scientific community) as being out of place in modern times. He seems an odd fellow to call upon when raising the question of whether the future will provide good narratives for women who work. Nevertheless, hear him out.

First, Royce valorizes averages. This gets him past the impasse of Ida Tarbell's historiography, which is based on sluggish progressions and reluctant exceptions that prove the rule—factors that make it unlikely for women to get on with it.[22] Second, Royce has faith that "habits" need not be negative forces that elicit negative reactions. He believes society's habits mature as nature (the eternal She) evolves. He is confident that social orders, minds, and moral processes move forward in unison, propelled by "the tendency of nature" toward "a more orderly arrangement." Third, this "more orderly arrangement" is precisely what the Tarbells, Taylors, and Walter D. Fullers work toward but seldom achieve in the workplace because they limit themselves to the mechanical, that which is "probably never exactly realized in nature" (2:733).

Actually, almost everything is wrong with Royce's notion of tendency and his belief in statistical ideology. He reverts to anachronistic notions of the stars dancing in joyous concert with the natural and the social, ideas that once stirred all good Neoplatonists and might have called Ralph Waldo Emerson back from the grave. His account has a strong masculine tone to it, and his ostensibly neutral numbers disregard the part sex plays in a fully developed worldview. On the other hand, Royce's faith in statistics breathes "vitalism" through ever-expanding narrative patterns; it allows room for narratives to escape the narrow essentialism that divides the universe into sexually prescribed work differences.

No single utopian vision ever offers a safe house to everyone. Something is always wrong for someone the moment self-proclaimed designers of better worlds advance their programs for the future. Run through some of the visionaries of the time: Karl Marx, Herbert Spencer, Edward Bellamy, Thorstein Veblen, King Gillette, Frederick Winslow Taylor, Josiah Royce, Charlotte Perkins Gilman. Whoever it is who sets down such narratives, disturbing qualities appear once we encounter that person's imagination of rational, logical, perfect places, places where pain and waste have been scientifically managed out of existence. Narrative elements of tendencies, averages, individuals, and aggregates get jumbled together. Inevitably, "my" or "your" preference or necessity gets left out. This, however, does not stop such stories from being written.

Strange things happen to the narrative impulse once it is handed over to programs of rationalism, scientism, or statistical correlation.[23] For example, it is difficult to derive any strong sense of what office work was like for the women involved from examining the graphs contained in Elyce Rotella's study, *From Home to Office: U.S. Women at Work, 1870–1930.* For another example: although quantitative disciplines are sternly unsympathetic to qualitative endeavors, which prefer to express themselves in terms of "the sense of" something or other, Taylor's constant introduction

of narrative devices indicates his desire to let in the breath of "the felt life."
The pressure of his engineer's need to make all things fit and function fully
is relieved somewhat (albeit problematically) by the stories he inserts, stories that extend beyond the edges of his flowcharts. For a third example:
Jacob Riis knew that statistics themselves constitute stories when he incorporated charts from the New York City Registry of Vital Statistics into
How the Other Half Lives. Just as surely, he realized that he had to supple-
ment those charts with verbal and visual anecdotes about the waste of human lives when he addressed audiences untutored in the skills of statistical
interpretation.

Turn the situation around. See what happens when three writers of
imaginative texts place working women within narrative structures determined by their favorite mental constructs, whether tendency, fatality, utopianism, biological necessity, or cultural urgency. Test what it is like to be
Marija Berczynskas in Chicago's Packingtown, Carrie Meeber at her
sweatshop machine or on the stage, or Una Golden slowly progressing
through a series of New York business offices. *The Jungle* by Upton Sinclair, *Sister Carrie* by Theodore Dreiser, and *The Job* by Sinclair Lewis are
all narratives with a sense of the future; all contain "average" working-
class women who struggle between being an aggregate or a particular. All
three texts help us to assess Royce's thesis: not its truth-value, but its
worth as a narrative theory suggestive of what the possibilities are for female characters once their authors convert them into "illustrative cases" of
the law of averages.

Questionable Heroines

Upton Sinclair's *The Jungle* suffers a complex fate as an instrumentalist
narrative. The overdetermined intentionality of the plot is saved, paradoxically, only in the final moments, if then. The victory the Socialists
achieved during the 1904 Chicago election was the incitement to human
agency Sinclair needed if he wanted to pull his hero, Jurgis Rudkis, from
the defeat enforced until that point by his own commitment to the literature of environmental determinism. Events taking place in history, outside the confines of the serialized chapters Sinclair was in the process of
sending to the journal *Appeal to Reason,* give his conclusion the look of
voluntarism. Unless one chooses to define history itself as a force whose
will cannot be abridged by individual action, these events have the capacity to break the fetters that lock Jurgis into a capitalist system of competitive economics and those that just as securely manacle Sinclair to a series
of episodic chapters with nowhere to go.

In an update of the conversion narrative (a genre at least as old as Augustine's *Confessions*), Jurgis erupts into a new faith in a new master. Joyous self-abnegation before the collective will of socialism replaces the dulling egocentrism that bound him to a destiny of powerlessness. He is theoretically restored to fullness of being at the very moment he vanishes as a fictional character. Upon *his* conversion, Upton Sinclair—also like Augustine—discovers the story he must tell. By imagining the force of a life of political activism, Sinclair as a writer is freed from a statistical nightmare. He can break past the novel's early image of an endless line of carcasses (animal and human) passing through the killing floors of Chicago's Packingtown, only to disappear into countless tins of lard and ropes of sausage: numbers passing into numberlessness, individuality annihilated in the slaughter of anonymous innocents.

Something odd happens to *The Jungle* when narrative voluntarism replaces abject environmental determinism, suggesting that writers may have to pay for freedom from "tendencies." The novel concludes with a vision of "radical Democracy left without a lie with which to cover its nakedness." With the "rush," the "tide," and the "floods" of outraged workingmen working together at last—organized, drilled, marshalled for victory—comes the promise, "Chicago will be ours! *Chicago will be ours!* CHICAGO WILL BE OURS!"[24]

Power comes to the people in the "real" world on the occasion of the 1904 Chicago election, but at a cost to Sinclair's fictive account. Power is drained from the text: perhaps in confirmation of the fears of Georg Lukács and other commentators on the complicated issue of Marxist aesthetics, perhaps because Sinclair was no Sergei Eisenstein, capable of vividly conveying the concept of the masses as hero. That the early chapters of *The Jungle* grip the reader's imagination may be the consequence of their allegiance to bourgeois expectations, or it may be an admission that the dark fatalism of these chapters compels the mind as utopian visions cannot.

The "social Darwinism" of Sinclair's novel is untenable to those who hold the socialist faith, but it grimly works as the source for narrative force. It would be difficult to surpass Sinclair's description of the Chicago winter, a setting that matches with metaphoric intensity the icy logic of Packingtown's economic system.

> It would come, and it would come; a grisly thing, a spectre born in the black caverns of terror; a power primeval, cosmic, shadowing the tortures of the lost souls flung out to chaos and destruction. It was cruel, iron-hard; and hour after hour they would cringe in its

grasp, alone, alone. There would be no one to hear them if they cried out; there would be no help, no mercy. And so until morning—when they would go out to another day of toil, a little weaker, a little nearer to the time when it would be their turn to be shaken from the tree. (97–98)

The cry uttered at the close of the novel by the nameless man who represents "the very spirit of the revolution"—"Organize! Organize! Organize!"—has (fortunately, from the workers' point of view) replaced the anonymous "hog squeal of the universe" uttered by the victims of the competitive system. But that same cry does irreparable harm to Sinclair's narrative. It is not a matter of doing damage to some detached, ahistorical quality called "art." The damage is done to the social and political instrumentality of the story itself.

To respond even more specifically to the consequences of Sinclair's narrative upon the lives it purports to represent, consider the figure of Marija Bercynskas. Is she (or any of the women workers in *The Jungle*) "saved" by Sinclair's socialist ending? Is the general cause of womanhood aided by Sinclair's story any more than it is aided by Taylorism's promise of a world cleansed of waste, or by Royce's vision of love attained through the power of statistical tendencies? It would seem not. The women who appear during the first half of the novel are wiped out as human agents long before Jurgis has his place usurped by the nameless voice crying, "Organize! Organize!"

Ona, Jurgis's sixteen-year-old bride, lasts less than two years and nineteen chapters. Before she is destroyed by anxiety, illness, and childbirth, her soul and body have been sold to the terrible routine of the packinghouse, and then resold to Connor the foreman in extension of Sinclair's prostitution narrative about the buying and selling of all his characters' bodies and souls. Marija, of the strong arms and broad shoulders, survives a little longer, but when she is last seen she has been reduced to a shadow: a drug addict and whore, her spirit is crushed, her body depleted. The one woman with the capacity to endure throughout Sinclair's novel is Elzbieta, but this is because she has no soul or self to lose. Elzbieta was

one of the primitive creatures; like the angleworm, which goes on living though cut in half. . . . She did this because it was her nature—she asked no questions about the justice of it, nor the worthwhileness of life in which destruction and death ran riot. (231)

Elzbieta's way is survival of the type with a vengeance—vengeance against all stories with pretensions to nurture the spark of individual humanity.

As represented by Sinclair, there is no place in the socialist vision for

women who work. This lack is disturbing to anyone concerned with all
the stories not being told about women, by this narrative in particular.
The battle cry "Organize! Organize!" that closes Sinclair's novel with the
promise that the great city will be "ours" projects but half a vision. Those
doing the organizing are men, as are those urged to take possession of the
city.[25] This half-told tale is especially hurtful in the case of Marija. Not
only is she formidable of body and spirit when we first see her in 1900;
she is depicted as the manager and boss, the "exception" whose commanding presence sends waves of energy through the opening pages of
the novel.

Within the Packingtown factory system Marija Bercynskas is no more
than a common worker; within her community she is the organizer, not
only of the wedding feast for Ona and Jurgis but of what the narrative
might have become.

> The occasion rested heavily upon Marija's broad shoulders—it was
> her task to see that all things went in due form, and after the best
> home traditions; and, flying wildly hither and thither, bowling every
> one out of the way, and scolding and exhorting all day with her tre-
> mendous voice, Marija was too eager to see that others conformed
> to the proprieties to consider them herself. (1)

Whenever the orchestra flags in its pace, "soldiering" on the job, Marija flies into its midst. She lashes the musicians into an accelerated pace of
performance no less demanding than that exacted by Taylorism. The
dancers are also powerless before the will of their powerful boss. But soon
Marija's genius as the manager of marriage folkways is cut short by "the
iron laws" of a fate that forbids her access to managerial power in the
workplace, where folkways are viewed as part of the waste that must be
excised.

The economic system Sinclair attacks is to blame for much of Marija's
diminishment as a potent social force, but blame also lies with a narrative
that is incapable of imagining Marija as a woman who could stand before
a political gathering of male workers, her voice raised in the cry "Organize! Organize!" Sinclair's failure is underlined when he opens the final
chapter (the one concluded by this cry) with Marija trapped in despair at
her current place of work (the brothel), telling Jurgis "indifferently," "I
can't do anything. I'm no good. . . . What's the use of talking about it—
I'll stay here till I die, I guess. It's all I'm fit for'" (394).

The original version of Theodore Dreiser's *Sister Carrie* concludes
with George Hurstwood, the erstwhile manager, beaten down in body,
mind, and spirit, also muttering "What's the use?" as he turns on the gas
jet before wearily settling down to die. Carrie Meeber occupies a different

narrative track than Hurstwood, however. *He* is part of Dreiser's story about chemisms, chance, and the iron laws that drain human agency and drag men toward those statistical "correlations" on suicide analyzed by Durkheimian sociologists.[26] Carrie is part of another arc, the agent of another tendency.

Sinclair's Marija is first seen in the Chicago of 1900, managing her work crew at the wedding feast at a merciless pace. Dreiser's introductory scenes in the Chicago of the early 1890s locate Carrie Meeber in a shoe factory, where she is assigned to punching eyeholes in uppers. "Carrie saw at once that an average speed was necessary or the work would pile up on her and all those below would be delayed."[27] Although she finds "relief from her own nervous fears and imaginings in the humdrum, mechanical movement of the machine" (28), she is dismayed by the dim light, the heat, the stool with no support for her aching back, and the insolent remarks made by brash male coworkers.

> Her hands began to ache at the wrists and then at the fingers, and towards the last she seemed one mass of dull, complaining muscles, fixed in an eternal position and performing a single mechanical movement which became more and more distasteful, until at last it was absolutely nauseating. (29)

The Dreiserian narrator of 1900 pauses to observe that Carrie arrived in Chicago a bit too soon to be involved either in a socialist narrative, which might mitigate her plight through political action, or in a narrative of advanced capitalism, which was just then introducing the benefits of industrial welfare programs.[28] Even so, no plot time is wasted before Carrie is removed from the factory world where she and the narrative would have remained "fixed in an eternal position and performing a single mechanical movement." Dreiser is much more interested in seeing Carrie market her personal wares and consume the world's goods than engage in any prolonged act of producing commodities. He quickly sends her forth into the arms, first, of Drouet the salesman, next, of Hurstwood the saloon manager. If Marija Bercynskas commences at the top of an arc with nowhere to go but down, Carrie's narrative arc is one of material ascent, while Hurstwood, in Marija's victim role, falls from the heights to the depths.[29]

Carrie's brief involvement in the world of industry is rapidly replaced by her complex engagement in the world of business. As has often been noted, Carrie's life is one of surplus value and false production, defined by illusory schemes of advertising, image promotion, and self-commodification.[30] Attention has also been given to the stage-world setting of Carrie's story and to the significance of her rise from the anonymity of the chorus line to star status. But it helps to examine the exact nature of the theatrical parts she plays since they suggest the kind of narrative Dreiser allows Carrie as a working woman.

Carrie Meeber's initial stage experience comes in Chicago during the Elks Club annual theatricals. She is given the role of Pearl, a typical figure in a typical melodrama, but during the performance she discloses an unexpected talent for representing the pathetic. Pathos is the emotion Carrie seems fated endlessly to express because of the "tendencies" of Dreiser's own philosophical stance, a pathos that would keep her from taking the powerful roles commanded by actresses versed in portraying tragic heroines. As chapters 4 and 5 have shown, the essential weakness of the pathetic mode was commonly affixed to working women of the period, whether by journalistic accounts or by popular fiction. But in the end it is Hurstwood, not Carrie, to whom Dreiser gives the female role of pathetic victim, the same role Sinclair confers upon Ona and Marija. Incapable of surviving as an angleworm like Elzbieta, it is Hurstwood who ends up as a suicide statistic, he who becomes one of the nameless corpses stacked in the Potter's Field of which Jacob Riis's charts took note.

In contrast, Carrie marshals enough willpower to find work as "a little soldier," even though—and this is significant—her success also stems from the innate aura she possesses that makes her stand out from the group. Carrie's escape from a tale of victimization paradoxically arises, in large part, from her particular talent for silently representing self-pitying young things like the little Quaker. Her pathetic twist of mouth and cast of velvety eye touch the imaginations of the men who come to the theater to buy a glimpse of what they most desire: the sign of their own essential pathos.

The strength of Carrie's character is questionable. Some have asked whether she even has "character." Is she any more responsible for her good fortune than Elzbieta is in escaping the fate of Sinclair's other females? One could view Carrie Madenda, née Meeber, as a weak figure of pathos from the beginning to the end of her story: she is trapped within that role by social and economic systems that render women vulnerable to defeat; she is also trapped within Dreiser's acquiescence to the way things are. On the contrary, one could argue that, in the final scene of the novel, Carrie is poised at the moment of her future ascent to the strong role of tragic actress, a role Ames has encouraged her to imagine for herself on stage and in life. But even if Carrie is deemed capable of both the passivity of romantic pathos and the force of the tragic mode, does this imply that she has the ability to cross over into the realm of a utopian tradition intent upon breaking past tragedy altogether?

Allegories of management provide one clue about where the narrative takes Carrie by the end (just as they provide clues, variously, in the cases of Maggie Verver and Marija Bercynskas). Hurstwood as manager (albeit his is a cosmetic role without financial or executive powers) fails and falters, his life consumed within a melodramatic plot of victimization by external forces; this is certain. But Carrie, glimpsed in the final paragraphs of the novel, opens up large questions of whether she will be able to manage her way out of the social abyss.

Marija's ways as a "driver" (although much good *that* does her in the world of Sinclair's novel) is never Carrie's way. By the last chapter Carrie has handed over the regulation of the material details of her life to Lola, her parasite, and to the ingratiating hotel manager. Further, there is that rocking chair.[31] Rocking chairs are an American invention. They symbolize the restlessness of the nation's population, urged to attain something unnamed and unreachable even while at rest. Rocking chairs are in constant motion but go nowhere. We might view a woman seated in such a chair the way we view anyone bound to the routine of factory shop or office. From dogs and convicts forced to supply the motive power of treadmills, to slaughterhouse practices that fix workers to one spot, endlessly repeating one task, and on to the automobile assembly line or the stenographic pool, the history of industrial technology is an endless reel of scenes of mindless motion. These routines produce either surplus value for owners and social alienation for workers (according to Marxist theories) or sound efficiencies and contented workers (according to Taylorist creed).

The original manuscript of *Sister Carrie* concludes with Hurstwood, the ex-manager, the female figure of pathos, saying "What's the use?" before putting a stop to the aimless rocking chair of his fate. The published version concludes with Carrie, the star, rocking to and fro. "Though often disillusioned, she was still waiting for that halcyon day when she should be led forth among dreams become real" (369). For every step already taken, others lie wearily ahead. The voice-over does not murmur "organize, organize!" (the admonition any author-as-manager heeds in shaping his narrative); instead, the words addressed to Carrie are "Onward, onward." "In your rocking chair, by your windows, shall you dream such happiness as you may never feel" (369).

Carrie comes out ahead of Hurstwood, but Dreiser's narrative denies her the chance to achieve the full status of a woman capable of managing the lives of others and her own life through possession of the will to "organize, organize!" If Dreiser had allowed his imagination to comply with either socialist or Taylorist utopias, Carrie would be saying, "Chicago is ours!" or at least, "New York is mine!" The fault lies—if fault there is—in Dreiser's willingness to tell an essentially genderless story about "blind strivings of the human heart" (369). His faith in a cosmos run according to universals and the law of averages proves the more powerful catalyst for his narrative than do social management programs that control or release individual energies, whether female or male.

Sinclair Lewis wrote *The Job* in 1917, three years before *Main Street* brought him fame as the American bard of the traps that small town hegemonies lay for the imaginative will of women. It tells the story of Una Golden, "a natural executive," as she moves slowly but inevitably toward her final position as the manager of a New York-based hotel company, a rise that takes her from Panama, Pennsylvania, where her fate would have been to remain "an untrained, ambitious, thoroughly commonplace, small-town girl." [32]

The Job juxtaposes realistic accounts of everyday averages alongside romantic exceptions. As Lewis's choice for his heroine, Una is the "one" sufficient enough to carry a sustained narrative while being "average" through and through; "a 'good little woman'—not pretty, not noisy, not particularly articulate." As far as her story serves as "an illustrative case" of the rare business success that proves the rule of averages, Una might just as well have been in Ida Tarbell's hands. But Una must do double duty, as Tarbell's cases never do. *The Job* opens with the two "mean" facts that characterize the double nature of Lewis's protagonist: Una I is "efficient" and "a matter-of-fact idealist"; Una II possesses "a healthy woman's simple longing for love and life" (5). It is determined form the start that she must figure in the public sphere as a modern corporate manager *and* in the private sphere as an old-fashioned girl.

Una's adventures in the big world of New York begin circa 1905, when Marija's life story has just reached an end. Whereas Ona's and Marija's souls and bodies are prostituted in Chicago's Packingtown and whorehouses, betrayed by the enticements placed beyond the reach of immigrant women, Una is quickly wooed by middle-class, nativist dreams about "the theory of efficiency, the ideal of Big Business" (25). Since Lewis has no quarrel to pick with either that theory or that ideal as long as they are touched by "a Fabian socialism" (235), he sees to it that Una's success keeps pace with the evolving success of the new management system: "the vision of an efficiency so broad that it can be kindly and sure . . . discernible at once in the scientific business man and the courageous labor-unionist" (26).

Una graduates from a commercial college, becomes the avid reader of "the new sorts of business magazines" addressed to men who "sought everywhere for systems and charts and new markets and the scientific mind" (27), and begins work in the office of the *Motor and Gas Gazette*.[33] But Lewis never loses sight of the double destiny his woman of averages must pursue. Quasi-Taylorist heroine that he makes her out to be, Una is also "representative of some millions of women" who keep "on inquiring what women in business can do to make human their existence of loveless routine" (147). At this very instant, Una meets Walter Babson. After many plot delays, Babson will be the means through which Una will interject routine with love, but just now Walter disappears from view so that Lewis can display Una's pilgrim's progress through the business world.

At twenty-six years of age, Una supervises two stenographers in an architect's office, but she is already "a woman of sterile sorrow" who derives her only pleasure from shopping or going to the movies to gaze longingly at the male stars.[34] Una moves slowly up the business ladder, very slowly, since Lewis's fairy tale of female success in the Big City of Big Business is concerned (like his later, more famous fables) with the homey details by which he domesticates the business of America. Step by step, we learn of Una's mastery of the modern filing system at a sleek new pharmaceutical firm, her education in caste systems and office politics while secretary to the head of the firm's advertising department, and her experience of the kind of efficient "social system in which time-saving devices didn't save time for anybody but the owners" (235). That Lewis's instructional reports retard the narrative pace is of little consequence, since this is a time of stagnation in Una's life. For the moment, she lingers at the sterile stage of office life where "Miss Ten-A-Week" is fated to remain forever.

Seeking any change from routine (just as the narrative seeks to move beyond daily logs of office duties), Una marries. Julius Edward Schwirtz is an early version of Lewis's big-hearted but weak-willed lout. But Schwirtz loses his drummer's job and settles into a life of leisure, bankrolled by Una until she orders him to hunt for a new job. It is a crucial moment for Una "when she took charge; began not only to think earnest, commonplace, little Una thoughts about 'mastering life,' but actually to master it" (272).[35] Just as Hurstwood fades from Carrie's life at a similar juncture, so does Schwirtz. Upon divorcing the man who is "two-thirds the old-fashioned brute" while she is "at least one-third the new, independent woman," Una is "free again" (300).

It is 1912 and Una is thirty-one, now a confidential secretary, but still fighting "her old enemy routine" (279). But unlike "Miss Ten-A-Week," Una shares Lewis's faith "that business was beginning to see itself as communal, world-ruling, and beginning to be inspired to communal, kingly virtues and responsibility" (280). Further, her new job affords the novel a thematically significant occasion: it points the way toward an acceleration in the rate of her managerial ascent as well as a noticeable pickup in the pace of the narrative plotting.

Una now works for a firm that deals in the design and sale of suburban family homes. Studying these designs causes Una II to dream of having children of her own; it also heightens Una I's interest in perfecting her grasp of real estate procedures and management systems. One day, in a scene filled with equal parts nineteenth-century womanliness and twentieth-century business acumen, Una brings off a major coup. She sells lots to the husband of the woman who has plied an ailing Una with beef tea and sympathy. (How lucky she is to suffer a "woman's complaint" during her work week!). In a single stroke Una "climbed above the rank of assistant to the rank of people who do things" (304). This scene is a brilliant exercise in "woman's fiction" that turns the tables on the common belief of male employers—that female biology entails a monthly loss of productivity. With it Lewis confirms Una's role in the forward momentum of history. On this score at least, he projects his heroine beyond those points of social and economic stasis to which pathetic Marija, the manager-manqué, and pathetic Miss Ten-A-Week, the eternal file clerk, are relegated.

Una never burns with the masculine fervor Jurgis Rudkus has when he envisions the revolutionary overthrow of corrupt systems. She is a social gradualist. Although intrigued by "the sunset-colored ideals" held by Mamie Magen, her socialist friend, she prefers slow change. Slow change also characterizes the narrative pace Lewis once again uses to diagram Una's move toward success, having allowed her life a momentary surge.

During the opening years of the Big War, Una Golden Schwirtz is resident salesman and director of a major suburban residential project; next she is a sales manager earning $2,500 annually, supervising five women in sales. At thirty-four, she considers adopting a child in order to fulfill her maternal needs, but she is sidetracked once her career suddenly takes an immense leap forward. There comes a time when Lewis has to forego narrative gradualism—a time when he, like Taylor, begins to administer the whip while holding out the plum as he "drives" his willing "little woman" onward.

Una is hired by the management firm, The White Line Hotels, as "a creator, a real manager." At dinner with her boss, Bob Sidney,

> she spoke deliberately, almost sternly. She reached for her new silver link bag, drew out immaculately typewritten schedules, and while he gaped she read to him the faults of each of the hotels, her suggested remedies, and her general ideas of hotels. (231)

Impressed that this woman can talk and figure like a man, Sidney makes a mild pass. Una adroitly fends it off, saying "sharply, 'Don't try that—let's save a lot of time [efficiency, again] by understanding that I'm

what you would call 'straight.' " He apologizes, calls her a "high-class ge-
nuwine lady," and Una's success as a careerist is assured (323). But Una I
has yet to succeed in regard to the second of Lewis's narrative promises:
the break past the "loveless routine" of business life in order to satisfy Una
II's "healthy woman's simple longing for love and life."

The plot had veered significantly at that earlier moment when Una
was mothered by Mrs. Boutell and when the fatherly Mr. Boutell purchased lots from the Villa Estates. This insistent family motif was also
reinforced by the brilliance of Una's proposal to Sidney that the White
Line Hotels serve as "cozy homes" for traveling salesmen. All now comes
into focus, and Una's final victory is decided when Walter Babson reappears. Una's public career as nurturer of wandering males will now be
matched by a private career in the same role.

When Walter turns up in her employ, Una's old feelings of dependency return for this charming, feckless male. When he proposes, "Her
head dropped. She who had blandly been his manager all day, felt managed when his 'Will you?' pierced her, made her a woman" (326).

The erotic penetration of Walter's words of proposal unsettles Una,
but she firmly assures herself, " 'I will keep my job—if I've had this world
of offices wished on to me, at least I'll conquer it, and give my clerks a
decent time,' the business woman meditated" (327).

Odd for Una to say business has been "wished on to" her. Interesting
that she will stay on at the office, not so much to prove her personal worth
as to look after her clerks with a motherly eye. " 'But just the same—oh,
I am a woman, and I do love. I want Walter, and I want his child, my own
baby and his' " (327).

There is much meaning in these words that bring *The Job,* this early
version of the female business success novel, to its conclusion. (1) Una
capitulates all too readily to Walter's "piercing" of her femaleness. (2) Walter is weak enough to need constant management and mothering by
an expert, and his presence will get her the baby she has always wanted.
(3) Her new private life now melds with her public success in the management of hotels systematized to mother lonely men. No wonder we ask
why Lewis felt he had to link his heroine's success in business with the
nurturing home sphere.

Why indeed! In 1917 popular stories about a woman's success in the
business world still had to fall into the pattern of the domestic romance
insinuated into the loveless routine of a scientifically managed office and
life.[36] Upton Sinclair's socialist vision cannot accommodate women workers in a world where success is defined by male political activism. Theodore Dreiser's apolitical imagination disregards the terms for "success"
taken seriously by persons committed to gender agendas. At least Sinclair

Lewis's paternalistic narrative does what the other two men could not and would not do: let the law of averages tied to the "tendencies" of Big Business sweep his heroine toward happiness as the manager managed.

Lewis is on to something very big in the double story he tells in *The Job*. He reports with accuracy on those new-century tendencies by which up-to-date business and management systems defined themselves through the mass selling of the happy home. In the form of imaginative fictions about females who yearn to "make human their existence of loveless routine," Lewis outlines the particular brand of domestic romance that businessmen were just then claiming as their own.

The Businessman as House Heroine

Captains in Conflict: The Story of the Struggle of a Business Generation is two novels in one—text and subtexts—about the manager as business hero and the male as domestic heroine. When it first appeared in serial form throughout 1926 in *System: The Magazine of Business,* the editors asserted that the author, Robert R. Updegraff, had "fashioned a story that no business man in America will want to miss." [37] Updegraff may be the nominal author, but he is actually only an amanuensis to history. *Captains in Conflict* is "a story that has taken 25 years in the writing, because it was written by business itself." But if business is the "dictator" of the "rationalized" text Updegraff dutifully records, subtexts well up from the deep currents of that system. [38] The text shows what business is for; the subtexts show what it is about.

The editors of *System* define the new "business fiction" as a mode of writing "released from the usual limitations of business writing." It is the prose romance "founded on the greatest romance in the world— BUSINESS" (50:602). But there is more to *Captains in Conflict* than meets the eyes of the *System* editors. Updegraff's use of the romance form to relate the grim battle for survival the Rowntree Stove & Range Company fights against the predatory moves of the Consolidated Stove & Range Company of North America is a telling reversal of Nathaniel Hawthorne's employment of the same mode, once he shook loose from the business of the Salem Custom House eighty years earlier.

Hawthorne unquestionably felt "released" from the office routine against which he had chafed. Let go from his job for political reasons, it pleases him to seize "the freedom of fiction" in order to reconstruct an account of the generational struggle between the old-time magistrates of the New England settlement and the (perhaps) revolutionary social changes introduced by a woman who maintains her own cottage industry as seamstress on the margins of society. In contrast to Hawthorne, Updegraff, however "released," stays with the Custom House scene, as it were. He continues to record what businessmen *do,* describing "hundreds of men, prominent in the fields of law, finance, economics, manufacturing, marketing, and politics" who have "contributed to the picture of the times"). On the other hand, although there is no place for a Hester Prynne in Updegraff's main text, *Captains in Conflict* contains Hawthornian family and domestic romances within its subtexts. But first there is the romance of business as management procedure to take into account.

The editors of *System* emphasize the historical importance of Updegraff's narrated events, events that cover the years 1900 to 1925. In 1900

> the old order, characterized by intense individualism, secrecy, and rule-of-thumb, was definitely passing. Men had begun to discover the power of combination; and the might of concentrated capital.

In the years that lead toward the 1920s

> cruel forms of competition were invented. Sinister methods were employed to further selfish ambitions. Small businesses were crushed or swallowed. In some cases the public interest was ruthlessly tramped upon.

Captains in Conflict is the "dramatic story" of the "epic struggle" out of which, by 1925, emerges a "new American business, not perfect, but cleaner, sounder, more efficient, and more human than the old." As *story,* it provides suitable fictive representations of all of these embattled forces—characters both typical and unique. It portrays average men embroiled in exceptional events—events that stand for the old order passing from view, for the tendencies of the intermediary phases, and for the triumphant order to which history will accord the victory: "the dawning of the ideal of Today which will further Tomorrow's business integrity and efficiency" (50:602).

Fowler Rowntree of Franklin, Illinois, dies symbolically in 1900—a time of heightened business consolidation—putting an end to a line of individualistic manufacturers of an earlier type, men of "simple nature, upright and uncompromising" (49:44). As Updegraff mythologizes him, Fowler had been the epitome of the businessman idealized in the late nineteenth century—a good man who is also a good man of business; a man who wonders on the day he dies whether his son intends to bring in "one of the new-fangled typewriting machines—and even to hire a young woman to operate it! Wouldn't it seem strange to have a woman in the office?" (49:45). Even Silas Lapham, Fowler's immediate fictional prototype, had typewriter and typist (a bit anachronistically). But Fowler is as much out of touch with modern times in 1900 as Mose, the faithful family retainer, who remarks, "Dat sure is a new one of dis nigger. Writin' a letter by machin'ry!" (49:142).

Rowntree Stove & Range is taken over by Fowler's son John, the hero of Updegraff's business romance. There are twenty-five years of history and an "epic struggle" to get through before John gains final victory over the text's villain, Hustus B. Lockhart. En route to the twelfth and concluding episode, Updegraff takes down "dictation" for the following events: U.S. involvement in the Philippines; British colonialist brushes with the Boers; business trusts in the hands of that man of "high character," President McKinley, and of President Theodore Roosevelt; the Panic of 1907; the pros and cons of various efficiency systems; strikes agitated by "wops" and other wild-eyed outsiders; businessmen's realization that they must "design and build sales just as we design and build" products; World War I fought on the home front under the leadership of Bernard Baruch of the War Industries Board; the rise of deferred-payment plans, which suit an "American temperament" that impatiently wants tomorrow's luxuries "without waiting to earn them"; the struggle to cut production costs after the wartime peak; Taylorist talk about having to make capital work "harder and faster"; the sharp turn toward a "service attitude" in business; and always the push toward growth, expansion, combinations, and consolidations.

The pleasure Updegraff takes in history defined as ever-evolving, ever-progressing business forces on the upswing is not shared by Thorstein Veblen. By 1921 Veblen had already anticipated a large part of the plot line Updegraff would lay out in 1926, but with at least one major difference: the role played by John Rowntree. Veblen's essay "The Industrial System and the Captains of Industry" (closely followed by "The Captains of Finance and the Engineers") also traces the generational history of the "captains in conflict." Although Veblen looks at much the same material as Updegraff, not only do his interpretations differ significantly but so does his cast of characters. This means that Veblen's story will not be "founded on the greatest romance in the world—BUSINESS."

Veblen is hardly willing to grant purity of motive to the "picturesque character" that Fowler Rowntree is intended to represent, but he acknowledges the accuracy of depicting a late nineteenth-century economic scene where the owner was all-in-all: inventor, designer, builder, shop manager, financial officer, and entrepreneur, who represented "a cross between a business man and an industrial expert." [39] Veblen is also keenly aware of the continuing presence of the Hustus Lockhart type, the man for whom business means making financial deals, not producing useful goods. But

Veblen's historical account contains no "dictation" about men like John Rowntree, the hero who balances industrial efficiency, engineering intelligence, business acumen, marketing savvy, and, as we shall see, many of the domestic virtues usually attributed to women.

The antiromance Veblen writes by means of his series of essays is a sorry story. Financiers control industrial production. Engineers (the heroes who would have figured in any work of fiction Veblen might have set down) struggle to survive. Managers of an overly specialized business enterprise have lost contact with the men who work with capital, the men who work with production, and the needs of the public in general. Veblen's narrative can never be "released" from "the usual limitations of business writing" by means of the "freedom of fiction"; it has no hero like John Rowntree, and no victory is predicted in its "epic struggle." When set over against the "scientific" structures and strictures of Veblen's historical review, Updegraff's reconstruction of the business world is exposed as sheer wish fulfillment, a result of his capitulation to the fictitiousness of the business system itself. But beneath the soft data of Updegraff's main text, certain truths emerge from the familial and domestic romances that form his subtexts.

Updegraff's account of John Rowntree's epic struggle sets out to prove the moral rightness of two forms of business organization: the small company (signifying the particular and the individualistic) owned by the man who can "do everything," and the big company (the general and anonymous type) overseen by corporate boards. Since both forms are "good" for the American people, suspense centers upon the question of whether the up-to-date owner-manager of 1920s can remain wedded to the nineteenth-century business ethic personified by Fowler Rowntree of Franklin, Illinois, a man who dies "worshiped" in 1900. The answer is yes on two crucial counts. First, the son shares with his father "a simple nature, upright and uncompromising" unaltered by the demands of "the new era." Second, the fact that the son's business principles are "scientific" and "modern" make them no less reliant upon the principles of virtue embodied by the father, since "business" and "ethics" derive from the same iron laws that define "American character."

"American character" remains unchanged throughout the main text of *Captains in Conflict*. It must only keep abreast of new *things* (Miss Hammond at her typewriter, in place of male clerks who pen their accounts; gas stoves instead of coal stoves; electric ranges rather than gas burners) and new *ideas* (marketing techniques; corporate financing; standardization routines; efficiency systems) while retaining the old *folkways* supported alike by Fowler Rowntree, the family's faithful "niggers," Mose and Marthy, and Fowler's son John.[40] As the plot winds down, the Rowntree Stove & Range Company merges with Consolidated Stove & Range Company of North America to become the Rowntree Division (a "laboratory" for the testing of innovative concepts). Both Lockhart and his outmoded villainy are dead, and "good" men of the new generation now control the huge combine. So goes "the business romance" Robert Updegraff told the readers of *System* in 1926.

The main text of *Captains of Conflict* is to the business enterprise of the first two and a half decades of the 1900s what Richard Harding Davis's *Soldiers of Fortune* was to the imperialistic business temper of the 1890s. These two "business fictions" are simultaneously transparent and opaque as ideological records of American history and business in the making. Davis's hero, Robert Clay, is the hero-as-engineer of an earlier decade. Just beyond the final pages of Davis's novel, Clay disappears into the maw of the corporate world, where Updegraff's hero, John Rowntree, waits to pick up the thread of this continuing narrative. The burden Updegraff places upon Rowntree is the abstracting "correlation"—the "statistical tendency" of the sociologist's chartings—that proves the business of America is business, not industry; finance, not production; marketing, not engineering. But John Rowntree, like Robert Clay, must also perform as a popular hero for his time.

What is interesting is the "averageness" Updegraff brings to John Rowntree. It points up how much Robert Clay, by contrast, functions within a slightly older romance tradition. The differences between the two men are not so much the result of the fact that Rowntree's battle campaigns are won at home rather than in the jungles of Latin America. Both are manly men who satisfactorily fulfill the code of masculine action earlier sanctioned by Davis and Roosevelt. Two other traits distinguish the hero of America's heartland from the hero of the Caribbean. One, Rowntree is more patently the average man whose exceptional achievements underscore his averageness. Two, the sex roles assigned to Rowntree do not repattern the romanticized heterosexual-homoerotic relationships found in *Soldiers of Fortune*. The nature of these roles is revealed more obliquely within subtexts that complicate, while confirming, the points Updegraff's main text makes about male aspirations to mastery in the business world.

Captains in Conflict is contained within the twin traditions of the familial romance and the domestic romance. It is not easy to explain how this is so until we look at the basic plot elements. Intricate shifts are taking place between the interchangeable roles of fathers and sons, husbands and wives, the greatest mother of them all, and nurturer of the hearthfire.

Fathers and Sons

Updegraff structures the conflict between several generations of business-men as a story of filial relations.[41] Fowler Rowntree's legacy to John is that of "the good father" whose reputation must be protected at all costs. Early on, John is tempted by his "bad father," Hustus B. Lockhart, to betray the family name when urged to "combine" with Consolidated Stove & Range Company. If he yields, the name Rowntree will vanish through absorption into the anonymity of Consolidated. Since this merger involves gulling the public with overloaded stocks, his father's reputation as a man of probity would also be destroyed. John resists this first of several temptations that would break his tie to his "good father" through the "murder" of Fowler Rowntree's identity and character.

The metaphoric intensity of father-son romances is familiar enough, but Updegraff stretches one's willing suspension of disbelief with a further "romance," one that controlled the dealings between Fowler Rowntree and Hustus Lockhart before John's birth and that will continue to fuel the conflict between Lockhart and the younger Rowntree. The question of whose "son" John will prove to be is complicated by the introduction of a "mother" who is not his biological parent and by a piece of paper with the power to dictate the family's fortune.[42]

John's own mother is never mentioned. The only "wife" Fowler Rowntree really had was his beloved Louise, who many years ago rejected him in order to marry Hustus Lockhart. (*Why* the angelic, beauteous Louise rejected Fowler, who was "worshipped" by all who knew him, for Lockhart—morally despicable and physically repellent, yet "worshipped" by his wife—is never explained.) Louise is John's "mother," the woman whom "the good father" never possessed and whom "the bad father" does in a childless marriage.

The plot thickens to the state of viscosity once we learn that, long ago, Fowler Rowntree decided to withhold a damning piece of paper exposing Lockhart's attempt to seize an important patent that was not rightly his. Fowler suppresses this information out of concern that Louise might believe that he, Fowler, seeks revenge against his rival in love. He conceals the paper within the pages of what his son jokingly calls his father's Bible: a 1810 volume titled *Jeffrie's Manual: Being a Survey of the Great Naval Battles from Early Times to Trafalgar; with Victories Where Earned.* Theodore Roosevelt and Henry Adams wrote their own histories of early nineteenth-century naval battles in order to define for themselves the nature of success and public conduct; Fowler and, later, his son John draw upon Jeffrie's account for the same ends.

John chances upon the family secret when he finds three items tucked within *Jeffrie's Manual:* a daguerreotype of Louise, Fowler's written explanation of why he delayed marriage and parenthood until he was past fifty, and a copy of the patent. Possession of the latter document would allow John to win the bitter battle Lockhart wages out of his unceasing hatred for the "son" who had earlier resisted the temptation to sign the contract that would have "combined" their destinies. But John puts aside the second of the temptations placed in his way. He honors the business code of his good father: a code not founded on considerations of capital, surplus value, and productivity; a code for which both father and son have "endured so many business hardships without flinching"; a code inspired both by the feminine ideal emblematized by "this face and that soul that shines" through Louise's portrait and by the masculine principles Jeffrie attributes to the figure of Horatio, Lord Nelson (49:800). The code extracted from early nineteenth-century naval warfare dictates the Rowntree business code of the early twentieth century: you earn victories; you cannot take them; you profit only through suffering and the war against fear.[43]

As the "epic struggle" rages between competing business interests throughout the next eighteen years, John continues to hide the document that would place immediate victory in his hands if he ever chose to reveal it. Only at the end does he bring the good father's document to light, thereby precipitating Lockhart's stroke and death.[44] John Rowntree has played out his role as the good son to the proper father, satisfying the demands of this aspect of the family romance, down to killing off the bad father.

Husbands and Wives

In 1900 John Rowntree is twenty years old, the average American male who will figure as the hero of a business fiction in the main text and as the hero of the filial romance of fathers and sons in the subtext. There is another subtext, however—a domestic romance in which John has to "know" a woman, if only to have a son of his own.

The surface of Updegraff's story is so resolutely masculine that there are very few references to female presences. There is the wraith of Louise; Marthy, the loyal housekeeper and wife of old Mose; and Miss Hammond, the loyal stenographer and go-between. But what about John's "woman"?

We are well into the second installment before Updegraff mentions that, on Sundays and Wednesdays, John regularly "called at a certain house on Walnut Street" (49:248). It is the fifth installment, and 1906, before readers learn that a young woman named Corinne Merriman is the reason for these "regular evenings." As they sit together in the porch hammock, John tells Corinne, "If things continue to look up, maybe some of these days we can begin to talk seriously about 'our day.' (John's ability to even discuss the possibility of marriage is the consequence of his having found a way "to get our gas-stove line under way" [49:678]).)

Three years pass before John permits himself the momentary distractions of domestic bliss, but the moment comes when Corinne lies at the point of death at the birth of John, Junior. When a business associate calls the hospital to inform John that the plant is in danger of being taken over by "wop" agitators, the nurse takes it upon herself to declare, "Business can wait. His wife needs him for the next few hours" (50:92). After this single instance of Corinne's claim upon her husband's attention, she disappears from the story in which she had barely figured. During the final six episodes, John makes an occasional reference to "my wife," and there is a flickering glimpse of Corinne and Little John holding Christmas presents in readiness for one of the rare evenings John is free to spend at home. Clearly whatever part John plays as the key figure in a domestic drama will not take place within his own household.[45]

Corinne's one big moment (reported from offstage) comes during World War I, when she is herself far from home. The reader's attention has been focused upon John's manly battle on the home front as a dollar-a-year man in Washington, D.C., working in league with Bernard Baruch of the War Industries Board to combat greed and inefficiency.[46] It is Walter Knox, John's loyal salesman, who has to inform him that "your wife is a wonder. Running the Red Cross work of the whole country now," and that Little John believes his mother is the image featured on the famous poster captioned "the greatest mother in the world" (50:328).[47] But Corinne's apotheosis as the manager of the Red Cross and mother to the globe (a twentieth-century amplification of the inspiration offered by the angelic Louise) carries little narrative conviction. *That* emotional impact is transferred to John's role as both father and mother of the business world and nurturer of hearthfires.

The Greatest Mother of Them All

It is no accident that the Rowntree firm manufactures stoves and ranges. In the big scene when John resists the temptation to combine with Lockhart in a shady deal that would destroy the memory of his father's integrity (as well as efface his father's name from the company letterhead), he articulates Fowler Rowntree's vision. John uses Thoreauvian terms—vital heat locked in a Manichaean battle with sterile chill—in order to distinguish the captain of principle from the captain of expediency.

"You and I don't speak the same language, any more than you and my father did. He always said you thought of stoves only as so much cold iron to be turned into so much cold cash, while he thought of them in people's homes, cooking their food or warming them and cheering them on cold winter nights." (49:242)

This contest between cold and heat is more than a linguistic or semiotic clash. It places Lockhart's devotion to "facts and figures" over against John's concern for "the people's needs" (the needs of those who produce stoves, those who sell them, and those who buy them). Cold and heat figure both in the subtext of the domestic romance in which John plays the roles of good father and mother and in the main text where he is the hero of "the new business forces."

Businessmen of the 1920s are meant to "keep in touch" with all aspects of a huge business enterprise, but plot details single out the nature of John's one true talent: the marketing of heat and light. What *Captains in Conflict* most wants to say is that the line of work good fathers and mothers do best is to supply the essentials of the happy life to "the little people" living in little houses around the land and sheltered within the workplace of the Rowntree family's factories.

Nurturer of the Hearthfire

Hustus Lockhart, the bad father, conceives his marketing strategies in significantly different ways from the manner in which John Rowntree sells his products, that is, in the name of the good father he emulates and in honor of "the face and the soul" of his true mother. Lockhart targets as his primary buyers men who are buyers of capital, financiers who have to be sold on the idea of the money to be made through stock deals and corporate mergers. To stimulate their desires, he commissions a set of huge photographs of the eleven factories that make up Consolidated, then angrily orders an artist to paint in black smoke and fires belching out of the chimneys, lest the factories look dead, closed down. For Lockhart "smoke means industry" (49:246). But for John and Walter Knox, the simulation of the warm glow of coal or gas that peeps out from a miniature model of the newest Rowntree stove is what inspires the little men who deal directly with the little women in the myriad households needing instruction in how much they want Rowntree products.

Model B—"The Rowntree Radiant"—is the big seller because of the marketing package carefully devised by John and Walter: a small-scale model with the look of a coal fire that leaps forth at the press of an electric switch; "ingenuous little drawings and colored diagrams"; "scientific test results"; and data based on scores of door-to-door calls. Lockhart's painted-in smoke is meant to impress big financial types in big Chicago offices. Rowntree's simulated coal fires stir the little people contacted directly throughout Illinois and Iowa. The former "de-personalizes" financial deals; the latter repersonalizes sales to the consumer (49:390, 392).[48]

John Rowntree identifies his management strategies with those followed by the men he reveres: Lord Nelson and John H. Patterson. Nelson insists that each man must intuit the direction of his leader's thought without having to wait for direct instructions. Patterson emphasizes teaching customers to want products, teaching workers to make the product right, and teaching organizations to cooperate. Nelson and Patterson stand for the leadership of fathers, a model that, in John's version, must also take the mother into account.

John never forgets the home truths he hands to his sales force:

> "We men don't know what a range should be like. I'm going to send you fellows out for a week to knock at back doors and get in women's kitchens. . . . Let them do the talking. Get all the criticism you can, and all the new ideas." (50:86)

John's penchant for going directly to the women in "typical towns" does not always get him data that he as a male can interpret with ease. Does the modern woman of 1912 like "to see fire under [her] pots and griddles," he wonders, or does she want "the luxury of doing everything by just turning a switch or pushing a button" (50:2104)? Marketing psychology is in its infancy; it is not yet all consumed by quantitative analysis and statistical charts. The desires of the populace, viewed as following the law of averages, can only be measured by means of intuition and fellow feeling. John's responses are those of the average male businessman, but he (exceptionally) trusts (and shapes) the needs of women—that mass of averages already in the first stages of being singled out as the greatest factor in the growth of American consumerism.[49]

The "corporate" nature of the two gender models John Rowntree follows is exemplified by the endless rounds he makes through his plants, talking as a father with one small group of men after another.[50] He appeals to their spirit of cooperation, asking each man to cut costs in every step of the production process. If all will work as members of one great family of workers, the Rowntree Stove & Range Company can fulfill its purpose: to act as the good mother by providing heat and light at a "people's price" to the one great family of American consumers. During the years 1875 to 1925, Rowntree manufactures countless models of home tabernacles glowing with vital heat. It is not only appropriate but necessary that the domestic romance running alongside the familial romance proves that

John is the true son of Fowler Rowntree and Louise Lockhart, and that he is father/mother and husband/wife to his workers and his customers. No wonder he has no need of Corinne Merriman.

The Rowntree Stove & Range Company dotes on the rule of averages, which promises the highest good in a land filled with average homes happy in the warmth of their hearthfires. Josiah Royce would have approved of this image: it affirms his philosophy of loyalty and community, and it confirms that homey averages can create a finer tomorrow.

We know better. Neither Royce's vision nor Updegraff's romance of the law of averages came true. But there is a certain truth at the core of *Captains in Conflict* that cannot be overlooked.

First, no matter what Sinclair Lewis achieved by depicting Una Golden, an average little woman who wins success in the business world, Updegraff's John Rowntree proves the better heroine. He not only figures as the successful businessman whom other businessmen of his generation were pleased to recognize as themselves; he is both the mother and the father that Una Golden becomes at the cost of submitting to Walter Babson. In the romances written by Updegraff and Lewis's generation, male averages are more potent than female averages. Male exceptionalism can be truly exceptional, unlike the exceptions grudgingly granted to women who exceed the destiny of most women in the work force.

Second, whatever stories were being written about women's new roles in the well-managed office, their efforts were still statistically weighed in terms of house management. In contrast, the male business of America was viewed as that of managing just about everything: not only the factory and office, but also the affairs of the household. Women were still expected to figure as good mothers in one guise or another, if they were to figure at all. Man, however, got to be both heroes and heroines.

By the 1920s cultural commentators such as Tarbell, Hoerle and Saltzberg, and Lewis attempted to revise previous procedures for telling stories about the new women confronting the new era. Notwithstanding their efforts (often well-meaning, usually lame) to break past inherited narrative forms, melodrama continued to be the mode of choice. What better way to contain social anxieties than by preventing female characters from realizing themselves as heroines, dressing them up (on occasion) as old-time victims or (more frequently) as updated go-betweens. Whatever the setting, factory or office, that space was converted into domestic space. Whatever enterprise the women undertook, it was diminished by the nature of the role they played. In contrast, as Updegraff's "business fiction" indicates through its various subtexts, the twentieth-century male had the protean romance form for the asking—a generous field of force, ready to appropriate for telling stories about the successful management of factory, office, and hearthside, all linked together in a powerful chain of command.

The next field effective managerial principles were to master? The making of ready-made houses and their marketing through the extended outreach of the mail-order catalogue. Henry Ford is the muse of choice, who will help to accelerate the process by which scientifically managed house lives were brought to the masses. Not even John Rowntree can do as much.

House Lives

By 1914 the Model T and the Five-Dollar-Day Plan had made Henry Ford both wealthy and famous. By 1917 he was fast becoming a legend with the aid of mythologizing narratives such as Rose Wilder Lane's *Henry Ford's Own Story,* subtitled "How a Farmer Boy Rose to the Power that Goes with Many Millions yet Never Lost Touch with Humanity."[1] Ford was only forty-six in 1917. He would have thirty years more to live, with the decade of the Ford Motor Company's greatest growth still ahead, but it seemed as though there were no time to waste in getting his model life before the American public.

By 1927 the Ford story was that of a man of untold power, the master of thousands of workers around the nation. What he had wrought is forcefully implied by Charles Sheeler's photograph of the River Rouge plant (figure 3), one of a group used as covers for the company's house organ, *Ford News,* between 1927 and 1931.

Vanity Fair presented Sheeler's "Criss-Crossed Conveyors" to the country at large in February 1928 as part of its series of full-page portraits of American notables. The copy that follows the caption—"By Their Works Ye Shall Know Them"—explains why this powerful geometric form has been substituted for Ford's features.[2] The thrust of the "chutes, elevators and power-house stacks" of the factory, which throw "its shadow across the land," delineates the physical space where employees spend their days turning out endless copies of the grand Idea formulated by "an almost Divine Master-Mind." In turn, *Vanity Fair* notes that the conveyors represent that Mind and its works.

> In hyperbole and anathema [the Ford motor works] has been compared, lyrically, reverently, vindictively, to the central ganglion of our nation, to an American altar of the God-Objective of Mass Pro-

Figure 3. Charles Sheeler, "Criss-Crossed Conveyers" (1927). From the Collections of Henry Ford Museum and Greenfield Village.

duction. But it is simply one man's monument to his own organizing and merchandising genius. . . . Surely Henry Ford, the name or the man, does not seem terrible or fabulous, yet to millions of Americans he is the present-day Colossus of Business, an almost divine Master-Mind. In a landscape where size, quantity and speed are the cardinal virtues, it is natural that the largest factory turning out the most cars in the least time should come to have the quality of America's Mecca, toward which the pious journey for prayer.

"How a Farmer Boy Rose to the Power that Goes with Many Millions yet Never Lost Touch with Humanity"

Vanity Fair, the big city sophisticate, comments from on high about what the American masses—"the pious"—consider sacred works and sanctified places. Together caption, text, and Sheeler photograph form a trademark "celebrity" portrait, one that keeps readers in the know by supplying them with new topics for chic social chat. Quite a different approach was taken the following year when the United Automobile Workers of America abetted the publication of *The Flivver King: A Story of Ford-America* by Upton Sinclair. Eschewing the flippancy of *Vanity Fair, The Flivver King* turns its frontispiece over to the sober query:

> What is Henry Ford? What have the years done to him? What has his billion dollars made of him? Here is the man, and the story of his life. Here also are his workers, a family of them over a period of three generations. What has the billion dollars done to *them?*[3]

The negative answers found in Sinclair's drama of the average man and his family ("the pious" gulled by the "Colossus" to their ruin) coincide with the response Reinhold Niebuhr gives to his own query of 1926, "How Philanthropic Is Henry Ford?" Together, Sinclair and Niebuhr rebuke what the Niebuhr finds is the "universal and inveterate habit of humanity to invest its heroes with moral qualities . . . and to insist *that the big man is also a good man.*"[4]

Back in 1917, when the legend of Henry Ford is in the making, the "divine Master-Mind" behind the yet-to-be-built River Rouge plant still wears a human face. Through the attention Rose Wilder Lane's biography lavishes upon the early days of the "farmer boy," Ford's business enterprise is thoroughly domesticated, made palatable for "the millions." The man is still life-sized, in "touch with humanity," his rise to future greatness keyed to the little house on Detroit's Edison Avenue where Clara Ford hovers by his side.[5] Lane's narrative provides the prelude to the painterly

rendition of "Henry Ford and Clara at Kitchen Sink" set down years later
by Irving Bacon (see figure 4), the Ford Motor Company's official lim-
ner—a domestic idyll in which the mythic male occupies, however briefly,
the homey work space of the woman's domain.[6]

Lane's account begins where it must. It attributes Ford's managerial
genius to Mary Ford, the "energetic, wholesome Holland Dutch wife" of
William Ford, mother of Henry and three other children, and mistress of
a large farm that took on twenty to thirty extra hands at harvesting time.
"All those tasks Mary Ford did, or superintended, efficiently, looking to
the ways of her household with all the care and pride her husband had in
managing the farm" (5). Mary dies, and the family has to be managed by
someone else, first by a married aunt and then by Henry Ford's youngest
sister, Margaret, who had to keep

> the house in order and superintend the work of hired girls older than
> herself. She was "capable"—that good New England word so much
> more expressive than "efficient"—but no one could take Mary
> Ford's place in that home. There was now nothing to hold Henry on
> the farm. (14)

After a stint in Detroit, Henry marries Clara Bryant in 1888. For a
time they live back on the farm, where Henry and a gang of men build the
house of Clara's dreams: "a good, substantial, Middle-Western home, 32
× 32 feet and containing seven rooms and a roomy attic" (48). Clara was
content in "that little country community" (49). She "kept the house running smoothly" while Henry managed the family farm (51). "His mechanical, orderly mind arranged the work so that it was done smoothly,
and on time, without overworking any one or leaving any one idle" (50).
But Henry becomes restless. In 1891 he informs Clara of his decision to
return to Detroit to pursue his dream of perfecting a horseless carriage, to
be built at a price that would make it available to the many.

> After her first protest Mrs. Ford accepted the situation and set her-
> self with what philosophy she might to packing her linen and wrap-
> ping the furniture. She had no great interest in the gasoline engine
> —machinery in general was to her merely something greasy and
> whirring, to hold her skirts away from—but if Henry was going to
> Detroit, of course she was going, too, and she might as well be
> cheerful about it. (64)

Here, in more detail, is Rose Wilder Lane's description of "the little
woman" who would do the right thing to insure that her husband would
become America's legendary "Colossus."

Figure 4. Irving Bacon, "Henry Ford and Clara at Kitchen Sink" (1938). From the Collections of Henry Ford Museum and Greenfield Village.

The rosy, teasing country girl who had kept Henry Ford from his beloved machines nearly five years before . . . had developed into a cheerful, capable little housewife—the kind of woman whose place is in the home because there she does her best work.

She could never invent a gasoline engine, but she was an ideal person to take care of Henry Ford while he did it, to keep the house clean and comfortable, cook good meals, cheer him a bit when he was depressed and never have "nerves." (64)

Up to a point all goes well. Husband and wife have separate workplaces to manage with calm assurance. But, alas, there comes the occasion when Clara Ford does have "nerves." One evening while her husband is in his toolshed behind the little house on Edison Avenue, fiddling with machinery after his workday at the Edison plant, the pregnant Clara flares up.[7]

It is not just any evening in 1893. Modern life will be changed forever in a matter of moments. It is the mythic day that will make industrial history and shake the nation's business enterprise to its foundation. Nonetheless, Lane carefully sets up the scene as a crisis in the domestic drama between a woman wed to the intertwined notions of house, home, and the good American life and a man whose invention will alter those notions almost beyond recognition.

Tears, almost hysterics, from the woman who . . . had been the quiet, cheerful little wife humming to herself while she did the housework—it was more than startling, it was terrifying.

Ford realized then, probably for the first time, how much the making of the automobile had cost her. (86)

Henry quiets Clara with the promise that he will put aside his work on the gasoline engine, that they will return to the family farm.

He took her into the house and made her a cup of hot tea. When she was sitting comfortably warming her feet at the heating stove and sipping the tea, he said he would just run out and fasten the shed door for the night. (86)

Inside Clara's kitchen all is warm. Outside it is raining and the toolshed is cold, but Henry lingers on, caught up once more in the workings of his machine.

He forgot about his wife, waiting in the house. . . . At midnight he was still working. . . . At 3 o'clock, grimy, hollow-cheeked, absorbed, he was hard at work when he felt a hand on his arm and heard his wife say, "Henry!" (87–88)

Clara has left her snug little house to come out to her man's workplace, to tell him,

> "I got to thinking—Henry, we mustn't go back to the farm.
> It was just a notion of mine. I guess I was tired, or something.
> I've changed my mind. We'd better stay right here till you get the
> machine finished."
> He laughed.
> "Well, little woman, I guess that won't be so very long. It's fin-
> ished right now." (88)

Within minutes Ford steps into the car. "Then, in the first Ford automobile, he rode away from the old shed," through the dark night where the "rain was falling in torrents" (89).

Lane's telling shapes the Ford legend from materials assembled from the tradition of the virtuous domestic romance—interchangeable parts that still appealed to a large segment of the American public, whose own notions of household arrangements were soon to feel the consequences of the automotive age. All the pieces for the assemblage are in place: the hard work expected of the average man who is also the all-American genius with the force to make exceptions; the loyalty of the "capable" and cheerful "little woman" who puts aside her (infrequent) bursts of rebellion (here called "hysterics") in order to hasten to her husband's side; the sequence of familiar home settings—from the substantial farmhouse in the rural landscape to the cozy bungalow in the industrial city—where soon the River Rouge plant with its criss-crossed conveyors will throw "its shadow across the land."

In contrast to the language *Vanity Fair* calls upon to project a sleekly rendered metal Moloch reminiscent of a DeMille cinematic epic, and also in contrast to the homey phrases of Lane's kitchen aesthetic, another kind of discourse is already in place by 1915, a discourse that will present business myths to the hardheaded masculine world of company office and workplace. With what ease this language appears to offer transparent expression to transparent answers, as when taking on the question posed by all mythic types, "What is Henry Ford?"

> Henry Ford's character is extremely simple and extremely easy
> to read; he is perfectly frank, is wholly self-reliant, is extremely af-
> fectionate and confiding by nature, is absolutely sure he is right in
> every wish, impulse and fancy, places no value whatever on money
> and has a passion for working in metals. . . . He has no sense of
> personal importance, meets his factory heads on terms of absolute
> and even deferential comradeship, and because he had, up to about

his thirty-fifth year, an intimate personal knowledge of day-wage life, his strong natural impulse to aid his workmen and bring some chance of happiness into their lives takes the form of increasing day-pay and shortening labor-hours of his own notion.[8]

This is the "professional" view, projected by a new breed of "business writers" who write blunt and unsentimental accounts for such journals as *The Engineering Magazine* (soon to be retitled *Industrial Management,* in part because of the success men like Ford had at making engineering a matter of management). Still, the "domestic" view Lane proposes (evident in portions of Horace Lucien Arnold and Fay Leone Faurote's *Ford Methods and The Ford Shops* as well) influences an even wider readership, made up of men as well as women, that likes its industrial folk heroes to represent home values as well as business values. For are not the two ultimately the same? Robert Updegraff claimed this fact for his hero John Rowntree in 1926, but Henry Ford's company had already confirmed its truth by 1915. Ford management was not just in the business of manufacturing family cars; its Sociological Department had authorized an all-purpose working model for the domestic romance, with which its thousands of workers were expected to comply.

The complex relationship between the Ford Motor Company and its employees, its employees and Americanism, Americanism and good conduct in factory and at home, between the right kind of housing and correct patterns of productivity at work: these concerns come together in *Helpful Hints and Advice to Employees,* the official code of conduct exacted of the Ford Man and his family. With this little manual we go from Henry and Clara's little house on Edison Avenue to all the good little houses occupied by all good Ford employees.

Printed in 1915, the same year Arnold and Faurote lauded the company's management of the factory environment, *Helpful Hints* defines correct house lives. Company practice codifies the principles that Lane's domestic tale asserts had been in the "divine Master-Mind" from the start, principles that had evolved from the influence exerted upon Henry Ford by Mary, Margaret, and Clara—those "capable" women managers of the Ford hearthfires, who sustained the man whose genius encompassed house space, toolshed, and the River Rouge.

Purportedly, *Helpful Hints and Advice to Employees* abjures the company as paterfamilias, acting as both hero and heroine to his dutiful children. The preface promises: "No rules or regulations, of a general nature, are employed. Each individual is given a chance to work out the very best condition for himself."[9] But our skepticism in regard to the worker's freedom of choice creeps in when we read the regulations outlined in the section "Home Comforts and Sanitation." Specifically targeted for rigorous control are the deplorable habits of "those of foreign birth," namely, their desire to crowd "the house with roomers and boarders," their predilection for "dark, ill-ventilated and foul-smelling" rooms, and their disregard of the cardinal virtue of cleanliness practiced by "the most advanced people."

> The Company expects employes [*sic*] to improve their living conditions, make their homes clean and comfortable, provide wholesome surroundings, good air and light, and to keep their households for themselves and immediate families.

The ignorant foreigner is the main obstacle to the Ford plan to inculcate the habits that had come naturally to the likes of Mary, Margaret, and Clara Ford. With this in mind, the company throws itself enthusiastically into the "Americanization" of its workers. The original raw material might be a Russian family like the one photographed in 1917 (figure 5). This material is passed through the assembly line of the American School for male wage earners, the final product dipped quite literally into a giant "melting pot" on graduation day (figure 6).[10] The metamorphosis that transpires affects not only the clothes and manners of the newly formed American but also his house life. A Ford manual entitled *Helpful Hints and Advice to Employees* illustrates the before-and-after stages of one dwelling place on its way to becoming the right and proper signature of "The Ford Man" and his family (figure 7).

Standardized "Records of Investigation"—compiled by teams of inspectors from the Sociological Department in the years prior to 1921—itemize data substantiating the presence or absence of well-managed house lives.[11] One such form scrutinizes the household of James O'Brien, paint shop foreman of the Minneapolis branch, with information supplied on the spot by Mrs. Mary O'Brien, labeled as "Wife." The single sheet of the inspectors' form covers a great deal of information: religion, savings passbook number, length of time in the U.S., number of children and their ages, value of house, name of family doctor, recreational activities, general conduct. At the end, the company man pens in his summation, deduced from the empirical evidence at hand.

> A small house on the outskirts of town. All neat and clean. She looks prim. They look thrifty, live happily. The yard is in nice shape. Plants all covered. You can see they take an interest in what they have and care for it.[12]

Workers across the nation *not* employed by the Ford Motor Company with its standardized principles for proper house lives often lived under deplorable conditions. Either their often-squalid living spaces were com-

Figure 5. Russian family (1917). From the Collections of Henry Ford Museum and Greenfield Village.

pletely controlled, as in the notorious "company towns," or workers had to struggle on their own to better their living conditions in the face of their employers' indifference.[13] Upton Sinclair's portrayal of the scams perpetrated by realtors against the immigrants pouring into Chicago's Packingtown area is one of the best-known narratives of the heartrending split between the promise of the American Dream House and the brutal actuality but it was not the only story waiting to be expressed.[14]

For Bread with Butter, a recent study of immigrant workers in the Pennsylvania mining area, records other sad tales from the early decades of the twentieth century, tales whose endings might in time turn out well enough, after a fashion. A young Serb named Nikola first comes to Johnstown in 1905. His pilgrim's progress follows a typical pattern: arrival in America, where he moves in with relatives in a boardinghouse; a brief trip back to Europe; return to Pennsylvania in 1910, once he realizes that life in Serbia entails even greater poverty than life in America; marriage in 1918 and crowding in with in-laws; after further struggles, a house of his own in 1926; eventually, the ability to have electricity, water in the house, food on the table, a radio, and the chance to dress "nice, American."[15]

If these stories were to end (even relatively) well, work lives, house lives, and "nice, American" lives required close attention to personal management. Only then might happy myths appear to beat out hard realities.

Designs for the Dream

Taylor had concentrated upon the man as laborer and, to some extent, as citizen. He paid no attention to the house environment to which the scientifically managed worker returned at night. In contrast, up to the 1920s the Ford Sociological Department insisted upon the tight fit between laborer, citizen, and homeowner, although it stopped short of sending ready-made Ford houses through the assembly line. It was the designers of ready-made houses who aspired to emulate Ford's formula for the rapid assembly of standardized components rolling off the line on a mass scale.

There was never a direct translation from Model T dream car to Model T dream house.[16] Nevertheless, all the components of the tripartite logic Fordism bequeathed to American house ideology were in place: (1) the good worker as the good family man (or the ambitious bachelor about to become one); (2) the good family abiding by the "American" model for the virtuous life; (3) the American model predicated upon ownership of one's own little house—modest perhaps, but tidy, clean, and warmed by the vital heat of acceptable conduct (and most likely a "Rowntree Radiant").

To implement the standardization of one element in this basic triad was to attempt the standardization of all three: the worker, the citizen, the single-family home. For generations the business of supplying house designs (diagrams printed in manuals or blueprints purchasable for nominal sums) convertible into material fact by client or local carpenter had been part of the American building scene. The concepts that lay behind the material designs—the republican family as efficient worker, dutiful citizen, and happy homeowner—had almost as long a lineage, and, as with any variation on the American Dream, as troubled a history.[17]

Merely to name a few points along this continuum is to retell much of American history: the open continent, which Congress laid out in grids in 1785; the Homestead Act of 1862, which rationalized the parceling of land for settlement; the segmenting of farm land into suburban vistas; the growth of the Garden City concept in the 1890s. In every instance, the

Figure 6. Graduation, Highland Park English School (1916).

From the Collections of Henry Ford Museum and Greenfield Village.

*A Ford employe's home before the inauguration of the profit-sharing plan,
January 12th, 1914*

*Four months after receiving a share of the profits an addition was built,
doubling the size of the house*

22

Figure 7. Ford Motor Company, *Helpful Hints and Advice to Employees* (1915).

The same employe's present quarters, fourteen months after receiving a share of the profits

show the dependent, is from infancy up until the age of 20 years. The formative period is from 20 to 30 years. The accumulative period is from 30 to 45 years. The efficiency period is from 45 to 55 years. The retrograde, or backward, period is from 55 to 65 years. Finally, comes the dependent period from 65 and on. It would therefore seem that these facts would lead any thoughtful person to the conclusion that a system of saving should be started early in life, in order that the greatest yield or returns from his savings or investment will fall to him when his earning capacity is on the decline, to avoid being dependent on others.

The Ford Motor Company is sharing the profits of its business with its employes so as to enable them to put by something for emergencies and old age.

A double purpose is served under the profit-sharing plan. First, to provide money for future needs; second, to foster self-control. The second is the more important of the two, because, having that, the first is quite assured.

The savings of an individual are pretty much the measure of his self-control. George Washington said, "Economy makes happy homes and sound nations; instill it deep." Abraham Lincoln said, "Economy is one of the first virtues. It begins with saving money." Bismarck said, "Saving leads to security, happiness and good citizenship. It makes men, while extravagance makes vicious and worthless members of society."

23

notion of planned spaces occupied by good families, right conduct, and efficient house space collides with all that is unplanned, sprawling, unfenced, and uncontrolled. The will of the planners was not to be denied, whether they set about designing farm buildings in middle Virginia, little houses on the prairie, or the cliff dwellings of the modern city.[18]

A plan for the "Prairie Cottage" (figure 8) is recommended in John Bullock's 1854 manual, *The American Cottage Builder: A Series of Designs, Plans, and Specifications from $200 to $20,000. For Homes for the People*. This hut of unburnt brick, intended for "settlers on the prairies in the Western States," is similar in size and kind (though not in materials or location) to the design proposed by another house-plan book published that same year, Thoreau's *Walden,* which also addressed the moral and material economy required of all who "confront" American frontiers.[19]

Three years later, Calvert Vaux's highly popular *Villas and Cottages* included a design for a log house nestled in a forest clearing (figure 9). Vaux's plan is not intended as a primitive space "in which a family of men, women, and children eat, drink, sleep, wash, dress and undress all together."[20] This plan will be adopted because it appeals to the American sense of beauty, utility, and moral character.[21] Recommended "for a well-to-do settler and his family," Vaux's plan is closer in scale to the living needs of Twain's Grangerfords than to Cooper's Ishmael Bush and his slatternly clan; in its ascetic purity and minimalist aesthetic aspirations, it is nearer to Thoreau's hut than to Bullock's prairie cottage. Dreams of rustic virtue continued into the twentieth century in the form of Rudolf Schindler's 1916 prototype for a summer house, one that swerves away from Frank Lloyd Wright's own Prairie House plans because of the literalism with which the Viennese expatriate held to the material appearance of log construction (figure 10).[22] Even so, by the 1890s log cabin life was no longer held up to the true American family as the ideal.

George F. Barber's *The Cottage Souvenir,* No. 2, originated in Knoxville surrounded by the majestic mountains of Tennessee. Barber insists in his preface that Southern states require different house plans than other regions. Such needs "cannot be described" and the "true principles cannot be shown" since the folkways of Southern house life exceed the materiality of construction.[23] Two photographs, which Barber captions "Uncle Tom's Cabin" and "Old Cabin Home," point to the difference between house plans intended for middle-class Southern whites and the actual dwellings of the Southern blacks.

Barber explains why he includes references, both visual and verbal, to Negro cabins: they serve as "contrasted architecture" to any of his own designs, such as No. 36 (figure 11). Mountain cabins are shown "for their oddity and picturesqueness. The contrast between these two houses and

CHAPTER IV.

PRAIRIE COTTAGE.

THIS DESIGN is for a cottage of unburnt brick, and is peculiarly adapted to settlers on the prairies in the Western States.

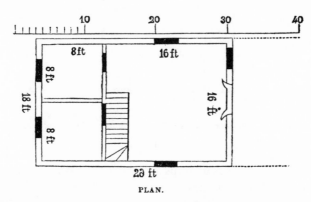

PLAN.

The above is the ground plan. The dotted lines show in what direction the building should be extended.

Figure 8. Prairie Cottage. From John Bullock, *The American Cottage Builder* (1854).

DESIGN FOR A LOG-HOUSE.

Figure 9. Design for a log-house. From Calvert Vaux, *Villas and Cottages* (1857).

those on the following pages gives us an idea of the advancement of modern architecture in this country."

Pattern books addressed to aspiring American families of the 1890s have no place for primitive houses designed for new settlers drawn from civilized races—not if they are whites, nor if they are blacks who raise themselves above their racial primitivism. Barber's reference to the "Old Cabin Home" style is used to highlight the modernity of his house plans. The same style also furnishes proof of the merits of Virginia's Hampton Institute.

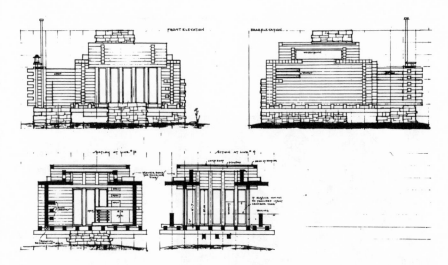

Figure 10. Rudolph M. Schindler, prototype for a log-house (1916).

Taken from the collection of forty-four photographs Frances Benjamin Johnston assembled during the years 1899–1900, figures 12 and 13 contrast "The Old-Time Cabin" with "A Hampton Graduate's Home." Writing of this pairing in his introduction to the 1966 publication of *The Hampton Album* by the Museum of Modern Art (temple of the American design ethos), Lincoln Kirstein observed:

> But with what relish does [Johnston] turn her page to show the triumphant advance of progress, this new dispensation of freedmen, in their decent, neat, immaculately hygienic homes, frozen as in habitat groups, almost, but not quite entirely—believable.[24]

Johnston's photographs rehearse the before and after modes for living available to the Southern black fortunate enough to receive training "for the sake not only of self-support and industrial labor but also for the sake of character." In similar ways, the Ford Motor Company emblematized the "almost, but not quite entirely-believable" making of Americans by contrasting the rude Russian family with the "good" Ford house in which the transformed "Americanized" Ford family lives. Nevertheless, too many lives were not making it into the pattern books underwritten by the American success story. Too many were left stranded in other forms of "planned housing."

In 1857 Calvert Vaux had pointed obliquely to the kind of house life

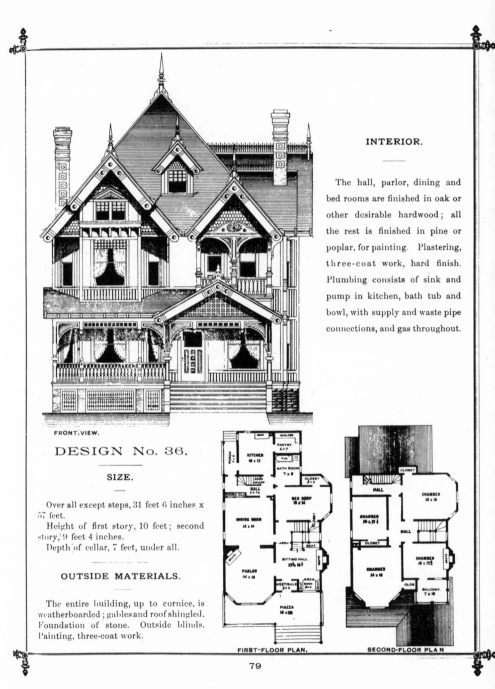

INTERIOR.

The hall, parlor, dining and bed rooms are finished in oak or other desirable hardwood; all the rest is finished in pine or poplar, for painting. Plastering, three-coat work, hard finish. Plumbing consists of sink and pump in kitchen, bath tub and bowl, with supply and waste pipe connections, and gas throughout.

FRONT VIEW.

DESIGN No. 36.

SIZE.

Over all except steps, 31 feet 6 inches x 57 feet.

Height of first story, 10 feet; second story, 9 feet 4 inches.

Depth of cellar, 7 feet, under all.

OUTSIDE MATERIALS.

The entire building, up to cornice, is weatherboarded; gables and roof shingled. Foundation of stone. Outside blinds. Painting, three-coat work.

FIRST-FLOOR PLAN.   SECOND-FLOOR PLAN

Figure 11. House design. From George F. Barber, *The Cottage Souvenir* (1891).

Figure 12. Frances B. Johnston, "The Old-Time Cabin" (1899–1900). Collection of The Museum of Modern Art, New York; gift of Lincoln Kirstein. Reproduced by permission.

his log cabin was *not* meant to accommodate: men, women, children eating, sleeping, working, dressing, and undressing in one confined room—brutal evidence of the American Dream gone wrong. But by the 1850s the urban tenement had already taken on that nightmare form. In fact, the tenement could be traced back to the early 1800s, when once sturdy middle-class, single-family urban dwellings began to be sliced up into smaller and smaller units, housing more and more people, resulting in the randomly arranged, inhumanly packed warrens of the mid-nineteenth-century city scene.[25]

Jacob Riis and other urban reformers shocked their native-born audiences with the fact that New York City (purportedly the world's most advanced civilization) had neighborhoods that rivaled Bombay (representative of primitive Asian culture) in population density. In the hands of

Figure 13. Frances. B. Johnston, "A Hampton Graduate's Home" (1899–1900). Collection of The Museum of Modern Art, New York; gift of Lincoln Kirstein. Reproduced by permission.

the speculators, "planning" led to profit, not morality. It meant packing every meter of horizontal space, while projecting verticals whose novelty in the 1890s was not entirely compensated for by the presence of Otis elevators, pride of the skyscraper, that monument to modern American technology.

Many members of the urban middle class hardly believed they were faring much better than the tenement dwellers of 1890 and 1895 pictured in figures 14 and 15. Charles Dana Gibson's 1897 sketch, "The Streets of New York" (figure 16) is a chillingly accurate representation (then and now) of life at street level. Henry Fuller's 1893 novel, *The Cliff-Dwellers,* is another disturbing portrayal of apartment angst (then and now) in which everyone, female and male, who occupies the Clifton, a Chicago apartment complex, is affected by one degree of neurasthenia or another (figures 17 and 18).

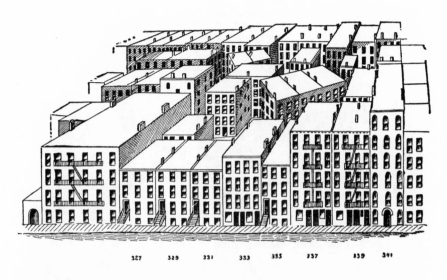

Figure 14. Charles Wingate, "Bird's Eye View of an East Side Tenement Block" (1890). From Jacob Riis, *How the Other Half Lives* (1901 edition).

What was the way out? The editors of *The Masses* thought that perhaps Edgar S. Chambless had an answer in 1911. Chambless appealed to fellow socialists to agree that "hasty, ill-considered, haphazard living centers must go," to be replaced by "the form and structure of the rational, co-operative dwellings of the future." [26] Three striking features distinguish Chambless's perfected city: (1) a single street extending "more than a thousand miles in length"; (2) an indoor railroad connecting one end of Roadtown to the other and the elimination of the new gasoline-driven automobile; (3) no separate houses owned by single families.

In one stroke, Chambless's socialist dream for Americans denies the sturdy "republican" tradition of the single-family house and the use of privately owned modes of transportation. Yet Chambless's concepts of construction and maintenance were based on the principles of collectivism, standardization, and rationalization currently employed by the new automobile industry and the ready-made house business. In common with his capitalist adversaries, this fervent socialist shared a belief in the means by which efficient service is conveyed to the greater American public.

The Roadtown monolith never left the realm of the printed page in 1911. Neither did Rudolf Schindler's log house of 1916. But unbuilt uto-

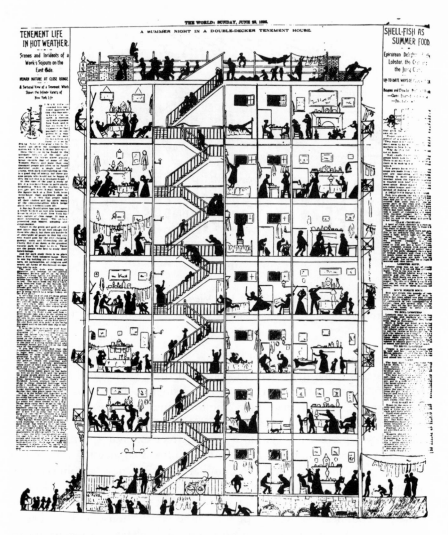

Figure 15. "Tenement Life in Hot Weather." From *The New York World* (1895).

pian models for house or city are not the focus here. What counts are the concepts and dreams for the single-family house that actually found their way into material forms of wood, brick, and stucco, whether or not those concepts and dreams provided fully adequate solutions for the historical moment. What also matters is that one of the consequences of creating "built America" was the construction of even more new narratives, narratives in which women figure as the heroine-managers of work spaces they have wrenched away from the John Rowntrees and the Henry Fords of the business and industrial world.

Taylorizing Women's House Space

The Roadtown scheme was but one attempt to bring order to the runaway complexities of modern living conditions. Taylorism and Fordism were committed to rationalizing and simplifying the materials, the tools, the human element, and the working environment in the shop and the office. The success of scientific management procedures was gauged according to how well the exactions of standardization and functionality were met. One of the most striking outcomes of the scientific management imperative in the first decades of the twentieth-century was the application of these methods and expectations to the management of household activities and the designing of efficient house space. It was claimed that, guided by sound management principles, the simple (read as "good," read as "moral") American life might be attained: externalized in well-managed house structures and internalized in republican virtues.

What exactly is "the simple life" that would be made manifest through rationally controlled house lives? The standardized plans for the farmhouses and outbuildings built throughout rural Virginia in the 1700s are completely unlike the elegance of Monticello, yet the mutual attention Jefferson and the anonymous farmers paid to rationality and functionality made them richly related. Downing's and Vaux's house plans, which extol the simple life enjoyed by both industrious mechanic and successful merchant, jumble together class demarcations, machine techniques, handwork, national pride, aesthetic properties, and moral pieties. Frank Lloyd Wright designs rational, functional, and breathtakingly sophisticated homes in the "prairie" style for wealthy clients, but he also expends time formulating Usonian models intended to bring sane living to the general public. Not only did the American Arts and Crafts movement of the early 1900s send out mixed signals,[27] so did the two-way path toward simplicity later taken by Richard Neutra in Los Angeles and by Le Corbusier and Walter Gropius in Europe, architects highly conscious of the relation of "scientifically" executed housing plans to complex ideological principles and economic needs.[28]

The idea of house plans and house lives designed to celebrate scientifically managed simplicity is ambiguous enough. We find even deeper contradictions once we consider how male and female roles were played out across the surface of these patterned houses.

In 1876 Frank Lloyd Wright's parents attended the Centennial Expo-

Figure 16. Charles Dana Gibson, "The Streets of New York." From *Life* (New York, 1897).

sition in Philadelphia. While there, Wright's mother visited the display devoted to Friedrich Froebel, celebrated as the Father of the Kindergarten, and came away with a set of Froebel building blocks for her seven-year-old son. Years later Wright wrote that these blocks pointed him toward his career as one of the country's preeminent designers of functional architecture for a modern machine age.[29]

One path traced by historians of builder's plans and/or architectural designs into the early 1900s goes straight from a children's sampler, which abstracts the blocklike house of the man who made building blocks part of his program for the training of impressionable young minds (figure 19)[30] to the imaginative development of the boy who would grow up to destroy the traditional block-shaped, box-sided house with elegantly iconoclastic structural arrangements. But if we follow this path keeping gender issues in mind, we raise other issues and ask different questions: (1) The schematized house sampler, featured in *The Woman's Book* to be "outlined in worsted by the children," is surely an act of commemoration executed by girls. (2) Anna Lloyd-Jones Wright brings her son Froebel blocks, and the boy grows up to become a dominant force in a profession

Figure 17. T. De Thulstrup, "She pressed him back into the depths of his great easy-chair." From Henry Fuller, *The Cliff-Dwellers* (1893).

Figure 18. T. De Thulstrup, "Then she fell back weakly and coughed violently." From Henry Fuller, *The Cliff-Dwellers* (1893).

April, 21, 1782

Figure 19. Card of Froebel's birthplace to be outlined in worsted by children in memory of the Father of the Kindergarten. From *The Woman's Book,* vol. 1 (1894).

largely dominated by men.[31] (3) Little girls stitch house images or play house mother while little boys construct houses with blocks—conventional gender roles borne out by figure 20, a tableau photographed circa 1900.

The business success of the Rowntree Stove & Range Company, which Updegraff writes up in the form of a domestic romance, points up the dual gender roles John Rowntree assumes, but in the end it is males like Rowntree who oversee the manufacture of cooking and heating equipment, as well as the radiators used in "cozy homes" where little girls learn to be little mothers (figure 21). Clara Ford shares the kitchen she keeps neat and tidy with her husband, who, using it as an annex to the toolshed, will perfect the automotive technology that will render American house lives less simple than they once had been thought to be. There was one area, however, in which women were encouraged to become their own scientific management experts, and, naturally, it was Frederick Winslow Taylor who was singled out as their inspiration.

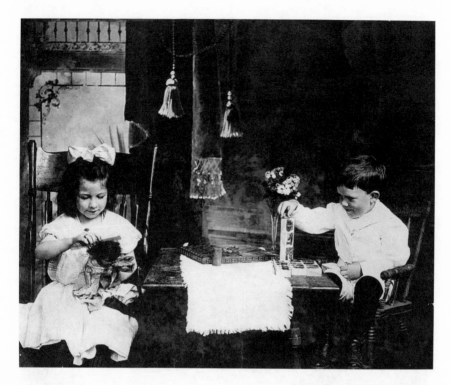

Figure 20. C. H. Anderson, boy and girl at play (c. 1900). Library of Congress.

By the second decade of the twentieth century, the principles of rationalization and standardization had been brought into factory lives and office lives; they also had made their way forcefully into women's space through the highly publicized introduction of Taylorism into the home.[32] The year the Columbian Exposition of 1893 touted the new academic disciplines of "domestic science" and "home economics" was the same year Henry Ford demonstrated the gasoline engine to Clara, his angel-in-the-house.[33] It was also the year Helen Campbell declared, in *The Easiest Way in Housekeeping and Cooking,* that before women could indulge themselves in the luxury of referring to intangible ideals of "home," they had to analyze the material facts of the house according to current methods of work management. Campbell compared what women did inside the house to what men did in the outside world of work. Skills expected of "the typesetter, the cabinet-maker, or carpenter"—men whose productivity depended upon their "ability to make each motion tell"—must now be transferred into the kitchen, "the housekeeper's workshop."[34]

Figure 21. Jessie Wilcox Smith, "Cosy Homes" (1910s). Library of Congress.

In 1893 it was novel to describe female housework in terms of skills required by the masculine work world, but Campbell restricts her references to manual craftswork. Within twenty years (the same time it took for Taylor's experiments in the metals industry to be carried over into the general industrial process) it became common to describe American houses as "the most scientifically planned of those in any country" and American housekeepers as "women skilled in managing the machinery of the house so that it runs easily, smoothly, and with least effort." [35] Women were now viewed as being masters of the modern machine, not of the preindustrial hand tool.

In 1893 Taylorism was no more than the shadowy yet unnamed idea hovering behind whatever attention was paid to the women who were beginning to incorporate "industrializing" skills into the domestic sphere. By 1914, however, Christine Frederick places the Father of Scientific Management front and center in *The New Housekeeping: Efficiency Studies in Home Management*, a book written with missionary fervor to inform all women how the "gospel of efficiency" might release them to a "higher life"—a happier existence freed from "drudgifying housework" and marked by "individuality and independence." [36]

Initially Frederick had been "only" a housewife and mother, but in 1910 she launched upon a public career by installing the Applecroft Home Experiment Station in her Long Island home. [37] As the newly appointed consulting household editor for *Ladies' Home Journal*, she wrote a series of four articles in 1912 that probed what "the new science of work was accomplishing for the office, the shop, the factory" and how it "could also be applied to my group of very unorganized industries—the home" (viii). *The New Housekeeping* (the collection of her articles) was quickly followed in 1915 by *Household Engineering: Scientific Management in the Home*. Founder of the League of Advertising Women, Frederick later won fame in 1929 with *Selling Mrs. Consumer*, her (admiring) assessment of woman's role as buyer. But it is her early championship of Taylorism for home consumption that merits our attention here, especially the adroit way she sets up her argument through a series of well-seasoned narrative ploys.

The New Housekeeping is a no-nonsense book that practices what it preaches about the efficient use of time and effort, yet it opens slowly with a homely little tale whose tone contrasts strikingly with what will follow. Frederick considers it necessary to convey what it felt like at that memorable moment when her isolated world of "drudgifying" housework was first penetrated by news coming to her from the outside, productive world of male management.

Like a latter-day Marmee March, Frederick is seated at her mending after a wearying day of home chores, half listening while her husband and his friend Watson talk over male matters. But when she hears the men "use several new words and phrases so often," she stops to listen. " 'Efficiency,' I heard our caller say a dozen times; 'standard practice,' 'motion study,' and 'scientific management,' he repeated over and over again." (3).

Unlike the Clara Ford whom Lane portrays as a woman who takes no interest in her husband's work life, Frederick "grew absorbed and amazed" (3). She begins to ask questions about a managerial approach to life, an approach that at first "sounds like a fairy tale" (5). Over the next hour her responses change markedly. Words descriptive of her feelings range from "skeptically" and "bantering" to "heatedly" and "eagerly." She inquires further into the mystery of how males manage the new era in new ways. She wants to know whether "you smart men and efficiency experts will soon try to tell me and all the other women that washing dishes can be 'standardized' " (6). In the end, she "concluded a little triumphantly" that "the principles of scientific management could be applied in the home" (8). The dissatisfied housewife has experienced a conversion as powerful as that experienced by Jurgis Rudkus. Knowing now what it means to answer the call "Organize, organize!" she announces the laws of her own revolution: "I won't have you men doing all the great and noble things! I'm to find out how these experts conduct investigations, and all about it, and then apply it to *my* factory, *my* business, *my* home" (10).

At this point fairy tale becomes treatise, muted domestic despair becomes utopian narrative of hope. Frederick's further method of attack is commensurate with the time-motion work forms filled out by Taylor's crew of management engineers. She discards the language of wonderment and magic, and immerses her readers in a world of scientific fact shaped by a prose style appropriate to her new mission. Yet it is important that Frederick began as she did with a scene of the wife silently bent over her basket of mending, repressing frustration over her lot; the husband and friend talking man talk beyond her sphere; then the wife awakening to the marvels of male management techniques that will allow her to control her material household existence as well as enter upon a professional career *out there* in the man's world.

Consider the tale Rose Wilder Lane told about Clara Ford. Clara the good wife remains forever fixed as an essential ingredient in the mythologizing of Henry Ford's achievements as industrial genius. In contrast, Christine Frederick productively utilizes a moment to recall the little woman she once was in order to banish that figure for all time from her treatise on "efficiency studies in home management."

For the sake of instructive comparison, let us briefly recall the look and feel of "the little woman" held within the roseate glow beautifying traditional house lives in nineteenth-century America. Since we already know how Lane memorialized the kitchen moment in which an earlier industrial age was transformed into the new without altering the woman's role acquiescently played by Clara Ford, we can turn to a man from "the old times," who is in the process of lovingly describing "my home, an ideal." [38]

Here are two kitchen scenes. The first, composed by Oliver Bell Bunce in 1884, is full of male nostalgia; the second, by Christine Frederick in 1914, briskly takes on the present. First, Bunce:

> I confess to no knowledge whatever of the economy or the necessities of the kitchen: but ignorance of the labors and the processes that pertain to this mysterious laboratory does not prevent me from realizing the possible felicities of such a place . . . which gentlewomen can enter with self-respect, comfort, and pleasure.
>
> The kitchen in my house . . . is well lighted . . . [and the] low, broad windows are embowered by vines and flowers. . . . There is a pleasant porch which opens into the orchard. . . . The floor is of hard wood, stained a mahogany color, and brightened with a few gay carpet-rugs. The hearth is very ample, and for a considerable space before it the floor is paved with tiles, which are easily kept spotlessly clean. . . . A splendid dresser . . . seems to have capacious arms for everything that pertains to the place, and its shelves are crowded with crocks of all kinds, with great bowls, with glittering utensils of metal—making a substantial and most interesting display of things that unite utility and homely grace.

Bunce's bucolic idyll lacks one needed touch of the picturesque: dream women at work in his sacred dream space.

> Had I now the painter's brush! See the piles of golden apples and reddened peaches and purple grapes heaped in yellow bowls; see the fresh, graceful, bare-armed women run their deft fingers through the fruit, and deftly prepare it for the waiting coppers.

Ignorant of what it means to preserve fruits in a suffocatingly hot kitchen according to the "craft" tradition, unaided by advances in processing techniques, the male dreamer concludes his painterly rendering of the goddess Pomona as American "gentlewoman."

> Is not fair woman when engaged in these womanly arts, under conditions that accord with her natural refinement, wholly charming? Why are not the conditions of her household work always made to accord with this refinement? A slattern at work is detestable; but seemly young women, sweetly attired, borrowing artistic contrasts

from the upheaved products of the garden or orchard, make a picture exceedingly delectable.

Now read Christine Frederick:

> The first step toward the efficiency of any kitchen is to have the kitchen small, compact, and without long narrow pantries and closets. Many women are under the impressions that a "roomy" kitchen is desirable. It may appear attractive, but a careful test of the way work is done in a "roomy" kitchen will discover waste spaces between the equipment, and hence waste motion between the work. Country kitchens are particularly apt to be large, and are often a combined sitting-room and kitchen. This plan seems cosy; but is inefficient because of the presence of lounges, flowers, and sewing. (47)

Having wiped out the myth of the delights of large spaces by her incorporation of the perspective of the woman at work, Frederick itemizes the materials (however unromantic) that assure efficiency.

> The most important point in the choice of fittings for the kitchen is that of "washability." I have been though the kitchens of one of the largest manufacturers of canned soups and similar products, the walls, floors, and ceilings of which were spotless tile—not only for looks, but because a tile surface can be washed, and sterilized if need be. . . . Open plumbing, tables covered with zinc, galvanized iron, or porcelain, are all essential to the sanitation of the standardized kitchen. (58)

Aside from a mutual liking for easy-to-clean tiles (which Bunce celebrates for their aesthetics rather than their usefulness), there are no similarities between these two kitchen scenes. Bunce's scene is an emotional delight; Frederick's foregrounds what is sanitary, functional, and efficient. One creates a setting where the male may enshrine his painterly dream of fair women. The other contains no women to be looked at for the viewer's pleasure; its space is controlled from the outside, by unseen women who manage its space for their own good. The one stays completely *inside* the kitchen: inside the male dreamer's consciousness, and inside an imagination of a time that already bears the marks of the past. The other goes *outside* the kitchen: by making references to canning factories and the world of commerce; by naming materials that are industrial and modern (zinc, galvanized iron, porcelain); by doing away with hardwood floors, crockery bowls, and rag rugs that connote days of yore; by looking through the present into the future, when "the new housekeeping" will be the standard for every woman's home life.

By 1914 women were being encouraged publicly (in some quarters, at least) to do what they had been doing at their own risk for some time: *to venture beyond the gates of their houses.* Charlotte Perkins Gilman had urged this in 1899.[39] Anna Spencer's *Woman's Share in Social Culture* (1912) detailed the "future double 'sphere' of womanhood" that promises "the heroism of pioneer adventure," since "the business of being a woman is precisely like that of being a man."[40] Yet another writer chided those who "fail to realize that the twentieth century is practically a new world," one requiring that "fundamental moral principles . . . be worked out on a new background."[41]

When Christine Frederick linked house to factory in 1914, she confirmed the strength of a notion whose time had come: new backgrounds, new foregrounds, perhaps even new stories yet to be told. Those front gates, however, had not opened all the way. For all the bright new visions, for all the glowing terms like "pioneer adventure," "new world," and "new background," *going outside* was still restricted by the nervous need to sustain the idea of family virtue lived snugly within the walls of the perfect house.

Some believed the happy solution was encoded by the words "open house," whereby the world would come to the woman.[42] Others spoke of the woman's entrance into "the great throbbing world of affairs."[43] But invitations to women to extend their lives into other realms were problematic; their ideological assumptions were questionable. Women might venture upon activities that connected private sphere with public world, but *home was where women were meant to return.* The single-family house was still considered the best place for the woman to act out her destiny as the all-purpose "go-between."

Tucked into the years that bridge adolescence and marriage, young women might enjoy a brief period of workplace "adventures." After marriage they were encouraged to expend many public hours as Mrs. Consumer, exploring the enticing realms opened up by the great department stores.[44] But the look of freedom in these forays "outside" was often just that: an appearance, not an actuality—a tautology of ideas pointing outward that continually pulled women back inside.

Christine Frederick insisted that Taylorism applied to household tasks might assist "in cutting from women the most dreary shackles" (ix), but *The New Housekeeping* never addressed the urgency the radical feminists expressed for taking collective action nor the socialists' wish to ameliorate the lives of the working class by undermining middle-class agendas. Frederick believed that women of wealth encounter no problems in home management since money "will buy service" (11). Nor do working-class women require special consideration. The housework of "the very poor" is kept "fairly simple," since such women "come from the class of servants."

> Their home-making is far less complex, their tasks simple, and society demands no appearance-standard from them. Added to this, organized philanthropy *is* by every means teaching the woman of the poor how to keep house in the most scientific, efficient manner. (11)

As far as Frederick was concerned, "the problem, the real issue, confronts the *middle-class woman* of slight strength and still slighter means, and of whom society expects so much" (11–12). Frederick candidly dedicates her book to "this middle class—to which I belong." Her gratitude to Taylor and his followers comes from her conviction that their methods will bring success to precisely these women, who are capable of being taught how to run—in all efficiency—the single-family household. Ultimately, Frederick's new housekeeping of 1914 is conducted according to the same ideology extolled in 1884 by Oliver Bell Bunce's *My House: An Idea.*

It follows that the mail-order catalogue copy, which was written to sell the idea of ready-made houses during the first three decades of the twentieth century, reveals as problematic an entanglement of the progressive and the reactionary, the scientific and the emotive, as everything else touched by Taylor's dreams of rationality, functionality, standardization, and simplification.

Negotiating the Middle Landscape

In his influential book, *The Machine in the Garden,* Leo Marx refers to "the middle landscape" as one means by which antebellum Americans tried to reconcile the brash aggressiveness of technology with the soothing domesticity of the lingering pastoral scene.[45] The glistening rails of the locomotive and the smoke puffs of the factories were given careful placement within the literature and paintings of the early decades of the nineteenth century. In George Inness's 1855 landscape, *The Lackawana Valley,* the male energies of the Iron Horse are located neither in the far distance nor in the immediate foreground. Rather, they are situated within the safe middle ground, where they announce masculine progress and prosperity without intruding too closely upon the feminine virtues embodied by the church and the tidy houses of this predominantly rural scene.

Marx contends that the conciliating mode of the "middle landscape" disappeared after the Civil War, once the masculine factors in American society closed ranks with technological advances. The following observations are intended to affirm in part, but also to qualify Marx's thesis. The commerce in standardized models for single-family dwellings that flourished long after the 1870s provides material evidence of *the continuing attempt* to mediate between machine and garden. Such house plans formed a "middle landscape" between the machine process pushing from the outside world and the inward turning of the hearthside, between what was allocated to the world of the male and to the realm of the female. When the house of wood, brick, stucco, or stone assumed the task of mediation, complicity rather than liberation, and betrayal rather than promises fulfilled, were too frequently the end result.

Just as there were notable precedents for Christine Frederick's 1914 descriptions of the management of house space and work activities within the kitchen, there were definite forerunners for the making and marketing of the ready-made house components, which achieved high public visibility between 1905 and the late 1920s. But because of the special conditions under which they were used, the early precut, sectional houses did not merit the attention of either established home dwellers or those aspiring to middle-class status. Corrugated iron buildings that satisfied the requirements of rude gold rush camps, Civil War army barracks, settlers on the edge of nowhere, or companies needing to shelter construction workers hardly met the dual test of material efficiency and the immigrant's dream of living "nice, American." [46]

The material efficiency of these houses was acclaimed almost from the start. The fact that precut sections of mill-worked lumber could be transported by railway car or farm wagon from the factory in Chicago, ready to be erected on site without "the services of a carpenter or skilled mechanic," resulted in products that met the criteria Taylorism exacted of any form of efficient production: simplified, rationalized tools and manufacturing procedures that assured that the job could be completed by the relatively unskilled worker. The marketing problem that still needed to be solved was how to give the ready-made house an aura of wish fulfillment. It had to be located, as it were, in "the middle landscape," away from the factory yard. It needed to show it could evolve just as automobile design did: from the Stanley Steamer (handsome, but too expensive for the masses) through Ford's Model N and Model T (utilitarian and cheap but aesthetically unexciting) to production of multiple models offering utility and economy as well as a soul-satisfying array of colors and design options.

Earlier efforts to produce prepackaged, trademarked houses made of mass-produced, standardized parts could only anticipate the golden years between 1905 and 1925, when evolving marketing practices enabled prospective customers to pore over catalogues featuring a wide range of styles and prices. Not even Thomas Edison's experiments in pouring concrete houses into cast iron frames had done the trick. When Pope & Cottle of Revere, Massachusetts, began manufacturing wooden sectional houses in 1905, they started the flood that only ran dry during the arid years of the Great Depression.[47] Just as Ford quickly edged out his early competitors, Sears, Roebuck soon became one of the leaders in mail-order house sales, but other names in the booming business must not be overlooked—such as the Aladdin Company and Sterling System-Built Homes, both of Bay City, Michigan, and Pacific Homes of Los Angeles.

The catalogue copy prepared by these energetic mail-order enterprises had a double game to play—one that matches its efforts to the other modes of discourse appropriated for the "selling" of scientific management as a way of life. First, customers were assured that they could count on the quality of the goods coming off the factory's assembly line; efficient shipping and delivery were guaranteed. Second, customers were repeatedly told about the time, motion, and money the company saved them every step of the way: at the point of purchase, delivery, and assembly—savings in time, motion, and money they would continue to enjoy as long as they lived in the well-designed house of their choice.[48] Last, customers were alerted to the moral and social benefits of houses that would provide them with far more than material advantages. As the Sterling System-Built Homes copy states in 1915:

> You get a *Home,* not a "house"—. . . a practical Home planned for your daily *comfort;* planned to save work for the wife or mother; planned to promote the *health* and *happiness* of the *entire family.* A Home that you can always point to with pride—that will stand as a monument to your good taste and sound judgment—that will be a credit to your locality.[49]

The frontispiece (see figure 22) and catalogue copy join in contrasting the anachronistic log-cabin ethic with the contemporary aspirations of those who dream of advancing into the new middle class—aspirations undermining the determined but frustrated efforts of American socialists and Marxists to repudiate bourgeois desires.[50]

"Be it
ever so humble,
there's no place like home"

FEB -8 1915 ©CLA395051

Figure 22. Frontispiece, *The Famous Fifty* (1915). Sterling System–Built Homes.

This picture tells a story which needs no explanation. Study it. Think of it. Appreciate the contrast. Here is the span of a hundred years in human happiness. On the same spot where the old log cabin was built a long century ago, the modern Sterling Home stands to-day. How great is the difference! How wide is the separation between these two kinds of Home.

We were happy with the little old log cabin because it was the best that could be had. But our home includes a host of comforts—conveniences—refinements and beauties of which our ancestors never even dreamed.

Things we demand not for *themselves,* but because we know they bring the greatest happiness and content.

After all, that's the sum total of earthly life.[51]

No matter that the painted scene contains its own nostalgic anachronisms: the little house in the country, the bonneted housewife in her garden, the chickens in the backyard coop, the husband and son at leisure in open spaces far from public view. No matter that the remainder of the catalogue is illustrated with grainy photographs of Sterling models set in sometimes stark urban and quasi-suburban settings. No matter that the Sterling model on display as "the last word" appears to be smaller in size than the log cabin it intends to replace. Image and words are at work to cast their sleight of hand over material fact.

One does not get very far by pulling up short with truisms about the deceptions practiced by the selling trades and the duplicities of advertising copy. In fact, the products being offered had much good in them, especially if buyers could be persuaded to accept certain material limitations as adding up to "something else" they had wanted all along. The point is to sort out how word and picture transformed the affordable space of actual houses into an object of desire, once the models fell into place along the basic dream continuum—the single-family house, the happy and virtuous family, a better America—aided and abetted by the basic principles of efficiency management.

Prospective customers who were able to spend between $250 and $2,213.50 had an enticingly varied selection from which to choose. House patterns, scientifically manufactured and marketed to enhance the scientific management of their owners' lives, encouraged dreams of individualism but also neighborhood pride, upward mobility for the future but also present contentment. Depending upon how we choose to view these patterned house lives and their accompanying copy, they either yield evidence for the most selfish and socially alienating of manipulated impulses or for the most pleasing of middle-class fulfillments. Either way, the texts are often in illuminating conflict with themselves.

Ready-made house-plan catalogues, placed in "the middle landscape," have a wonderful knack for the sense of ambivalence that confirms their "squint-eyed" nature (recall William James as cited in chapter 1): standardized houses presented as exemplary machines; house plans that reinforce the ideal of home life yet resist the encroachments of an industrialized society. Before we take on these ambivalences, however, three gender issues demand our attention: (1) how texts written to describe model houses and house lives use metaphors to designate impulses as either male or female; (2) how women householders appropriate language formerly associated with male enterprises taking place outside house boundaries; (3) how men and women, besieged alike by modern times, start to formulate stories out of their need to retreat farther into house spaces previously allocated to women alone.

The Final Bastion Betrayed

Is there such a thing as male space? If so, is it an essentialist property or a matter of cultural conditioning? Psychologists, biologists, and cultural historians are still sorting out the data in the controversy over the origin of gender-based impulses. Eric Erikson, for one, believed that his experiments in children's free play indicate that little girls like to put together abstracted house spaces where figures are placed in static postures within wall-less interiors. In contrast, little boys construct buildings with elaborate towers and facades, setting toy figures in motion outside the high walls. Erikson added (one hopes, wryly), "boys play with the idea of collapse; ruins are exclusively male constructions."[52] Erickson's hypothesis may never be verified, but it might explain Alexis de Tocqueville's exclamation, uttered in the 1830s as he looked upon the chimney stumps left behind in New England by restless American males who were abandoning home sites to push on across the young country, "What! Ruins so soon!"

Forty years after Tocqueville's observation, the American motto had become "Let men construct and women decorate."[53] Also mandated was the man's duty "to rule the house" from his vantage point in the ever-shifting outside world while the woman's task was "to regulate [the] eternal movements" of the home's moral nature.[54] But what contractual arrangement binding male, female, and home—however reified—did this imply?

In the centennial year 1876, when numerous Americans were congratulating themselves on their progress and their possessions, Henry Adams concluded his Lowell Institute lecture, "The Primitive Rights of Women," by making a pronouncement about the universal nature of male desires: "the most powerful instincts in man are his affections and his love of property . . . on these the family is built."[55] Chief among these proprietary claims was the woman located within the house the man owned, a point Thorstein Veblen seconded in his 1899 *Theory of the Leisure Class.*

The house owned is the woman and the family possessed. In Adams and Veblen's view, ownership, not virtue, was what the man desires. But others tried hard to merge the material fact of having a house of one's own with bland notions of happiness, beauty, and goodness, disavowing any strife. For such folk, even admitting the problematics and diversity of gender, race, and class was not part of living "nice, American."

> A beautiful home has the power to attract attention, improve conduct, compel respect, bind families and friends together, form communities, found states and nations. Children reared in and among beautiful homes acquire good taste from them and seldom if ever do a very ugly thing.[56]

The American literary imagination is packed with views and counterviews both warning against and commending house lives. On the one side, Walt Whitman's vision pries through domestic walls in his determination to become an honorary member of the national family group. Mark Twain's Huck Finn needs the home comforts and relief from loneliness he finds with the Grangerfords and the Phelpses, just as much as he needs raft flights. But irony, not homage, most frequently marks the literary representation of these family types: Hester and Pearl at the edge of Bostontown; the unhousing of Frederick Douglass, Uncle Tom, and the Invisible Man; Mr. and Mrs. Ahab and the whole Glendinning clan; the extended families of *Pudd'nhead Wilson;* the Hurstwoods of Chicago and the Johnsons of Rum Alley; Mr. and Mrs. Osmond and the odd relational geometries of *The Golden Bowl;* Wharton's big houses and diminished hopes; Fitzgerald's Buchanans and Divers; Faulkner's claustrophobically interrelated McCaslins, Compsons, Sutpens, Sartorises, and Snopes. Consider, too, the actual house lives of the Jukes and the Kalikukes, the Hatfields and the McCoys; and also of the Adamses, the Jameses, the Clemenses, and the Howellses, for whom sanity, serenity, and just plain house normalcy were in all too short supply.

The purpose of scientifically managed house space and house lives was the attainment of normalcy. It was a normalcy shaped by three assumptions that the house-plan manuals never questioned: (1) a man's primary life exists outside his household; (2) a man's status in the community is affected by the facade his house turns toward the public thoroughfare, no matter how much he seeks refuge inside its walls; (3) a man is responsible for obtaining the good house by whose means his family is promised the good life.

Underlying these assumptions—tacitly agreed upon by the catalogue copy that accompanies floor plans, elevation sketches, measurements, and costs—is another stratum of modern folk wisdom: men may run the house-plan industry and men may purchase its services, but it is women who dictate the way houses are made to meet the vaunted look of scientific management, inside as well as out.

Early in 1882 Eugene Gardner insisted in his aptly titled *The House that Jill Built* that husband Jack is a dull boy if he fails to take his wife's lead in pointing the way toward effective functionality.[57] Of course, Gardner's Jill remains *inside* the house, checking pipes and drains in the basement, surveying the work spaces in the back, and managing the upstairs storage closets and bathrooms, but whenever Jack ignores her wise advice, he repeats the bad old male mistake of opting for wasteful cost and external display.

The sound logic of putting women in charge of creating and constructing entire buildings was not fully accepted in the early years of the twentieth century, just as it is not today, but Gardner's suggestion that women be consulted in the planning of the inner workings of the house was so much a commonplace by 1900 that the men who sold ready-made houses complained about the situation.[58] By 1915, however, the Sterling System-Built Homes catalogue reflects a cheerful acceptance of woman's role as the "constructor" of the proper "decor" for the American home. A woman spends 90 percent of her time at home; the house is her "constant environment," "her work-shop" and "place of entertainment." Because the house is her all—the very *insideness* of her being—she seeks to control its design.[59]

The men of Sterling System-Built Homes supply words to define a woman's "inside" life; their language takes for granted that her heart lies within a middle-class household space that signifies her value and purpose. There were, of course, other voices, other vocabularies, that led in different directions—away from the discourses of established institutions or the new strategies for marketing "sterling" and "model" house plans. There was a growing body of women's tales, tales that rejected the sanctification of the home as "pure and holy" and that repudiated the concept of an *inside* that keeps women from ever living fully *outside*.

In her trilogy, *Women and Economics, The Home,* and *The Man-Made World,* Charlotte Perkins Gilman thoroughly debunks "the domestic mythology." She supplies a strong story line that demythologizes the house as heaven.[60] She points out that the male use of words such as "family," "home," and "children" conspires to make the woman "home-bound" under conditions in which "the moving world" of men enforces the existence of "the unmoving house" (*Home*, 6).

Yes, home is the "very oldest thing" (*Home*, 29), but this means that women shut up within "the house habit" (*Man-Made World*, 65) are trapped within "an incarnate past," left "far behind the march of events" (*Home*, 6, 29). In this hellish place without exit, they are forced to endure "married prostitution" and "scab-labor," whether as mother, sister, or wife (*Women and Economics*, 98, 110). Often expensive, ugly, unhealthy, and unhappy, homes are, in fact, those spaces in which women *suffer the most* (*Home*, 77, 79).

Gilman acknowledges the primal need for permanence, the comfort of being in an enclosed "box" where there are "cushions and more cushions and eternal lying down" (*Home*, 28). Also comforting is the lulling effect of existing in "the same place over and over,—the restful repetition, rousing no keen response. . . . All this from our first consciousness. All this for millions and millions of years" (*Women and Economics*, 221). Then she suddenly jolts the reader from the misleading languor of her sentences and the imaging of home as harem with the sharp questions about the different expectations created when modern house structures are gendered.

There is more to the house than men think, as the women who are held within its walls (whether patterned with yellow wallpaper or not) know. Houses can enfold their occupants soothingly, but they are also treadmills where women seldom have time to sit. Male absorption in the dream of perfect security "gives the subtle charm of sex to a man's home ideals," but it also gives "the scorn of sex to a man's home practices" (*Home*, 22). That is, on the one hand are the house and its kitchen as gazed upon by Oliver Bell Bunce, on the other are the same spaces experienced by Gilman herself.

Something terrible is taking place, which Gilman is ready to point out. Ideas of home as heaven and house as haven are intended to harbor the middle-class family within fantasies of stability and seclusion. They not only allow each member of the family to shut out the rest of the world, but—and this is the shocker—to shut out the others who live within these sheltered spaces. Whereas later scholars analyze the nineteenth-century home in terms of the haven it gave the family from the heartless world beyond the front gate,[61] Gilman exposes the urgent need to find a haven from the family itself.

In *The Children of the Poor* (1892) and *Children of the Tenements* (1903), Jacob Riis writes of the young who flee from the squalor (material and emotional) of their living conditions into the streets beyond. Middle-class families own houses intended as buffers against such outer reaches. However, alongside the ample male fantasy literature depicting home-havens built to express a siege mentality, there is another body of material: literature rising from the female awareness that (as Henry James, that most feminine of sensibilities, commented) true privacy is "the highest luxury of all, the supremely expensive thing." [62]

Here are two examples of the dream means women used to seek corners of calm within houses besieged from without, houses that, had in turn, become battlefields. These dreams might further the aims of the middle-class wife and mother, but the lower-class woman was given no such chance.

Mary Gay Humphreys contributed an essay on house decoration to *The Woman's Book* of 1894.[63] Amidst talk of draperies and Oriental carpets, Humphreys suddenly interjects a disquisition on the various sanctuaries lying at general removes from the "public" rooms where family members gather as a group. Men have a "growlery"—"the den"—where they burrow deep within a space hung with the trophies of the "mighty hunter" and the "virile" ornaments of antlers and buffalo hides, a place where males need grant "no consideration to anybody." [64] But Humphreys's greatest concern is with what the wife and mother craves—her own "retiring room." Located on the uppermost floor, it is a faraway space where the woman "can go and pull herself together"; where she may "shut out the distractions of the household"; where she is able "to plan the campaigns, and map out the household operation" like a weary general. It is also a temple of blessed indolence where she "can lie on a couch in the blazing sunshine; she can toss a book on the floor and let it lie, and, unabashed, can enjoy the fascinating confusion of things out of place (2: 139–41).

Only in her "retiring room" the woman "can take her grief and . . . her joys too sacred to be submitted to other eyes." Only there does she find a true sanctuary "where no one can enter unasked, not even the husband of her bosom, nor the babes . . . on the lower floor" (2:141–43). But if this special place under the eaves gives the woman a house-haven out of reach of the maddening crowd below, it also forbids her from reaching out to the public world that feminists were insisting was her due.

In 1903 Charlotte Perkins Gilman also deplored the continual invasion of the home by tradesmen, callers, servants, and children, persons who can only be kept at bay through the newest technology: the dumbwaiter, the speaking tube, the telephone.[65] This is not enough. With a rising sense of drama, Gilman narrates the woman's flight from the outside world as she is forced back, back, past successive lines of entrenchment within the house. Her militaristic discourse shares resonances with Humphreys's account, but Gilman's communiqué from the battlefront is more tense since more is at stake. The woman *must* escape the prying eyes and ears of "the others," lest she blurt out that shame, the dread secret she shares with the house.

What is the nature of this shame? The betrayal of ideals in whose rightness she believes, ideals that the woman and house together are meant to represent.

> A beautiful, comfortable house meeting all physical needs; a happy family, profoundly enjoying each other's society; a father devotedly spending his life in obtaining the wherewithal to maintain this little haven; a mother completely wrapped up in her children . . . children, happy in the home and growing up beautifully under its benign influences.[66]

Lies, all lies! What, then, can still be said in the mail-order catalogues promoting ready-made houses and American middle-class family virtue, privacy, and pride?

First, sales copy made much of the innovations architects and builders offered in the area of construction methods, material, and rational design, but additional appeals were made to physical comfort, individual mental peace, and cultural stability. These multilayered selling points were aimed, scattershot, at the men and women of the family. The result is some confusion over which—the new techniques or the traditional values—are meant to have the most "masculine" appeal and which the most "feminine." Because of this somewhat erratic attribution of different needs to different sexes, the language the catalogues use to assess the multiple wants of their unseen audience understandably contains its own loose ends.

Second, copywriters had to deal with housing problems that were material in their origin yet heavily freighted with emotional value. If a house is meant to be a haven, structured to protect one from the other inhabitants, that house must provide space for retreat. Unfortunately, the cost of furnishing extra nooks and crannies, attics and dens, had become overwhelming by the time of World War I. Somehow the copy for houses that were getting smaller by the year had to make a virtue of coziness and snugness at the very moment that the psychology of beleaguered middle-class family life demanded expansiveness.

The third point copywriters treated with care was the relation of the exterior of the house to the rest of the community. Should there be a front door and front porch that extended an invitation to one's neighbors? Or should house facades stand aloof, proclaiming taste and financial success but denying "open house" to passersby? These relations would change in the years surrounding World War I.

The following choices were at issue in the copy used to promote scientifically managed, ready-made house patterns: (1) interior spaces, ample or constricted; (2) exteriors as facades to attract public attention or as walls to the world; (3) desires shared or rejected by the members of the family, despite or because of sex or generation; (4) scientifically managed material arrangements or their subordination to the meeting of emotional needs; (5) irrational personal desires satisfied or frustrated by the introduction of rational, standardized designs. A variety of narrative devices were used to convey the urgency of resolving these issues.

Ready-Mades and Dream Copy Revised

Ready-mades were the apotheosis of almost everything set in motion by Taylorism, Fordism, and the nativist fervor in the decade prior to the start of the First World War and the decade that followed. The Depression of the 1930s put a stop to this particular phase of the capitalistic patterning of American lives. The 1940s and 1950s would give Henry Kaiser, William Levitt, and Foster Gunnison an entirely new role to play in the mass construction of the American single-family house, ranged row upon row in an ever diminishing chance for choice.

Many Americans today find yesterday's dream of the simple life in the pages of old Sears catalogues. Such a life is no longer simple to maintain, even if found intact, but worth it all the same to people like the woman in Takoma Park, Maryland. In 1985 she writes Sears, Roebuck about her house, Modern Home No. 167 (figure 23), which was built for $754 back in 1909, the year after Sears entered the mail-order house-model business.

The three-story structure, measuring 25 × 50½ feet at each level, that the Maryland woman describes is real, and the life she lives in it is real, including home-management problems that complicate her current dealings with plumbers, house painters, roofers, and electricians not used to such anachronistic amplitude. Notwithstanding these difficulties, her letter makes clear that No. 167 represents her dream of spaciousness, "unabashedly American," much closer in kind to Oliver Bell Bunce's ideal of 1884 than to the model of efficient compactness Christine Frederick extolled in 1913.

> Inside, the rooms and hallways are large and airy. There are high ceilings, protruding bays, paneled doors, soft pine floors and oddly shaped closets for children to hide in. The third floor, once the attic, provides a quiet hideaway, a place where model trains can be left up

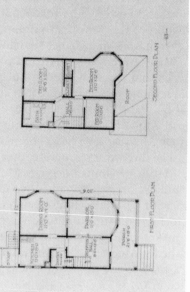

Figure 23. Sears Modern Home No. 167 (1911). National Trust for Historic Preservation in the United States. Photo: Sears, Roebuck and Co.

all year long, a spot from which you can look down at the tree tops and watch squirrels building nests.[67]

Our concern here is not with whatever it is about life in the 1980s that makes this 1909 house elicit such impassioned reveries. Instead, we will focus upon the rhetorical strategies used to sell the increasingly constricted ready-mades that followed Sears No. 167 in the years between 1913 and 1938.

The amplitude allowed by the 1909 house plan is precisely what is absent from the majority of house designs available from 1910 onwards. Extravagant visions of "the great good place" could only frustrate potential customers after the First World War, for they could not secure what the housing market was unable to supply. Ways had to be found to redefine their needs and redirect their desires.

In the 1880s, prior to the ready-mades, a house costing $3,000 offered 2,000 to 2,500 square feet. By 1905 a house at that price had shrunk to almost half its former size, a shrinkage that accelerated during the war years and afterwards. High ceilings and roomy third floors survived into the earliest years of the twentieth century, but against increasing odds. By 1920 they were almost out of the question. Mounting costs were introduced at every stage of construction because of available materials, labor, house lots, finance charges, and technological improvements.

True, between 1900 and 1917, 75 percent of American city dwellers saw their average income double, reaching a figure of $1,500. True, in 1910 many low-income families were still able to finance a two-bedroom house. But between 1904 and 1918, housing costs increased 25 percent. With the housing crisis that followed the close of the war, a dwelling that had cost $3,000 in 1918 demanded $6,000 to $8,000 by 1920.

Under conditions affecting the entire house-building market, companies that sold "pre-cut and fitted" houses realized they had to celebrate the benefits of the absence of space that home buyers had enjoyed in the years between the 1870s and the early 1900s. Catalogues were driven to offer buyers of model houses sound reasons to like what they got. "Better a house too small for a day than too large for a year," sang one brochure of 1921.[68] The catalogues promoted the advantages to be gained through the scientific management of house lives, but even these arguments had to be redeemed from the look of excessive practicality by the careful overlay of the discourse of desire. The result was copy that reads as though written in a collaborative effort by Oliver Bell Bunce and Christine Frederick.

Over the fifteen years between 1913 and 1938, the catalogue copy changes significantly. Each new catalogue shifts the emphasis given to five principal sales features: (1) the social status one could achieve through the display of the exterior of the house; (2) the dual nature of the house that incorporated up-to-date conveniences in the interior but embellishes the facade with nonfunctional touches evoking romanticized moments from the American past; (3) dimensions that either give the appearance of "dignified" space and/or make a virtue of smallness; (4) an inward-turning floor plan that will enfold the family's private life within the walls of the house; (5) the relative weight given to the straightforward presentation of material facts or to the interweaving of wishes yearning to be fulfilled.[69]

Two Sears models from 1913 give us a standard against which we can measure later alterations in the basic dream narrative. The first, No. 119 (figure 24), has nine rooms, one bath, and sells for $1,731. The copy is as utilitarian as the design. It does not seem to have to strain to persuade readers of its special merits. It simply points out that No. 119 has "a good substantial design, constructed with a view to economy and affording a great deal of room" (232). On the other hand, No. 159 (figure 25), at $762, comes with six rooms and a bath, but the room sizes are noticeably smaller. *This* is the type of house with which many American homeowners would have to make do by 1920.

The copy for No. 159 is restrained; it lacks the hyperbole that later characterized the catalogue of the 1920s. Nonetheless, effort is expanded to make this smallish house *sound* good. Whereas No. 119 is praised for the economy of its construction and materials, the kind of "economy" No. 159 offers comes from the fact it is "well arranged, having no wasted space." Really big houses, it appears upon second thought, are foolishly wasteful; small houses, by contrast, are sensibly compact. The word "large" appears three times in the copy block for No. 159, but in reference to quite different matters: (1) the windows whose large size assures that rooms will be "well lighted and ventilated"; (2) the popularity of the model has caused it to be "frequently built in large numbers, proving [it] to be a very good investment"; (3) the width of the front porch and the seeming size of the exterior, described through some masterful waffling as being "practically two full stories high"—with the consequence that the "good" appearance of the house insures that it "rents well" (233). Since interior spaciousness can hardly be claimed for No. 159, other means are used to insinuate virtues of "largeness." At the same time, the positive lack of *wasted* space is singled out for commendation.

The 1915 Sterling System-Built Homes catalogue contains far more verbal zip than the 1913 Sears catalogue in pushing the desirability of two of its models: The Heather ("a cozy cottage" of three rooms, marketed at $250—see figure 26) and The Vernon ("a wonder of wonders" for $2,213.50 that answers to "man's supreme ambition" and "woman's highest aspiration"—see figure 27). The merits of The Heather rest on the fact

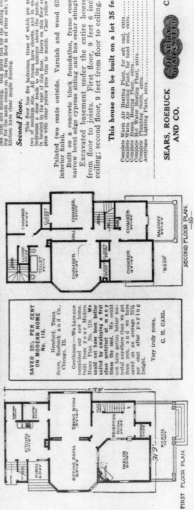

$1,731.00

For $1,731.00 we will furnish all the material to build this Ten-Room House, consisting of Mill Work, Siding, Flooring, Ceiling, Finishing Lumber, Building Paper, Pipe, Gutter, Sash Weights, Hardware, Painting Material, Lumber, Lath and Shingles. NO EXTRAS, as we guarantee enough material at the above price to build this house according to our plans.

By allowing a fair price for labor, cement, brick and plaster, which we do not furnish, this house can be built for about $3,345.00, including all material and labor.

For Our Offer of Free Plans See Page 3.

THIS is a good substantial design, constructed with a view to economy and affording a great deal of room. It has a large front porch, 7 feet wide by 24 feet long, with balcony over part of it 8 feet 6 inches by 12 feet.

First Floor.

The front door is made of clear red oak and glazed with leaded art glass. A large reception hall in which there is an open oak stairway to the second floor. A convenient closet is located right under this stairway. We furnish a grille for the opening leading from the reception hall into the parlor, in which there is a handsome mantel. There is a cased opening between the sitting room and parlor. Cement cottage window glazed with colored leaded art glass for the front parlor. There is a bay window in the sitting room. The kitchen can be entered from the sitting room and dining room. Large pantry and storeroom located convenient to the kitchen. We furnish oak-cross panel clear oak interior doors for the first floor with clear oak finish. Maple flooring for the kitchen. All flooring for the main rooms on the first floor is of clear oak; the pantry and kitchen have clear maple flooring.

Second Floor.

This floor has five bedrooms, three of which are quite large and two of medium size. All rooms have closets, and in one of the front bedrooms a door leads to the balcony above the porch. A bathroom is located in the rear of this floor. Doors on this floor are clear yellow pine with clear yellow pine trim to match. Clear yellow pine flooring.

Painted two coats outside. Varnish and wood filler for two coats of interior finish.

Built on a concrete block foundation, frame construction, sided with narrow bevel edge cypress siding and has cedar shingle roof.

Excavated basement under the entire house, 7 feet 4 inches from floor to joists. First floor, 9 feet 6 inches from floor to ceiling; second floor, 9 feet from floor to ceiling.

This house can be built on a lot 35 feet wide.

Complete Warm Air Heating Plant, for soft coal, extra......... $121.87
Complete Warm Air Heating Plant, hard coal, extra............... 125.67
Complete Steam Heating Plant, extra............................ 199.65
Complete Hot Water Heating Plant, extra........................ 230.16
Complete Plumbing Plant, extra................................. 130.10
Acetylene Lighting Plant, extra................................ 25.10

SEARS, ROEBUCK AND CO. CHICAGO, ILLINOIS

QUALITY GUARANTEED

MODERN HOME No. 119

SAVED 33⅓ PER CENT ON MODERN HOME No. 119.

Herford, Texas.

Sears, Roebuck and Co., Chicago, Ill.

Gentlemen:—We have now completed our new home, built from your Modern Home Plan No. 119. We could not have been better suited by employing a first class architect at many times the cost. We could not have gotten better material anywhere than we got from you, and we have saved on an average 33⅓ per cent after paying freight.

Very truly yours,

C. H. CARL.

FIRST FLOOR PLAN.

SECOND FLOOR PLAN.—85—

Figure 24. Sears Modern Home No. 119 (1911). National Trust for Historic Preservation in the United States.

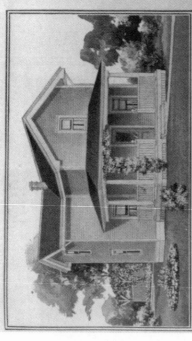

MODERN HOME No. 159

This house has been built at Aurora, Ill., La-Porte, Ind., Boston, Mass., Ely, Minn., Fulton, Mo., Paterson, N. J., Bay Shore, L. I., N. Y., Canton, Ohio, Waynesboro, Penn., Mt. Pleasant, Tenn., and other cities.

FIRST FLOOR PLAN

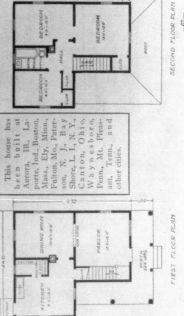

SECOND FLOOR PLAN

$699.00

For $699.00 we will furnish all the material to build this Six-Room Two-Story House, consisting of Lumber, Lath, Shingles, Mill Work, Ceiling, Siding, Flooring, Finishing Lumber, Building Paper, Pipe, Gutter, Sash Weights and Painting Material. NO EXTRAS, as we guarantee enough material to build this house according to our plans.

By allowing a fair price for labor, cement, brick and plaster, which we do not furnish, this house can be built for about $1,171.00, including all material and labor.

For Our Offer of Free Plans See Page 3.

THIS house is well arranged, having no waste space. Has six good size rooms well lighted and ventilated with large windows. Is suitable for suburban or country home and has been frequently built in large numbers, proving to be a very good investment. It rents well, as it is practically two full stories high and of good appearance. It has a large front porch, 33 feet 6 inches long, with Colonial columns.

First Floor.

Parlor with staircase leading to second floor. Cased openings from parlor to dining room. Has a large front window facing the street. Dining room and kitchen are of good size.

Second Floor.

Has three good size bedrooms, three closets and bathroom.

At the above price we furnish a massive front door, 3x7 feet, 1¾ inches thick, glazed with bevel plate glass. Interior doors are five-cross panel with Nona pine rails and stiles and yellow pine panels. Clear yellow pine interior trim, such as baseboard, casing, molding and clear yellow pine staircase. Clear yellow pine flooring throughout house and porches.

This house is built on a concrete foundation, frame construction, sided with narrow bevel clear cypress siding and has cedar shingle roof.

Painted two coats outside; your choice of color. Varnish and wood filler for two coats of interior finish.

The rooms on the first floor are 9 feet from floor to ceiling; rooms on second floor, 8 feet from floor to ceiling.

This house can be built on a lot 27 feet wide.

Complete Warm Air Heating Plant, for soft coal, extra .... $ 70.98
Complete Warm Air Heating Plant, for hard coal, extra 73.95
Complete Steam Heating Plant, extra 145.45
Complete Hot Water Heating Plant, extra 181.17
Complete Plumbing Outfit, extra 106.17
Acetylene Lighting Plant, extra 47.90

QUALITY GUARANTEED

SEARS, ROEBUCK AND CO.   **CHICAGO, ILLINOIS**

Figure 25. Sears Modern Home No. 159 (1911). National Trust for Historic Preservation in the United States.

This Cosy Cottage—$250

Specifications and Terms

Price, $264   Cash Discount, 5%
Net Price, $250.80
3 Room Home   Size, 20 x 16   See page 14

All lumber furnished will be hemlock, red cedar, yellow pine, and white pine, or spruce of Sterling quality.
Height of ceiling, first floor, 8 feet 6 inches.
Floor joist, 2 x 6 inches.
Center sill, 6 x 6 inches.
All ceiling, joists, studding, rafters and plates, 2 x 4-inch stock.
Joist, ceiling joists and studding spaced on 16-inch centers.
Sheathing for wall and roof boards, 1-inch hemlock.
Bevel siding, 6-inch red cedar, or shingles, clear and knotless.
Shingles, red cedar, extra Star-A-Star grade, clear and knotless.
Flooring, ⅞ x 3¼-inch yellow pine, clear and knotless.
Outside finish and trim, white pine or spruce.
Inside finish, yellow pine or fir, kiln dried, and smoothly sanded, will take fine polish, clear and knotless.
Sash, 1⅜ inches thick, primed and glazed with double strength glass.
Doors, inside and outside, 1⅜ inches thick, 2 feet 8 inches x 6 feet 8 inches.
Builders' hardware for complete house, including lock, sets, hinges, sash locks, weight, cord, nails, building paper, etc.
Best wood lath and plaster, or patent plaster board if desired.
Plenty of paint, stain and varnish for two coats, inside and outside.
All steps from grade to first floor, unless cement.
We do not furnish basement stairs or basement windows at above price.

The Heather

CHOSEN because for a small Home nothing has ever been found that is more practical.

The Heather is a plain, simple, little Home, with three rooms. Yet it is just as durable and as strongly built as any of "The Famous Fifty."

The finish is all knotless Sterling lumber, every inch. The windows, the flooring, the siding — everything inside and out is the same standard grade that you find in all Sterling Homes.

Here is a tasteful little place with a degree of originality in extended roof, porch-shelter and Craftsman door.

"Be it ever so humble" — just so it's a Sterling Home.

Some of the greatest men in America have lived in far less comfort and they often say that those days were their happiest.

Your choice of these plans may depend on the position of your lot. The rooms are the same size in each except the living room is longer and narrower in one case — shorter and deeper in the other.

The porch entrance in plan A is somewhat unusual since the living room is entered from the side.

These living rooms are remarkably spacious. Just half of the Home is given over to a fine, large lounging room. Stove may be placed in the center near the flue and the corners offer splendid possibilities for comfortable furnishing.

Our women advisers have some very pleasing suggestions to make on the furnishing and decoration of The Heather. Simple touches that cost very little yet add immensely to home comfort and refinement. This information will be gladly given to any who are interested. Our Home Planning Department is the central exchange for thousands of Home ideas, and it will pay you to get them.

Any able-bodied man can fit this home together in a week since all pieces are cut, marked and ready.

Our charts show where each piece is to go and everything is furnished even to the nails.

Color card will be sent giving choice of paints and before you realize it, The Heather will be finished, furnished and ready to occupy.

You will save nearly $200 on this home. You will get the very best materials.

You will have real pleasure in putting it together.

And you do not have to wait on hand-saw, hand-measure methods.

In ordering please write very plainly which plan you prefer. You will be delighted with The Heather.

Plan A

Plan B

The Sterling Stamp on Your Home Means the Same as on Your Silver

Figure 26. The Heather (1915). Sterling System-Built Homes.

The Finest of the Famous Fifty

The Vernon

TO own such a Home is man's supreme ambition. To live in this wonder of wonders expresses woman's highest hopes. To design a Home more perfect is utterly impossible. We know. For here is the finest of all The Famous Fifty. And The Famous Fifty, by common consent, is the world's leading class of Homes. No description or picture can do this Home half justice. This photograph, which the owner took exclusively for us last Christmas morning, does not begin to tell of the charm and splendor of this Home of Homes — The Vernon.

Try to imagine what it must mean to call this Home, "My Home." Gaze on its beauty. Picture its comforts. Revel in its refinements. Live in its loveliness. Never was there another such Home. Never will there be again this opportunity to own it.

After you have gone through The Vernon and have explored every corner, discovered every comfort and convenience, admired every point of its artistic refinement—then write to us. Let us tell you more about this Home—the finest of all The Famous Fifty.

Two of our architects spent a year on this one plan. They answer, personally, all questions regarding it.

First Floor Plan

Second Floor Plan

Specifications and Terms

Price, $2330	Cash Discount, 5%
Net Price, $2213.50	10 Room Home
Size, 38 x 24	See page 14

All lumber furnished will be hemlock, red cedar, yellow pine, and white pine, or spruce of Sterling quality.

Height of ceiling, first floor, 9 feet; second floor, 8 feet.

Floor joist, first floor, 2 x 10 inches; second floor, 2 x 8 inches.

Center sill, 6 x 8 inches.

All ceiling, joists, studding and plates, 2 x 4-inch stock; rafter, 2 x 6 inches.

Joist, ceiling joists and studding spaced on 16-inch centers.

Sheathing for sub-floor, wall and roof boards, 1-inch hemlock.

Bevel siding, 12-inch red cedar, clear and knotless.

Shingles, red cedar, extra Star-A-Star grade, clear and knotless.

Flooring, ⅞ x 3¼-inch yellow pine, clear and knotless.

Outside finish and trim, white pine or spruce.

Inside finish, yellow pine or fir, kiln dried, and smoothly sanded, will take fine polish, clear and knotless.

Sash, 1⅜ inches thick, primed and glazed with double strength glass.

Doors, inside and rear, 1⅜ inches thick,

2 feet 8 inches x 6 feet 8 inches; front, 3 x 7 feet, 1¾ inches thick.

Builders' hardware for complete house, including lock, sets, hinges, sash locks, weights, cord, nails, building paper, etc.

Best wood lath and plaster, or patent plaster board if desired.

Plenty of paint, stain and varnish for two coats, inside and outside.

All steps from grade to first floor, unless cement.

We do not furnish basement stairs or basement windows at above price.

The Sterling Stamp on Your Home Means the Same as on Your Silver

Figure 27. The Vernon (1915). Sterling System-Built Homes.

that it is "a plain, simple, little home" that "any able-bodied man" can assemble, yet it is "just as durable and as strongly built" as other Sterling models. Potential customers are informed that "be it ever so humble," all is well "just so it's a Sterling Home." They are reminded that "some of the greatest men in America have lived in far less comfort and they often say that those days were their happiest." What is more, the statement that "half of the Home is given over to a fine, large lounging room" helps to disguise the fact that the entire floor plan measures only 16 × 20 feet (38).

The Sterling copywriters are hardly going to undercut their top-of-the-line model, The Vernon. Any family able to afford its $2,200 price tag will be thrilled by this ten-room home of "charm and splendor" whose two levels each measure 24 × 38 feet. But the copy leaves little to chance as it launches upon a series of imperatives: "Try to imagine what it must mean to call this Home, 'My Home.' Gaze on its beauty. Picture its comforts. Revel in its refinements. Live in its loveliness." Readers are also confronted by warnings prefaced by the fateful word "never": "Never was there another such Home. Never will there be again this opportunity to own it" (69).

The Sterling catalogue has it both ways. It associates The Vernon with George Washington's stately home while endowing The Heather with the value of everything *wee* and *cozy* about Scottish Highland cottage life. If Washington's house furnishes the prototype for The Vernon, the Sterling copy for The Heather draws emotional energy from the stories of American presidents, such as Harrison and Lincoln, who began their careers in spaces even more "humble." (Never mind that the preface had already informed its readers that log-cabin life was long gone.) In the Sterling catalogues, spaces, large and small, are given the full "American" treatment by linking them to the successful life, past and present.[70]

The 1921 Sears catalogue contains The Homeville and The Stone Ridge, listed at $1,896 and $2,229, respectively. The primary feature of The Stone Ridge (figure 28) is the visual impact it has upon one's neighbors. Its facade identifies its "owner as a person of good taste and judgment" since it is "of a type that will conform to the architecture of the best neighborhood and will be a place of distinction anywhere." Readers are also reminded that The Stone Ridge is a "large, comfortable house" for the family nestled *within* its walls. Cicero is cited as having lauded "the delights of a fireplace" of the kind enhancing its living room. But whatever "cheer" the family enjoys at the hearthside is reoriented toward the view from the sidewalk, where the rugged chimney "adds much to the exterior" (206). Good things hidden inside also function outside to assure the approval of the public at large.

The Homeville copy takes a different tack (figure 29). It has six rooms

Figure 28. Sears, The Stone Ridge (1921). National Trust for Historic Preservation in the United States.

Figure 29. Sears, The Homeville (1921). National Trust for Historic Preservation in the United States.

to the five offered by The Stone Ridge, but The Stone Ridge delivers large spaces: it has a relatively ample kitchen area and two somewhat bigger bedrooms in place of the three small sleeping spaces offered by The Homeville. Clearly, The Homeville cannot compete either in terms of the actual dimension of its floor plan or in regard to the largesse of public prestige that makes The Stone Ridge "a place of distinction" for "the best neighborhood." Catalogue copy for The Homeville has to stir feelings of snug protection from the weather outside as well as a certain smugness about the aesthetic sensibilities of its owners.

> That big exposed chimney . . . promises security against winter blasts. The French windows and French doors, together with the columned entrance, imparts just the right artistic touch. When painted pure white in contrast with red or green roofing, this little home will be recognized as an architectural gem in any community. (93)

With what care the phrase "this little home" has been prepared so that it may work in favor of the house design. With what deftness the phrase "architectural gem" has been placed to connote something rare and wondrous *because small*.

By 1925 a four-room Sears house tagged for $993 (model 3217) is all too obviously a downscale model in the postwar national economy. Catalogue customers limited to such a design might be expected to yearn instead for that year's Americus model—six fair-sized rooms for $2,173. (Recall that The Vernon offered ten rooms and more square footage for the same amount ten years earlier.) But, as usual, the Sears copywriters are ready to sell both high and low sales models. They take great pains not to let the brute facts of a society divided increasingly between haves and have-nots get in the way of the enticements they have to offer.

The two-story Americus (measuring 26 × 26 feet on each level—see figure 30) "is a fine home that any American can be proud of and be comfortable in. It is a dignified, substantial house that will stand out among its neighbors and never go out of style" (289). Not much more has to be said. It is a design intended to sell itself on its own merits as being one of the best, and the biggest, amidst the ever-dwindling house spaces available to homeowners in the 1920s.

In contrast, economy model 3217 is dollar-cheap precisely because it is *very* small (figure 31). It compresses a living room, dining room, two bedrooms averaging 9 × 10 feet, and a kitchen into a square box measuring 22 × 28 feet. But upon examining the name Sears gave to this little box, and the descriptive copy that floods its page, one realizes that the copywriters did not resign themselves to a lost cause. The Fairy features

Figure 30. Sears, The Americus (1921). National Trust for Historic Preservation in the United States.

FOUR ROOMS AND BATHROOM

Honor Bilt

The Fairy
No. 3217 "Already Cut" and Fitted.
$965.00

See Description of Honor Bilt Houses on page 9.

THE FAIRY is a comfortable bungalow home, with shingle siding. It has many features that will appeal to the housewife. There is quality in every foot of material. Yet, we will furnish all the material to build this bungalow at the very low price quoted. The splendid value is made possible by our modern and successful system of "Honor Bilt" homes.

The Living and Dining Room. The porch affords a pleasant place for warm summer evenings. The half glazed front door enables the housewife to see the caller before opening the door.

Having entered you find the living room combines with dining room. Hence the most economical use of floor space, without sacrifice of appearance. This combination living and dining room is about 12 feet wide by 15½ feet long. There is room for a piano between two windows on the outside wall. Your dining table and chairs may be set at the end of room nearest the kitchen and hidden by a screen if so desired. There is ample space for other furniture as shown on plan.

The Kitchen. A swinging door leads from the dining and living room into the kitchen. Here is a well planned kitchen, room to place cabinet, table, sink and range to make work easy which reduces the housewife's work and saves many steps each day. Two windows give plenty of light and air.

A door connects the kitchen with the rear entry, which has space for ice box, that can be iced without tracking dirt into the kitchen. From the rear entry, stairs lead to the outside and down to basement.

The Bedrooms. The front bedroom opens from the living room. It has a fair sized clothes closet with shelf.

A small hall is open from the living and dining room and gives privacy to rear bedroom and bath. Bathroom is just the right size and is conveniently located.

Basement. Excavated under entire house. Cement floor.

Height of Ceilings. Basement is 7 feet from floor to ceiling. Main floor rooms are 8 feet 6 inches from floor to ceiling.

What Our Price Includes.

At the price quoted, we will furnish all the material to build this four-room house, consisting of:
Lumber, Red Cedar Shingles for Siding; Lath;
Fire-Chief Shingle Roll Roofing, guaranteed for 17 years;
Framing Lumber, No. 1 Yellow Pine;
Flooring Interior Floors, Clear Yellow Pine; Porch Floor, Clear Edge Grain Fir;
Porch Pergola;
Finishing Lumber;
High Grade Mill Work (see pages 86 and 87);
Interior Doors of White Pine with Two Cross Panels of Fir;
Trim, Clear Yellow Pine, choice grain and color;
Windows of California Clear White Pine;
Medicine Cabinet; Building Paper; Sash Weights;
Eaves Trough and Down Spout;
Stratford Design Hardware (see page 113);
Paint for Three Coats for Outside Trim;
Stain for Two Coats, for Shingles on Walls;
Varnish and Filler, for Inside Trim and Doors;
Complete Plans and Specifications.
Built on concrete foundation, cement blocks above grade.
We guarantee enough material to build this house. Price does not include cement, brick, concrete blocks or plaster.

Can Be Built on a Lot 28 Feet Wide.

FLOOR PLAN.

This house can be built with the rooms reversed. See page 3.

OPTIONS.

Sheet Plaster and Plaster Finish to take the place of wood lath and plaster, $90.00 extra. See page 88.

Storm Doors and Windows, $48.00 extra.
Screen Doors and Windows, galvanized wire, $29.00 extra.

Oriental Slate Surfaced Shingles instead of Fire-Chief Roofing, $30.00 extra.

For prices of Plumbing, Heating, Wiring, Electric Fixtures and Shades see page 95.

Page 24

SEARS, ROEBUCK AND CO.

Figure 31. Sears, Model 3217, The Fairy (1925). National Trust for Historic Preservation in the United States.

the worthwhile human economies that come from cutting back on the
time and effort necessitated by large spaces.

No direct mention is made of the meager dimensions of The Fairy,
but its name evokes the particular charms possessed by diminutive things.
The copy insists upon the comfort and convenience that compactness has
to offer—the quality that the ever-useful word "cozy" instantly converts
into a virtue. It is an approach meant to be especially potent when addressing the mistress of the household.

> The Fairy is a comfortable bungalow . . . with many features that
> will appeal to the housewife. The combined living room and dining
> room allow the most economical use of floor space, without sacrific-
> ing appearance. The well planned kitchen has room to place a cabi-
> net, table, sink and range to make work easy, which reduces the
> housewife's work and saves many steps each day. (50)

The Fairy copy remarks on the "quality of every foot of material"—
a fact of interest to the man of the house, who is expected to meet its
payments, but it mainly caters to the workingman's wife, persuading her
(in the tone of Christine Frederick's *New Housekeeping*) that she will experience the money saved as pleasurable convenience, not as squalid
crowding. How else could this design be viewed as an alternative to the
rented apartments that the manufacturers of ready-made houses had to
counter every step of the way in their attempt to sell the idea of home
ownership to families with little buying power?[71]

Buying power was at its lowest ebb during the Great Depression, but
Sears struggled to sell its ready-mades in the dwindling market, focusing
on the middle-class families that still had money to spend. The Webster
and The Torrington of 1933 both cost a little over $3,000; both contain
seven rooms, two and one-half baths, living room fireplace, and an attached garage. Their brick and wood exteriors also call upon the architectural vocabulary indicative of the era's fixation on styles derived from
America's colonial past.[72] Both are houses that only those escaping the
hard times devastating the nation's economy could contemplate owning,
yet no allusion is made to the world that exists outside the dream-life of
the catalogue's pages.

Copy for The Torrington (figure 32) could just as well have come
from the house models featured in the 1920s. It foregrounds a woman's
concerns "with convenience in room arrangements; with features that add
to the appearance of interior and exterior; with the many modern-day improvements that help lighten the task of housekeeping" (237). A note for
the 1930s is introduced into the selling of The Webster. This model, however nostalgic its colonial facade, meets "today's needs." These needs are

THE TORRINGTON ..

▲ SEVEN ROOMS, TWO BATHS, GARAGE AND DINER

MODERN HOME
No. 3355
ALREADY CUT AND FITTED
PRICE $3189⁰⁰

MEN are concerned with ruggedness of construction—with quality of material and in an economical plan to finance the home—and women are, too. But women are interested in other things as well—with beauty and with style. They are concerned with the convenience in room arrangement; with features that add to the appearance of interior and exterior; with the many modern-day improvements that help to lighten the task of housekeeping.

This beautiful Colonial design is planned with outside walls of siding and brick. The gable ends and front and back walls of the wings are of face brick while the center portion is of siding.

THE FLOOR PLANS

Not only has careful thought been given to the front entrance, dining room bay, well balanced dormers and other exterior details, but the floor plans are ideal for a home of this size.

The First Floor: Entering the main stair hall you have large arched opening into the dining room on the left and living room on the right. Size 14 feet by 22 feet with three exposed walls, the living room lends itself to many happy arrangements of furniture with the fireplace as the pivot of interest.

Just one surprise after another as you continue to study this plan. The back hall or passage contains additional closet and lavatory; dining alcove with space for china cases; the most convenient kitchen you would ever hope for; attached garage and cellar entrance next to the rear door. The porch at the front of the garage has a French door entrance from the dining room.

The Second Floor: Four large bedrooms, each with two or three exposures, fine wall space and good closets will be just to your liking. The master bedroom, located over the dining room, is planned for private bath but could be rearranged with door into hall if so desired. The rooms are made additionally attractive by good windows.

We do not furnish stone, brick or any masonry material. Our base price includes all materials according to Specifications 11B, also 6-panel interior doors, Colonial backband trim, cabinets, oak flooring, LaTosca hardware, linoleum for kitchen, bath, lavatory and diner, with four coats enamel throughout.

SECOND FLOOR PLAN

FIRST FLOOR PLAN

Modern Homes Division

Figure 32. Sears, The Torrington (1932). National Trust for Historic Preservation in the United States.

not economic; rather, they are needs for self-enclosure and emotional in-
sularity. The Webster is likened to the

> newest homes, designed [to face] away from monotonous passing
> traffic, with living and dining rooms toward the garden. . . . From
> the kitchen an eye can be kept on both approaches. The large porch
> may be enjoyed without the family being on public view. (188)

By the close of the 1930s, Sears had to shut down its house-model
business, printing its last ready-made catalogue for the year 1940.[73] Yet
there is no way to tell from anything overt in the copy for The Bayside of
1938 (no price given) that the nation is economically distraught (figure
33). One can, however, read between the lines of the lush copy (as if from
the pen of Oliver Bell Bunce) that offers this bucolic design as a refuge
from modern times. Here is The Bayside—ironically, that consummate
product of the standardization and rationalization of the industrial process
and the business enterprise—disguised as a relic from the old days:

> Rarely will you be able to find a home so fully enraptured in solace
> and restive quietude as this substantial home, a replica of the type to
> which time-honored fisherfolk of the eastern seaboard were wont to
> repair after a strenuous day. Properly nestled on a partially wooded
> lot, this home with its wide shingle siding, picketed gate and shel-
> tered front entrance will prove a source of ever-growing delight.
> (105)

Gone in 1938 is the language once used to single out the "public"
features favored by the ready-made house plans of the 1920s; gone is the
"inviting front porch," the "friendly front entrance," or the veranda that is
"the ideal place to enjoy pleasant weather." True, copy for The Fairy back
in 1925 had commented that the "half glazed front door enables the housewife to see the caller before opening the door." But this expresses nothing
like the nervousness about possible intruders found in the copy for The
Webster, or for The Hampshire of the same year, which "turns its back on
an endless procession of autos" and "sets its entrance to the side where
those within can see all those who approach"—people like the tramps,
who were knocking upon the side doors of America asking for work and
some food.

The Bayside of 1938 looks back to the preindustrial, precorporate
days of sturdy fisherfolk, whose only storms were those of wind and rain.
The Hampshire is said to recall Paul Revere's house in a century whose
anxieties ceased with the winning of the nation's glorious revolution. But
take note that these 1930s excursions into nostalgia are not prompted by
memories of the *size* of houses from days of yore. Instead, the Sears copy

THE BAYSIDE ▲ ▲
▲ FIVE ROOMS AND BATH

CHARMING NEW ENGLAND DESIGN

RARELY will you be able to find a home so fully enraptured in
solace and restive quietude as this substantial home; a replica of
the type to which time-honored fisher folk of the eastern seaboard were
wont to repair after a strenuous day. Properly nestled on a partially wooded
lot, this home with its wide shingle siding, picketed gate, and sheltered front
entrance, will prove a source of ever-growing delight.

WELL ARRANGED INTERIOR PLAN

The interior arrangement is beyond compare. Every foot of space is put
to good use. All the rooms are comparatively large. There is a guest closet
off the hall. A notable feature is the stairway arising from the central connecting hall to the large attic. There is sufficient headroom for the installation of one or two rooms at a later date, providing additional space for the
expansion of the family, or for den, sewing room or recreation room.

Refer to specifications in the fore part of this book, and permit us to
quote you a delivered-to-your-station price for the materials required including plumbing, heating and lighting.

WHAT OUR PRICE INCLUDES

Our base price includes all the material needed for this home consisting of
lumber, lath, millwork, flooring, shingles, building paper, hardware, metal
and paint material according to general specifications shown on Pages 8, 9,
10 and 11. All Lumber furnished in convenient lengths.

Study introductory pages of this book and select the options which are
carefully explained for your convenience. Buy your home from *Sears* and
become a happy satisfied home builder.

SEARS, ROEBUCK AND CO.

MODERN HOME
No. 3410
NOT ALREADY CUT

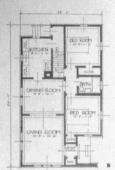

Floor Plan
Can be built on a lot
30 feet wide

641   Page 23

Figure 33. Sears, The Bayside (1938). National Trust for Historic Preservation in
the United States.

of the late 1920s points to the myth of better times when citizens were safe. If the desire for more space is replaced with a longing for coziness, this coziness has nothing to do with scientifically managed compactness; it has to do with the sense of security seized upon by people who burrow far inside, well away from the anxious outside.

Somehow the sales texts of the Depression years had to avoid mentioning the America of the moment, even if this meant ignoring the era's exemplary accomplishments in technology and the fetish for the rational treatment of material space. Also missing is the emphasis the 1910s and 1920s placed upon economies of construction, quality of material, and the thrill of owning a house that draws all eyes upon itself. Instead 1930s house models are celebrated as private spaces that coil in upon themselves. They strive to articulate a house dream that had not been voiced with such fervor since the likes of Oliver Bell Bunce.

In 1927 Herbert Hoover wrote the essay "Home Building and Home Ownership" for *Child Welfare Magazine*. Further notations on the subject were included in Hoover's foreword to *How to Own Your Home,* published in 1929 by the Better Homes of America. In 1931 Hoover as president was still making the same appeal—"to achieve home ownership" for the sake of "good business and good citizenship"—by merging his earlier statements into the opening chapter of *The Better Homes Manual.*[74]

It was not long before appeals began to come from the other direction, as beleaguered citizens began to address the country's top executive. These were not, however, appeals to Herbert Hoover (who had been the nation's best-known engineer and management expert throughout the 1910s and 1920s) but to Franklin Delano Roosevelt, once the electorate concluded that Hoover had mismanaged the times.

> I am an old Citizen . . . about 75 or 6 years old and Have Labored Hard all My Days until depression Came on and I Had No Job in three years and I have a Little Home I Bought when times were good and I managed to Pay my state and County tax But they claim I owe about 15 fifteen do City tax and going to sell my Little Home for that and will you Please sir Help me out the government Can Have a Lean on the Little House until I Get some way to Pay Back Please Sir do what you Can for me I am to old to be turned out of doors.[75]

Deep attachment to the idea of the family house led the imagination of Cecilia Beaux in yet another direction. In 1938 when Beaux, the well-known painter, set down memories of her Philadelphia girlhood in the 1860s and 1870s, she did not dream of the townhouses of that constricted little city, nor of the smallish house in which she grew up. The scene she records during the Depression years rises from her heart's desire. It is an image of

> deep quiet houses that stood in gardens, with tall trees and slopes. . . . There were high ceilings with windows to the floor of large rooms . . . [and there were] long wide halls, softly carpeted and curving stairs, mounting up to regions where running and peeping could be slyly enjoyed. There were views, too, of great bedrooms, where everything was ample and spatial, big smooth pillows, white bedspreads, heavy furniture, for which there was plenty of room, and spotless comfort everywhere.[76]

Although Cecilia Beaux's dream life seems to float in a world of its own, beyond the covers of the Sears and Sterling System-Built Homes catalogues, it might have been lived out in Sears Modern Home No. 167 or in other ready-made house plans made available prior to the 1910s and 1920s. But by 1930, whatever Herbert Hoover might have tried to wish into being by applying the newest management practices, the language of such space, such privacy, such "spotless comfort everywhere," existed only to recount one's dreams.

The discourse of reality, expressed by the old man in danger of losing his "Little Home," is heard again in words addressed by an old woman, not to President Roosevelt this time but to the president's wife: "Dear Mrs. Roosevelt. It's hard to be old and not have anything."[77]

In 1935 Laura Ingalls Wilder, mother of Rose Wilder Lane, the mythologizer of kitchen scenes in the little house on Edison Avenue, wrote *The Little House on the Prairie*. Like Cecilia Beaux, Wilder set down in loving detail house dreams located in the 1870s, but instead of the spacious, gracious Philadelphia houses Beaux envisioned, Wilder's houses were snug and cozy one-room "immigrant's cottages," in which the vaunted virtues of American family life assumed material form out in the free Western territories. Indeed, Wilder's children's book concludes with the Ingalls family having to push even farther west, dispossessed of the house left empty upon an endless horizon of lushly waving prairie grass. But the Ingalls family (as remembered from the distance of sixty years) still has all the pre-Turnerian time and space it needs to take roots on down the open trail of the open frontier.

In contrast, the Joad family, as written up by John Steinbeck in 1939, is cast off land now managed by anonymous groups, groups angry men cannot even track down to kill in retaliation. Lacking any "middle landscape" whatsoever, the family house the Joads leave behind may never be replaced by anything better than a Hooverville. As for the old man and the old woman who expressed themselves in plaintive letters to the Roosevelts, it is no longer a question of how much space they can have, but of what it means to have no space at all. The Sears, Roebuck and Sterling companies cannot come to their aid; nor can Hoover with his faith in scientific management; nor, just then, can the New Deal, through which Roosevelt's administration tried to reintroduce the revised principles of Taylorism to a country whose business enterprise, industrial process, and house lives seemed to have lost all semblance of the rational, the functional, and the efficient.

Society's Wastrels

To FOREGROUND FRAGMENTATION and/or alienation as the all-informing trope characterizing American narratives by World War I would misrepresent the cultural scene. For every prototypical plot line, clogged with dismembered body parts and anticipating *The Texas Chainsaw Massacre,* there are other narratives that are just as inherently interesting. Before turning toward *those* narratives, however, let us review some of the fragmentation stories that do indeed form part of the texture of *Taylored Lives.*

There is Rheta Childe Dorr's tale about Catherine, whose arm was (literally) chewed off by the jaws of the giant printing press. There is the charge made by the president of the International Association of Machinists in regard to the (metaphorical) decapitation effected by Taylorism: "Mr. Taylor says, 'Give us strong men with big physical bodies, but take their heads off; we do not want men with heads. . . . We will do their thinking for them.'"[1] And there is the observation Max Weber made in 1904—that Chicago is "like a man whose skin has been peeled off and whose intestines are seen at work."[2]

Whether one culls examples from the hard evidence of industrial accidents attributed to the speeding up of the work process and to the bosses' indifference to safety precautions, or makes tabulations of figurative references to the dismemberment of mind, soul, and body taking place in factory, office, and home, any study of modern times inevitably reinforces what Thorstein Veblen had feared all along: the functional derangement of business, industry, and society.[3]

Functional Derangements

Take Henry Ford for example: not for the purpose of a fast cut to polemical equations between oppressor and oppressed, controller and controlled, but in order to get a slant on the tangled organizational relations that obtained at the Ford Motor Company among worker, production line, product, and head man.

It is an oft-told tale that Ford intended the Model T to stand as a technological achievement with the die-cut completeness of an eternal Platonic form, so right as the ultimate mode of transportation for "the human motor" that it need never be altered. Once it rolled off the Highland Park assembly line for the first time in 1908, universalized by the color black, its total efficiency and utility satisfied (Ford believed) the full extent of the human capacity for desiring.

As it turned out, the car-buying public harbored desires and the rival manufacturers encouraged design aspirations: both exceeded what the Model T had to offer. Ford's one true theory about the relationship between perfect mechanisms and consumer wants was rejected in the face of a diversity of notions about what it means to own such a sacralized thing. These responses, which Ford identified as the result of the creeping growth of "nasty Orientalism" (read "Jewish"), forced him to redesign his production plans in 1927 in order to meet demands based on the nonutilitarian pleasures of style and fashion.[4]

Keep this situation in mind: Ford counted on the Model T as the "closure" to the narrative of his lifelong endeavor to achieve complete efficiency in both product and production. Then realize that the same man was never able to organize himself as the Model T of the perfected self.

Ford's contemporary Charles Cooley (followed shortly by George Herbert Meade) argued that the whole man entails "mental unification." Proponents of the new psychology and new sociology knew this just as surely as Ralph Waldo Emerson did when, writing on the verge of the nation's plunge into industrialization, he defined the "penny-wisdom" that results in "a half-man."[5] Although Ford was a reader of Emerson and although he, like Emerson, felt himself to be a "Child of Destiny" in pursuit of "'The Plan,' a shadowy Calvinistic belief in Fate or Foreordination," Ford never caught on to the faultiness of his self-manufacture.[6]

Samuel Marquis, in and out of Ford's employ as director of the Sociological Department between 1917 and 1921, has just been referring to Ford's propensity for throwing his executives on "the scrap heap." He sums up "the explicable and ironical contradiction" about Ford, this man of "shadows" whose dispersed qualities of greatness never cohered. Although

> a genius in the use of methods for the assembly of the parts of a machine, he has failed to appreciate the supreme importance of the proper assembly, adjustment, and balance of the parts of the mental

and moral machine within him. He has in him the makings of a great man, the parts lying about in more or less disorder. If only Henry Ford were properly assembled! If only he would do in himself that which he has done in the factory![7]

One of Ford's most loyal critics, Reinhold Niebuhr, railed against the social derangements that he, like many others, attributed to the production of "Mechanical Men in a Mechanical Age."[8] Niebuhr's charge against Fordism is familiar enough: although we desire to be whole, strengthened through "organic unity" with both the universe and human society, we are forced into lives of isolation, set adrift in a series of "mechanical relationships"—a bleak condition that can be relieved neither by "pure science" nor by the "engineers" but only by the coming of a band of "prophet-technicians."

For all Niebuhr's rejection of "pure science" and the "engineers," his solution is similar in many ways to the solution proposed by Veblen and others filled with a rising enthusiasm for "prophet-technicians." That this solution just compounds the problem it wishes to solve is one of the ironies with which we, as the legatees of an ever-expanding culture of management, have to deal today. As a story that places its emphasis upon the mechanistic dismantling of organic entities whose fragments are wastefully strewn upon the winds of change, it is typical of its time and all too familiar in ours. Thus it is time to shift from twice-told tales toward those "more interesting" ones. Consider, then, stories about individuals compacted—not dispersed—by the mechanization of society into an indivisible mass, their pleasurable dreams of organic unity replaced by fantasies of machine-made wholes.

The Great American Compacting Machine

Upon his belated return to his homeland in 1904, Henry James is not off the ship before he becomes a fascinated witness to the "applied passion" of New York City. Confronted by a level of "power" and "energy" whose like he had never experienced, James makes a valiant attempt to release language energetic enough to meet the hyperbolic force of the city's harbor on its own fantastic terms: the "bold lacing together . . . of the scattered members of an enormous system of steam-shuttles or electric bobbins"; the "web," the "colossal set of clockworks"; the "steel-souled machine-room of brandished arms and hammering fists and opening and closing jaws."[9] In the months to come, as he restlessly wanders around the American scene, caught up within the pulsating energies of advanced capitalism and late industrialization, James tries to discover what manner of product this "steel-souled machine-room" is grinding out, what its "brandished arms and hammering fists and opening and closing jaws" are doing to human lives.

Ellis Island and the Yiddish theater district on the Lower East Side are two of the sites James visits in search of answers. His reactions to the influx of "aliens" are complex enough. He senses that he and his kind are being dispossessed by a flood of peoples whose presence defamiliarizes not only the streets of old New York and the general social landscape but the decor of his memories as well. Yet if James, exasperated and anxious, has much to say about the effects of the "new people" upon "his people"— of changes that displace the remembered pastoralism of his boyhood city with the "applied passion" of "mechanical men in a mechanical age"—he is also alert to the perhaps harmful transformations being wrought upon "them."

Once James perceives that Ellis Island is a door that rushes thousands of the aliens through "an intendedly 'scientific' feeding of the mill," he realizes what the "colossal set of clockworks" positioned in the harbor is doing there. First ingested, then spewed forth by "the clock that never, never stops," the aliens have become the main product of "this visible act of engurgitation on the part of our body politic and social."

James next traces the movements of the newly "engurgitated" Jews on the Lower East Side. As a rapt spectator at the Yiddish theater, he again considers the question of the "foreigners." One melodrama he attends involves the escape "the virtuous heroine" makes from the clutches of the villain; she sets off the mechanism of "our superior Yankee machine," the Murphy bed that swallows the scoundrel "as in the jaws of a crocodile." In this effective plot closure, the heroine releases herself from her plight, but what matters to James is that this bit of stage action provides an apt simile for what may be happening to those pulled through the massive maw of Ellis Island.

James queries whether the incredible energy of "our superior Yankee machine," the spell of "our offered mechanic bribes," will efface the aliens' instincts for picturing life. Will not *what they once were*—the various places and cultures that gave them their original "organic unity"—now be eliminated, their diverse individualities be replaced by the mechanic unity of the "applied passion" of that machine process known as "Americanization"?

Unity through Americanization was an established part of the Ford Motor Company's plan for enhanced production. As we saw in chapter 7, immigrants were taken through an assembly-line process intended to transform them into good citizens and loyal workers. Aliens in alien dress carrying alien flags stepped into a large melting pot to emerge in American clothes waving American flags, representations of the company's role in the mass production of the American Way.

Once Murphy beds and ceremonial cauldrons are introduced, the plight of the mechanical man in the mechanical age has a certain comic edge not found in the stilted earnestness of Reinhold Niebuhr's fulminations. Murphy beds have provided a useful prop for many a stage farce and two-reel comedy. Patriotic pageants of the kind performed at Ford's English School are somewhat risible. There were, however, serious-minded reactions to the assembly-line production of Model T Americans, some of them quite favorable.

Israel Zangwill's 1908 play *The Melting Pot* won praise from Theodore Roosevelt and others whose Progressivist hopes were supported by any such conceptualizations. It assured those who preferred a nation comprised of citizens whose ethnic edges were polished smooth, cut to patterns designed to function efficiently within normative work environments and social situations.[10] Melting together suggested wholeness, not the feared dismemberment of the old America into political factions and class conflicts; it augured the triumph of "transcendental materialism"— "a totalizing phenomenon that subordinated all social activities to production."[11]

Others were less sanguine. They viewed the products extracted from raw material, first chewed then spit out by the great American machine, with trepidation. The assembly-line process did not bring wholeness but leveling off, not democracy but socialism, not the authority of the best individuals but the disorder of a coagulate mass.

Henry James had complex and unresolved feelings about the two-way effect this circulating process would have upon "us" and "them." The unadulterated hatred Henry Adams felt for the new forms unity was taking in the age of the dynamo is well known. Less familiar are the warning statements made in 1884 by Melusina Fay Peirce, one of the heroines of material socialism, who expended prodigious amounts of energy to forward the cause of cooperative housekeeping.[12] Peirce (a descendant of Anne Hutchinson and former wife of Charles Sanders Peirce) said many worthy things about the rights of women in a world dominated by men, but when it came to the homogenizing effects the new industrial process had upon women of education, breeding, and intellectual fineness, her class instincts took over. Once women were run through the "iron hopper," Peirce cautioned, they would be disgorged not as persons of value but as that unwanted collective unit, factory workers of the "most repulsive and degrading" sort.

Peirce's observations come from the 1880s when the effects of the industrializing process initiated in the Lowell textile mills during the 1830s were intruding ever more blatantly upon the American scene, although they had yet to reach the level of the "bold lacing together" powered by the "enormous system of steam-shuttles or electric bobbins" James witnessed in the early 1900s. By the 1920s, even more Americans (old and new) felt the force of the "brandished arms and hammering fists and opening and closing jaws." Melusina Fay Peirce, Henry Adams, and Henry James were not the only ones to react against a notion of wholeness that entailed fitting everyone to a single pattern. Old-style Americans objected to the perceived loss of specialness because of their allegiance to traditions of individuality supposedly shared only by so-called *real* Americans. But resistance to modern management principles also came from women like Helga Crane, descendant of an enslaved race, which had had no say about being chewed up by the American Way long before the industrial process was introduced.

Helga Crane, the protagonist of Nella Larsen's 1928 novel *Quicksand,* is furious over what is being done to her by Naxos, the Negro college that has more than a passing resemblance to Booker T. Washington's Tuskegee Institute. She feels trapped by "its air of self-righteousness and intolerant dislike of difference" and its "cold, slowly accumulated unreason." Lest she become a victim of "a machine" that she likens to "a big knife with cruelly sharp edges ruthlessly cutting all to a pattern, the white man's pattern," she must try to escape—just as surely as her future fellow victim, the Invisible Man, must avoid being blended into one white mass of "Optic White" at the Liberty Paint plant, where "*we the machines inside the machine.*" [13] By this time, no one of any class, gender, or race seemed safe from the mighty forces of Taylorism and Fordism, forces producing a nation whose notion of wholeness was inspired not by Emerson's man redeemed from the ruins but by the Model T.

One of the cleverest (perhaps too clever, but more on that later) critiques of the ethos of the mechanical man in the mechanical age is Nathanael West's 1931 comic novel, *A Cool Million; or, The Dismantling of Lemuel Pitkin.* West forcefully demonstrates that it is not the acts of dismemberment that endow modern times with optimum horror-story qualities so much as the process of *reassembly,* which pulls scattered parts into strange new wholes and surrealistic consumer products.

Who has never experienced the primal shiver at seeing the stitches that seam the face of Boris Karloff in *Frankenstein,* a film appearing the same year as West's novel? The assembled whole brought into being by men of science, crazed or not, terrifies. Shudders run deeper still when the result is not some alien monster, birthed in some alien Transylvanian province, but (as in West's novel) the young American of Emerson's vision—torn apart, then sutured back together as the all-American boy, martyr for a nation freed at last from "the aliens."

Nathanael West is an apt author to shape this narrative of the fall and rise of Lemuel Pitkin. West—who practiced first at remaking himself from the nice Jewish son of a prosperous building contractor into an approximate representation of gentile wit and obnoxiousness—writes as though he had discovered just in time that he was not, after all, the son of Horatio Alger, or the grandson of Benjamin Franklin, or the nephew of Ralph Waldo Emerson.[14] His true lineage comes to him from Mark Twain as grandfather, Thorstein Veblen as father, and Henry Ford as uncle and evil genius.

West takes up the narrative grotesquerie native to Twain's rendering of Jim Blaine's "symmetrically" drunken tale about Miss Wagner, who has a glass eye, wooden leg, and bewigged bald scalp, and William Wheeler, who "got nipped by the machinery in a carpet factory and went through in less than a quarter of a minute," leaving his widow with a roll fourteen yards long to honor at his funeral.[15] But in West's hands, the frontier specificity of Twain's humor expands to encompass an entire nation and its destiny. The joke he wants to tell must push beyond anecdote; it warrants a novella-length narrative shaped by the "symmetrical" outrageousness of his uninebriated wit.

West's novel opens with the old saying, "John D. Rockefeller would give a cool million to have a stomach like yours."[16] Such suggested trade-offs structure the entirety of West's narration of Lemuel Pitkin's adventures. Body parts extracted from Lem's original "organic unity" are constantly being exchanged to serve the greater needs of the American corporate (read as "political") enterprise.

Lemuel Pitkin initially embodies one of America's proudest possessions: the hero of the combined Franklin/Alger narrative. He is a package complete with youth, health, high spirits, boundless optimism, sterling virtues, and full faith in the work ethic, supplemented by the obligatory widowed mother, genteel poverty, and childhood sweetheart. But this product, based upon a merger of inherited plot lines, is no longer marketable in the America that first produced it. Narrative attributes appropriate for the young American's tale of success are the first things to be stripped away. By the end of the opening chapter, West has dispossessed Lem of this now obsolete plot line. He hands Lem over to another, updated narrative tradition—one marked by nightmarish details of the kind the later Mark Twain utilized in lieu of the genial mutilations typical of his *Roughing It* period.[17]

In terms of bodily dispossession, Lem in short order loses all of his teeth, an eye, his left thumb, one leg, and his scalp, his vigor, his youth, and his wits. Only now can he become a contributing member of the society represented by Nathan "Shagpoke" Whipple, the dark genius of the tale into which Lem has been tumbled without ever knowing it.

By this point, Lem's maimed body and depleted mind has been incorporated into Sylvanus Snodgrasse's "Chamber of American Horrors, Animate and Inanimate Hideosities" (162). Whipple denounces Snodgrasse's touring show as a conspiracy supported by Jews, Catholics, unions, and the like, since it highlights a history of violence, rape, and murder. It also foregrounds a welter of consumer products, including Venus de Milo with a clock set in her abdomen; Hiram Powers's "Greek Slave," with elastic bandages at every joint; Hercules bound by a surgical truss; and objects made of paper that look like wood, wood that looks like paper, rubber disguised as steel, and steel passing as cheese.

In the melee that results when Whipple commandeers the Chamber of Horrors for his own purposes (a riot that ends with the heads of Negroes paraded on pikes, a Jewish salesman nailed to his hotel room door, and the rape of the Catholic priest's housekeeper), Lem manages to escape, but not for long. His finest hour lies just ahead, the narrative purpose for which he has been destined all along by Shagpoke Whipple.

Lem's current occupation is that of a "stooge" in a stage act. His surrogate body parts fly off when the team of Riley and Robbins whack at him with an enormous mallet labeled "The Works." Rescued by Whipple from this base existence, Lem is featured in a pageant as a victim in a nation taken over by degenerate foreigners. During the opening performance, a man wearing false whiskers suddenly appears and shoots Lem through the heart, killing him. The remaking of Lemuel Pitkin is completed with the creation of a martyr in whose name Whipple leads his National Revolution to victory and himself to supreme power.[18] Thereafter Lem's birthday is observed as a national holiday. His name and the memory of his mutilated body now represent all that is whole and pure.

Lem Pitkin's story concludes with society "purged of alien diseases," with "America become again America." "All hail, the American Boy!" (179). Lem may not have received "a cool million" in exchange for his body parts, but the Rockefellers, Fords, and Whipples have gotten exactly what they need: a preassembled package of symbolic goods to sell to the American people.

The American System

Although it meant wasting their talents, Ford was not hesitant to "scrap" his executives. But Ford also made news because of his unusual utilization

of workers whom other industrialists did (and still would) discard. Inspired by the adage "waste not, want not," the Ford Motor Company
employed a legion of disabled workers: in 1914, 680 legless men, 2,637
one-legged men, two armless men, 715 one-armed men, and ten blind
men.[19]

Ford, the man who was never "properly assembled," developed (although he did not originate) the production-line system. He incorporated
the work activities of the disassembled human bodies itemized above into
the making of cars whose technological triumph lay in the canny use of
interchangeable parts. Notwithstanding the problems Ford's method
caused "the human element"—workers who were not born into the world
as "pieces of metal that were all alike"—the cars assembled from "more
than five thousand separate parts, made of many different materials, and
of many sizes and shapes, *were* put together to make a magical whole."[20]

Ford became one of the leading legends of the American Way of business success because he pushed the "thorough identity of parts" to the
point of perfection. His achievement of true interchangeability recalls
some of the aims of the so-called "American System." This series of manufacturing procedures, first introduced in the 1850s and developed during
the Civil War when small arms factories were urged to make rapid field
replacements feasible, was adopted by a widening group of other industries throughout the final decades of the nineteenth century.[21]

"The American System" (a term first used by British observers at the
Springfield Armory) refers to an overarching project that was bent on replacing individualizing handwork with standardized mechanization for
the purpose of lowering production costs. "The New England System" is
now accepted as the correct term for speaking of the inception of precision
manufacture that abets interchangeability of parts. Scholars of the history
of technology rightly insist that one avoid oversimplifying methodological linkages between later developments in the manufacture of small arms,
sewing machines, and motor cars. What cannot be ignored is the increasing application of concepts and techniques of scrupulous measurement
modeled upon the tooling of military weaponry, first in the design of dress
patterns, next in the ready-made garment industry, and finally in the assembly procedure Fordism made famous.

Briefly stated, the complex story that plots the desire for *industrialized
likeness* contains these elements: (1) the vaunted "Yankee enterprise" that
Henry Adams praised in his account of the crafting of sloops of war during the War of 1812—that national flair for invention that turned the making of clocks, guns, locks, and, later, sewing machines, bicycles, and cars
into the American miracle, a knack that requires organizational talent as

much as technological innovations; (2) the impetus of the Civil War, which furthered the government's bureaucratization of armory manufacture in order to augment the design and production of interchangeable parts; (3) the creation of that vast coagulate, the Union Army, which needed not only workable guns but also uniforms in great quantities, a situation that led to the establishment of "Government Tailors' Shops" and the codification of male body measurements; (4) the postwar merchandizing of women's dress patterns by entrepreneurs such as Madame Demorest, once they solved the measurement problems caused by the "irregularities" of the female form; (5) the singular success of the Singer Sewing Machine Company after it incorporated precision manufacturing lessons learned during the war; (6) the rise of the ready-made garment industry during the 1890s, with all its industrial, economic, and social consequences, such as the "democratization of clothing," the sweatshop system, the strike of 1910 when 20,000 women shirtwaist-makers walked off the job, and the Triangle fire; (7) the establishment of Platonizing procedures, which rationalize every step along the way—nowhere more apparent than in the making of women's clothing, from the devising of the original design, to the "sloper" that is "draped," "drafted," and "corrected" upon the dummy, to the snip of scissors in the cutting room, which transforms the "standardized prototype" into the "assorted" pieces "assembled" by "operators," which results (the bosses hope) in a "runner," not a "lemon."[22]

What can we extract from these intertangled histories? Just this: that the relation of parts to wholes was both the leading principle in the standardization procedures considered necessary to modern industrial production and the guiding trope for lives led within a culture of management.

What this relation was *not* supposed to entail was what Whitman found when he searched for his brother George in the countryside near Fredericksburg just after the battle of December 13, 1862: "a heap of feet, arms, legs, &c., under a tree."[23] The prosthesis business would flourish after the war in attending to the tragic dismemberment of human bodies,[24] but a more cheerful side of the war was the systemization of methods for measuring the human body while still in one piece.[25] (At the time soldiers were issued their uniforms, they had not yet entered the battles that might tear them apart.)

There was *direct measure* and there was *proportional measure*. It is the latter of these two methods that coincides with the concepts informing nearly every area of nineteenth-century scientific classification. Proportional systems relied on the principle that human bodies had set proportions and, therefore, that one measurement was the key to the rest. . . . [They] attempted to reduce measuring and cutting to a series of mathematical calculations which in theory eliminated human error and wastage.[26]

Pattern-makers and amateur home sewers, and later, cutters in ready-made garment shops, came to depend on "uniformity." Clothing was made to fit a series of predetermined norms in the expectation that people would conform to the clothing. In contrast, direct measure was the older, more haphazard method that remained the province of the bespoke tailor and the custom dressmaker. In reverse of the expectations of proportional measure, its tools conformed to the individual human body (see figure 34). This essentially laissez-faire notion would not do for the mass dispersal of Butterick patterns or the cutting of ready-mades, which followed the ideal laid down by the small arms manufacturers in the 1850s. And an ideal it was. "The entire system was based on a model or pattern weapon. For armsmakers, *model* was used in the Platonic sense of an *ideal form*."[27]

Reliance on Platonic forms (backed by standardized mathematical calculations) made possible the move from custom-tailoring[28] to mass-produced ready-mades,[29] just as the faith in universals and mathematical calculations aided in the refinement of products ranging from armaments, clocks, and bicycles to cars, portable radios, and office furniture.

Even when considered apart from the techniques and technologies it shares with the design of military weaponry, the clothing industry as an economic, cultural, social, and political enterprise is not, of course, entirely innocent. In their essential forms, dress patterns and shirtwaists are sufficiently benign objects, but despite the emphasis that clothing manufacturers place upon the fitness of each part to the final whole, they also allow the whole to be seen as a series of detachable parts.

The troublesome quality introduced by the look of fragmentation is made manifest in pages taken from garment catalogues and pattern books. Louis Adler, manufacturer of cloaks, presents an endless line of headless, armless models (figure 35). *The Delineator* floats upon its page sleeves with the surrealistic look of poisonous mushrooms or the nauseous swing of elephants' trunks (figure 36). Once we carry through on what "essential forms" might mean in a society gone a bit mad over measurements, standardization, classification, and the interchangeability of parts, we quickly arrive at territory staked out by the proponents of human engineering.

Human engineering, under which eugenics was subsumed, was called "euthenics" by Ellen H. Richards in 1910. The full title of Richards's book is *Euthenics: The Science of Controllable Environment. A Plea for Better Living Conditions as a First Step toward Higher Human Efficiency*—a clear assertion

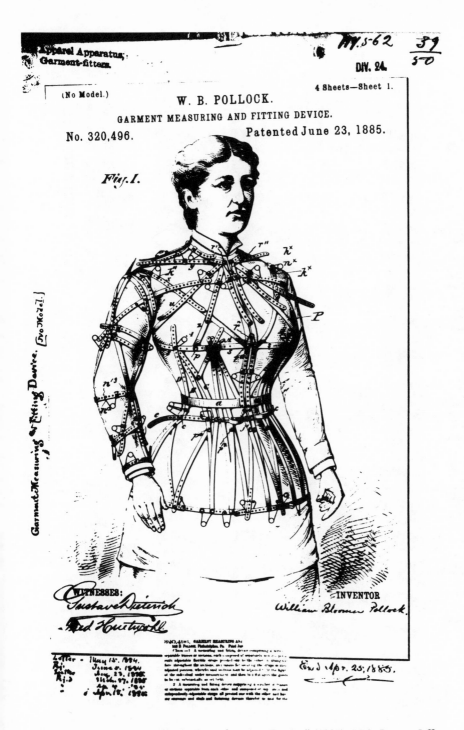

Figure 34. William B. Pollock, "Conforming Device" (1885). U.S. Patent Office, No. 320,496.

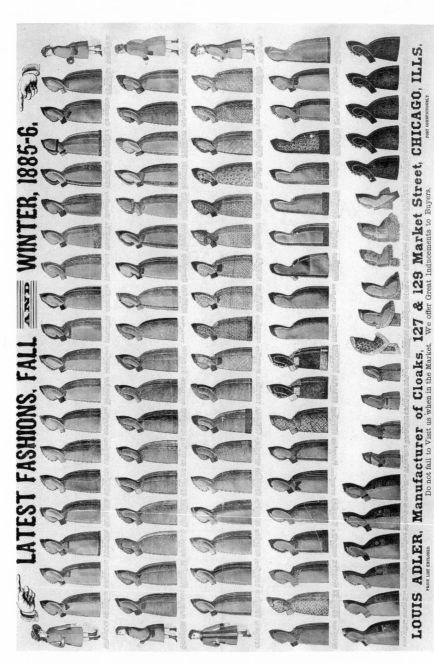

Figure 35. "Latest Fashions, Fall and Winter, 1885–6 . . ." Chicago Historical Society.

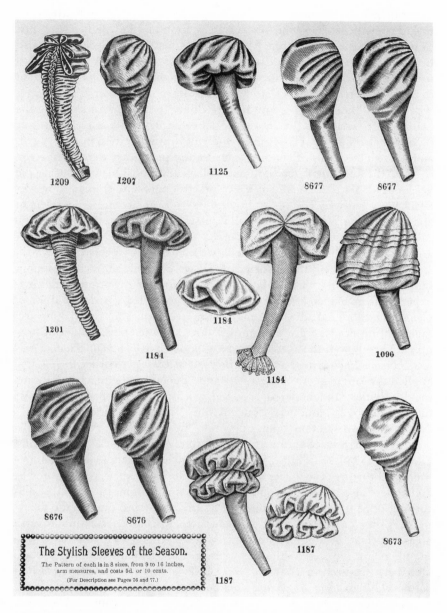

Figure 36. "Stylish Sleeves of the Season" (1897). From *The Delineator*.

of her belief that personal efficiency, sought by means of the scientific control of societies, is her "one best way" for attaining the "higher" life. Just as striking is the fact that the Massachusetts Institute of Technology also became the site for such an experiment, however briefly. A 1928 endowment funded a series of lectures, conferences, courses, and texts dedicated to the proposition that MIT students must learn how to convert knowing what to do ("knowledge") into how to do it ("power"). Anticipating the "Humanics" activities, Erwin Schell delivered *The Million Dollar Lecture* before the MIT senior classes in engineering administration in 1920, 1921, and 1922. The "rules of conduct" this lecture promoted were guaranteed to save "the Tech man" ten thousand dollars additional income during the years ahead. Further benefits came to practitioners who studied (however anachronistically by the 1920s) how to be "a loyal citizen," a "gentleman and a Christian."[30] It is the Lem Pitkin story taken seriously, not satirically, whereby wholes are disarranged into detachable parts, then rearranged according to needs defined by the human engineers.

Prestigious institutions such as MIT were not alone in championing human engineering. In 1923 J. J. Dorey, a former mechanic, efficiency expert, and manager of a detective agency, compiled *The Daily Workers' Counsellor*. It offered advice on engineering techniques for the making and saving of money, the prevention of failure, and the enhancement of progress. Throughout the 1920s and 1930s, books like *The Man-Building Process, Human Engineering,* and *The Business of Living: Personal Engineering* applied the language of "blueprints" and "operating the machine" to human activities, and lingered over the words engineers privileged most highly: "doing," "conduct," "purposeful," "control," "clean," "orderly," "simplicity," "discipline," and, of course, "power."[31]

Mechanisms used for measurement, like W. B. Pollock's Conforming Device of 1885 (see figure 34), conjure up ancient instruments of confinement and torture. Garments molded upon absent bodies (as in figures 35 and 36) are also visually disquieting. But human engineering is most disturbing once it spreads the touch of its invisible hand outside the dressmaker's shop and ready-made garment factory. Its infiltration into diverse areas of private and public life suggests the possibility of a society whose members are reduced to the "interchangeable elements forming a body alphabet," featured in *The Grid: A Modular System for the Design and Production of Newspapers, Magazines, and Books*.[32]

The "remarkable signage system" designed for the Munich Olympics is illustrated in figure 37. Nonetheless, once terrorists broke through the grids enclosing the Israeli compound, history and politics proved stronger than the ideals of "simplicity," "control," and "purposefulness" comfortingly sequestered within the margins of the grid based on the *De Divina*

Figure 37. Otl Archer, signage for Munich Olympics (1972).

Proportione, "the golden section," of Phidias. If human engineering cannot guarantee Olympic athletes the full benefits of the "controllable environment" Ellen Richards called for, what chance does Lemuel Pitkin have of enjoying Shagpoke Whipple's use of his "interchangeable parts"? What chance does Theodore Dreiser's Clyde Griffiths have to beat a "signage system" that tells its own story lacking in simplicity, discipline, control, purposefulness, and power?

Perfect Fits

At last we have a hero and heroine who fit the perfect plot, which resolves the suggested agon between "the human element" and "the industrial body" by disclosing that they are one and the same (see figures 38 and 39). Finally, the dream of attaining that "point of maximum productive output and minimum exhaustion" can be fulfilled, a dream that, for management and workers alike, is "the *summum bonum* of modern society." Possessing physiological measurements that have no quarrel with the newest technologies, these new bodies function "without fatigue, without discontent, and without aversion to work."[33]

Joe and Josephine are the great-grandchildren of the hopes projected by both Hermann von Helmholtz and Karl Marx. Platonic forms created by the well-known product designer Henry Dreyfuss, they also require no "moral qualities" and contain no "immoral qualities." Using numbers, they match "the laws of nature with the laws of production."[34] When viewed as the incarnation of the culmination of the shift from "labor" to

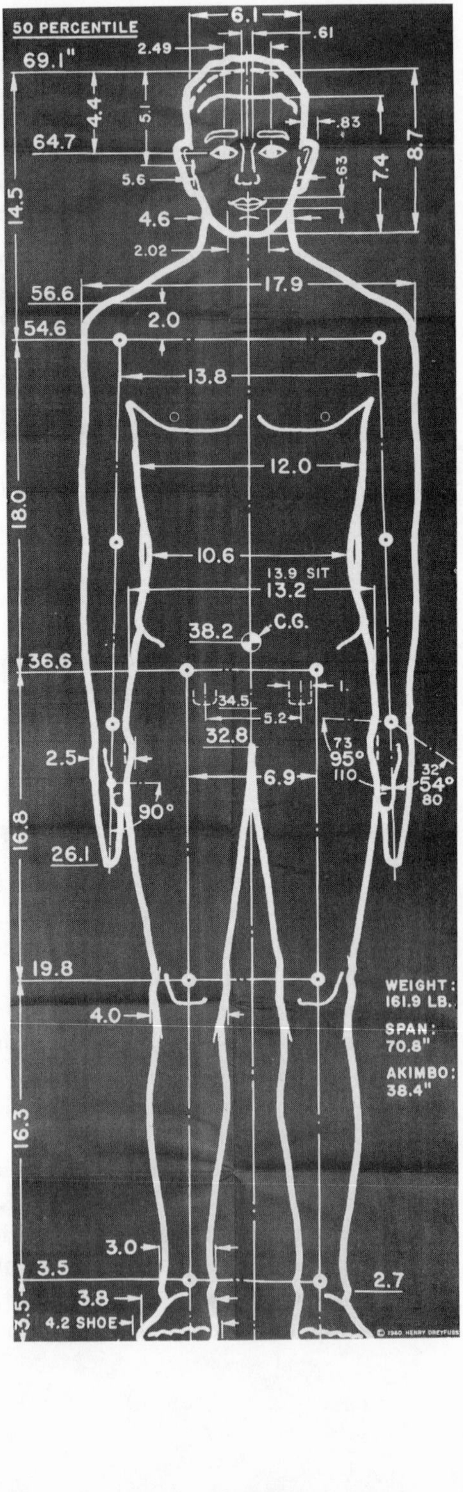

Figure 38. "Joe." From Henry Dreyfuss, *The Measure of Man* (1959). (c) Whitney Library of Design.

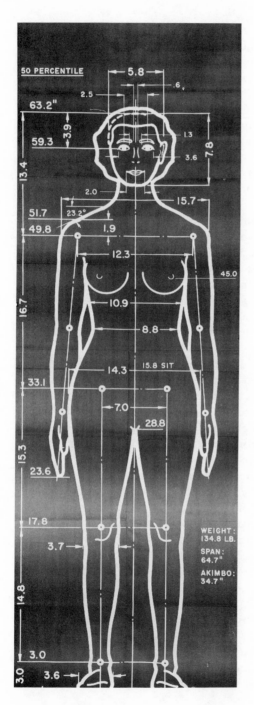

Figure 39. "Josephine." from Henry Dreyfuss, *The Measure of Man* (1959). (c) Whitney Library of Design.

"labor power," Joe and Josephine represent work as "a potentiality that can be marketed and measured in units of time."

Unencumbered by "human will, moral purpose, or even technical skill," these artificial forms replace mortal laborers whose wastefulness derived from their anachronistic commitment to work that is "at once productive, rational, and moral." They embody the "natural language of the phenomena" of activated physical forces; they are participants in a wordless discourse "superior to all other modes of expression." Once Joe and Josephine are placed within their designed work spaces, earnest reformers no longer need listen to "moral exhortations, the idealization of the 'true worker,' and the reflections of political economists on the needs of the worker." [35]

The story of Joe and Josephine is *about* the perfection of the working body, the work task, and the work environment as authored by Henry Dreyfuss. Computed to be the theoretically average male and female, their schematized figures serve as the means to the end of solving complex design problems. They indicate how far the new profession of industrial engineering has come in its use of rationalized models placed in functional contexts—that crucial first step in model-making that will lead to product designs that are safe, comfortable, and effective in the elimination of fatigue and wasted motion. [36]

In Dreyfuss's words, Joe and Josephine exist as an " 'encyclopaedia' of human factors data . . . presented in graphic form." [39] Proof of the "underlying affinity between physiology and technology," they demonstrate how the human physique can be accommodated to standardized workplace "applications," such as reach, sight lines, and sitting posture (see figure 40). [30] But once we move away from the privileged plane of paper patterns, percentiles, graphs, and grids, the *absences* in the story of Joe and Josephine reveal a fatal flaw, and perhaps the presence of monsters in our midst. [39]

In what manner of dramatic action can encyclopedic data be engaged? It is true that these forms are defined by specific work functions and work sites, such as shipboard maintenance, machine tools, farm and industrial equipment, missile systems, and military vehicles. If a "human element" were added to his blueprint, Joe could be made the protagonist in a narrative of sailors at sea, or of an airman in a gripping scene who flies his plane into combat, or of the operator of a giant crane breaking ground for a visionary dam project; Josephine, at the least, could figure (although with less dramatic flare) in episodes from the life of a stenographer, a housewife, or the driver of a drill press. This is not the case, however.

Although the potential narrative spread of their work worlds is sufficiently wide, Joe and Josephine are limited to roles defined by their occupational functions within specific settings. Even though their graphics are

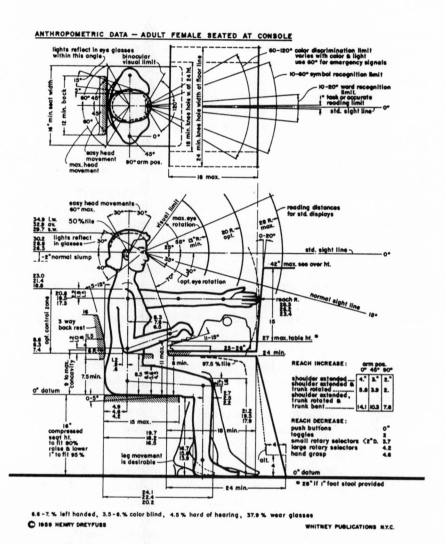

Figure 40. "Anthropometric Data—Adult Female Seated at Console." From Henry Dreyfuss, *The Measure of Man* (1959). (c) Whitney Library of Design.

life-sized, they appear as mere dots within a vast panorama of industrial, agricultural, and military space, through which they are moved by the invisible hands of the designers in charge.

Even Joe and Josephine's anthropometric possibilities are limited. Much of Dreyfuss's data was supplied by the armed forces, thereby predetermining a bias toward stories of men at war. Dreyfuss acknowledged that even though his percentiles included data for small, medium, and large body types, they were limited in regard to race (few minorities were included in his tabulations), age, and geographic location.[40] He also realized that his static graphic examples cannot account for the dynamic qualities the bodies of real Joes and Josephines introduce into design spaces. More than most, Dreyfuss was aware that product designers, as authors of mathematically based work narratives, must add "thought" and "imagination" to the raw percentiles used to chart any "theoretical group based on average dimensions."

Dreyfuss was sensitive to the need to take the dynamics of "the industrial body" into consideration, but he did not (indeed could not, given his particular conception of industrial design) take other "human factors" into account. It is conceivable that designers apply thought and imagination in order to anticipate how Joe's work capacity would be affected if he were to suffer from hemorrhoids while seated in the cab of a Caterpillar tractor. They may even write into their design narratives featuring Josephine at her stenographer's desk appropriate suggestions for dealing with impairments to her day's work if ever she is wracked by migraines brought on by her menstrual periods. It is unlikely, however, that even the most innovative of the industrial engineers and product designers will offset the passivity diagramed into a Joe or a Josephine; the schematic measurements of these representations eliminate moral and immoral qualities, and with them eliminate emotional needs and intellectual doubts.

Take the way a new employee perceives his work space when entering upon his new life at the Griffiths Collar & Shirt Company.

> And there, amid a thunderous hum of machines, Clyde was led to the extreme west of the building and into a much smaller department which was merely railed off from the greater chamber by a low fence. Here were about twenty-five girls and their assistants with baskets, who apparently were doing their best to cope with a constant stream of unstitched collar bundles which fell through several chutes from the floor above.[41]

Certainly Samuel Griffiths or his son Gilbert, keen as they are to foster efficient production procedures, ought to call in industrial designers for expert advice on how to remedy misuse of the work space within and adjacent to the stamping room. There are other concerns, however, that they will never think to address and that Dreyfuss could never manage to answer: the ways in which the work environment at the Griffiths plant affects the narrative lives of a Clyde Griffiths and a Roberta Alden introduced into a room filled with the bodies, thoughts, and imaginations of those "employed so mechanically as to leave their minds free to roam from one thought of pleasure to another" (1:243).

> For it was summer—late June. And over all the factory, especially around two, three and four in the afternoon, when the endless repetition of the work seemed to pull on all, a practical indifference not remote from languor and in some instances sensuality, seemed to creep over that place. There were so many women and girls of so many different types and moods. And here they were so remote from men or idle pleasure in any form, all alone with just him, really. (1:242–43)

As mere "representations"—graphics charted with formal precision upon the surface of sheets of paper—Dreyfuss's Joe and Josephine are shielded by the "rawness" of their data from the exquisitely calibrated, however mechanistic, desires felt, for instance, by Faulkner's Joe (Christmas) and Joanna (Burden).[42] The "average" male and female forms serve as surrogates for living flesh. Although intended by their makers as instruments for advancing the bodily ease and safety of real workers, and for reducing chances for discomfort or jeopardy, Joe and Josephine cannot themselves be hurt.[43]

What allowances are made, for instance, for the passions unleashed in a Faulkner novel when a man, that tool-using animal, discovers the exact instrument he requires to confront the effrontery of the world's energy? The Tall Convict in "Old Man" learns that a tin can of food can be used for other purposes than eating. Driven by terror and rage over the unthinkable fact that the woman he has been transporting across a waterscape gone mad in floodtime has just borne a child on an Indian mound writhing with snakes, poised just above the crest of biblical waters, he converts the edge of the can into a tool for cutting through the infant's umbilical cord. Under extreme duress, the Tall Convict also learns how to use a knife to slay a monster (an alligator to those in the know) whose like he has never seen before, a monster that would drag him under the waters of the swamp if it could. Then there is Popeye from *Sanctuary,* who seizes upon the right tool—the corncob conveniently at hand in the crib where Temple Drake lies—to enact the rape that is beyond the capacity of his impotent human motor. None of these violent acts of cutting, slitting, and slashing recorded by Faulkner takes place within the sanctuary of a designer's laboratory. His life stories happen because of, not despite, the unholy irrationality of the ungridded scene and the incalculable situation.

Platonic models used in the design of products or of work environments vicariously absorb our potential encounters with bodily injury or work fatigue. Although incapable of feeling desire, they are an important means of stimulating product desire, because they incorporate new concepts of aesthetics and psychology as well as the most advanced engineering techniques. They cannot, however, aid us in our living, up to a point. They have become our lives, up to a point; but not all the way, not in all things.

Joe and Josephine are Platonic entities predicated on proportional "rightness." They are functionaries in controlled design systems that stand apart, somewhat out of sync with the sprawl of experience that is never fully curbed. Through them designers correct the mistakes of Nature, God, and Society—this, despite the fact that people existing outside the design studio continue to contend with the consequences of exactly those mistakes. Created as a "theoretical group based on average dimensions," they share a wholeness found only in "clear, rational" models. Theirs is a clean, ahistoricized sanctuary of blueprints and graph paper wherein they are defined in terms of "a style beyond style, a world of permanently valid forms."[44]

In 1934 the Museum of Modern Art placed on exhibition stunning examples of what could be built from such design models—desk chairs, telephones, radios, lamps, and so on. When the museum selected as its epigraph Plato's definition of beauty—"straight lines and circles, and shapes plane or solid, made from them by lathe, ruler and square"—it left no doubt as to what kind of public narrative it presented within its privileged space and what kind of protagonists peopled its plot line: *Plato's best*.[45]

By the time of the MOMA show, an arresting thing had happened to the nature of object design. Ford's criterion for efficiency had always been smoothness in the production process, whereby "demoralizing" changes in design were kept to the minimum,[46] but by the 1930s friction of any kind between the parts of the product itself was being eliminated. Rounding of edges and streamlining of shapes brought them to "smooth impersonality." Objects without aesthetic individuality or passion functioned best and had the greatest consumer appeal.[47]

Ergonomics was (and is) the analysis of man-product relationships for the sake of industrial development. Literary productions (to this point in time, at least) also dealt with the analysis of man/product relationships. The approaches ergonomics and literature took to these overlapping fields of action were different in kind but closely allied.

It is difficult to separate literary works of the 1920s and 1930s from the ergonomics that inquire into either functional derangements or functional wholeness, the former in particular.[48] Such literary narratives often contain representational Joes and Josephines; these narratives share in the concepts of time, motion, and environmental imperatives used in the design models that plot the making of products appropriate for scientifically managed societies. Nevertheless, some literary narratives resist the final rounding off of edges and streamlining of shapes; they pay attention to precisely those irregularities unacceptable to object designers, for whom the perfect wholes of a Joe and a Josephine require absolutely interchangeable parts.

The American Tragedy: An Uninteresting Life

Clyde Griffiths's story is often read as the tragedy of an indecisive young man in a decisively determined universe, an Olivierian Hamlet transplanted from Elsinore to Lycurgus, New York, who cannot make up his mind whether to murder or not to murder. But it is more to the point of his times to gloss his tale as being about a young man who is unable to apply the principles of the American System to others with the adroitness to which they are applied to him.

As a child growing up within the aura of the Star of Hope Mission, Clyde is hardly seven before he begins to sense that his parents' dependency upon "praying their way out" of unfavorable situations is "a rather ineffectual way" (1:12). From remarks Clyde overhears about his father's brother (a kind of upstate New York Claudius), he concludes that Samuel Griffiths is "a shrewd, hard business man" who was "plainly different from all this." Early on, Clyde imagines that there are those who might do "certain things" for him if they "but would" (1:13).

Clyde's disdain for manual labor is a twentieth-century response toward work Dreiser believed to be "the general American attitude toward life" (1:14). He quickly settles upon a formula for drawing himself into the field-force of success: get people who are "interesting" to do "certain things" by being "interesting" to them, at the same time doing what is "interesting" to oneself.

Now, doing interesting things and being interested in one's work formed the heart of Frank and Lillian Gilbreth's time-motion studies.[49] Unfortunately, Clyde will never experience the traditional joy in work that the Gilbreths insisted upon as an essential adjunct to their innovative techniques for labor management.[50] Clyde belongs to the generation whose taste for instant gratification rejects the delays inherent in the age-old doctrine (almost theological in nature) of preparation through apprenticeship.[51] This is clear from Clyde's first job as assistant to a soda-water clerk. In Clyde's eyes, the clerk's activities are glamorous, but he becomes discouraged when he realizes he will have to wait before being allowed to do interesting things in front of the audience of pretty girls drifting in from the theater next door.

Waiting is replaced by doing once Clyde realizes the quick way up
may be attained through smooth manners and good clothes. He signs on
as a hotel bellboy; under the eye of his supervisor, Clyde learns the job
skills of being "clean and neat," "willing, civil, prompt, courteous," "on
the dot" (1:34). Although Clyde is repulsed by one aspect of the hotel
world (the presence of men who try to "interest boys" for sexual reasons),
he finds what he does "interesting—yes, delightful and fascinating—
work" (1:51). Still, he senses he will not remain content; his hotel work
will not "interest him forever" (1:61).

Clyde is trapped within the spiraling effect of needing to be interested
yet always having what interests him at the moment fade before the anticipation of future enticements to his imagination. Not only is his work
world ruled by those wants, his leisure hours are caught within "the opening and closing jaws" of his sexual needs. As it is with Hortense Briggs,
so it will be with Roberta Alden and Sondra Finchley: "His one dream
was that by some process, either of charm or money, he could make himself interesting to her" (1:84).

Up to this point, Clyde Griffiths has managed to survive with partial
impunity. Yes, there is the drunken evening, the hit-and-run accident, the
child lying dead in the road, the need to flee town, but that is nothing in
the life of a young man in the early stages of learning how to make the
best use of his particular talent for being attractive. He is already part of
"an American tragedy" created by the cult of personality, the rage for consumerism, the alienating force of advanced capitalism. Nonetheless,
Clyde has managed to stay just outside the range of the direct impact of a
Taylorist system, a system that would have ground him up and spat him
out for not being enough like Little Schmidt, forever content to move pig
iron; he has avoided falling under the all-observing eye of the Gilbreths,
whose notion of "interesting work" is hardly his own; he has yet to be
judged by the American System in terms of whether his parts are
precision-made and readily interchangeable. But now his predetermined
path draws him into the "web" that radiates out from the Griffiths Collar
& Shirt Company, as powerful a force in Lycurgus as the web Henry James
saw functioning in New York's harbor.[52]

For those familiar with the American System, the signs are clear that
Clyde must fail. Clyde's face and build are almost duplicates of his cousin
Gilbert's. But being "almost like" is not sufficient; it lacks the precision
required of interchangeable parts, the precision that enables two guns to
perform with equal effectiveness on the battlefield. Gilbert has the manner
and force, "much colder and shrewder," that has been left out of the assemblage of Clyde, "his western cousin" (1:155, 186). Clyde will rise for
a time on the basis of the Griffiths look—the quality that makes him "in-

teresting" to Sondra Finchley and the young social crowd; he will fall because he does not possess the Griffiths' "executive" abilities. Whereas Clyde is "soft and vague and fumbling," Gilbert stands for "force and energy in business," all that is "authoritative and efficient" (1:186, 221–22).

While Clyde shares the Griffiths name as well as the family look, he does not possess what that name stands for: "reserve and ability and energy and good judgment." Nor does he care for the purposes to which that name is used by his Lycurgus cousins: for him the name is supposed to open up his life to what is interesting; for them the name is good "for business" (1:232). The genetic production line has been replicated within the Griffiths male line in terms of physical appearance, but unfortunately Samuel's brother Asa and his nephew Clyde bear character traits of softness, vagueness, and inefficiency for which Samuel and his son have no patience. The Griffiths name was not in good hands with Asa and his wife, who rely on "praying their way out." The marketability of the name will not be in good hands with Clyde, who counts on the "certain things" that people "might do for a person" like himself.

Dreiser has been building up carefully the many layers of social exchange in this complex narrative. Once Clyde enters upon his Lycurgus life, Dreiser has an even greater need to note meticulously the stages through which a young man goes before the "web" entangles him past the point where he can be saved. Since what Clyde "really was" is made up of a variety of personalities, each with its own "averages," Dreiser, like Dreyfuss the design engineer, provides him with a sequence of "environments" that test those "averages."

Clyde's uncle places him at "the very bottom" of the factory in the shrinking room. The Griffiths' business creed is based on *beginnings* (the basement where "lower individuals" experience the difficulty of getting money, "the clear mark of necessity and compulsion" [1:180–81]) that logically precede *endings* (the executive offices upstairs). Before workers may aspire to the gratifications of social prestige, money, security, and the virtues of the "conservative, respectable, and successful" life, they must become "inured to a narrow and abstemious life" that is "good for their characters" (1:158, 101). Samuel Griffiths's work ethic, like that of Henry Ford, lags well behind the technological advances in evidence within his factory. Clyde never benefits from this technology; it is the work ethic alone he must contend with, the belief that "the only really important constructive work of the world—that of material manufacture"—requires total commitment to the need "to be drilled, and that sharply and systematically, in all the details and processes which comprise that constructive work" (1:181).

Deep in "the basement world," Clyde is set apart from the other workers. He cannot understand how they could be interested in what is uninteresting to him, nor can he realize that they, too, have to contend with lives without interest. Then he is lifted up a floor to the stamping room. Given the title of assistant foreman, he is charged with enforcing "due decorum and order" in a work space where everything acts against efficient performance of such a duty (1:233).

Once again we see the disjunctions among the work ethic touted by the owners, the work procedures laid down by the managers, the machine technology installed in the factory, and the human element introduced by the employees' desires. As was shown above in the passage describing the room where Clyde presides, the warm June afternoons that insinuate "languor" and "sensuality" along the rows of young women, set to stamping the collars sliding down through the chutes, do not lend themselves to a scientifically controllable work environment.

The labor process itself—an "endless repetition" that leaves the young women's minds "free to roam from one thought of pleasure to another"—cuts against Samuel Griffiths's intention that his workers constantly meditate upon the relation between the difficulty of making money and the inner satisfaction gained through "constructive work." [53]

Finally, there are the employees, recalcitrant individuals who, like Clyde, pursue one line of conduct by day (the one enforced by the Griffiths work code, which forbids contact between management and employee)[54] and an alternate line of conduct by night, urged on by the moods and dreams that factory existence seeks to deny. That those same moods and dreams are themselves deeply affected by the overarching "manufacture" of Lycurgus life is a matter that we, if not the employees, must take into account.

In addition to the double life the ethos of the plant produces as an unexpected commodity, Clyde becomes involved in yet another doubling effect. The Clyde who goes out after work hours with Roberta Alden is the night self forbidden by his being a Griffiths. The Clyde whom Sondra Finchley picks up as one of her acquisitions is one of the selves connected with his being a Griffiths, although not the day self that languishes in the stamping room as a lesser member of the family.

Sondra first addresses Clyde because he is a Gilbert look-alike, but what she finds "interesting" is that quality of Clyde that is not interchangeable with Gilbert. Sondra's preference for Clyde-in-Gilbert stems from the fact that he mirrors her vanity, whereas Gilbert-alone rejects that mirroring. She seeks the young man who is interesting to her because he finds her so interesting. It is a perfect match, an efficient interlocking of needs, a merger of corporate energies upon the social and sexual scene. It is, however, a match that fatally contradicts the requirements of "constructive work" exacted by the American System, in which Clyde could win only if he and Gilbert were interchangeable parts in the executive offices.[55]

Clyde becomes "part and parcel" of Sondra's crowd because those who are free of the world of work find him interesting and attractive. But then Roberta realizes she is pregnant, and Clyde is assigned his first, and most crucial, task of scientific management. What the Gilbert side of the Griffiths line could do, Clyde cannot. Inept, ignorant, procrastinating, he is unable to determine the means by which Roberta can efficiently abort the unwanted, because potentially unproductive, fetus.

Neither Clyde nor Roberta has the "real skill to meet such a situation." Neither receives aid from factory or community.[56] Unable to manage this problem on their own and unable to think beyond the hope that "chance in some form should aid," they "drifted, fearing to act really" (2:3, 5).[57] Together they face a common problem, but Roberta's solution (marriage) is not Clyde's solution. For Clyde the issue is "how to avoid that and to win to Sondra after all" (2:36).

When it is too late for him to solve his management problem by conventional means, Clyde reads of a drowning accident in which the woman dies and the man disappears. Not an originator, only a borrower, Clyde appropriates the plot of this accident as the prototype solution to his own plight. Even so, he is incapable of meeting the contingencies that ensnare him in the consequences of sexual impulse. (He never does have the ability to be patient, to be the apprentice, in terms of his pursuit of love.) The only way left for him to prove his merit for efficient conduct is through the imagination of murder.

Murder would remove the work load Roberta has become, freeing Clyde to succeed at having Sondra, whose scientifically measured possession would bring him everything he wants. He must, of course, be cooly irrational and convert himself into a cleverly mad scientist/engineer/manager ("decent, sane people did not think of such things" [2:26]). The unmanageable problem is that there are too many Clydes: not just the one who can't murder and the one who can, but the one who is too soft to be a true Griffiths and the one who now will attempt to be "a shrewd, hard business man" (1:13).

Conventional moral issues raised by the scene on the lake—not only in the minds of those who put Clyde Griffiths on trial, but in the minds of all Dreiser's readers—tend to get put aside by the nature of Dreiser's telling. More "interesting" is the way the scene testifies to what happens to young men who fail at being what the business enterprise and the industrial process expect of them, and what happens to the young women whose fate is intertwined with the young men's inadequacies.

In the rowboat Clyde experiences "the most urgent need for action." Yet he feels "a sudden palsy of the will—of courage—of hate or rage sufficient" (2:76). His failure is written on his face—the face that has drawn Sondra to him and that links him to Gilbert, the cousin who never would have gotten into such a scrape and certainly would have known how to get out of it. His face, "weak and even unbalanced," reveals "a balanced combat between fear" and the "desire to do." It classifies him as "a static between a powerful compulsion to do and yet not to do" (2:76–77).

Issues of social ethics, moral decency, the state of one's soul, the fate of identity—all the "oughts" and "shoulds" that the "powerless" worry over when judging the good or evil of such acts—are pushed aside (and out of the novel). The single fact remains that Clyde Griffith fails at the only test he needs to pass: he has not been able to manipulate to their fullest the rules of scientific management guiding the culture into which he was born.

In the rowboat on the lake, Clyde leaves to accident what he should have carefully planned (by means of Taylorism, Fordism, Dreyfuss's design engineering, the New England armory system, whatever). He thinks to himself that "an unintentional blow [to Roberta's head] on your part is now saving you the labor of what you sought, and yet did not have the courage to do" (2:78). His inability to adhere meticulously to a planned schedule is compounded by his deplorable sense of timing. He botches the process through which murder plots are successfully enacted. And so he will go to the executioner's chair as punishment for his lapses in effective management method.

Several hundred pages intervene between the "accident" on the lake and Clyde's walk down death row. Dreiser uses this narrative space to detail further the discrepancies between people's plans and their ability to bring them to completion, between outmoded moral passions and the new-style principles of a management culture.

During the hours before Clyde's complicity in Roberta's drowning is found out, Sondra scolds him with the mother-to-baby talk in which she disguises "the infatuation that now dominated her." "And Sondra planning everything for you!" she tells him, "You ought to have a good spanking."[58] But all Clyde can think is, "Oh, God! The folly of all his planning in connection with all this to date! The flaws! Had he ever really planned it right from the start" (2:123, 131).

For a time it appears that Clyde might be saved by the efforts of the

perfect manager, his uncle Samuel, who is lauded by the hortatory language favored by the contemporary business press: "The power of him!
The decision of him! The fairness of him in such a deadly crisis!" (2:178).
But once Clyde's uncle discards him as a bad business asset, his destiny is
in the hands of those who have their own managerial plans to push to
completion in ways satisfying to themselves.

The lawyers for the defense and for the prosecution, the reporters
covering the case, the jurors, and the general public miss the point of what
Clyde's situation signifies, although they are actively part of that point.
Fred Heit, the "old, moral-religious-political-commercial coroner," me-
thodically attends to the details that will help to convict Clyde (2:109).
Mason the prosecutor, who views Clyde as one of society's ne'er-do-
wells, a member of the "wretched rich," the "idle rich," the "wastrel and
evil rich," gives Clyde's actions a fine Marxist reading, although he is a
man to whom Marxist thought would be abhorrent (2:108). The defense
layers, Belknap and Jephson, do with Clyde what Taylor did with Little
Schmidt: they drill him over and over in a routine whose gestures will
"give him courage—teach him to act it out" (2:205). Jephson, exuding
"iron and power," most closely approximates Taylor's model for the ideal
manager. He is "so shrewd and practical, so very direct and chill and indifferent and yet confidence-inspiring, quite like an uncontrollable machine of a kind which generates power" (2:198, 223). But even Jephson's
efforts are ineffectual before jurors ("with but one exception, all religious,
if not moral") whom even Taylor would have been incapable of "driving"
toward a "correct" response (2:231).

The jury is asked to decide whether to exact the death penalty for a
shrewd planner (one who successfully completed his work task of murder) or whether to acquit on the grounds that the accused is an inept bum-
bler—a young man of "*perhaps too pliable and sensual and impractical and
dreamy mind*," caught up in an accident that was "unpremeditated and
undesigned" (2:294, 327).[59] Either Clyde will be released for *not* being effective as the scientific manager of murder or much of anything else, and
thereby will labeled as the worst kind of failure American business (or
MIT's human engineers) can identify; or he will be sent to death praised
(though damned by such praise) as one who had a clever plan that just
missed being shrewd enough to carry him through. In the end the state
has its way: it gets to punish inefficiency while rejecting the notion that
one of its attractive young men is totally unprepared to plan his life according to the tenets of keen business practices and the self-enhancing
techniques of human engineering.

On his side, Clyde denies "the false form" advanced by his defense, which maintains he held opposing views toward Roberta's murder but was simply too weak-willed to be efficiently evil (2:381). As he begins to sense who he "really was," he realizes it was "not that he was not guilty." It comes down to the fact that his feelings were "all too human" (2:401).

No one else pays attention to Clyde's newly received self-knowledge—neither the lawyers, nor his mother, nor the Reverend McMillan, all of whom try in different ways to measure the amount of innocence or guilt in the case; all of whom drill Clyde to say what they think the public wants to hear; some of whom expect Clyde to attain an efficient life in the next world through the redemptive process that turns earthly flaws into heavenly perfection. *To measure* is to control, and how could those sympathetic to Clyde's cause hope to control the unmeasurable energy of thwarted dreams, based as they are upon Taylorized needs? *To drill* is to coerce others into patterns of behavior, patterns that deny the desires that society management methods both create and fail fully to accommodate. *To accept* redemption is to be interesting in the sight of the God-fearing, but not necessarily in the eyes of God, and certainly not in the eyes of Sondra and her crowd.

Clyde is perceived as having lost out on the benefits of control, drill, and redemption. His managers wish to gain those qualities for themselves even in the last moments of his life. This is why society has the kind of prison system it does—one that imitates the principles Uncle Samuel attempted to impose within the Griffiths factory. Within a system that "moved automatically like a machine without the aid or the hearts of men," the guards are "iron," "mere machines, automatons," filled with "hollow words," as they push Clyde toward "that little door" to death (2:401–2).[60]

What becomes of those who represent the way of management and the way of the Lord?

Samuel Griffiths faces the fact of his own defeat. He must begin his business life over again, transfer his company to South Boston, and take his wife and daughters away from the gossiping tongues of Lycurgus, where the value of the family name has been ruined forever. And it was all his own fault. Because he lapsed from his own principles when he took Clyde in, on the basis of his "interesting" Griffiths face, he failed to live up to the essential managerial code he had always prided himself upon upholding: "Had not a long, practical struggle with life taught him that sentiment in business was folly?" (2:338).

As for Clyde's mother, she returns to the Star of Hope Mission, out of whose "little door" Clyde had escaped on his way toward the "little door" of death row. She gives her young grandson, Esta's boy, an ice cream for Clyde's sake, but will the boy find an occasional treat "interesting" enough to bind him to a life whose sole notion of what human engineering entails is to pray one's way out?

The entropy of "being interesting" rules Dreiser's dominion in *An American Tragedy,* setting its unfamilied characters "adrift" in an interlocking series of management cultures, with no way out. This is not what we find when we enter Faulkner's narrative realm of the familial romance, where "taking interest" means alternating jolts of energy committed to breaking free with counterjolts devoted to keeping matters under control.

N I N E

Ways Out

Henry Dreyfuss compiles anthropometric data to assure that his average (Anglo-Saxon) Joe is programmed for success within work environments tailored to corporate needs. The data Nathanael West and Theodore Dreiser accumulate guarantees the fatal averageness of Lemuel Pitkin and Clyde Griffiths, American boy types utterly incapable of surviving the clashing jaws of a social machine powered by the business process. Betty Prail and Roberta Alden are no less significantly "average" than Lem and Clyde, and their fates are no less sordid, but these two Josephines are treated as incidentals to the male-centered plots that consume them. This is not the case with certain other women, however. Although they are placed within situations dictated by cultures of management patently antagonistic to a woman's will, these women win a kind of managerial success. Through their resistance to averages, they make the claim that any woman has the right to be the exception.

That these women are Charlotte Rittenmeyer, Eula Varner, and Linda Snopes, created by a man known for the narrative violence he does to his fictive females, may cause surprise. Hardly surprising, though, is the controversial nature of the managerial goals Charlotte, Eula, and Linda set for themselves. The nature of the success they attain is just as controversial. For these women are managers of love, consumers of living, and producers of meaning within the cosmic work environment envisioned by William Faulkner.

The Management of Love

"Wild Palms" first. The narrative Faulkner wove together with "Old Man" and published in 1939—in which Charlotte Rittenmeyer defiantly pulls Harry Winterborne back into life and, still defiant, is pulled into

304

death—bears the marks of the classic plot of doomed lovers: lovers who reject, yet comply with, their society's devotion to narratives of original sin and the necessary punishment of that sin.[1]

> She grasped his hair again, hurting him again though now he knew she knew she was hurting him. "Listen: it's got be all honeymoon, always. Forever and ever, until one of us dies. It cant be anything else. Either heaven, or hell; no comfortable safe peaceful purgatory between for you and me to wait in until good behavior or forbearance or shame or repentance overtakes us."
> "So it's not me you believe in, put trust in; it's love."
> She looked at him. "Not just me; any man."
> "Yes. It's love."[2]

If Charlotte escapes the feminist sin of giving all for the love of any one man—if she is no Shakespearian Cleopatra tricked by her male author into giving up independence and authority for the sake of that hollow man, Marc Antony—she still stands accused of commitment to the ideal of a transcendent act. Moreover, it is this innate Platonism that aligns Charlotte with the product designers and scientific managers, the men who shape the society against which she rebels. But this is what one should expect from a Faulkner narrative. The complicity that ties Charlotte to those she defies helps to define "Wild Palms" as yet another of Faulkner's many tales of familial conflict.

But do not be misled. We are not tied to those old-time myths that pit preindustrial wilderness lives of love against the dread "other," the modern capitalistic city.[3] Quite the opposite. "Wild Palms" attests to "the logics and erotics of machine culture," which forever couple "bodies, machines, and money."[4] However, just because nature is not the fated enemy of the machine, this does not mean that every person caught up in the energy of their interchange submits passively to the web that connects them. Charlotte is a fine example of someone who fulfills her role in society precisely because she is so much a part of what she resists.

In this telling, the friction is between Charlotte and Frederick Winslow Taylor, who believed in "the one right way"; between Charlotte and the New England arms-makers, who set up the American System; between Charlotte and the statisticians, the eugenicists, and MIT's human engineers; between Charlotte, who combines "grids" with "blots," and design engineers, who deal with grids in isolation.[5] The crucial difference between her Platonism and theirs is that Charlotte's ideal is Love, with its outrageous demand that she disregard the norms of social and business conduct, while her opponents' ideal is Business, which makes Money rather than Eros its bond servant.

Faulkner quickly clears out the underbrush. Although "Wild Palms" provides an ample supply of tangible social data about people, places, and diurnal events, these details, whose verisimilitude lend the story its look of naturalism, lie along the surface. The true allegiance of the narrative is to allegory—allegory characterized not by the flat or the thin but by depth and richness, because of its relentless focus upon the radicalizing energies of love pitted to the death against the conventionalizing forces of money.

In its race against final closure, Charlotte and Harry's story dismisses Marxist-minded arguments about capitalist economics being an abstract exercise not connected to passionate living. The way the lovers live out their narrative, the theories of Adam Smith and Thorstein Veblen are beside the point. Their universe is self-defined, ruled by the invisible hand of fate and the conspicuous consumption of love. As essentializing an author on matters of economy as Thoreau, Faulkner grants his equally essentializing heroine an austere vision pared down to a single question: how much money does it take to stay alive so that one can really live? The one fact Charlotte and her lover must face is "the strong reason we cant beat even if I cannot believe or understand that it could be just that, just money, not anything but just money" (49).

Charlotte admits her inability to understand why money should have the power to sanction or forbid love, but she knows innately that money cannot be beaten. (Because Charlotte does not consciously comprehend why money affects loving, she is unlike Henry James's Charlotte Stant or Kate Croy, women who, being social creatures to the core, have always realized the connections between getting money and being allowed love.) But if Charlotte has this lesson still to learn, no one has to teach her about managing the occasions in which love is seized.

Charlotte has to coach Harry, the typical Faulknerian male innocent, in how to conduct an assignation at a cheap hotel. A friend tells Harry that no woman, including Charlotte, needs prior experience to know exactly what to do in such a situation, because the sex possesses "that instinctive proficiency in and rapport for the mechanics of cohabition" (54). "She could turn up with a bag of her own and a coat and a veil and the stub of a Pullman ticket sticking out of her handbag and that wouldn't mean she had done this before. That's just women" (45).

Yet Charlotte is naïve in her own way. In the face of all reason, she retains hope that love won't be denied.

Not as long as we are worthy of keeping of it. Good enough. Strong enough. Worthy to be allowed to keep it. To get what you want as decently as you can, then keep it. Keep it. . . . That's what I'm going to do. Try to do. (88)

Charlotte is like many of Faulkner's Platonists, partially blinded by belief that worth, strength, and goodness *should* make a difference in the battle against one's foes. She also voices the classic Faulknerian statement of self-deluding faith in a just system of economics. After she tells Harry, "I like bitching, and making things with my hands," she adds, *"I dont think that's too much to be permitted* to like, to want to have and keep" (88; my emphasis).

Charlotte's and Harry's tragedy is given specifically "American" dimensions because of their unending, day-by-day bargaining with fate, fate that locks their lives into the nation's money ethic wherever they go: New Orleans, Chicago, the Wisconsin woods, the Utah mine, San Antonio, the Mississippi coast. But "Wild Palms" is a cosmic tragedy as well.

The implacableness of hard numbers denies the intangible solidity of love's passion: numbers such as the $1,200 Harry finds in a wallet dropped on the sidewalk; the check Rat Rittenmeyer uses to hold the departing lovers to a binding contractual agreement; the $100 here and the $28 there that Charlotte makes as a designer of department store displays; the dwindling line of food cans on the lakeside cabin shelf; the money Harry makes writing sob-story confessions of victimized women; the four months Harry lacks of an twenty-four-month internship that would have given him official license to practice medicine; the days that Charlotte marks off when she does not menstruate and the days that lapse before her abortion becomes fatally dangerous. *"I have been confounded by numbers,"* Harry says (85), speaking for all humanity, which is caught up in a culture of management obsessively dedicated to the sacred power of numbers.[6]

Only once does Charlotte veer away from the worth, strength, and goodness of her war against the insidious, outflanking movements of the enemy. The moment comes when she and Harry get too busy making money to love; they regress to the point where "we had to rent and support a room for two robots to live in" (129). Charlotte knows better, of course; so does Harry. Having been tutored by this fierce efficiency expert in the management of love, Harry senses how easy it is to turn into Joe and Josephine. Charlotte has taught him "that it is one of what we call the prime virtues—thrift, industry, independence—that breeds all the vices—fanaticism, smugness, meddling, fear, and worst of all, respectability" (133).

That bad time came about when the two Platonists were "solvent, knew for certain where tomorrow's food was coming from (the damned money, too much of it; at night we would lie awake and plan how to get it spent . . .)." For a single moment they lost sight of the truth that

> it's idleness breeds all our virtues, our most bearable qualities—contemplation, equableness, laziness, letting other people alone; good digestion mental and physical: the wisdom to concentrate on fleshly pleasures—eating and evacuating and fornication and sitting in the sun—than which there is nothing better, nothing to match. (133)

Charlotte, with her proud belief in her independence, faced yet another threat when she stayed in the Chicago apartment creating a "home" decor. She had put on an apron, cooked chops for dinner, cleaned up after the meal. This was dangerous, but she thought she was still safe as long as she came to Harry at night with "the compactly simple rightness of the body lines, the sober intent yellow stare," capable of offering to life what a Josephine never could: "The hell with it. I can still bitch" (93). Her only fear was that she might become too busy being respectable to bitch.

Eventually "the others" get them. In a reversal of the tragedy that awaits Roberta and Clyde, Charlotte demands that Harry abort her pregnancy in order to bypass respectability and deadness. (We cant have the kid. It costs money to raise a kid and we cant have money, respectability, and love as well.) In performing the abortion, Harry's hand shakes from his love and fear of losing her; and, since he is a true Faulknerian male, also from his need for revenge upon her body and from his fear over the mastery she might continue to exert over his will. Charlotte dies, and Harry is sentenced to life in prison for the murder of the woman he loved and feared—who loved and feared not him or any man but Love.

Charlotte and Harry do not have a chance. In general, however, Charlotte does so admirably in managing the business of their life together that she delays the moment when they are beaten by the power of numbers. But even she made a strategic mistake, one that anyone adept in the management of work environments could have warned her against.

There was that instant when Charlotte should have stopped long enough to prevent her douche bag from freezing in the cold of the Utah winter, but, in her haste to leap into Harry's embrace, she does not take the necessary time or make the necessary movement across the room to hang up the bag out of harm's way. Because of this oversight she is impregnated. Dreyfuss's paper-pattern Josephine never has to take such fleshly matters into account within her programmed work life, but real women pay the cost exacted by the biology of bitching. What happens is what Harry sensed from the start. Charlotte and he fortified themselves against society's pull of money and respectability, yet what chance did they have against the shrewd "business" of biological systems that will not countenance unproductive expenditures of energy, that threaten to upset the cosmic balance?

> So They will have to find something else to force us to conform to the pattern of human life which has now evolved to do without love. . . . So I am afraid. Because They are smart, shrewd, They will have to be; if They were to let us beat Them, it would be like unchecked murder and robbery. (140)

The War Continues: The Snopes Trilogy

The greasy smear of Flem Snopes's progress leaves its trail across the pages of Faulkner's trilogy, separately titled, *The Hamlet, The Town,* and *The Mansion.* Sharing a complicated composition history, and published respectively in 1940 (with a 1956 update), 1957, and 1959, the narrative time of the three novels spans roughly the years between 1904 and the close of the Second World War. This time frame enables rural and small-town Mississippi to be introduced to the benefits of finance capitalism; it also allows a depiction of how the South is responding to the managerial methods stirring Yankee business and industry. Flem's smear, however, extends well beyond the times and places located within these fictional texts. Our historians have recognized Snopesism along with Fordism and Taylorism. Snopesism has become another tag for identifying many of the more unpleasant, yet energizing qualities of twentieth-century American society.

Faulkner's trilogy supplies material for the analysis of the sociological, anthropological, political, economic, and cultural mechanisms that made Snopesism take hold in this outlandish territory, a territory that dropped out of "history" at the close of the war. In Faulkner's telling, Snopesism is born in the small, tight hamlet of Frenchman's Bend, a community so ingrown that Negroes from elsewhere in the county avoid passing through its margins at night. Anyone who lives outside the riding range of Will Varner's fat white horse is viewed, suspiciously, as a stranger, whether the Texan who sells off dreams in the form of spotted ponies or McCaron, who tries to steal dreams in the shape of Eula Varner. Women are expected to know their place, either as battered wives like Mrs. Armstid, cheerful housewives like Mrs. Varner, or hard-working surrogate mothers like Mrs. Littlejohn. The soil is poor, the working lives of the sharecroppers—necks reddened under the beating sun—verge on desperation, and the cash-poor economy is based on a rudimentary exchange system in which time and labor is bartered for the barest necessities. This is hardly the place to expect Platonic models for either modern business or love to take hold, but, leave it to Faulkner, they do.

Eula Varner Snopes and her daughter Linda are less single-minded, less obsessed in their battle in the name of love against the Snopes Principle than Charlotte Rittenmeyer is in her rage against respectability. Relatively speaking, Eula is more interested in Eros than Agape, and Linda is more focused upon Agape than Eros, whereas Charlotte—with "the compactly simple rightness" of her body and "the sober intent yellow stare" of her eyes—tries to balance both.

As Faulkner tells it, Eula's ripe body, which flows outside her clothes, and her blue gaze make it impossible to ignore that she is a pagan goddess who antedates the complicating concerns introduced by Christianity and capitalism. In contrast, Linda's tall, spare body and her hyacinth eyes represent modes of thought and action that postdate Augustine and Marx. But both Eula and Linda, like Charlotte, contain a force and live by a creed that defies, even as it in part reinscribes, any view of money and respectability as the sole aims of human endeavor. It is a creed that defies Flem Snopes, husband to one and titular father to the other.

The following factors shape the prolonged familial conflict within the Snopes family drama:

The Visible Hand Made Invisible

According to the evolution of business practices traced by Thorsten Veblen, Flem Snopes displaces Will Varner in the hierarchies of power. Varner incarnates in bawdy flesh the rapscallion figure of predatory culture, which antedates the coolly calculating methods of pecuniary culture that Snopes brings to Frenchman's Bend. Will's old-style entrepreneurship means that men approach him "not in the attitude of *What must I do* but *What do you think you think you would like for me to do if you was able to make me do it.*"[7] For Will, the invisible hand of classic economic theory, even though viewed on the slant, is made visible and audible. In contrast, invisibility and silences are the palpable forces Flem uses to disguise his moves. Even a shrewd fellow like V. K. Ratliff can only sense what has happened but not quite how.[8]

> Snopes had sold the new [blacksmith] shop—smith clientele and goodwill and new equipment—to Varner, receiving in return the old equipment in the old shop, which he sold to a junk man, moved the new equipment to the old shop and sold the new building to a farmer for a cowshed, without even having to pay himself to have it

moved . . . at which point even Ratliff had lost count of what profit
Snopes might have made. (*The Hamlet,* 67)

The Southern Way of Management Control

Frenchman's Bend eliminates the possibility for nuances of change—
nuances that, up North, mark the distance between the point where Will
Varner stands as the old-time, out-in-front entrepreneur and the point
reached by advanced capitalism, as made manifest by Flem's machinelike
methods. Nuances are what Northern business has had the luxury of time
to indulge in, but not post-Reconstruction Mississippi. The welfare programs John Patterson pleasurably provided for his employees are something the rural South does without, just as it does without staffing its enterprises with formally trained engineers and managers. Further, Flem's
down-home managerial style encourages nepotism, that swarm of untutored relatives Taylorism was meant to discourage. The very names of
Flem's kin, however, trace the newest Yankee developments in early
twentieth-century business history: IOU, Wallstreet Panic (although this
cousin later disqualifies himself through his outrageous decency and honesty), Montgomery Ward, and Watkins Products, as well as Grover Cleveland and Admiral Dewey, named after historical figures who helped to
create the conditions that bred Snopesism.

Creeping Snopesism

His kinfolk aside, Flem is not the only man in Yoknapatawpha County
infected by Snopesism. (Snopesism, by the way, is not conveyed through
the female; it is an entirely masculine trait.)[9] Just about every (white) male
in Frenchman's Bend and Jefferson is implicated in what it means to think
Snopes thoughts. If Gavin Stephens escapes full immersion in the Snopes
way, this is because he is not really a male; his principles are those of the
women, but without a female's force behind them.
    V. K. Ratliff is a nice Snopes, but the inner tendency is there nonethe-
less. If the essentials of Snopesism are what Charlotte taught Harry Winterborne to despise—"thrift, industry, independence, fanaticism, smugness, meddling, fear, and worst of all, respectability"—then Ratliff has
journeyed into the pit: he digs for buried treasure; he puts a stop to Ike
Snopes's love overtures to his beloved heifer out of his own need "to be
right"; he meddles as naturally as his pulse beats; he attempts to beat Flem
at his own flimflam paper shuffles. Just in time, Ratliff recognizes his unconscious complicity with Snopesism: in time, but late enough to have

smeared himself with Flem's taint; late enough to be able to serve as one of Faulkner's more prescient narrators.[10]

Ratliff maintains an inside-outside position. He knows what Snopesism is because of the terror it has caused him. This knowledge and this terror together enable him to be the chronicler, commentator, and, on occasion, active antagonist of Snopesism (using Snopesian methods, of course). He is also aided by the marginality his celibate state confers. He is neither impotent, like Flem Snopes (which is another matter), nor a tormented misogynist like Jack Houston. If Ratliff were a male slave to love, he would be as incapable of narrating the friction (and compliance) between love and erotics as, say, would Labove or Gavin Stephens.

Snopesism Rejected

Certain members of the Snopes clan reject their genes the way transplanted organs reject the bodies into which they are sutured. There is Ike Snopes with his female thighs and his Platonic love for the forbidden cow. In his idiocy, he is impervious to monetary bribes and the demands of respectable conduct. There is Wallstreet Panic Snopes, so innately decent that it is difficult to call him a Snopes. Even so, the "simple automatic fierce Snopes antipathy" of Wall's wife (together with Ratliff's loan) is needed to defeat "it" (*The Town*, 147)—that dread miasma of Snopesism against which Wall and his wife pit the "outrageous un-Snopesish method of jest telling ever body exactly what they thought they was buying, for exactly what they thought they was going to pay for it."[11]

Mink Snopes, Old and New

Mink Snopes's role is greatly affected by the changes that take place over the thirty-four years of the narrative, as Faulkner discovers the implications of the way Snopesism jockeys for power with its competitors in the modern business economy. Over the course of the trilogy sympathy will mount for Mink, and his final role will be that of the avenger. But initially Mink is conceived as a murderous varmint, and also as a victim: first as a victim of the harsh, irrational, old-time business practices used by Varner and Houston; then as a victim of Flem's new-style system, which forever keeps the visible hand of managerial power invisible.[12]

In Faulkner's world, to be a victim is to be complicitous with your victimizers. Although Mink ends his life with agency, in the beginning he has no way to resist Snopesism. First he has lessons to learn about the relation of labor power to speed and to patience.

Mink Snopes's initial enslavement to hand/land labor is what Taylorism intended to remedy, but Faulkner graphically describes the nightmare Taylorism could become, whether practices on the factory floor or the hard scrabble soil or rural Mississippi. Mink's work life is that

> constant and unflagging round of repetitive nerve-and-flesh wearing labor by which alone that piece of earth which was his moral enemy could fight him with, which he had performed yesterday and must perform again today and again tomorrow and tomorrow . . . this until the day came when (he knew this too) he would stumble and plunge, his eyes still open and his empty hands stiffening into the shape of the plow-handles, into the furrow behind the plow, or topple into the weedy ditch, still clutching the brush-hook or the axe, this final victory marked by a cenotaph of coiling buzzards on the sky until some curious stranger happened there and found and buried what was left of him. (*The Hamlet,* 192).

Mink's will to endure comes from his belief that patience allows him to control the relation of time to work motions. This runs counter to the Taylorist need to speed up the pace of the task, controlling that pace through an invariable routine with no goal but to go on producing itself forever.

> He now had a kind of peace, freed of hurry and haste . . . marking off one day less which meant fifty cents less toward the recovery of his cow. But with no haste now, no urgency. . . . Because patience was his pride too: never to be reconciled since by this means he could beat Them; They might be stronger for a moment than he but no-body, no man could wait longer than he could wait when nothing else but waiting would do, would work, would serve him. (*The Mansion,* 22)

Mink's principle of patience predates the Taylorist obsession with consuming time for the purpose of speeding up production. By suppressing urgency, Mink's labor beats Them. The suppression of urgency also entails the denial of impulse. Mink is aware of this: he knows that They "couldn't beat him with money or its lack, couldn't outwait him; could beat him only by catching him off balance and so topple him back into that condition of furious blind earless rage where he had no sense" (ibid.).

But, back near Frenchman's Bend, impulse is precisely what beats Mink, this man impervious to the lures of money or respectability. The old-time capitalists "topple him back into . . . rage" when he learns that he will be charged "one dollar more" as a "pound fee" for pasturing his cow. Because of rage, he loses whatever power he had in managing his own conduct and in laboring without haste on his own terms. Because of rage, he is sentenced to years of unremunerated toil at the Parchman prison farm.

At last Mink is released from prison. At this point in time, as Mink steels himself to conquer "Them," he is no longer battling the tangible code harshly upheld in the old days by a visible foe—like Houston, whom he could shoot down. Now the invisible workings of Snopesism are out to beat him, as they had been all along if only he had realized it. His one hope is that he will be able to utilize one remaining weapon: the renewed patience to wait to take the path he has laid out for himself.[13]

Dismantlements and Assemblages

Snopesism picks men apart, disrupting the harmonious equilibrium of perfected design models. This is evident in the person of Flem himself when he first appears in Frenchman's Bend,

> a thick squat soft man of no established age between twenty and thirty, with a broad still face, containing a tight seam of mouth stained slightly at the corners with tobacco, and eyes the color of stagnant water, and projecting from among the other features in startling and sudden paradox, a tiny predatory nose like the beak of a small hawk. It was as though his original nose had been left off by the original designer or craftsman and the unfinished job taken over by someone of a radically different school or perhaps by some viciously maniacal humorist or perhaps by one who had had only time to clap into the center of the face a frantic and desperate warning. (*The Hamlet,* 51–52)

Flem's clothing also identifies him as a man of the times he is helping to mold, for it comes straight from the mass-production line and the sweatshop process. The "tiny machine-made black bow which snapped together at the back with a metal fastener," that "tiny viciously depthless cryptically balanced splash like an enigmatic punctuation symbol against the expanse of white shirt," which Flem wears the day he enters Varner's store to take over as clerk, will be "made for him by the gross" once he becomes president of the Jefferson bank (*The Hamlet,* 57–58).

Snopesism mass-produces *itself,* not just snap-on ties.[14] Along comes IOU, the second clerk to infiltrate Varner's store. He is

> exactly like the old one but a little smaller, a little compacter, as if they had both been cut with the same die but in inverse order to appearance, the last first and after the edges of the die were dulled and spread a little. (*The Hamlet,* 160)

Snopes males are incomplete; their parts lack connection. I. O. Snopes buttons his coat "hurriedly about the paper dickey he wore in place of a shirt (the cuffs were attached to the coat sleeves themselves)." Discarding his lensless glasses, his gaze has an intentness that "seemed actually to be no integral part either of the organs or the process behind them, but seemed rather to be a sort of impermanent fungus-growth on the surface of the eyeballs" (*The Hamlet,* 200).

In a way each Snopes is all of a piece, whether "exactly like the old one" (The Old One, meaning the Devil), "but a little smaller, a little compacter." For all his dismantling, Lem Pitkin is all of a piece, too, pulled together into a single representation ("All-American Boy"). And for all his disarray, Henry Ford coalesces as "Fordism." After the same manner, the bits and scrapes of individual Snopeses mean something—have power—once they are brought together as "Snopesism." Fragmentation, yes; alienation from the group, no. Emersonian individual integrity, no; collective assemblages, yes.

Faulkner Women

Whether or not they choose to live and die by the demands of love's inefficiency, Faulkner women are realists, levelheaded managers in shrewd pursuit of their goals. In contrast, Faulkner males tend to be addled by idealism and have a bent for nominalism that makes it difficult for them to name things according to empirical evidence.[15] Males fear what they view as female irrationality, immorality, and extravagant conduct while they pride themselves on what they call the masculine principles of logic, rationality, and prudence.[16] The paradox lies in the Faulkner truth that it is women's realism that connects them with love and other aspects of things as they are, and that it is men's idealism that commits them to reified creeds of honor, money, power, and convention.

Vis Inertia

The fact that neither Eula nor Linda is called upon to speak directly offers no proof that Faulkner is casting aspersions on the female sex. Rather, their silence points toward Faulkner's realization that the ideologies of Snopesian society are voiced by the ideologues. Those placed on the slant to Snopesism—to the side where money and respectability are not considered the motors that regulate the universe—need no direct say; however qualified, their force requires no words.

Eula Varner stands in blatant, almost frightening contrast to the male principles of Snopesism, the Mississippi version of twentieth-century management and engineering practices, practices committed to progress, productivity, and profit. From girlhood, Eula has represented what Henry Adams defined as the power of vis inertia resistant to progress— mechanistic indeed, but hardly efficient in the sense blessed by scientific management. She never partakes as "a living integer of her contemporary scene, but rather [exists] in a teeming vacuum," because "she already knew there was nowhere she wanted to go, nothing new or novel at the end of any progression, one place like another anywhere and everywhere" (*The Hamlet*, 95).

Eula can easily be denounced as a retrograde force, a force radical politics fears as much as the progress-committed conservatism of the Snopesian way. Furthermore, Eula slides directly out of Nature, created as "some symbology out of the old Dionysic times" (ibid.). Nature is by nature mechanistic, and no more so than in the way Eula's erotics represent a machine going nowhere. But Nature's mechanisms and Eula's "logics and erotics" are at odds with the Apollonian aspirations of the "new" machine process.[17]

Since Eula's origins are in *another kind* of mass-production system, and since she remains unduplicable as an "original," she is alien to the system of mechanical reproduction Walter Benjamin describes. Instead, she contains the "aura" that is lost once "a work of art," with "its presence in time and space, its unique existence at the place where it happens to be," is banished to make way for its copy.[18] Therefore, she is ahistorical, apolitical, a danger to us all, no matter what position we take vis-à-vis the business enterprise, the machine process, and the agency of the sexes.

Gavin Stevens comments, "That's what you thought at first, of course: that she must of necessity repeat herself, duplicate herself if she reproduced at all." But

> immediately afterward you realised that obviously she must not, must not duplicate; very Nature herself would not permit that to occur, permit two of them in a place no larger than Jefferson, Mississippi, in one century. . . . Because even Nature, loving concupiscent uproar and excitement as even Nature loves it, insists that it at least be reproductive of fresh fodder, for the uproar and the excitement. Which would take time, the time necessary to produce that new crop of fodder, since she—Eula Varner—had exhausted, consumed, burned up that one of hers. (*The Town*, 133)

Because of the precision of her movements, no existing machine is capable of duplicating Eula for mass consumption or of turning her into the kind of consumer mandated by the crudities of the existing industrial process. In fact, she is what Karl Marx defined as the perfect machine. In contrast to the common worker who "consumes his provisions during pauses in the labor process," Eula is an entity that "consumes what is essential to it *while it is still functioning*."[19]

The real American tragedy is misuse of the perfect machine. Just as Anzia Yezierska declared, it means the waste of the glorious gift of productivity. By the time the second novel of the Snopes trilogy ends, Eula has committed suicide, driven, some say, by her need to leave a legacy of respectability to her daughter Linda, although respectability was never anything she cared about for herself. But the truer reason is probably the one Ratliff hits upon: that she was bored. Weeping at the sorry part he has played in Eula's progress through the earthly kingdoms of Mississippi, Gavin Stevens gets it right when he says,

> "She loved, had a capacity to love, for love, to give and accept love. Only she tried twice and failed twice to find somebody not just strong enough to deserve, earn it, match it, but even brave enough to accept it." (*The Town,* 359)

He most likely gets it wrong, however, when he comments upon "The waste. The terrible waste," as though it were Eula who had done the wasting. "To waste all that, when it was not hers to waste, not hers to destroy because it is too valuable, belonged to too many, too little of it to waste, destroy, throw away and be no more" (*The Town,* 358). This is like blaming perfection for not being fully appreciated; or chastizing Nature's abundance because no one knows how best to use it; or censoring love's consumption out of infatuation for the methods of consumer capitalism; or saying hers was the tragedy, not ours.

Conclusions: Grief or Nothing?

What can stop Snopesism, Taylorism, or Fordism once a culture of management has been established according to their rules, a culture that infiltrates all institutions and conditions all individuals, even those offering resistance? Whatever the solutions, if solutions there are, they will take place outside the pages of novels by authors like Nathanael West, Theodore Dreiser, and William Faulkner. But let us look at how these authors—Faulkner in particular—conclude their narratives. With this focus, we may at least see more clearly what the real problems are.

"Wild Palms" ends with Harry Winterborne's decision against using suicide as a means to escape life in prison for his part in the death of Charlotte Rittenmeyer. Suicide would bring Harry rest; it would silence the palms whose ceaseless rustling has been the leitmotif of fate throughout the novel. His death would also ensure that Charlotte had never lived. Her struggle in the cause of love against money and respectability would be erased if his memories of her were to drop into the void, and memory requires that he keep his grip on the body that sustains the mind that remembers. Between grief (the richness of the pain he must suffer in order to honor the pain she suffered) and nothing (the zero of death canceling life), he chooses grief.

Our most energetic social critics tell us that responsible texts should not end this way. They continually accuse the tragic mode and the tragic conclusion of being in league with the enemies of the good life. Radical politics from Emerson on teach us that grief is itself nothingness, nothing more than the self-importance of the isolated individual. It paralyzes action and silences dissent. What, then, can we say of the final episode of *The Mansion,* the last of the three-part history of Flem Snopes and his contributions to the culture of management in which the invisible hand become visible once again becomes invisible?

Vengeance is taken against Flem because he represents the forces that corrupt in the name of money and respectability, but this annihilating act does not—cannot—annihilate Snopesism without reconstructing the foundations of an entire culture. Besides, the deed is done by a man (Mink Snopes) and abetted by a woman (Linda Snopes Kohl) whose methods and motives throw their collaborative deed into question as a generally viable political response and as a particular counteraction against codes of managerial control.

These are the stern charges that *could* be laid against the way Faulkner closes the Snopes trilogy:

Count 1

On the surface, the shot Mink Snopes fires, which kills his cousin Flem, fits neatly into the standard formula for personal revenge (*He did wrong to me and I will make him pay for it*). This action, extracted from the "familial romance" tradition, has nothing to do with making society accountable for its history of unrelenting injustice; it seems to strike no blow against the legal, economic, or social systems molded by the tenets of Snopesism. Nothing has changed in Yoknapatawpha County or in the rest of the Western world.

If the scope of Mink's act is narrowly personal, it is also as broad as the cosmos. Political praxis is ineffective in either the inner life or the transcendent sphere, but these two realms are precisely where Faulkner's narrative locates its action.[20]

Count 2

Once Mink Snopes successfully completes his self-assigned task—one that required him to wait patiently in silence down through his years at Parchman—his response is to return, permanently, to silence. The cry that concludes *The Jungle*—"Organize! Organize! Chicago will be ours!"—is neither for him nor for Faulkner. The pistol shot speaks for Mink. He is now ready to give himself over to the earth, whose death pull he has hitherto resisted with all his will.[21]

Throughout the development of scientific management, human engineering, and the science of work, there has been stout resistance to any notion of the lure of rest and sleep as the means of escape from the fatigue of labor. If humankind ever depletes the energy allotted it by the law of thermodynamics, it might yield to a *"compulsion to rest."* [22] Rest was one of Adam Smith's favorite things; he equated it with "liberty and happiness." Karl Marx, however, fiercely denounced rest, which he viewed as "idleness," not the productive leisure that brings true freedom to the worker who "steps to the side of the production process instead of being its chief actor." [23]

Henry Armstid is pulled back into the annihilating void once he begins, like an automaton, to dig his own grave as he searches for buried treasure at the Frenchman's place. This is not "good work" in either Marx's or Faulkner's view. Where Faulkner parts ways from Marx is in the way he conceives the universe of force and reasons why Mink Snopes yields to rest.

Marx accepted Helmholtz's notion that the cosmos is "an industrialized automata" in whose image the human "working body was thus recast." [24] In contrast, Faulkner's cosmos is aristocratic, hierarchical, sublime—the realm of "Helen and the bishops, the kings and the unhomed angels, the scornful and graceless seraphim." This kind of transcendent glory neither solves diurnal labor-management problems nor projects a proletarian paradise. But the starry spheres toward which Mink gazes—in league with the soil upon which he rests once he "steps to the side of the production process"—promise him equality and freedom through entropy. Life's energy goes down through the grass blades and roots, the little worm holes,

> down and down into the ground already full of the folks that had the trouble but were free now, so that it was just the ground and the dirt that had to bother and worry and anguish with the passions and hopes and skeers, the justice and the injustice and the griefs, leaving the folks themselves easy now, all mixed and jumbled up and comfortable and easy so wouldn't nobody even know or even care who

was which any more, himself among them, equal to any, good as any, brave as any, being inextricable from, anonymous with all of them. (*The Mansion,* 435–36)

True "industrial democracy" at last! But this is democracy located well beyond the factory floor.

Count 3

It looks well (from the perspective of revolutionary thought, although not from the standpoint of family decorum) that Flem's death is helped along by Linda Snopes Kohl, not his blood daughter but raised as his only heir. One can argue that Eula Varner Snopes's wasted life has been avenged when her daughter conspires in the murder of the man who murdered love. Linda's action can be seen as defending courage and honor from becoming mere "habit," that is, from becoming part of Snopesism itself.[25]

Linda has the look of a heroine of the people, up to a point. Women who arrange the deaths of their fathers interest not only Freudian analysts but also political theorists and feminist activists. But Linda is an odd case, one who resists easy accommodation to the radical mold. Faulkner sees to this by converting her, by the symbolic fact of her deafness, into "the inviolate bride of silence."

Count 4

Words (whether too many or too few) and silences present a major obstacle to anyone planning to appropriate the Snopes trilogy into the canon of social protest literature. In *The Hamlet* Eula Varner, for all intents and purposes, speaks only twice: (1) when Labove advances toward her at the start of what will prove his futile attempt at rape, he says, "Don't be afraid," and she says, "Afraid? Of what?"; (2) when he grapples with her, "whispering his jumble of fragmentary Greek and Latin verse and American-Mississippi obscenity," and she knocks down this dismantled would-be master, saying, "Stop pawing me. You old headless horseman Ichabod Crane" (*The Hamlet,* 120–22).

In *The Town* Eula Varner Snopes speaks more, but what she says is not particularly interesting, except when she advises Gavin Stevens to stop talking and start acting. Rather than attributing her indifference to language to Faulkner's disbelief that women are capable of linking thought with speech, it should stand as the sign that Faulkner considers language itself suspect. Besides, what does this woman have to say to a society that has no notion of how to use her abundance efficiently?

In contrast to the careless disregard Eula has for ordinary speech acts, there is Gavin Stevens's endless flow of talk. Based on sheer volume, there is little difference between all his words and those turned out on the assembly line of gossip and political machinations by I. O. or Clarence Snopes. The quality of the discourse Gavin produces is higher in terms of vocabulary and ostensible content, but it is wasteful verbiage just the same.[26]

Flem Snopes is most effective as a force when he is not only invisible but (largely) silent. When the original description of Flem as a man chewing a quid of tobacco is replaced by the image of a machine whose jaws chew on air, Snopesism is portrayed brilliantly. Snopesism means being powered by a mechanism that exists on air and produces nothing, even as the silent movement of Flem's mouth repeats the ominous image of the clashing jaws Henry James found in control of the American scene.

Flem's force as a fictional character is noticeably diminished once he moves from the quest for money to the quest for respectability, despite Ratliff's highly important observation that while money and power allow a man "some place where he will stop," respectability curses one with a lifetime of endless toil (*The Town*, 259). As long as Flem silently pursues money and power, he casts terror over Hell itself.[27] The old terror is sustained as long as Flem is seen seated in silence, inside the bank cage where the money is. But once his silent jaws chew their way toward respectability he becomes impotent as a potent narrative force. This is, of course, the sorry fate of the capitalist in decay, who figures in most versions of proletarian fiction: "the capitalist himself . . . who had begun life as a nihilist and then softened into a mere anarchist and now was not only a conservative but a tory too; a pillar, rock-fixed, of things as they are" (*The Mansion*, 222).

The figure who should worry us most as we try to sort out whether Faulkner's trilogy is able to move responsibly past the self-defeating stasis of things as they are is not Flem but Linda Snopes Kohl. Meddlesomeness is apparently the impulse that moves Linda to threaten her name-father; meddlesomeness, if you recall, is one of the vices Charlotte and Harry were driven to defy.

The late 1940s have brought relative "peace and plenty" to the New South, but Linda is bereft: no war in Spain in which to fight against fascism; no world war with ships to rivet; not "even the downtrod communist shoe patchers and tinsmiths and Negro children" she took it upon herself to manage upon her return to Jefferson. "She has done run out of injustice," and so it looks as though she must hunt up something to manage (*The Mansion*, 361). Mink Snopes's unrelenting quest for justice against Flem seems just the thing for Linda to take as her cause. That this new cause brings her into direct confrontation with Flem is both necessary to the momentum of the plot and inconsequential to the conclusion of the narrative.

Linda is also inconsequential in the sense that any mission, not only Mink's, would have served just as well to activate her managerial talents. Linda is the necessary agent for ridding Yoknapatawpha County and the novels of Flem. No one else has been effectual in doing either (killing Flem or giving Faulkner's prolonged novel-making its release into rest). Gavin Stevens and Ratliff realize that Linda is one of the instruments (Mink is the other) that fate needs in order to erase the man who represents Snopesism, even though Flem's murder will result only in *his* death, not the death of Snopesism itself.

Whatever the prompting causes of the part Linda plays (whether accidental or fated), their significance is partly determined by the fact that she is deaf: "immured, inviolate in silence, invulnerable, serene." Her special gift, given to her when the bomb goes off during the war between Franco and the Republicans, is that eternal absence from human corruption possessed by one of Faulkner's beatific icons, the Keatsian Grecian urn. It is also the work/world environment enjoyed by Dreyfuss's Josephine. "If there were no such thing as sound. If it only took place in silence, no evil man has invented could really harm him; explosion, treachery, the human voice" (*The Mansion,* 203). Clyde Griffiths is harmed by the voices that explode around him, by their betrayal of the truth of what human beings are like when, trapped in the human element, they send him through "the little door" of the prison's execution chamber. Linda's silence protects her from ever having to go through the door traditionally flung open to trap women at "the altar and the long line of drying diapers; fulfillment the end."

> Not in motion continuous through a door, a moment, but immobilised by a thunder-clap into silence, herself the immobile one while it was the door and the walls it opened which fled away and on, herself no mere moment's child but the inviolate bride of silence, inviolable in maidenhead, fixed, forever safe from change and alteration. (Ibid.).

Linda thus shares with Flem the condition of stasis, "fixed" with things as they are. But paradoxes abound. Acting as the instrument for the opposition that brings him down with a pistol shot she will be unable to hear, she is a character in a silent film melodrama. Still, Linda's actions do not fit the standard protest movie plot formula. As Kay Sloan demonstrates throughout *The Loud Silents,* the cinematic businessman's daughter aids in her father's redemption so that the oppressed may be uplifted by the end of the movie. She relieves the people of their angers by means of the lesson of benevolence she teaches to her father. In this instance, however, Linda the daughter of the oppressor leagues with the oppressed in order to give him his patiently awaited moment of revenge.

There is another distinction, too. Linda does not need Mink as her go-between to "speak" to Flem about his coming death. Mink did have to think about his need to call out, "Look at me, Flem," as he lifts his pistol, so that his foe might realize that justice was being done at last. But because Linda and Flem both exist in silence, the latter knows without hearing what the former has to say. Throughout his lifetime, Flem has made use of two words: "one being No and the other Foreclose," but Linda is "forever safe" from being hurt by whatever Snopesism has to say. She exists

> in that chastity forever pure, that couldn't have heard him if he had had anything to say to her, any more than he could have heard her, since he wouldn't even recognise the language she spoke in. The two of them sitting there face to face through the long excruciating ritual which the day out of all the days compelled; and nobody to know why they did it, suffered it, why she suffered and endured it, what ritual she served or compulsion expiated—or who knows? what portent she postulated to keep him reminded. (*The Mansion*, 216)

Linda's "duck's voice" was "dry, lifeless, dead. That was it: dead. There was no passion, no heat in it; and, what was worse, no hope" (*The Mansion*, 217).[28] Linda has gone beyond "the human element" that even the idiot Ike Snopes possesses. Ike's only words "Ike H-mope," express the blend of hope and sadness that is the common plight of "all us sons of bitches." If Ike H-mope's position is not the best from which to launch effective literary (much less, political) protests against Snopesism, Linda's position is even less promising. Ike still exists in the world where love's disarray and irrationality struggles against management's hope to achieve an order and rationalism that pontificates, *Men dont love beasts. It's not normal, not respectable, not productive.* Linda exists between the mundanity of Jefferson and the poetic realm of "Helen and the bishops, the kings and the unhomed angels, the scornful and graceless seraphim"; she also exists in the realm of product design, where grids, graphs, averages, and pictograph figures provide the universalized "signage," requiring no words to transmit meaning.

Rosalind Krauss is among the brave souls who try "to declare the modernity of modern art."[29] She has done it by advancing the grid and its import. The grid stands opposed to the tradition of naturalist perspective, "the science of the real." Grids lie along a spatial plane that is "flattened, geometricized, ordered, it is anti-natural, anti-mimetic, anti-real." The grid is "a naked and determined materialism"; it is also "Being or Mind or Spirit," "the staircase to the Universe" (2). As one mounts like a twentieth-century Peter Bembo toward the stars, space and time merge; all is subsumed within the structuralist mode through which myths and emblems are read.

In league with physiological optics, the grid functions as "a matrix of knowledge"—that point of vision afforded by "the separation of the perceptual screen from that of the 'real' world" (5). Both centrifugal and centripetal, it works "outward, compelling our acknowledgement of a world beyond the frame," while also bringing movement "from the outer limits of the aesthetic object inward" (6). Repetition, not development, is the proper way of designating this "paradigm or model for the anti-developmental, anti-narrative, the anti-historical" (8).

Let us appropriate Krauss's paradigm of the grid to explain, in part, the paradigm Faulkner provides at the conclusion of the Snopes trilogy. It is a paradigm that illustrates what Pierre Janet called *psychasthenia,* the "inhibition to action" that comes about once inertia overcomes will.[30] This, too, is Faulkner's vision of what happens to those caught up in Snopesism, whether its progenitor or its rebellious progeny. Energy draining, tired to the bone, strangers to hope, enveloped in silence, yearning for rest, Flem waits for death, Mink waits to bring death, Linda waits to be its handmaiden.

What does this do to the entire narrative sequence, one that put Faulkner to the strain of finding an expressive form capable of representing what the culture of management feels like once it pervades every corner and fold of society? Oddly enough, the conclusion of the final volume of Faulkner's Snopes trilogy pours energy *back into* a narrative process that had begun to flag noticeably by the second volume. In the last scenes of *The Mansion,* Faulkner reacquires the quality of Bakhtinian polyphony that characterizes his most powerful works. Here, silences work as dialogic debates, far more effective than the garrulous talk spun out by Gavin Stevens, V. K. Ratliff, Charles Mallison, and the Faulkner narrator.

This is the magical paradox: that the Platonizing quality so pronounced in Faulkner's "big books"—the quality that, in *The Mansion,* takes us up "the staircase to the Universe" beyond narrative, beyond history—makes for a smashing return to narrative and historical power. Faulkner perceives, brilliantly, that you fight fire with fire, making certain all the while that your blast of heat masters the fire you wish to contain.

If the visible hand made invisible through Snopesism reaches everywhere, then the author must include everything: melodrama, fable, tall tale, tragedy, farce, words, silences, history, myth, empirically perceived particulars, cognitive abstractions, emblems, grids, grit. Those who fight human engineering are human engineers; the reformers are part of what they would reform; the monomaniacal pant in eagerness to pit their own "one true theory" against another's "best way." Mink and Linda (as well as Stevens and Ratliff) are what Flem *is,* no matter how much "nicer" they may be in the way they play out their particular agon. What matters is that Faulkner the storyteller not fall to the temptation to think *his* tale says it all.

As long as any author follows through on the full implications of Emerson's laissez-faire dictum to search for an absolute theory that will explain everything, knowing that "all" will never be touched (not even by "Helen and the bishops," who are but part of the totality)—as long as the storyteller responds to William James's admonition to plunge deeper and deeper into the dark bushes beyond the "sunlit terrace" of the classical scientific tradition—that narrator stands as a new-style totalist who celebrates the open universe of the narrative act, not a conventional absolutist who lacks trust in the possibility of energy abounding in the midst of entropy.

Nathanael West's *A Cool Million* is a brilliant little tale. It is perfect, but perfect because complete. It is complete because it captures within its narrative grid all there is to say about the flip side of cultures of management. It is self-contained within the form of the satiric parable, a self-repeating pornographic mechanism, a Rube Goldberg assembly line that can only reassemble itself.[31] West's tale lends itself beautifully to the kinds of diagrams that pattern the books written by our most profound narratologists. The significant thing is that their diagrams and West's novel follow in the tradition of model-making utilized by the professional designer. Indeed, a page taken from the writings of narratologists Seymour Chatman and Mieke Bal *looks* very like the blueprint taken from the studio of the product engineer.[32]

In contrast to *A Cool Million* (given that matters of taste always enter in, of course), Dreiser's *An American Tragedy* is more successful at offering a critique of the excesses of management culture because of its imperfections, because it tries to include too much. Dreiser never lets up; he never allows himself to say it has all been said. The final pages of Clyde's story expose how busily the people around Clyde (even his mother) are making up stories about him, stories they can "sell" in a marketplace that has an insatiable passion for consuming tales of money, redemption, respectability, and lust.[33]

Walter Benjamin's essay, "The Author as Producer," projects the hope that we may escape being consumers of stories by becoming our own producers. He notes, however, that many difficulties prevent even the most enlightened member of the bourgeoisie from ever proletarizing his or her work.[34] Benjamin's thesis has been confirmed over and over in these pages: both the necessity for, and the obstacles to, ending the need to convert our stories into routines that would manage our lives too tightly, too narrowly.

Many of the debates currently agitating, and energizing, literary and social criticism concern *where* one must be positioned in order to tell truths about things as they are so that things may be changed for the better. Some anti-theorist theories insist we can never find an Archimedean point outside the broil of conditions that need exposing. Others—more sanguine, more foolish, or more brave—say there are places where a somewhat clearer view can be had. Some speak from deep within the pit of complicity and call this truth. Some go outside, at real risk, to look inside. But whether inside or outside, acquainted with breadth or with depth, there seems to be no sure place where we can escape being part of "the web, the iron-thin warp and woof of [our] rapacity but withal yet dedicated to [our] dreams" (*The Town*, 316)—which is why Faulkner elects to be one with the web, one with the grief. If it were otherwise, his stories would pretend to partake in the purity that means death of memory and death of meaning.

"Meaning" is a dangerous word, but who believes one can escape danger when writing stories or thinking about their authoring? Meaning can be frozen within monuments. Flem Snopes's impoverished life is finally defined by three such edifices: the town's water plant, the tombstone placed over Eula's grave, the mansion. "Meaning" is also problematic if it is a thing *given to* us, as Benjamin knew when speaking of the passivity of the consumer mentality.

Pierre Janet made up stories with "good" endings to replace the "bad" stories that had paralyzed the will of his patient Marie (a kindly effort on Janet's part, which goes well beyond what either Belknap or Clyde's mother is capable of doing in attempting to rewrite that particular American tragedy). It is well and good that Marie is returned to some sort of "normalcy" by this creative and benevolent act of narratology. Yet many continue to contend that it is better all around when each of us writes our own story. Of course, they argue, we are not yet in the position to possess the ability to make them fully "correct." Naturally, we are still partially held back in our imaginations by the conditions under which we and our society function. But why wait?

Mink Snopes stopped waiting after thirty-eight years. He set out down a straight road to impose his notion of a good ending upon his story: a pistol shot and then rest, his vital energy not wasted but reabsorbed into earth and universe.[35] There are surely other endings more appropriate for us than the one Mink chooses. That is the point: *my good ending may be your bad one.* The thing is, at the very least, to question the manager's dearly held belief that there is "one best way" for us all.

NOTES

Preface

1. Brown, introduction to the "Theory of Literary History" issue of *PMLA* (107, no. 1 [Jan. 1992]: 22), paraphrasing Robbins's argument in "Death and Vocation."

Introduction

1. This summation of the "new" system of work regulation is from Kendall's "Unsystematized, Systemized, and Scientific Management," a paper delivered at the first Tuck Conference in 1912. For comments on these influential conferences, see Beniger, *The Control Revolution,* 397.

2. Taylor, "Workmen and Their Management."

3. Dos Passos, *The Big Money, U. S. A.,* 3:55.

4. Lears stresses the centrality of language in determining relations between culture and power under capitalism. Language leads to "the spontaneous consent" by whose means hegemonies seek legitimation. People are "spoken by language," but they also "speak," thereby participating in the creation of cultures. Lears, "The Concept of Cultural Hegemony," 568–69, 589, 592.

5. MacCabe, for one, resists discourse locked into polarities of "difference," which "simply reduplicates certain traditional forms of cultural pessimism and denies any effective form of engagement with contemporary culture" (MacCabe, "Defining Popular Culture," 3). Foucauldian theorists tend to disagree. Since their position forms an important part of the intellectual osmosis of our day, there is no need to run through the specifics of their arguments; they exist here as one of the givens of any current discussion of the nature of social disciplines. Seltzer's *Bodies and Machines,* however, represents an excellent point of reference.

6. This is the fear Lears expresses in "Man the Machine," his review of Rabinbach's *The Human Motor.* He calls for hard looks at the continuing consequences of a culture still devoted to productivity.

7. Anthropologists point to "vestiges" left over from more "primitive" periods that affect later, supposedly more progressive eras. Veblen promoted this idea in *The Theory of the Leisure Class,* as did Mumford in *Technics and Civilization.* In "Social Dramas and Stories about Them," Turner discusses the effect these residual impulses have upon the narrative process. His remarks also may help to explain the complexity of the new "progressivist" professionals' response. Robert Lynd and the Middletown project is an excellent example. Lynd was both a critic of an overly "managed" consumer society and an active agent in that society, both the

analyst of the problem and part of the problem itself. See Fox, "Epitaph for Middletown."

8. Faulkner, *The Hamlet,* 166.

9. Washington, *Up from Slavery,* 56–57.

10. See Rabinbach, *The Human Motor,* as well as Henry Adams's 1910 "A Letter to American Teachers of History," on the era's obsessive concern with wasted energy at every level, from the cosmos down to society and the private individual. Gies points out in "Automating the Worker" that Ford's innovations in assembly-line procedures greatly exacerbated problems introduced by Taylorism. However, two misunderstandings concerning the connections between Taylorism and time must be corrected from the outset: (1) Taylor did not originate time-motion studies. (2) Although Taylor paid great attention to methods for speeding up the work process, speeding is *not* what defines scientific management. The essential elements of scientific management include (a) the breaking down and analysis of each phase of the machine process; (b) the hastening of the demise of the skilled craftsman and jack-of-all-trades, and their replacement by unskilled workers assigned to isolated units of a work process rationalized to match machine standards; (c) the employment of functional foremen restricted to single tasks; (d) the addition of a new layer of managerial elite.

11. The literature on Taylorism is filled with references to the warp caused by this single-minded emphasis upon the money motive and the denial of human feelings. Elton Mayo's subsequent discoveries of the importance of on-site work relationships during "the Hawthorne experiment" led to the development of industrial psychology. The aims of management were still the same (to get as much effective work as possible out of the labor force), but Taylor's "plum" shifted from economic enticements to psychological appeals. For discussions of the repercussions of Mayo's studies, see Gies, "Automating the Worker"; Beniger, *The Control Revolution;* and Bendix, *Work and Authority in Industry.*

12. Veblen would appreciate Washington's demonstration of "the instinct of workmanship" that made him care deeply how well he wielded his broom.

13. Washington progressed beyond the lessons in self-management instilled at the Hampton Institute. As director of the Tuskegee Institute, he became "the master instead of the servant" by means of the work schedule he put into effect, a schedule that started with the 5 A.M. rising bell and dissected the day into discrete units (*Up from Slavery,* 171, 281). His 1901 book, *Up from Slavery,* preceded Taylor's published statements, which would not receive attention from the general public for another decade; Taylor was still unknown when acclaim was being heaped upon Washington. Like Taylorism, Bookerism was geared to character formation (students kept "out of mischief" through a rationalized work routine) as well as to the production of goods and services. It was also a concerted effort to change the idea whites had of blacks as an inefficient labor force, a belief that embedded the culture of slavery within the economic system long after the Civil War ended.

14. Chapter 8 comments upon the reactions against Bookerism found in Larsen's *Quicksand* (1928) and Ellison's *Invisible Man* (1952).

15. Washington, *Up from Slavery*, 162.

16. Chapter 7 deals with the relation between the abundance myth and the actuality of lack, which shaped the appeals mail-order catalogues made to potential purchasers of ready-made houses.

17. Faulkner, *The Mansion*, 382.

18. Ibid., 260.

19. Faulkner, *The Wild Palms*, 114. Deep within the pages of the Snopes triology, Faulkner offers us a glimpse at one possible solution to the effective satisfaction of human desires. As V. K. Ratliff, shrewd salesman and business entrepreneur, puts it, "So what you need is to learn how to trust in God without depending on Him. In fact, we need to fix things so He can depend on us for a while. Then he wont need to waste Himself being everywhere at once" (*The Mansion*, 321).

20. Or, as Seltzer puts it in *Bodies and Machines*, his important examination of managerial culture, such studies commonly reveal "a miscegenation of the natural and the cultural, the erosion of the boundaries that divide persons and things, labor and nature, what counts as an agent and what doesn't" (21). Indeed, Seltzer's entire argument is based on the "double discourse of the natural and the technological" that "makes up the American body-machine complex" (4). For Seltzer, it is not simply machines replacing bodies, or people already being machines, or technologies making bodies; what is radical is the "intimate *coupling* of bodies and machines" (12–13). Whether Faulkner goes this far remains to be seen.

21. On "the political ambiguity" that runs throughout *Modern Times*, see Maland, *Chaplin and American Culture*, 149–55.

22. Comments made by Floyd Dell in his 1914 critique of Theodore Dreiser's lack of radicalism, "Mr. Dreiser and the Dodo."

23. Rube Goldberg's biographer, Peter C. Marzio, expertly argues that Goldberg (like Keaton) captures the incongruity of new inventions and traditional patterns of life. Goldberg took classes from S. B. Christy, an avid Taylorite, during his student days at Berkeley. He made his start as a cartoonist in 1904, the year the first successful Ford car was assembled. By 1912 Goldberg had discovered his own expressive style for rendering the complexity, unreliability, angers, despairs, and longings of the little people who live amidst "dreamlike creations of disparate pieces precariously arranged" (Marzio, *Rube Goldberg*, 179). Unlike Ford Motor Company products, Goldberg's machines cannot be mass-produced; they eventually collapse into an entropic heap. Like Keaton, who also uses laughter that resists the tragic mode, Goldberg portrays life as adaptation to new things by people whose essential nature never changes.

24. Stein, *Three Lives*; the primary quotations below are from 12, 28, 37, 52, 62, 77, 82.

25. Living "regular and quiet," "good and regular" is the aspiration of Herman,

the husband of "the gentle Lena" (the third panel of Stein's triptych), and of the black community represented by Dr. Jefferson Campbell, Rose and Sam Johnson, and even, at times, Melanctha, the central figure of Stein's three portraits. This aspect of the culture of management reiterates Booker T. Washington's manifesto in *Up from Slavery*. As voiced by Jeff Campbell, it is a program for social control: " 'I want to see the colored people like what is good and what I want them to have, and that's to live regular and work hard and understand things, and that's enough to keep any decent man excited' " (ibid., 117). Problems arise when "romance" and "excitements" replace "peace and quiet" as the highest values for Melanctha and the Good Anna.

26. Taylor's biographers cannot avoid discussing his neuroses, but Kakar's analysis goes all the way in relating Taylorism to Taylor's private compulsion to master every aspect of his existence. See Dos Passos's version, which traces Taylor's control mania to the mother who "laid down the rules of conduct: self-respect, selfreliance, selfcontrol and a cold long head for figures" (*The Big Money*, 44).

27. Van Vlissingen, "Ardsley Thinks Out His Problem," 754.

28. Dell, "Mr. Dreiser and the Dodo," 17.

29. This attack against "high literature" and its affiliation with pessimism and purity is made in Calkins, *Business the Civilizer*, vii. For Calkins (notable in the 1920s advertising world), for Feather (the "100 percent American" is bored by Ibsen but will "cheer and exalt his business men above all others" [see "A Fourth of July Speech—New Style"]), and for the editors of *System*, right conduct and the good society result from codes laid down by the "masculine" business community, not the outmoded arbiters of genteel morality. See Mulcare on the anti-intellectualism of Taylorism in "Progressive Visions of War in *The Red Badge of Courage* and *The Principles of Scientific Management*."

30. Van Vlissingen, "Ardsley Thinks Out His Problem," 864.

31. Otte, "As Deever Does It," 480.

32. Grossman, "History and Literature," 5–6.

33. Robbins, "Death and Vocation," 39.

34. Jordan's work-in-progress, "To Engineer a Modern America," emphasizes the reformers' appropriation of engineering discourse. My own study differs in two ways: (1) it looks at the ways in which "the engineers" took up the expressive modes of social and private reform; (2) in addition to looking at language, it stresses narrative strategies—structures, plottings, and genre transformations.

35. What constitutes "the rest of us" is itself a question. In *Working-Class Americanism*, Gerstle observes that workers gradually lost control of their own "marginal" radicalized discourse once it was overlaid and absorbed by mainstream "nativist" conservative rhetoric. The famous *Life Magazine* coverage of "Middletown" in May 1937 has a Margaret Bourke-White photograph of a disabled steelworker, father of thirteen, and WPA relief recipient who reads Spencer, Darwin,

Marx, the Bible, *The Power of Will,* and *Power for Success.* If this worker's social views were constructed of such patched-together clusters of discourse, think of the variety of "made" narrative structures available to his generation.

36. "As we continue to talk of plots and plotting, we shall be paying ever greater attention to dramatizations of telling and their relation to implications of listening" (Brooks, *Reading for the Plot,* 236–37).

37. Docherty, *Reading (Absent) Character,* 253. Whereas Docherty works through tensions between realism and postmodernism, Knapp is concerned with the troubled relations between the "usefulness" exacted by scientific management and discourse affected by "pragmatic instrumentality"—the "triangulation" obtaining between "knowledge, history, and work" prevalent in modernist fiction. Knapp, *Literary Modernism and the Transformation of Work,* 3, 16.

38. White, "The Value of Narrativity in the Representation of Reality," 3.

39. The dual nature of the discourse intellectual elites deploy when addressing one another and when speaking to "ordinary people" is clarified by distinctions Spinoza made between "an acceptable truth when one is speaking with the vulgar and an acceptable truth when one is speaking philosophically." See Hampshire's review of *Spinoza and Other Heretics,* 40. Whether or not Spinoza was correct in arguing for the necessity of "a two-tier system of persuasion," because there are in actuality Jewish prophets (the bona fide elite) and the Others (the vulgar), we treat this duality of discourse between Us and Them as resulting from socially constructed self-perceptions.

40. Houser, *What the Employer Thinks,* 226.

41. Genette, *Narrative Discourse,* 216. Scholes also remarks, "To speak of the future is to prophesy or predict or speculate—never to narrate" ("Language, Narrative, and Anti-Narrative," 206).

42. Bremond's discussion, "The Logic of Narrative Possibilities," demonstrates both the lures and the limitations of reform literature. His elaborate charts map narrative cycles of "amelioration" and "degradation" and narrative endings that allow injustices to be prolonged, avoided, or eradicated (390–91, 394, 400). Keep Bremond's remarks in mind as chapter 6 examines Upton Sinclair's *The Jungle* in light of what happens when the narrator chooses *not* to "limit himself to mentioning the performance of the task" or to "the nature of the obstacle encountered," but proceeds to propose "the structure of measures taken to eliminate it" (394). As narrative, Sinclair's amelioration process merges its methods with those used by managers who try to eradicate obstacles to perfection.

43. Quoted in Ross, *The Origins of American Social Science,* 252.

44. Gerster concedes that "man's worst offenses are aesthetically upgraded by sufficient distance," but he insists that "redemption through distance is the one drawback of an approach that otherwise has only advantages" (*Grand Design,* 11–12).

45. Ibid., 12.

46. The first quotation comes from Kipnis, "'Refunctioning' Reconsidered," 28; the second comes from Grossman, "History and Literature," 31.

47. Here Grossman verifies views held by Prosper de Barante ("History and Literature," 35).

48. Turner, "Social Dramas and Stories about Them," 159–61.

49. Genette, *Narrative Discourse,* 253.

50. Van Kleeck, "The Social Meaning of Good Management," 10.

51. Weber, *Max Weber,* 287.

52. Meyer, *The Five-Dollar Day,* 39, 40; quoted from a 1914 article.

53. The first quotation comes from Culler, describing Genette's activities as a narratologist (introduction to *Narrative Discourse,* 13); the latter is Genette's defense against the charge made against him by Dorrit Cohn in *Narrative Discourse Revisited,* 116.

54. Henry Adams, the amateur scientist and accomplished narrator, was "forced to write science because our purpose is science, and cannot be rendered by narrative." Damned whether he intended to instruct or to amuse, he was left in the midst of a literary experiment, trying "to find the exact point of equilibrium where the two motives could be held in contact" (Adams, letter of March 1909, *Letters,* 6:238). In the world of scientific management, this duality might be split between cocreators of efficiency texts. Frank Gilbreth set down the facts of time-motion procedures while Lillian "spun the stories" about the people they affected (Gilbreth and Carey, *Cheaper by the Dozen,* 29). Adams and the Gilbreths would find a support in Hayden White, who leads the group concerned with the importance of "metaphorical statements" that exceed the technical language some historians believe is the guarantee of truth. In White's view, we familiarize an unfamiliar event through the use of figurative language, without failing in our common task of "defamiliarizing" and "demystification." Riffaterre argues that the value found in fiction's "truth" is not a matter of "factuality" and that "fiction is a genre whereas lies are not." Reinitz concludes his examination of Progressivist historiography by agreeing that analysis of the "literary" kind aids in interpreting historical events. See White, "The Historical Text as Literary Artifact," 51, 56, 61; Riffaterre, *Fictional Truth,* xiii, 1; and Reinitz, "Niebuhrian Irony and Historical Interpretation," 126.

55. Godden, *Fictions of Capital,* 9. Godden insists that we ought not view matters of commodity as theoretical abstractions in the absence of historical contexts for consumption.

56. Marquis, "Memo on the Ford Profit-Sharing Plan," 17.

57. Genette, *Narrative Discourse,* 29–30.

58. Grossman, "History and Literature," 10.

59. White, "The Narrativization of Real Events," 253, in response to Louis O. Mink's rebuke of his earlier essay, "The Value of Narrativity in the Representation of Reality." Taylor's "engineering" methods ally him to students of semiology of

the Bremond school, as evidenced by Bremond, "The Logic of Narrative Possibilities," 387. In a note appended in 1986, Bremond chastises himself for his 1980 essay, saying it is "not false but it is not economical." Striking the note found throughout Taylor's narratives, Bremond tells himself that he will "bring together categories of analysis," reduce the "number of actions," "grade units," and "make this model operative" (407). In "Death and Vocation," Robbins remarks that some theorists believe narrative, "if somewhat paradoxical," grants authority to critics "because it *undermines* authority—because it acts as an agent of relativism, unreliability, or 'literariness' loosed subversively into the world of 'scientific' or authoritarian truth" (42).

60. Brooks, *Reading for the Plot*, 4, 6, 10, 12.

61. Genette, *Narrative Discourse Revisited*, 129.

62. Barthes, quoted in Brooks, *Reading for the Plot*, 18–19. This inclusion indicates that Brooks himself goes well beyond the limitations of Taylorite plots.

63. Robbins, "Death and Vocation," 42.

64. Genette characterizes Balzac as being more conservative in his manifestos, less conservative in his novels (*Narrative Discourse Revisited*, 142–43). We can say the same of a number of the authors whose texts appear throughout this book.

65. Scholes, "Language, Narrative, and Anti-Narrative," 208.

66. Dell, "Mr. Dreiser and the Dodo." *The Masses* directly equated Darwinistic theories of evolution with a reactionary politics that was either resigned to the impossibility of social change or desirous of retaining the status quo.

67. The first comment by Dell is from "Talks with Live Authors"; the second is from "Mr. Dreiser and the Dodo."

68. Genette asks, "what would theory be worth if it were not also good for *inventing practice*?" (*Narrative Discourse Revisited*, 157).

69. McDonnell, "'You Are Too Sentimental,'" 629–30. Marx then and others now would displace the emphasis (often nostalgic) given to culture and psychology over economics and politics. See MacCabe, "Defining Popular Culture," 4, 8, and Cohen, "What Kind of World Have We Lost?" 680. *Taylored Lives* deals (without nostalgia) primarily with matters of culture and psychology, but without dismissing political and economic concerns.

70. McDonnell, "'You Are Too Sentimental,'" 629. Russell's 1913 attack in *The Masses,* "The Invisible Government," mocked the "smug gentlemen" of the National Association of Manufacturers for the "lying and hypocrisy and slimy fraud there was in their pretenses about 'freedom of contract' and 'law and order.'"

71. Sumner, "The Forgotten Man," 1:476. Besides adumbrating today's arguments against welfare assistance, Sumner's essay echoes arguments that were being made in the contemporary "social Darwinism" debates. See Bannister, *Social Darwinism*.

72. Quoted by McDonnell, "'You Are Too Sentimental,'" 629.

73. Feather, "A Fourth of July Speech—New Style," 14.

74. Throughout 1914 *The Outlook* featured "The 'Big Business' Man as a Social Worker." Manufacturers like Gary and Cyrus McCormick were "sentimentalists" who acted so that "we have no trouble with labor." McCormick "flees the word" socialism (creature of "parlor impossibilities"); he replaces "the field of feudal business" with the "something new" of welfare systems.

75. V. G. Rocine had mixed feelings about Rockefeller as the ideal American, but none about Theodore Roosevelt, the model for productive, antientropic Americans. See Banta, *Imaging American Women,* chap. 2.

76. Dell, "Mr. Dreiser and the Dodo"; Sloan, *The Loud Silents,* 52.

77. Ross, *Changing America,* 89. Adams more neatly fits the portrait of the muckraker as pessimist in his habit of squirreling away newspaper clippings in which he "harvested the woe and misery . . . in order to pound home his theme of social decrepitude" (Samuels, *Henry Adams,* 42). See the useful studies of the connections among muckraking journalism, the reformist mode, and literary productions by Fishkin, *From Fact to Fiction,* and Wilson, *The Labor of Words.*

78. Sloan, *The Loud Silents,* 24.

79. Peter Brooks believes that melodrama is "the most remarkably distinctive and valuable thing" about American culture (quoted in Lang's *American Film Melodrama,* x). Lang distinguishes between *tragedy* (aware of the part ideology plays, thereby subject to confusion about what is right or wrong) and *melodrama* (less intelligent, likened to "hysteria," but better able to fight against the evils it perceives) (18–20, 25–26). Also see Reinitz's comments about the melodramas of history written by Gabriel Kolko in which "the leaders of America are powerful, manipulative, and guilty; the masses are powerless, manipulated, and innocent," a narrative that "is very comforting" to anyone "who identifies with the people rather than the leadership" ("Niebuhrian Irony and Historical Interpretation," 125). Mulvey's essay, "Melodrama in and Out of the Home," instructs us that early nineteenth-century British melodrama was identified with "the people" and only later became "respectable" in its effort to appeal to middle-class family audiences.

80. Ford's attack against "mushy sentimentalism" and "professional charity" appears in *My Life and Work* (206–7, 267) as a defense of his code of self-reliance. In *Changing America,* Edward Ross, the influential sociologist, picked up on both Theodore Roosevelt and Frederick Jackson Turner in arguments that (typically for the times) try to merge "Western" individualism and self-control with the conviction that it is the duty of the professional class to guide the "lower grades" of immigrants and women into a more efficient society.

81. Pierce, *Co-Operative Housekeeping,* 6, 29.

82. See Graebner, *The Engineering of Consent,* 189.

83. Tichi's *Shifting Gears* mounts vivid evidence of the ways in which the figure of the engineer captured the popular imagination at the turn of the century, becoming the hero of modern efficiency.

84. *The Masses* reprinted Russell's article "The Invisible Government" from the *International Socialist Review* in July 1913. It addressed contemporary activities that Alchon analyzes after the fact in *The Invisible Hand of Planning.* For Russell, the National Association of Manufacturers, in covert league with members of Congress, exerts power over government policies to the detriment of the labor movement. For Alchon, the "invisible hand"—located midway between laissez-faire practices and "statist" collectivism—rapidly spread its touch to nonindustrial areas, among them, the professions of social work, public relations, and (benignly) library science (as with the inception of Melville Dewey's decimal system).

85. For Engels's 1878 remarks, which include the admonition "Thou Shalt Not Steal," see *The Marx-Engels Reader,* 726.

86. Belief in organized morality was advanced by the new-style sociologist Charles Cooley as part of his influential 1902 study, *Human Nature and the Social Order.* It would be an injustice to Cooley to classify him with the oppressors because of this phrase. His insistence on the moral weight of "ought" as a necessary antidote to the amoral callousness of "is" involves the dangers any reform program invites (as chapter 3 will elaborate), but Cooley's views of human nature ("warm, fresh, outward-looking") are among the more human voiced by the social theorists of his age. See Cooley's chapter titled "The Social Aspect of Conscience."

87. Marquis, "The Ford Idea in Education."

88. The remark made by Mark Twain's friend, Mr. Ballou, in chapter 33 of *Roughing It.*

89. Links between personal morality and business conduct were made with the greatest self-confidence in *The Universal Self-Instructor and Manual of General Reference* (1883) and Hill's *Right and Wrong, Contrasted* (1884). Later decades would experience the "controlled pessimism" of the New Deal (see Kemler, *The Deflation of American Ideals*) and the gloom that Brick claims characterizes the 1940s (see *Daniel Bell and the Decline of Intellectual Radicalism*).

90. "So far from the new conditions created from time to time being dangerous," Andrew Carnegie promised, "they are progressive [*sic*]; not revolutionary, but evolutionary, the last stage being better than what it displaced" (*A Rectorial Address,* 21).

91. Kendall, "Unsystematized, Systematized, and Scientific Management," 139, 141. Note that Kendall's observations concern women factory workers. Champions of Taylorism maintained that the human element had been its concern from the start (see Van Kleeck, "The Social Meaning of Good Management"). Fordism always had a more tenuous connection to the moral process, but even there lip service was paid to "the making of men" as "Mr. Ford's business," however much the quality of life experienced by his "made men" might be in doubt (see Marquis, "The Ford Idea in Education"; "Reminiscences of Charles Sorensen"; and Meyer, *The Five-Dollar Day,* 40).

92. Dewey and Tufts's *Ethics,* for example, was concerned with proving that "the social end is the rational end." What is "more rational" is simultaneously "more social" and "moral" (12, 314).

93. James, "Frederic Myers' Services to Psychology," 156; the next quotation is from the same essay. See Ross, *The Origins of American Social Science,* on the value (male) professionals in the social sciences placed on the "realism" of "hard facts and hard science," which they set against the "romantic fantasy" of female subjectivity. Also see Fitzpatrick, *Endless Crusade,* on the roles played in the new social sciences by women emerging from the University of Chicago.

94. White's *Social Thought in America* emphasizes how contemporary thinkers benefited by shaking free from abstractions. Purcell's *Crisis of Democratic Theory* looks at the opposite response: the fear of those who discovered that irrationality and "wild facts" might be more "real" than rational, predictable, "good laws," and their efforts to insure that science and scientism would continue to set standards for objectivity and reason. If anyone believes that these aspirations and anxieties no longer exist, read Martindale, *The Clockwork Muse,* which is ardently committed to the premise that "nothing is random" and that "the universe is governed by deterministic laws." Martindale is opposed to "the negativistic, pessimistic, and melancholic attitudes of humanism," which are so "caught up in details" that they cannot accept "the uniformity principle" allowing aesthetics to be reduced "to basic behavioral science" (1–4). The debate continues undiminished. In Robbins's words, although "narrative means militant indeterminacy or relativism to some, to others it is something excessively determined, a hyperstructured vehicle of dogmatic belief that desperately needs to be relativized" ("Death and Vocation," 42).

95. The dream of transforming the inchoate wilderness into a successful commercial nation linked by a network of roads and canals began very early with George Washington's 1770 proposal for "practicable trade routes" (reiterated by John Quincy Adams in 1804). See Adams, "The Heritage of Henry Adams," *The Degradation of Democratic Dogma,* 13–21. More recent studies have pointed up the American desire to map, web, and grid the continent, among them Boelhower, *Through a Glass Darkly;* Jackson, *American Space;* and Fisher, "Democratic Social Space."

96. Emerson, "Nature," *Complete Works,* 1:4.

97. Du Bois, *The Souls of Black Folk,* 241. This description also applies to Fordism, which relied on the belief that Ford was "extremely simple" and "absolutely sure he [was] right in every wish, impulse and fancy." See Arnold and Faurote, *Ford Methods and the Ford Shops,* 16.

98. See the "promotion literature" compiled by Dorson, *America Begins.* Two scholarly theses predicated on assumptions of American abundance are Fitch's *Architecture and the Esthetics of Plenty* and Potter's *People of Plenty.*

99. Lynd and Lynd, *Middletown,* 13–14.

100. Feather, "A Fourth of July Speech—New Style."

101. Rabinbach's main argument about "the science of work" focuses upon its origin in fears over loss of energy. See chapter 3, "The Political Economy of Labor Power," *The Human Motor*.

102. Reinitz, "Niebuhrian Irony and Historical Interpretation," 119.

103. James, "The Hidden Self," 105–7; quotations in the following paragraph are also from this essay.

104. In "The Historical Text as Literary Artifact," White accuses psychoanalysis of "overplotting," weighing in masses of fantasy against modicums of truth (50), but in James's essay it is Janet the analyst who clears away the excesses that have left his patients at the mercy of unhappy fantasies. Keep in mind that Charles Sanders Peirce wrote in "How to Make Our Ideas Clear" that "to be masters of our own meaning" it is necessary to be one of those "whose ideas are meagre and restricted" rather than "such as wallow helplessly in a rich mud of conceptions." Peirce also worried about America's ability to overcome "a vast, unfathomable deep of ideas" (288).

105. Sloan relates the way in which William Sulzer, the impeached governor of New York, starred in the 1915 film melodrama *The Governor's Boss*. In this attack against the Tammany Hall machine that divested him of power, Sulzer "took the unique opportunity that film provided to rewrite his own history with a happy ending." In place of his actual role as victim, he concluded his rewrite with the victorious defeat of his opponents (*The Loud Silents*, 10–11).

106. Hall, "Gramsci and Us," 19.

107. Engels in 1887 and 1892, from *Marx and Engels on the United States*, 282, 327. In 1892 Engels still voiced the hope this "colossal energy" will "one day bring about a change that will astound the whole world. Once the Americans get started it will be with an energy and vehemence compared with which we in Europe shall be mere children" (328).

108. See Ross, *The Origins of American Social Science*, 144–46. *Social Justice without Socialism* was published in 1914 by John Bates Clark, a leading liberal economist and Veblen's former teacher.

109. James, "The Hidden Self," 90–91; quotations in the following paragraph are from this essay.

110. James, quoted in Lentriccia, *Ariel and the Police*, 110.

111. Emily Dickinson being spontaneous in her garden is different from Zelda Fitzgerald dancing in the Paris streets or from Charles Manson practicing "helter-skelter." Hester's Pearl, Daisy Buchanan, and the Invisible Man gone underground all act out spontaneity in their own ways; in each case, their wildness is also part of a control system.

112. Adorno, "Culture and Administration," 105.

113. These chemical terms, drawn from the language of insurance companies that must take into account the susceptibility of paintings to change, are taken from Updike's review of an exhibition of Albert Pinkham Ryder's paintings

("Better than Nature," 17). It is time we stopped limiting ourselves to metaphors drawn from mechanisms and biology, susceptible as they are to excessive traits of behaviorism and determinism.

114. See Banta, "The Boys and the Bosses," which draws upon Basalla's discussion of "idle curiosity" in *The Evolution of Technology*. Whether free-floating curiosity in the purist sense exists in a managerial world is debatable. Researchers with IBM, Dow, and Bell Laboratories are paid to be curious; their activities are hardly "idle."

115. Marx, *The Eighteenth Brumaire of Louis Bonaparte*, quoted in Anderson, *In the Tracks of Historical Materialism*, 1.

116. White, "The Historical Text as Literary Artifact," 47.

117. Hernadi, "On the How, What, and Why of Narrative," 199.

118. *The Works of George Herbert Meade*, 1:196–97. These notes from lectures Meade gave between 1900 and 1934 make clear that he was not a "bad" behaviorist, as his attacks on John B. Watson show. Chapters 5 and 6 of Cooley's *Human Nature and the Social Order* (1902) similarly promote the attainment of "the whole man" through mergers between "me" and "the social self."

119. Kipnis, *'Refunctioning' Reconsidered*, 33.

120. Lears, "Man the Machine," 43, 44, 45; the following phrase about history left "in a museum case" is also from Lears's article.

121. Nor defined as Martindale does, when he asserts that revolutions "differ only on the surface. On an abstract level, the same sequence of events always happens" (*The Clockwork Muse*, 6), which means that it matters little whether it is George Washington or Lenin who runs affairs.

Chapter One

1. In "The Politics of Pragmatism and the Fortunes of the Public Intellectual," a review essay of George Cotkin's *William James: Public Philosopher*, Posnock distinguishes the effect James's "voice" has had upon his admirers from the highly problematic contradictions of his logic. Posnock argues that James's pragmatic philosophy was impotent in the world of practical politics and that he shared affinities with the very men he attacked. In his chapter "The Imperialist Imperative," Cotkin suggests that, prior to 1899, James's anti-imperialist stance was similar to that of the Mugwumps in their anxiety over involvement with "barbaric" racial groups abroad. (For a classic example of this stance, see Sumner's bitter essay, "The Conquest of the United States by Spain.") While fully granting the aptness of Posnock's and Cotkin's reservations about the vaunted rightness of James's position, this chapter centers precisely upon James's "voice": (a) his force as a storyteller in providing alternative tales to those of the "war men"; (b) his awareness as a student of "the double self" that alternating waves of coldness and hotness (similar to the physical process that makes possible the expansion that follows upon contraction) enter into the making of dangerous stories of expansionism.

2. James, "The Philippines Tangle," 225; the following quotations are from 225–26.

3. Posnock is quick to point out that McKinley, Roosevelt, and James shared a belief in American exceptionalism and that in this instance, as in others, one ought not draw too hard a line separating James from his adversaries ("The Politics of Pragmatism and the Fortunes of the Public Intellectual," 571–72).

4. The following paraphrase, together with quotations from 216, 218, draws upon chapter 9 ("The Conversation of Archaic Traits") of Veblen's *Theory of the Leisure Class.*

5. Riesman, "The Social and Psychological Setting of Veblen's Economic Theory," 450. Robbins compares Genette's account of the process by which the "vulgarity of story" flows through "sophistication of discourse" to "a social allegory of evolution from barbarism to civilization." This is also the same set of textual moves, says Robbins, that Hayden White discusses in *Metahistory*—moves that shift "from (barbaric) metaphor to (civilized) irony" ("Death and Vocation," 46).

6. Veblen, "The Place of Science in Modern Civilisation," *The Place of Science in Modern Civilisation, and Other Essays,* 1–2; the following quotations are from 26–27.

7. While Veblen concedes the lure of the "dramatic play of passion and intrigue" for those fatigued by too much "science," he distrusts what results when professional "students of literature" try to ape scientific models. They should stick to "that discipline of taste and that cultivated sense of literary form and literary feeling that must always remain the chief end of literary training, as distinct from philology and the social sciences." Any "straining after scientific formulations in a field alien to the scientific spirit is as curious as it is wasteful." What is appropriate to true science—the "theoretical statement" and the "air of scientific acumen and precision"—has no place in the activities of "myth-makers" involved in "the humanities generally" (ibid., 27–28). However, Veblen introduces yet another twist in his handling of the "idle curiosity" that stirs myth makers and scientists alike. See Posnock, "William and Henry James," 13–14, and chapter 9 below on the advantages science gains from the storytelling imagination.

8. Riesman comments on Veblen's acceptance of the same "crudities and self-deceptions" he attacked in nineteenth-century thought. "All of us suffer from the illusion that we are outside what we are criticizing," and Veblen was no exception. In supporting the ostensible advances of a technological culture, Veblen tended to reintroduce outmoded conceptions of human relations governed by "a market economy" and "rationalistic individualism" ("The Social and Psychological Setting of Veblen's Economic Theory," 450, 459–60). What Posnock's essay "The Politics of Pragmatism" (568) has to say about the conversion of William James into a cult hero by "left romanticism" (Cornel West's term) applies just as well to Veblen. Dos Passos swears that Veblen dismissed "the business of the day" in the hope "that the engineers, the technicians, the nonprofiteers" might yet "take up the fight where the workingclass had failed." But even Dos Passos senses that the

answer is "no" to his posing of Veblen's question, "Was there no group of men bold enough to take charge of the magnificent machine before the pigeyed speculators and the yesmen at office desk irrevocably ruined it . . . ?" (*The Big Money, U. S. A.*, 97, 103–4). For what did happen, see Ehrenreich and Ehrenreich, "The Professional-Managerial Class," and Segal, *Technological Utopianism in American Culture.*

9. Fiske is quoted in Martin, *American Literature and the Universe of Force,* 74. Also see chap. 12, "Imperialism and the Warrior Critique," of Bannister's *Social Darwinism.*

10. Morris, *The Rise of Theodore Roosevelt,* 470, 550. Roosevelt constantly used phrases that verbally fight a war of opposites: *the bad:* "feeble renegades," "the thin-skinned," the "over-soft natures," "the weakling or the coward," "willful sterility," "sheer unmanliness and cowardice," "shrunk from the contest"; *the good:* "robustly patriotic," "sound, healthy minds," "a race of good fighters and good breeders." See Roosevelt, "True Americanism" and "The Manly Virtues and Practical Politics" (both 1894), "The Duties of American Citizenship" (1893), "The Strenuous Life" (1899), and "Citizenship in a Republic" (1910), all from vol. 15 of *The Works of Theodore Roosevelt.* The December 1914 issue of *The Masses* printed Amos Pinchot's piece, "The Failure of the Progressive Party," which speaks of the sense of betrayal felt by the working class that had turned to Roosevelt to lead them in "a campaign against privilege and injustice." They had believed he "would fight courageously" in the battle they had joined "with the fervor of a religious crusade." But he had failed them with his repudiation of Eugene Debs's socialism. "The masses" did not reject the quasi-religious bellicosity of the Rooseveltian ethos of manliness. Roosevelt was rejected when they found him a coward in battle.

11. Weber, *The Protestant Ethic and the Spirit of Capitalism,* 166; Lenin, "Raising the Productivity of Labour," 417.

12. Ford, *My Life and Work,* 263, 267; Feather, "A Fourth of July Speech—New Style," 14.

13. In his chapter "The Machine Process" in *The Theory of Business Enterprise,* Veblen indicates his awareness of "the modern warlike policies . . . entered upon for the sake of peace, with a view to the orderly pursuit of business" (186–89). He notes the battles taking place between "archaic" business practices and "modern" technology for control of future societies and institutions, but his prose style is not up to the tragic conditions he attempts to analyze.

14. Comment in *Life* [New York], 15 Feb. 1900, 124.

15. De Forest, *Miss Ravenel's Conversion from Succession to Loyalty,* 257.

16. "The Army of the Potomac," 331.

17. This and the next two quotations are from *Battles and Leaders of the Civil War* 3:163, 179, 188.

18. Crane, *The Red Badge of Courage, The Works of Stephen Crane* 2:63. Earlier, Fleming (who has moments of feeling as though he were "grimy and dripping like a laborer in a foundry," [2:37]) likens the battle to "the grinding of an immense and terrible machine" whose "complexities and powers, its grim processes, fascinated him" in its ability to "produce corpses" (2:50). But war to Fleming is also "the red animal" and "the blood-swollen god" that sends men forth uttering "a wild, barbaric song . . . strange and chantlike" (2:25, 35). Eleven years later in 1906, Upton Sinclair's *The Jungle* would portray the plight of people caught within barbarian narratives simultaneously filled with beast imagery and tropes for the modern machine process.

19. Whitman, *Specimen Days, Complete Prose Works,* 35.

20. This praise for Howard's moral qualities comes from the chapter devoted to him in L. P. Brockett's *Men of Our Day* (1868), which also traces Howard's checkered career as the first head of the Freedmen's Bureau. Howard's trials at the bureau are reviewed further in Du Bois, *The Souls of Black Folk.* "Good" man; inept administrator.

21. *Battles and Leaders of the Civil War,* 3:184.

22. Ibid., 3:198; the next quotation is from 3:202.

23. See Kaplan, "The Spectacle of War in Crane's Revision of History," for an acute discussion of Crane's responsiveness to the rise of the imperialist spirit. In "Progressive Visions of War in *The Red Badge of Courage* and *The Principles of Scientific Management,*" Mulcare disagrees, since he reads Crane's novel as a statement of support for business, Taylorism, and war imperialism. He manages this, however, by appearing to conflate Henry Fleming's responses with those of the narrator. That Crane placed himself neither with the anti-imperialists nor with the pro-expansionists is suggested by the comment he made during an interview published in the *London Outlook* (4 Feb. 1899). He is quoted as saying, "The people of the United States consider themselves as a future Imperial Power only vaguely and with much wonder. The idea would probably never have occurred to them had it not been for foreign statements and definitions. . . . As far as I see, there is no direct American sense of Imperialism" (*The War Dispatches of Stephen Crane,* 243).

24. Emerson's narratives of the 1840s, although written in the prophetic mode, may seem to place his stories within the "prior" imagination of naively peaceable "savages," particularly when they are compared with the avant-garde nature of Marx's prophetic texts of the same decade. However, the narrative positioning of Emerson's 1861 essay "War" relocates Emerson (in imaginative time) in the aftermath of the war stories told by Theodore Roosevelt and places him in close proximity to Veblen. That is, Emerson and Veblen stand within modern times, looking back upon an earlier barbaric era in which Roosevelt rides by at a gallop in quest of honor and glory. Even though Roosevelt acts in the name of latter-day, quasi-predatory tales filled with the urgency to reform inefficient institutions and human conduct, he is one with "such wide, passionate, needy, ungoverned,

strong-bodied creatures," whom Emerson describes as belonging to the early "tribe" ("War," *Complete Works* 2:151).

25. Sims, "Roosevelt: Historian and Patriot," preface to Roosevelt's *Naval War of 1912,* in Roosevelt, *Works,* 7:ix; hereafter cited parenthetically in the text.

26. "Scenes in the War of 1812," the lead article in the May 1863 issue of *Harper's Monthly Magazine,* opens with the account of the court martial of William Hull, brigadier general of the U. S. Army, who was "accused of treason, cowardice, and neglect of duty." Found guilty of the last two charges, he was condemned to be shot for having surrendered Detroit and the entire Michigan Territory to the British, but President Madison remitted his sentence. In the same issue that features this tale of grevious mismanagement during the land war of 1812, an article titled "The Drift of American Society" laments the "social and civil drift" threatening the nation's survival. Eerily, the next two issues of *Harper's* will detail the debacle at Chancellorsville. Faulty planning at every level of society calls out for the introduction of some kind of scientifically managed society.

27. Morris, *The Rise of Theodore Roosevelt,* 154.

28. Roosevelt never missed a chance to rag Jefferson. In his biographies of Gouverneur Morris and Thomas Hart Benton, both published in 1887, he scorns Jefferson as "helpless" and as a "scholarly, timid, and shifty doctrinaire." While acting secretary of the navy under McKinley in 1897, he continued his attacks in private letters and public speeches, characterizing Jefferson's accession to power as "a terrible blow to this nation" and chastising Jefferson's timidity in covering the coastline only with defensive gunboats. See ibid., 334, 379, 547, 570.

29. In his *Autobiography* Roosevelt attacks both efficiency "based on unscrupulousness" and inefficiency resulting from "purely negative virtue." But at least the men behind "the machine" (which "as such had no ideals at all") possess the vigor lacking in "the aesthetic" types, "the silk-stocking reformers," with no means "to achieve results, and not merely to issue manifestoes of virtue" (*Works,* 22: 319, 328).

30. See Adams on those who figure as "types of character, if not as sources of power," in *History of the United States of America During the Administration of James Madison,* 1333–35; hereafter cited parenthetically in the text. Good material for the psychologist; lean evidence for the historian.

31. I wish to thank Charles S. Adams for his observations concerning Adams's ambivalence toward the means and ends taken during the War of 1812 and throughout the Jeffersonian years. Henry Adams had to consider the same painful questions in regard to Jefferson's bold "Yankee" move to acquire the Louisiana territories while circumventing Congress. Whereas Roosevelt scorned Jefferson for lacking aggressiveness and for relying too much upon traditional means to cautious ends, Adams's Jefferson always runs ahead of the pack. See Adams, *History of the United States During the Administration of Thomas Jefferson,* 615, 849. In his 1876 review of von Holst's *History of the United States,* Adams notes the aggressive power moves made by Jefferson (even though the President chided opponents for

similar behavior), which "may prove that Jefferson was an unscrupulous politician"—even though, the review continues, "it also proves . . . that the American political system was stronger than the individual" (353). On the other hand, Adams agrees with Roosevelt about Madison's passivity and his inept handling of the war. See Adams, *History of the United States During the Administration of James Madison*, 116, 249. Also see Watts, *The Republic Reborn*, for recent scholarship on the making of "the culture of capitalism" introduced by Jeffersonian Republicans.

32. Adams, *History of the United States During the Administration of Thomas Jefferson*, 11, hereafter cited parenthetically in the text.

33. See Baym, "Early Histories of American Literature," 466–68.

34. Bourget, *Outre-Mer*, 128–29.

35. Taylor, "Workmen and Their Management."

36. Dos Passos, *Nineteen Nineteen*, *U.S.A.*, 143, 148.

37. Adams, "Recognition of Cuban Independence," 34. The following quotations extracted from Adams's report are from 23–25. At the 1988 Modern Language Association convention, John Carlos Rowe presented a paper that is part of a larger project focusing upon the new diplomacy of imperialism championed by Henry Adams and John Hay.

Chapter Two

1. See Rotundo's essay, "Boy Culture," in *Meanings for Manhood*, a phenomenon characterized by "energy, self-assertion, noise, and frequent recourse to violence" (19). See also Dallek's comments in his chapter, "Imperialism: A Crisis in National Self-Confidence," in *The American Style of Foreign Policy*, about the disorder in the Cuban campaigns that pointed up the problem of assertions of individual will during military engagements requiring discipline (20), and Dos Passos's depiction in *Nineteen Nineteen* of the Cuban scene, where rain, disease, and heat did not make it "bully" for the regulars left behind once the amateurs went home (*U.S.A.*, 144–45). Amy Kaplan also provides important insights into the relations between adventure romance fiction, the imperialistic bent, and assertions of rugged masculinity in her essay "Romancing the Empire: the Embodiment of American Masculinity in the Popular Historical Novel in the 1890s," where she makes direct reference to Richard Harding Davis' *Soldiers of Fortune*.

2. Roosevelt, *The Rough Riders*, *Works*, 13:149, 163; hereafter cited parenthetically in the text.

3. Dallek, *The American Style of Foreign Policy*, 20.

4. Disregarding what it might be like for men in the ranks, Roosevelt asserts that the manager-leader "has positively unlimited opportunity for the display of 'individual initiative,' and is in no danger whatever either of suffering from unhealthy suppression of personal will, or of finding his faculties of self-help numbed by becoming a cog" (*The Rough Riders*, 13:37).

5. Particulars supplied by press correspondents in Cuba supported Roosevelt's general allegations of mismanagement. Although the war meant excellent business for the journals, reporters were quick to point out martial managerial deficiencies. See Milton, *The Yellow Kids,* 229, 312, 320, 330–31. Among the reporters was Stephen Crane, whose feelings about "the general incompetence and idiocy existing in several departments of the army" are conveyed through the angry words of "A Private" whose "Memoirs" were "Dictated to and Taken Down by Stephen Crane." See *The War Dispatches of Stephen Crane,* 213–15.

6. Brave under fire during his stint as war correspondent in Cuba, Crane was always candid about his own fears (*The Yellow Kids,* 305). Roosevelt could not countenance such admissions from a manly man.

7. Army regulars in Cuba did not admire Roosevelt and his men; they scorned them as mere amateurs (ibid., 329–30).

8. Davis, *The Cuban and Porto Rican Campaigns,* 6; hereafter cited parenthetically in the text.

9. Morris's *Rise of Theodore Roosevelt* details the substandard accommodations with which the men on board the transport ships had to contend, both before and during the debarkation from Key West to Cuba. This data is given short shrift in both Roosevelt's and Davis's accounts.

10. Davis sent a dispatch that stated bluntly that the campaign was "prepared in ignorance and conducted in a series of blunders," but his dispatch was withheld (*The Yellow Kids,* 334).

11. Davis admits that early newspaper accounts spoke of a fiasco at Guasimas. This happened because some newsmen posted wild rumors. Real "historians" like himself "correct" the "falsehoods" that make it seem as though Colonel Wood and Lieutenant Colonel Roosevelt needlessly sacrificed their men's lives. He also tips readers off to the "inside story" of the Seventy-first New York, facts "well-known to everyone who was present at the fight." While it was true that the men "certainly did not behave well," the fault was "entirely" that of a few officers who "funked the fight" (*The Cuban and Porto Rican Campaigns,* 238).

12. See *The War Dispatches of Stephen Crane* for the remarks Davis and other correspondents made about Crane's activities in Cuba. In addition to statements of admiration for his fellow professional, Davis includes "a lonely picture" of a grievously wounded white lieutenant seemingly influenced by Crane's novel: an expressionistic, color-coded scene in white, black, and red. The officer is surrounded by black soldiers "crouching at his feet like three faithful watch-dogs, each wearing his red badge of courage, with his black skin tanned to a haggard gray, and with his eyes fixed patiently on the white lips of his officer" (*The Cuban and Porto Rican Campaigns,* 211). Similar comments about the loyalty of black soldiers (reminiscent of Amasa Delano's good-natured bigotry in Herman Melville's "Benito Cereno") appear in *The Rough Riders* (13:108), which speaks of the responsibility white officers have to lead black soldiers.

13. "The Europeans can say to our discredit, that we failed to feed our soldiers in the field, and to care for them when they were wounded and ill; but they cannot say that the soldiers did not do their share, even though republics were ungrateful and political officials incompetent" (Davis, *The Cuban and Porto Rican Campaigns,* 300).

14. In citing the soldier's remark, Davis quotes from Crane's article, "Stephen Crane's Vivid Story of the Battle of San Juan," published in the *New York World,* 14 July 1898 (see *The War Dispatches of Stephen Crane,* 180). "Vivid" as Crane's reports may have been, in his "War Memories" he insisted that "you can depend upon it that I have told you nothing at all, nothing at all, nothing at all" (ibid., 295).

15. Davis's account of the passing of power from Old World Spaniards to New World Americans gives no sign of the irony Melville provided in "Benito Cereno" regarding Spain's decline and America's rise.

16. In *Drive to Hegemony,* 62–63, 69–71, Healy outlines how American businessmen eager to take over the fertile land of new territories put their faith in a market agriculture, a faith betrayed when industry replaced agriculture as the main source of twentieth-century wealth. Also see Healy's chapter "Assumptions, Biases, and Preconceptions" for further reasons American expansionists gave for thrusting themselves into the Caribbean: among them, the notion of "international law," disgust over the inefficiency of local governments, and belief in the moral imperative for "modern business enterprise to push its way into the preindustrial world" in order to correct "barbarism, enervated by certain civilized forms, without barbarism's vigor."

17. Healy observes of American business interests, "Self-serving they certainly were, but not necessarily insincere. It is, after all, easiest to believe what is welcome; belief and self-interest typically run hand in hand" (ibid., 69–70).

18. Lloyd, "In New Applications of Democracy," 14. In "The Instinct of Workmanship," Veblen comments that "nearly all those who *speak for war are at pains* to find some colorable motive of another kind. Predatory exploit, simply as such, is not felt to carry its own *legitimation*" (84).

19. Veblen, *The Theory of the Leisure Class,* 227, the next quotation is from the same page.

20. Weber, *The Sociology of Religion,* 100–101.

21. In "The Moral Equivalent of War" (reprinted in both *McClure's Magazine* and *Popular Science Monthly* during 1910), James again speaks of "civilized opinion" as "a curious mental mixture." "At the present day," James writes, "'peace' and 'war' mean the same thing, now in posse, now in actu" (213). He acknowledges the thrill war has for men, himself as well as Roosevelt: "War is the strong life; it is life in extremis" (211). Like Veblen, James traces the apparent need for violence back to "piratical" wars waged by Greece, but he focuses upon the current barbarism in which "the popular imagination fairly fattens on the thought of

wars" (213). Because of their emphasis upon the archaism of the war spirit, James and Veblen disagree with Roosevelt, who believes that it takes men of the advanced, "civilized" breed to lead the United States towards peace. In contrast to "barbarians" like Indians, the "civilized man finds he can keep the peace only by subduing his barbarian neighbor" (Roosevelt, "Expansion and Peace," published in *The Independent,* 21 Dec. 1899, included in *The Strenuous Life,* 31). In a review of Roosevelt's essays, Henry James attacked the "puerility of his simplifications" (Morris, *The Rise of Theodore Roosevelt,* 576).

22. See Healy's chapter "Agents of Hegemony" in *Drive to Hegemony,* in which he relates the activities of regular American military forces and the irregular forays commanded by two soldiers of fortune, Lee Christmas and Samuel Zemurray. Also see Davis's *Real Soldiers of Fortune* (1910), in which he mythologizes the men who carried out private imperialist expeditions throughout the Caribbean and Latin America.

23. Tichi's *Shifting Gears* documents the elevated stature accorded the engineer in the popular mind.

24. Pagination for Davis's *Soldiers of Fortune* will be given parenthetically in the text.

25. See Banta, *Imaging American Women,* for its analysis of Davis's *The Princess Aline* (1895), illustrated by Charles Dana Gibson, and the turn-of-the-century "norms" set for the masculine and feminine types.

26. See Banta, "The Boys and The Bosses." Whereas Hank Morgan, boss at the Colt Revolver Factory in the late 1870s, nicely represents the earlier type of all-round mechanic, Robert Clay represents the success story of the 1890s: the engineer both specialized enough and adaptable enough to take on assignments as varied as building bridges, roads, and forts, and administering a mining operation.

27. In his seminal 1903 address, Taylor stated that "good manners, education, and even special training and skill . . . count for less in an executive position than the grit, determination and bulldog endurance that knows no defeat." See Taylor, "No. 1003—Shop Management," 1417–18. Clay conveniently lacks the education and specialist's training that Taylor says is of little importance to the successful engineer. What matters for Davis's narrative is that Clay has both the grit Taylor calls for and the sufficiently good manners required of any hero of popular barbaric fictions.

28. Engineers make good marksmen. The eyes of Clay's men "had been trained for years to judge distances and to measure space, and they glanced along the sights of their rifles as though they were looking through the lens of a transit" (Davis, *Soldiers of Fortune,* 340).

29. After all, Clay's father was a "filibuster" who "went out on the 'Virginus' to help free Cuba" in 1873 and was "shot, against a stone wall" (ibid., 177). See Davis, *Real Soldiers of Fortune,* particularly about William Walker of Nicaragua fame, called "the last of the filibusters." See also Foner, *A History of Cuba and*

Its Relations with the United States, 2:244–47. Both books narrate attempts at "missionary" takeovers in South America and Cuba.

30. In Clay's bitter recounting of the rough life he was forced to lead since boyhood, he refers to Indian squaws and the girls of dance houses and gambling hells as the only kind of female "companions" he has known (151); but the question of whether he ever "knew" them carnally is left in abeyance. Clay must appear to be the kind of manly virgin that Roosevelt himself was on his wedding night.

31. *The Cuban and Porto Rican Campaigns* (265–70) provides an extended description of the hero's reception given to Captain Richard H. Hobson, a scene second in its emotionality only to Davis's allegorization of the coming of "the son and heir" who conquers the Caribbean. In contrast, see Crane's "Hobson's Exchange," *War Dispatches of Stephen Crane,* 289–91. Crane makes sharp distinctions between moments in which men act "simply, honestly, with no sense of excellence, earned out of blood and death" and moments when "suddenly the whole scene went to rubbish." Rubbish is when men say and do things with a self-consciously grand air; it is absent where there is "the mere exchange of language between men."

32. Morris, *The Rise of Theodore Roosevelt,* 467–68.

33. James, *The Wings of the Dove* 20:405; hereafter cited parenthetically in the text.

34. A notable exception is Seltzer's examination of *The Golden Bowl* in *Henry James and the Art of Power,* 58–95.

35. James, *The Golden Bowl,* 23:17; hereafter cited parenthetically in the text.

36. Weber, *The Protestant Ethic and the Spirit of Capitalism,* 19. It frequently has been observed that James's characterization of Adam Verver does little to persuade readers that Verver was capable of becoming one of the age's great industrialists and financiers, however much Verver fits Veblen's description of what happens to capitalist barbarians once they decline into the sloth of leisure. Admittedly, the Verver we see *within* the narrative seldom matches the description given of the qualities Verver possessed prior to the opening of the story: "The essential pulse of the flame, the very action of the cerebral temperature, brought to the highest point, yet extraordinarily contained—these facts themselves *were* the immensity of the result; they were one with perfection of machinery, they had constituted the kind of acquisitive power engendered and applied, the necessary triumphs of all operations" (James, *The Golden Bowl,* 23:127–28). However, we are shown Verver in the act of conveying *the look and feel* of businessmen who know how to apply the principles laid down by Taylor and analyzed by Weber. As Verver formulates his plans to marry (to incorporate) Charlotte, he acts "not in precipitation, flurry, fever, dangers these of the path of passion properly so called, but with the deliberation of a plan, a plan that might be a thing of less joy than a passion, but that probably would, in compensation for that loss, be found to have the essential property, to wear even the decent dignity, of reaching further and of providing for

more contingencies" (23:211). Verver's plan of action is, of course, precisely the one taken by Charlotte herself; it is the reason why she succeeds as a top manager as long as she does, until the time comes when she is unable to keep down the "precipitation, flurry, fever . . . of the path of passion."

37. McWhirter gives a fine reading of *The Golden Bowl* with which I cannot agree on two counts: (1) that Maggie is able to engage the two sides of the prince; and (2) that, because she has replaced desiring with loving, her triumph is complete and the marriage is restored to an authentic wholeness. I believe Maggie has held back from exploring the "other" Amerigo, and that, although she has indeed gone far in the ways of loving, the situation remains a tragic one—"tragic" in the sense that all of James's mature works are tragic, because of their economics of cost. One person's gain is always another's loss. It is precisely the one who loves profoundly who is most aware of this terrible fact. In response to all of us who find sadness, not triumph, in the final embrace of the novel, McWhirter has a ready answer: "they expect too much, and want the impossible rather than the attainable." See *Desire and Love in Henry James*, 151, 197.

Chapter Three

1. Silcox, "Discussion," in "Workers' Participation in Management," 25.

2. Veblen, *The Theory of Business Enterprise*, 31.

3. Mumford, *Technics and Civilization*, 215.

4. In 1901, in the same issue of *The Congregationalist* and on the same page as Lloyd's encouraging words concerning the benefits of imperialistic brutality (the means to the end of imperialism), Helen Campbell writes that science (once "counted almost purely materialistic") is becoming "one with spiritual law." "*Love* is entering in" ("In Home Life," 14). Silk and Vogel's *Ethics and Profits* (whose introduction is titled "Looking for Love") records the bewilderment of employers as to why they are viewed as villains, unable to comprehend that "periodic public vilification is the price American business pays for the absence of a serious socialist challenge" (29). But if many tried to redefine science and business in terms of love, others (represented by Jack London's Wolf Larsen) took "altruism," "morality," and "right conduct" to be words from a strange language that intruded upon a brutal world of materialism.

5. Houser, *What the Employer Thinks*, 113; the following quotations are from 108–9, 114–16.

6. *The Marx-Engels Reader*, 550.

7. Ibid., 726; the following comments, including the admonition "Thou Shalt Not Steal," are from the same page.

8. Kloppenberg's *Uncertain Victory* is an excellent study in the relations of American pragmatism to radical European social thought. See chapter 4, note 24 below for reference to treatments of American socialist thought vis-à-vis nineteenth-century Marxism.

9. This and the following quotations are from Veblen's *Theory of Business Enterprise,* 25–26. Brandes cites the unsettling mix of democratic ideals and bureaucratic techniques permeating the texts of the times in *American Welfare Capitalism, 1880–1940,* 9. An unpublished paper by Daniel Borus, "Thorstein Veblen and the Distopia of Commodities," addresses the problematic nature of Veblen's own writing style and authorial tone. I agree with Borus, and with White's appraisal of Veblen in *Social Thought in America,* that Veblen was more moralistic than he admitted (as in his use of "invidious" and "waste"). The constant emphasis Veblen placed upon the supposedly impartial, unfeeling, unbiased nature of scientific thought is, as Borus notes, often annulled by the myths he makes about the "spell" cast by *things.* Yet, although Veblen came under the sway of "the hegemony of commodities," and although his text "reveals its involvement in the logic it aims to overthrow," Borus views Veblen as maintaining his adversarial linguistic stance.

10. Ford, *My Life and Work,* 9; the following quotations are from 154, 207, 278. In this instance and others, Ford's "writings" consist of Samuel Crowther's careful reorganization of Ford's free-flowing talk during a series of interviews, which he supplemented with material written by William J. Cameron for "Mr. Ford's Page" in the Ford-owned *Dearborn Independent.* The relationship among the *langue,* the *parole,* and the *écriture* supplied by Ford, Crowther, and Cameron would make fascinating study.

11. Ford, with Crowther, *Today and Tomorrow,* 269.

12. Bendix, *Work and Authority in Industry,* 199.

13. From Fay Leone Faurote's compilation of interviews with Ford, *My Philosophy of Industry,* 34; the following quotations are from 34–35, 37, 38, 40.

14. Ford, with Crowther, *Moving Forward,* 75; the following quotations are from 75, 78.

15. Ford, *My Philosophy of Industry,* 88.

16. Lenin, "Raising the Productivity of Labour," 417. Also see Afanasyev, *The Scientific Management of Society,* for a more recent assessment of the value placed upon Taylorism by the Soviet industrial system. Marxist-Leninist texts, of course, require the same critiques one exacts of bourgeois writings.

17. Veblen, *The Theory of Business Enterprise;* this and the following quotations are from 14–15.

18. Chapters 6 and 8 look at the desk-bound office manager of the 1910s and 1920s, no longer imaged as the intrepid engineer out in the field or engaged head-on with workers on the shop floor.

19. DuBrut's comments are included in Taylor's "No. 1003—Shop Management," 1457; hereafter cited parenthetically in the text. Taylor first presented his ideas at the ASME meeting of 1895, but, according to Nadworny, his message was largely ignored. The year 1903 is generally recognized as the "day of creation" during which Taylor became the Father of Scientific Management.

20. In "New Aspects of Employer's Welfare Work" (1904), John Graham Brooks addresses the employers' desire to "secure more contentment and stability" by "manipulation of" (not "participation with") the workers—a difficult task, since business must deal with "that spirit of labor independence from which, for good or ill, we never again shall be free" (6). Independent workers; enslaved bosses.

21. For ways in which technological metaphors have invaded everyday life, see Connolly, *The Terms of Political Discourse,* and Edge, "Technological Metaphor," in *Meaning and Control,* ed. Edge and Wolfe. An unpublished paper by John M. Jordan, "The Engineers and the Discourse System," demonstrates how nonengineers drew upon the language of engineers and thereby moved away from metaphors of morality. My emphasis tends in the opposite direction: the incorporation of nontechnological language and narrative techniques into areas of industrial discourse, and the technologists' concern over matters of conduct and moral values.

22. In *Desire and Love in Henry James,* McWhirter makes an important distinction between the writer whose text is controlled by his desires and the author who controls his text. "Writer" and "author" are both useful terms when speaking of the personal and private strands contained within Taylor's texts, but a major distinction must be made between McWhirter's argument and mine. McWhirter shows, brilliantly, that Jamesian authors pledge themselves to realistic narratives while Jamesian writers stay with the self-deceptions of romance and "modernism." In Taylor's case, acts of writing and authoring alike tend to fix Taylor as the romancer.

23. See Rowe's remarks in "Henry Adams," 645–67.

24. Speaking in 1914 of "the routine of the machine industry," Veblen remarks that "this routine and its discipline extend beyond the mechanical occupations as such, so as in great part to determine the habits of all members of the modern community" (*The Instinct of Workmanship and the State of the Industrial Arts,* 311).

25. In "Technological Metaphor," Edge defines metaphor as the overlaying of two puzzling images. We find a good example in Taylor's paper, where the language of "the machine process" constantly overlays the image of the donkey (untamed primal energy) with that of the "first-class" horse (purposeful discipline).

26. See Taylor's account of the merry means by which the head of the American Screw Works of Providence, Rhode Island got children to do "a fair day's work" ("No. 1003—Shop Management," 1374). Taylor's anecdote demonstrates the callousness over child labor shared with others of his generation; it also suggests the way different ideologies offer different slants on the nature of humor, as do the stories Taylor tells about Pat and Mike and the stupid little "Dutchman."

27. See ibid., 1411, 1415, 1454. The antagonism of Taylor and his disciples to welfare work is hammered home in Nelson and Campbell's essay, "Taylorism Versus Welfare Work in American Industry." Petersen modifies the Nelson-Campbell thesis in an unpublished analysis, "Henry Gantt's Work at Bancroft."

28. In Taylor's version of the counterrevolution, men "must be brought to see"

that bosses are "friends," not "antagonists." Those who do not "acquiesce in the new order of things," because they are "either stupid or stubborn," "must drop out" (No. 1003—Shop Management," 1411–12). "Fairness" will end turnover, contain unrest, and further the industrial process, even if workers must be forced into accepting its benefits. See Fisher's 1917 Department of Labor report, "How to Reduce Labor Turnover."

29. Taylor bases his objections to the Towne-Halsey Plan on a view of human nature that rejects his rivals' privileging of old-fashioned notions of self-reliance into which every American can tap (No. 1003—Shop Management," 1421).

30. Job specialization disrupted traditional categories of boss, mechanic, and laborer. The consequences of specialization for both labor and management are detailed in Hounshell, *From the American System to Mass Production, 1800–1932,* and Meyer, *The Five-Dollar Day.* Taylor also comments upon the changes his practices initiated in "No. 1003—Shop Management," 1347.

31. Elsewhere Taylor the Good Shepherd lavishes upon the employer the attention he gives single erring workman. The "ninety-nine men out of a hundred" in management shall also be led toward the light of his production methods ("No. 1003—Shop Management," 1479).

32. Lears, "Man the Machine," 45.

33. Taylor accuses the Towne-Halsey Plan, his competition in "the management war," of sharing with piecework "the greatest evil of the latter, namely that its very foundation rests upon deceit, and under both of these systems there is necessarily . . . a great lack of justice and equality" ("No. 1003—Shop Management," 1355). But when Halsey charges that Taylor's plan denies workingmen initiative and intelligence, he does not condemn it for reasons of character malformation; rather, he claims it invalidates the "economic soundness" of their wages (1467).

34. Taylor is willing to explain his work practices to the laborers, "patiently, one man at a time," but only "a series of object lessons" will make the new theories "stick" ("No. 1003—Shop Management," 1412–13).

35. Gramsci, "Americanism and Fordism," 279; subsequent quotations are from 296, 298, 302, 317.

36. In *Capital,* Marx repudiates the process that turns into Taylorism and Fordism: the "constant labour of one uniform kind [that] disturbs the intensity and flow of a man's animal spirits which finds recreation and delight in mere change of activity" (1:4:322). However, the age of Taylor and Ford that enfolded Lenin and Gramsci set its values against "animality," unless the flesh could become the untiring metal of the machine.

37. The texts referred to below, in order of publication, are: James, "The Moral Philosopher and the Moral Life" (1901); Cooley, *Human Nature and the Social Order* (1902); Ward, *Applied Sociology: A Treatise on the Conscious Improvement of Society by Society* (1906); Dewey and Tufts, *Ethics* (1908).

38. James, "The Moral Philosopher and the Moral Life," 344; Cooley, *Human Nature and the Social Order,* 361; Ward, *Applied Sociology,* 29; Dewey and Tufts, *Ethics,* 496–97.

39. Cooley, *Human Nature and the Social Order,* 364–66, 373.

40. James, "The Moral Philosopher and the Moral Life," 350.

41. U.S. Congress, *Report of the Industrial Commission on Relations and Conditions of Capital and Labor Employed in Manufacturers and General Business,* 14:350–51.

42. Samuel Crowther, who honed his hortatory talents in his many books about Henry Ford, told Patterson's story as the "Pioneer of Industrial Welfare." But Crowther's 1923 book was published when praise for Patterson's achievements of the early 1900s had waned, when the overt paternalism of his former methods was already being viewed as outmoded.

43. Patterson, "Altruism and Sympathy as Factors in Work Administration," 579; subsequent quotations are from 578, 579, 584, 600.

44. Typical of prevalent attitudes is a little book from 1905, *The Competent Life: A Treatise on the Judicious Development, Direction and Employment of Man's Inherited Ability to Aid in the Betterment of Labor.* Written by Thomas D. West, "Journeyman, Foreman and Manager," it is dedicated to "the Caucasian Race whose Strength, Intelligence and Sacrifice have excelled all others in uplifting Humanity, but whose elevating and industrial Power can wane if Ability to develop and maintain competency is not more fully exercised."

45. Taylor insisted that intelligence was not required for the average factory job, only for the fulfillment of the duties of "the first-class men" holding managerial positions. Lester Ward agreed that the lower classes lacked intelligence, but he identified this condition as the cause of all social inequalities, one to be remedied by raising the working class through education.

46. Lewis, "Uplifting 17,000 Employees," 5939, my emphasis; hereafter cited parenthetically in the text. The Colorado Fuel and Iron Company, whose welfare programs Lewis praises highly in 1905, became the site of the infamous "Ludlow Massacre," which took place on April 20, 1914 after a fifteen-month-long strike (see Eastman, "Class War in Colorado"). Even in 1905, Lewis feels the need to place the touchy word "interfered" within quotation marks. It is as though he were already on the defensive against the objections the radicals made to all forms of management control.

47. McDonnell criticizes the sentimentality of Herbert Gutman's liking for the comradely drinking bouts common to workers in turn-of-the-century America. McDonnell, like Bill Haywood at that period, views drunkenness as a serious working-class problem; attempts by industrial welfare programs to correct excessive drinking should not, therefore, be damned out of hand. See McDonnell, "'You Are Too Sentimental,'" 635.

48. Lewis alludes to the 1903 strike yet another time when he tells of the company's solicitude for the camp children. Guards escort them past the strike line to their school; Christmas trees and toys are provided for their holiday pleasure;

mothers are duly grateful for the kindnesses shown. The Ludlow Massacre of 1914, however, would leave two women and eleven children dead.

49. Nelson's *Managers and Workers* contains useful information on the formation and goals of the NCF.

50. The following quotations are from Beeks, "What Is Welfare Work?" 5–6. In 1905 an article by H. F. J. Porter, titled "The Higher Law in the Industrial World," appeared in *The Engineering Magazine*. The editors prefaced the piece by noting, "The statement in this instance is forceful, not only by the manner in which it is put, but because it is supported by recent, practical, and successful trial, and indeed is the record of actual results under working conditions." From the start, welfare work needed validation through the "manner" of one's text and the "actual results" one achieved.

51. In *Managers and Workers,* Nelson provides a perspective on the way welfare secretaries (the majority of whom were women) were uncomfortably situated between employers and workers on the workplace ladder. Also see Ehrenreich, *The Altruistic Imagination,* and Graebner, *The Engineering of Consent.*

52. However, when Beeks points out that it is "but humane to furnish a couch on which a prostrated woman may be restored, instead of permitting her to lie on the floor or on two chairs," she does not go to the main office in order to insist on its practical benefit to the employer (6). She *remains with* the image of the ailing woman.

53. Taylor, "The Policy of Being Human in Business," 8. On Taylor's active aid to workingmen and his role in instituting graduate studies in the social sciences, see Wren, "Industrial Sociology," 313, and Fitzpatrick, *Endless Crusade.*

54. National Civic Federation, *Welfare Work;* quotations below are from 5, 7, 15, 23. Also see Vreeland, *Welfare Work.*

55. Wilhelm's profile of Cyrus H. McCormick makes the industrialist the hero of his own "welfare work" narrative, as do Wilhelm's portraits of Judge Gary of the Steel Trust and Dr. Steinmetz of the General Electric Company. The style of presentation for the McCormick story is strongly reminiscent of the interview Bartley Hubbard writes for "The Solid Men of Boston" series in Howells's *Rise of Silas Lapham.*

56. Comstock, "A Woman of Achievement," 445; the following quotations are from the same page.

Chapter Four

1. See Copley, *Frederick W. Taylor;* Haber, *Efficiency and Uplift;* and Kakar, *Frederick Taylor.*

2. Drury, author of the first study of scientific management (*Scientific Management,* 1915; rev. ed. 1918), cites the Brandeis Eastern Rate case of 1910–11 as the occasion that gave Taylor's methods their name. The ideas "in the process of formation for about thirty years" that Taylor "fortuitously" named in his 1903 paper

remained "unfamiliar to most persons" until a small conference was held in October 1910 to decide on "a single term" that "would apply to the system as a whole." Drury includes statistical data for the spread of the terms "scientific management" and "efficiency" between 1898 and 1913, proof of their rising popularity. See Drury, *Scientific Management*, 36, 38, 41. Haber describes the founding of the Efficiency Society in 1911, its waning by 1915, and its demise by World War I. See Strum's study of Brandeis, *Louis D. Brandeis*, chap. 10, on the relations among Brandeis, Taylor, and the labor movement. Note Bill Haywood's remark that Brandeis was "dangerous" because he was "the whitest man who ever mixed up in the class struggle." Workers, trusting Brandeis's honesty, might be led away from socialism toward support of Taylorism (168).

3. Taylor, "The Principles of Scientific Management," *Scientific Management*, 44–45. Taylor's imaginary conversation with the imaginary Schmidt is a comedy skit, punctuated by dialect humor made familiar by early twentieth-century vaudeville acts. It plays the stupid, stubborn little foreigner and his comic accent off against the straightforward American speech of Taylor, his boss. Taylor teases, joshes, and flatters until he gets the pig-iron handler to admit he "vants $1.85 a day." In (perhaps pretended) exasperation, Taylor states, "Oh, you're aggravating me. Of course you want $1.85 a day—every one wants it! You know perfectly well that has very little to do with your being a high-priced man. For goodness' sake answer my questions, and don't waste any more of my time" (44–55).

4. Taylor, "Testimony Before the Special House Committee," *Scientific Management*, 9; hereafter cited parenthetically in the text.

5. Three sample riffs: (1) Taylor reminds listeners that the virtues of drill and obedience, which some are so misguided as to view as inimical to American labor, are familiar to "most of us . . . since we were small boys. . . . I refer to the management of a first-class American baseball team" (ibid., 46). (2) He introduces the phrase "the atmosphere of scientific management" as part of "the relations that ought to exist between both sides," then explains what he means by this, since a word like "atmosphere" may make listeners think he is "a little highfalutin'" (50, 49). (3) Sensing he must head off rejection of his claims about "the science of shoveling," he comments, "You gentlemen may laugh," then gives details about the number of pounds shoveled under the new systems (50). Chairman Wilson picks up on the baseball team analogy when he asks if Taylor does not realize that members of professional baseball teams are "bought and sold like cattle on the market." Caught off guard, Taylor says he had not realized this. His illustration was drawn from his experience with the Phillips Exeter team, where they "never bought and sold me" (219).

6. Gies's article, "Animating the Worker," mentions that the most violent rejoinders to Taylor's testimony were left out of the permanent record.

7. Wilson's committee arrived at a decision against Taylor. Even though it urged that workers ought to be consulted in the matter of their working conditions, however, no legislation was recommended in labor's cause. See "The Taylor System—Report," 156.

8. See Sollors, "Immigrants and Other Americans," 568–88, for a review of the many print forms used to voice minority views. In 1907 Sinclair listed a number of contemporary American socialist papers; see *The Industrial Republic,* 21–24.

9. The NCF included an employers' welfare department to protect the interests of owners. Among those in attendance were August Belmont, George Perkins of U.S. Steel, Pierre DuPont, Cyrus McCormick, H. J. Heinz, Jacob Gimbel, and Jacob Wertheim.

10. Mitchell, "Efficiency Not Acceptable to Wage-Earners," in *Eleventh Annual Meeting,* 114. Mitchell remarked on the resistance to bonus wages by "the American and the English-speaking employes [*sic*]." He provided a chart that indicated that "persons whose names indicate they are Americans protested against the acceptance of the new plan" (114). (Mitchell left the NCF the same year, once affiliation was forbidden by the United Mine Workers.)

11. Emerson's offer is from *Eleventh Annual Meeting,* 75. Quotations from Stone's talk, bannered in the record of the proceedings as "Railway Engineer Opposed to Efficiency" (itself a put-down on the part of the NCF), are from 103–6.

12. Goldmark's prior experiences readied her to evaluate the connections between the "driving" procedures of Taylorism and the fatigue suffered by workers under that system. The ambiguities introduced by her experiences will be discussed in chapter 5.

13. Goldmark, *Fatigue and Efficiency,* 3; the following quotations are from 197.

14. For the importance of statistical studies during the Progressive era, see Rodgers, *Contested Truths,* 188–89, and Thompson, "Clarification and Symbolization."

15. Goldmark, *Fatigue and Efficiency,* 226–27, 235. Goldmark extracted these quotations from earlier studies dated 1895, 1901, and 1909. Her distaste is echoed in *The Pittsburgh Survey,* vol. 1 of Butler's *Women and the Trades: Pittsburgh, 1907–1908,* 355–56. For views then and now, which do *not* take exception to workers' enjoyment of "cheap amusements," see Glenn, *Daughters of the Shtetl;* Parker, *Working with the Working Woman;* Patten, *The New Basis of Civilization;* and Peiss, *Cheap Amusements.*

16. Note the 1907 pamphlet, *The Trade Unions' Attitudes toward Welfare Work,* in which J. W. Sullivan states that he speaks for the workers. They must educate their employers; they have brought about better working conditions, not the other way around. Sullivan's bias against nonskilled, non-"American" laborers is apparent when he comments that welfare work deals with three areas: (1) "American white-working people," (2) "negroes removed by a gulf" from the others, and (3) immigrants who are as far removed from the whites as the Negroes (a sentiment with which Taylor concurred). On the hostility between "American" workers on the one side, and blacks and immigrants on the other, see Haydu, *Between Craft and Class;* Mink, *Old Labor and New Immigrants in American Political Development;* and Walling, "Class Struggle within the Working Class."

17. Hoxie, *Scientific Management and Labor,* 2; hereafter cited parenthetically in the text. My emphasis throughout.

18. Taylor is the chief sinner named in charge 7. He is labeled "an enthusiast" and "an idealist." In his fond belief "that he had discovered industrial laws and methods of universal applicability," he "failed to distinguish between what might be and what is" (114). Compare Eastman's July 1913 editorial for *The Masses,* "Knowledge and Revolution," in which he assails the harmful idealism of upper-class altruists and disciples of economic progress whose activities foster "brother-hood as an artificial emotion." According to Eastman, the workers believe, "We simply hold our idealism to be more scientific."

19. Drury, "Democracy as a factor in Industrial Efficiency," 15.

20. Hopkins, "Democracy and Industry," 58; hereafter cited parenthetically in the text. Hopkins rebukes those who view "industrial democracy" as an X-factor, "the unknown quantity in the equation" that acts as "a counter-irritant" to "what-ever is, is right," by proposing "whatever is, is wrong." Addled reformers think the solution is to identify the X-factor with the workers' authority, a solution that "was to give us better conditions all around" (59). If power were shifted to work-ers under the guise of "industrial democracy," society would lose out on that "which most consistently breeds efficiency and stimulates output in production"; it would also suffer the "*sacrifice in character* of the individuals who compose it, through their being so little called up to acknowledge authority to anybody or anything" (63; my emphasis). The following quotations are from 58–59.

21. Russell, "The Invisible Government," 3.

22. Robinson, "Intellectual Radicalism," 21.

23. Taylor, *Scientific Management,* 216; the following quotations are from 218.

24. As for just how "radical" the move by American labor to achieve "indus-trial democracy" was, see Kloppenberg *Uncertain Victory;* Brick, *Daniel Bell and the Decline of Intellectual Radicalism;* Denning, "'The Special American Condi-tions'"; Herreshoff, *American Disciples of Marx;* Lipset, "Why Is There No Social-ism in the United States?"; and *Marx and Engels on the United States.* All shed light on the controversy as to whether early twentieth-century American political thought resisted Marxism, and, if so, what forms of modified socialist belief took its place.

25. Silcox, "Discussion," 25; the following quotations are from the same page.

Chapter Five

1. Clark, "Editorial: Industrial Efficiency," 131; Tarbell "The New Place of Women in Industry—I," 265.

2. Dorr, *A Woman of Fifty,* 194; Glenn, *Daughters of the Shtetl,* 191.

3. Tarbell was a highly successful career journalist but no advocate of women's social, economic, or political equality. Charlotte Perkins Gilman and Helen Keller ridiculed her and characterized her as "one of the most conservative women speak-

ing out." Originally an outspoken critic of the business enterprise, as in her attacks against Standard Oil for *McClure's,* Tarbell ended her writing career praising management. See Brady, *Ida Tarbell.*

4. Clark, "Editorial," 131; the following quotations are from the same page.

5. Tarbell, "The New Place of Women in Industry—III," 400.

6. For an instructive cross section of contemporary responses to the influx of women into factories during World War I, check vol. 102 (July–Dec. 1918) of *The Iron Age,* which includes nine articles and notices about the assets and problems caused by the mass entry of women into the metals manufacturing industry. Tarbell believed the "new epoch" resulted from women having caused "one of the industrial surprises of the war." Both managers and women were caught unaware. "The things [the woman worker] did were so different from those the world had been seeing her do, they so often proved unfounded even her own notions of what she could or wanted to do, that her exhibit took on the quality of a discovery" ("The New Place of Women in Industry—I," 265). This discovery is a happy one in Tarbell's view, not a frightening revelation that releases hidden horrors to writers of tragic narratives. Had not managers found that the women replacing men going off to war as soldiers did not "soldier" on the job? See Porter, "Detroit's Plans for Recruiting Women for Industries," and Braybon, *Women Workers in the First World War.*

7. Tarbell, "The New Place of Women in Industry—V," 137.

8. Goldmark, *Fatigue and Efficiency,* 3. Lord's 1917 article, "How to Deal Successfully with Women in Industry," sarcastically refers to the refusal of "our novelists" to believe that employers provide proper working conditions for women. He implies that these authors relish tales of cruelty inflicted upon helpless women. Their acknowledgment of the actual relations between management and labor would force them to publish happier stories (839).

9. Goldmark, *Fatigue and Efficiency,* 3. Anderson's 1919 article "Wages for Women Workers," draws attention to the fact that employers are "curiously illogical" in their responses to women's war work. On the one hand, they reserve high praise for the quality and quantity of women's productivity; on the other hand, they give women lower wages than they previously had given the ineffectual male workers the women replaced. "Statements" by still other employers that *they* give equal pay for equal work "will not bear analysis". Furthermore, managers level the same arguments against women they used to level against men. Women must "scientifically" scrutinize the language used by employers who pride themselves on their rationalism, lest they be harmed by men's illogicality (123–25).

10. Kessler-Harris's landmark study, *Out to Work,* demonstrates many times over that the "transformation of women's work into wage labor" continually brought into question "the relationship between wage-earning and family roles: the tensions between them as well as their mutually reinforcing aspects." One must pay close attention to "the reciprocally confirming system of values" that linked "the tendency of women to enter the work force" with "the changing

household itself" (ix–x). Those wishing the household to remain unchanged did all they could to thwart women's search for alternative ways to earn wages. Also see Faue, *Community of Suffering and Struggle;* Groneman and Norton, eds., *"To Toil the Livelong Day";* and Weiner, *From Working Girl to Working Mother.*

11. Thompson, "The Truth about Woman in Industry," 751, 756, 760; hereafter cited parenthetically in the text.

12. Thompson credits her own journalistic career with having done harm to her family (ibid., 757–58). Fear of race suicide was intense at this time because of the drop in birthrate among native-born "Americans" and the belief that the new immigrants were breeding like rabbits. Three such arguments, drawn respectively from works of 1903, 1912, and 1910, are: (1) Edward A. Ross fears that "the high-strung, high-bred, feminine type that is our pride" will be replaced by the "Flemish mare type"—"squat, splay-footed, wide-backed, flat-breasted" (*Changing America,* 75–76); (2) Theodore Roosevelt's letter, which the Van Vorsts used as the preface to *The Woman Who Toils* (discussed in further detail later in this chapter), describes the "most melancholy side" of women's desire to work as being their substitution of personal pleasure "for the practice of the strong, racial qualities without which there can be no strong races"; because of this shift away from "the greatest thing" a woman can be ("a good wife and mother"), the nation has cause "to be alarmed about its future"; (3) MacLean, *Wage-Earning Women,* 178.

13. Rodgers's chapter, "Idle Womanhood: Feminist Versions of the Work Ethic," in *The Work Ethic in Industrial America,* outlines the strongly divergent views of women in the work force, which tapped "an immense reservoir of moral feeling." The language in which these views were expressed was also affected: "even conservatives [moved from] the language of sentiment and into the language of jobs and labor," leading to distortions of meaning that allowed "the rhetoric of the work ethic" to become "a tyrannizing commonplace" (209).

14. Tarbell remarks that the "fine masculine chivalry" of the manager "makes him revolt at the idea of opening wider the industrial field" to women. This observation (hardly ironic, one fears) is from "The New Place of Women in Industry—II," 329.

15. Carpenter, "More Truth about Women in Industry" 222; hereafter cited parenthetically in the text.

16. See Banta, *Imaging American Women,* chap. 2 and passim, for the era's many representations, negative and positive, of the New Woman.

17. See Hendler, "The Limits of Sympathy," for an examination of Louisa May Alcott's struggles in writing her 1873 novel *Work.* Alcott attempted to expand the sentimental genre (with that genre's own "covert struggle with domestic ideology") "into new territory, extending the genre's figurative feminization of culture into the public sphere" (703).

18. Abbott, "Are Women Business Failures?" 496.

19. "Minimizing the Controversy," 105; the following quotation is from 106. Gompers, Brandeis, Henry Moskowitz, Belle Israel Moskowitz, and Lillian Wald

stood behind the Protocol of Peace; the I.W.W. opposed it (107). See Glenn, *Daughters of the Shtetl,* 171, and Elisabeth Israels Perry, *Belle Moskowitz: Feminine Politics and the Exercise of Power in the Age of Alfred E. Smith* (New York, 1987), chap. 5.

20. Glenn provides the phrase *Mentshlekhe bahandlung* (*Daughters of the Shtetl,* 174).

21. Robins, "Fatigue and Efficiency," 297.

22. Goldmark, *Fatigue and Efficiency,* 3, my emphasis; hereafter cited parenthetically in the text. Controversy continues over the role Goldmark and other reform groups (such as the Women's Trade Union League and the National Consumers League) played in restricting women's hours in the name of protecting them from the hardships of industrial work. Kessler-Harris's *Out To Work* is an excellent source for details; see chaps. 5–7, in particular 184–98.

23. Currently under scholarly scrutiny is the question of whether abolitionist fiction was primarily legalistic or pathological in its concentration upon the ownership of bodies, as is the question of whether legal and scientific narratives are masculine by definition.

24. Goldmark quotes here from Clark and Wyatt's *Making Both Ends Meet,* 266.

25. Strains caused by the "speeding process" were constantly evoked by writers across the political spectrum. See the following examples: Becker, "The Square Deal in Works Management—IV," 39, 43; Becker, "How to Increase Factory Efficiency," 813–26; Ross, *Changing America,* 69, 71, 77; Clark and Wyatt, *Making Both Ends Meet,* chap. 4; U.S. Bureau of Labor, "Speed Rate," 108–11; Nestor, "A Day's Work Making Gloves," 138.

26. James, *The American Scene,* 74–75; Brann, "Max Weber and the United States," 19.

27. See Brann, "Max Weber and the United States"; Bourget, *Outre-Mer;* and Weber, *Max Weber.*

28. Glenn, *Daughters of the Shtetl,* 193, 212.

29. Glenn reports that when Mary Dreier, a society woman deeply involved in Women's Trade Union League activities, joined the pickets at the 1909 Triangle strike, her presence "turned the spotlight of the press on the brutal treatments of strikers by local police and brought the plight of the shirtwaist workers to the attention of the entire city" (ibid., 168).

30. Dorr, "Bullying the Woman-Worker," 458; hereafter cited parenthetically in the text. Dorr's lifelong endeavors to write "good lives" for herself and all women deserve even greater attention. See her autobiography, *A Woman of Fifty,* and the entry in vol. 1, *Notable American Women.*

31. Dorr's reform articles were recommended reading in sociology departments; students found them easier to grasp than books by "authorities" (*A Woman of Fifty,* 104).

32. A recurring criticism (as exampled by Sinclair's *The Jungle*) concerns the lack of frequent, cheap transportation to and from work. See "Jessie Davis," "My Vacation in a Woolen Mill."

33. Dorr, *A Woman of Fifty*, 105.

34. While writing her *Harper's* piece, Dorr worked on the projected series, "The Woman's Invasion." Overwhelmed by "reams" of material she was unable to organize, her nerves were made raw by her awareness that women were "a race of dispossessed." Her investigations first appeared under the name of a colleague, William Hard, who viewed the women as "a triumphant army of invasion." Dorr felt she had been "silenced," since her intent was "distorted beyond recognition." What she viewed as tragic realism, Hard presented as epic romance (ibid., 193–97).

35. Carpenter's article, "How We Trained 5000 Women," refers to women's initial fear of machinery: "when new girls came into the shop they were very nervous—badly frightened—and . . . they would often break down and weep because of the actual fear that took hold of them when they first stood before a big machine tool the like of which they had never seen before, the uses of which they could not conceive, and which looked like a veritable monster to them" (354). Also see "Jessie Davis," "My Vacation in a Woolen Mill," 538–40, which characterizes the typical industrial plant as an ominous Gothic castle, with high walls, iron gates, and an interior like a prison. Even the cars transporting the workers home have the same prisonlike atmosphere as the shop (538–39).

36. After the accident (for which her employers took no responsibility), Catherine was given a new job with the weekly pay of seven dollars. Her previous salary was twenty-five dollars.

37. Critics have attacked (and defended) Stephen Greenblatt's new historicism for the way it continually incorporates anecdotes, from which Greenblatt draws heavily moral meanings. Conscious of her own inability to "build a structure four square from foundation to roof," Dorr gave this description of her compositional method: "'Once upon a time there was a little dog and his name was Fido,' and they all end 'Come to Jesus'" (*A Woman of Fifty*, 202). But her best work resulted from the way she pointed to morals by telling a string of affecting tales.

38. "'I Make Cheap Silk,'" 7; further quotations are from the same page.

39. The famous "Pageant of the Paterson Strike—performed by the strikers themselves"—was held on June 7, 1913. Although it drew wide attention, it failed as a fund-raiser, and the Wobblies lost the strike. See Heller and Rudnick, eds., *1915, The Cultural Moment*, 32–35.

40. Redfield, "The Employment Problem in Industry," 10.

41. Dorr had little use for the Van Vorsts. Their articles described "not heroism but 'children to be led to freedom'" (*A Woman of Fifty*, 206–7). For details about the Van Vorsts, see *American Women Writers* 4:293–97, where distinctions are made between Bessie's rigidly upper-class biases and Marie's more sympathetic approach.

42. Van Vorst and Van Vorst, *The Woman Who Toils,* 4; hereafter abbreviated parenthetically in the text.

43. That investigative reporters in search of on-the-spot experience ought not be accused automatically of patronizing attitudes is supported by the (ironically) titled "My Vacation in a Woolen Mill" by "Jessie Davis." This New England college graduate, a veteran of years of studying labor conditions for state and federal agencies, generally provides the appropriate tone and response.

44. One of many such pronouncements in *The Woman Who Toils* is that "industrial art" is proper for women who work because they wish to buy more luxuries but not for those women who work out of economic necessity. Because hand labor calls "into play higher faculties than the brutalizing machine labour," the "new, higher, superior class of industrial art labourers" must be encouraged. According to the Van Vorsts' double standard, women who work to survive are fated to put up with lives of "squalor and sordidness"; the woman of a better sort uses her taste and skill in ways "consistent with her destiny as a woman" (see 56, 159, 162, 163).

45. Yezierska, "America and I," 20; the following quotation is from 29.

46. Cited in Glenn, *Daughters of the Shtetl,* 2.

47. Clark and Wyatt, *Making Both Ends Meet,* xi; hereafter cited parenthetically in the text. Material for this book originally appeared as a series of articles for *McClure's Magazine,* perhaps the best-known muckraking journal of its day.

48. The importance women attributed to being able to talk freely among themselves while working in the shop is constantly emphasized, although this habit was exactly what Taylor tried to eliminate (see "No. 1003—Shop Management," 1384) and what Mrs. Van Vorst found to be "vulgar and prosaic" chatter. In contrast, "Jessie Davis" and Constance Stratton Parker realized that conversation is the working woman's lifeblood. Mothers of working women often agreed with Taylor, however, since talk during work hours lowered their daughters' production level and cut back on their wages. See Gilson, "The Relation of Home Conditions to Industrial Efficiency," 287–88. Some managers, however, stressed the importance of "making workmen cheerful, happy, and content." Such conditions resulted in "better men and women and better producers"—a situation that, in turn, "yields good interest upon the investment" (quoted from Becker, "The Square Deal in Works Management—IV," 53–54, 57). Also see Knoeppel, "American Women in War Industry—I," 483. Knoeppel was pleased to report on shops that "allow women the right to sing as they work." Anzia Yezierska, on the other hand, had little use for men who extolled "The Happy Worker and His Work," men who wished to bring comfort and joy to themselves by getting higher productivity from "contented" workers (Yezierska, "America and I," 29).

49. Taylor's pronoun references are always masculine. *Making Both Ends Meet* insists upon the feminine factor, although recognizing that "Scientific Management as applied to women's work in this country is, of course, very recent" (267).

50. For those who insist that problems caused by machine speeding result from

the misapplication or partial use of Taylorism, the villain is the boss who neither understands nor trusts the new doctrine. See Robins, "Fatigue and Efficiency," 367.

51. Dorr, *A Woman of Fifty*, 129.

52. Jewish Sadie is hit by her foreman. Rheta Dorr takes her to municipal court to file assault charges and to corroborate every detail of her experience. The judge declares, "The story is incredible," and dismisses the case (ibid.). For others who struggled to tell their own stories, see Richardson, *The Long Day*, and Schofield, ed., *Sealskin and Shoddy*.

53. Alchon, *The Invisible Hand of Planning*, 167.

54. Van Kleeck, "The Social Meaning of Good Management," 10.

55. F. R. Still, "Women as Machinists," 654.

56. Bendix, *Work and Authority in Industry*, 314. According to Mayo, this revised image applied to owners as well as to workers. This caused a quandary: in order to manage well, the men in charge had to stop being illogical even if the workers could not. One consequence was the technocratic elite's conscious struggle to "free themselves from emotional involvement" in order to handle workers' emotions more effectively (315–16).

57. Gilkeson's *Middle-Class Providence, 1820–1940*, 262–63, discusses the Gilbreths' 1911 relocation to Providence, Rhode Island, where their efforts as "systematizers" matched efforts by the city's middle-class municipal activists to integrate individuals into the social fabric, thereby preserving the value of each citizen's actions while subordinating them to the public interest. Also see Yost, *Frank and Lillian Gilbreth*, and Trescott on Lillian Gilbreth in "Women Engineers in History."

58. "It is *interesting* to note here not only the *interest* aroused in the subject of motion study itself," but also "in the correlation of processes in the industries with general processes outside." Further, "this intensive and extensive *interest* is aroused in all those engaged in motion studies, whether as observers or observed" (Gilbreth and Gilbreth, "The Effect of Motion Study upon the Workers," 274; my emphasis). The following quotation, from 276, was set in italics by the Gilbreths. *Taking interest* as the motivating spring of self-creation was also crucial to the new philosophy advanced by William James, Josiah Royce, and John Dewey.

59. "Jessie Davis" wondered "about the beneficent effects of women's on-rush into industry" because of the poor working conditions they experienced, but she was careful to register that "the work itself is satisfying" and that women preferred factory labor, where they had companionship and a sense of pride in accomplishment, to the solitary drudgery they suffered at home ("My Vacation in a Woolen Mill," 541).

60. Tarbell, "The New Place of Women in Industry—IV" and "The New Place of Women in Industry—V"; Knoeppel, "American Women in War Industry—I" 480.

61. Carpenter, "More Truth about Women in Industry," 217.

62. Thompson, "The Truth about Women in Industry," 756.

63. Becker, "The Square Deal in Works Management—IV," 38.

64. Tarbell, "The New Place of Women in Industry—III," 399.

65. For a variety of views on the effort required of managers to deal with women's ailments, nerves, and morals, see the following: Tarbell, "The New Place for Women in Industry—III," 400; Patterson, "Altruism and Sympathy as Factors in Work Administration," 584; Hubbard, "Some Practical Principles of Welfare Work," 90; Lord, "How to Deal Successfully with Women in Industry," 838–43; Becker, "The Square Deal in Works Management—IV," 43–54; Becker, "How to Increase Factory Efficiency," 820; Carpenter, "How We Trained 5000 Women," 354; Woods and Kennedy, eds. *Young Working Girls,* 23–26; Redfield, "The Employment Problem in Industry," 124; and MacLean, *Wage-Earning Women,* 3. Reports on class, ethnic, and racial snobbery include Bruce, "Comments," 22; Still, "Women as Machinists," 650–53; and Knoeppel, "American Women in War Industry—I," 481–82. Contemporary management discussions say little about black women shopworkers. These women are so marginalized by these texts that they appear (if they appear at all) over in the corner, sweeping up in silence. For one example, see Van Vorst and Van Vorst, *The Woman Who Toils,* 91. In "The New Place for Women in Industry—IV," Tarbell praises the "natural" relations between "the white and colored girls" who chat on their way to lunch, although "they had separate tables" (54). One exception is Parker's account of her various work experiences, *Working with the Working Woman,* which includes black women as a natural part of the factory scene.

66. Knoeppel, "American Women in War Industry—I," 480.

67. Barnes, "Women in Industry," 116.

68. Tarbell, "The New Place for Women in Industry—IV," 56–57.

69. No longer "victims" of old-time narratives, these women are still not heroines except in the "charming" sense—like Shakespeare's young things, who wear britches until their femininity is discovered by the right young men, men who return them to their proper place through marriage. Tarbell's 1921 article, "The New Place for Women in Industry—IV," depicts Polish women workers in a manner reminiscent of the way Cather depicts her delightful "boy" heroines in *My Antonia* (1918). Cather's Bohemian, German, and Scandinavian "hired girls" are lively and very pretty, yet definitely viewed as social inferiors by "respectable" American women.

70. Quoted by Lord in "How to Deal Successfully with Women in Industry," 844. The Ford Motor Company classified all women, no matter what their age or economic status, as "youths"; as a consequence they were ineligible for welfare benefits (Meyer, *The Five-Dollar Day,* 140).

71. Tarbell, "The New Place for Women in Industry—III," 400.

72. Tarbell, "The New Place for Women in Industry—IV," 56.

73. Tarbell, "The New Place for Women in Industry—V," 135.

74. Emerson, "Efficiency Principles Applied to Measurement and Cure of Wastes," in *The Twelve Principles of Management,* 391.

75. Tarbell, "The New Place of Women in Industry—V," 135.

76. Emerson, "Efficiency Principles Applied to Measurement and Cure of Wastes," 377.

Chapter Six

1. Yezierska, "America and I," 30–32. No documents are available to pin down the dates of Yezierska's birth or of her family's departure from the Russian-Polish border for the United States. Conjectures place the former around 1883 and the latter circa 1892. At seventeen she was working in sweatshops and factories; in 1915 she began the writing career that allowed her to "give out" her "difference." Key works examining Yezierska's life and writings are by her daughter, Louise Levitas Henriksen, and Carol B. Schoen.

2. Tarbell, "The New Place of Women in Industry—V," 136; the following quotations are from 136–37.

3. Hoerle and Saltzberg, *The Girl and the Job,* 3; hereafter cited parenthetically in the text.

4. Girls are not as strong as young males and tend to be absent for illness, but they do not duck off to ball games. Because more "willing and cheerful, less impudent and lazy," they are "fast succeeding the office boy" (ibid., 6).

5. Trained under Henry Gantt (an ardent Taylorite), Wallace Clark was a consultant hired to rationalize office operations. He was credited with having turned the stenographic department of the Remington Typewriter Company into one of the best in the country. Pagination for "Getting the Office Work Done—II" will be cited parenthetically in the text.

6. Shirtwaist culture, as opposed to factory-uniform culture, suggested a higher social status, greater opportunities for better wages, more interesting work, and enhanced chances for advancement. Or so *that* story went, as related in newspapers, magazines, and novels. Nevertheless, status tensions characterized both shop and office, reflecting the rage to classify, which the popular press and the scientific community reinforced. Women did not want to associate with other women who existed on the other side of the line demarcating superior from inferior. See Kessler-Harris, *Out To Work,* 132–36, and Tarbell, "The New Place of Women in Industry—IV," 56–57.

There were further divisions among women doing clerical work. Factory office staff resented women working in business offices "uptown," while *those* women ranked themselves according to the hierarchy that placed stenographers above file clerks. The one advantage supposedly shared by all office workers was their avoidance of demeaning manual labor. By the 1920s native-born women had a long history of resisting entry into domestic service, since this struck them as being an obvious master-slave relationship. In similar ways, stenographers told themselves the stories they wished to hear: "If I'm slaving at my desk, I'm still a Cinderella waiting to be taken to the palace." These distinctions did not always make sense, however. Heavy-duty factory toil aside, shop women sat for long hours before bolted-down work surfaces under artificial lighting fixtures, plying their machines under conditions scarcely different from those that placed stenographers for long hours before their fixed work surfaces under artificial lighting fixtures plying *their* machines.

7. Rotella, *From Home to Office,* 37.

8. Performance reports led to the posting of charts that ranked work force productivity. It was public knowledge who met the standards and who stood exposed as "an unduly expensive individual." What fine lunchbreak drama! See Fuller, "Standardization in Office Work," 14, and "Application of Scientific Principles to Office Management," 507.

9. Bennett, *Women and Work,* 19; hereafter cited parenthetically in the text.

10. "Miss Ten-A-Week's Plea," 42.

11. Barnes, "Women in Industry," 124.

12. Stigler, *The History of Statistics,* 2.

13. See Fuller, "Standardization in Office Work," 506, for this and subsequent remarks.

14. Fuller consistently refers to the ideal office manager with the pronoun "he." Casual references suggest that the majority of the staff are female. Those assigned to "standardization work" are occasionally identified as women. Never in doubt, however, is the fact that men are the managers.

15. This quotation from Geddes's and Thomson's *Problems of Sex* (1912) is cited in Russett, *Sexual Science,* 130. The next quotation, drawn from Geddes's and Thomson's *The Evolution of Sex* (first published 1889, revised 1901), is from ibid., 137, as is Russett's astute reading of the significance of this shift in attitude toward the biology of sexual difference.

16. See Stigler, *The History of Statistics,* and Porter, *The Rise of Statistical Thinking, 1820–1900.* Bush's *Halfway to Revolution* also emphasizes the importance of statistical thinking in the development of the science of sociology (10). Hacking's *The Taming of Chance* is imperative reading for the field at large.

17. See Boudon and Bourricaud, *A Critical Dictionary of Sociology,* 406–7). Also see chap. 2, "The Laws that Govern Chaos," in Porter, *The Rise of Statistical Thinking,* for a discussion of the effect Quételet's search for certainties via concepts of tendency and the teleological had upon the new sociological theory.

18. Emerson, "Fate," from *The Conduct of Life, Works,* 6:17. Both Seltzer's 1987 essay about Henry James's *The American* (material reincorporated in his *Bodies and Machines,* 83) and Barbara Packer's paper, "Emerson, Statistics, and 'Fate,'" delivered in 1989 at the American Literature Association conference, have called atten-

tion to this passage from Emerson and its reference to Quételet in regard to the notions of race supported by mid-nineteenth-century statistical theory.

19. Boudon and Bourricaud, *A Critical Dictionary of Sociology,* 274; hereafter cited parenthetically in the text.

20. The entry on Spencer in *A Critical Dictionary of Sociology* is much more favorable than most. In many ways, this portrait of Spencer mirrors traits usually associated with William James: openness of mind, distrust of generalizations, pleasure in the unplanned, faith in the power of human activity to make things happen. This is hardly the view usually taken by critics of Spencer, or by James in his "Remarks on Spencer's Definition of Mind as Correspondence" (1878) or "The Dilemma of Determinism" (1884).

21. Royce, "The Mechanical, the Historical, and the Statistical," *Basic Writings,* 2:719, my emphasis; hereafter cited parenthetically in the text.

22. Edith Abbott's 1907 study of gender changes taking place within the cigar industry, "Employment of Women in Industries: Cigar-Making," suggests a similar story in which real social gains were made via "history" and "tendency." Women dominated the cigar-making industry in the early 1800s but were displaced by men after the Civil War. Another turnaround occurred by 1900, when the men were pushed aside by women. Royce would agree with Abbott's view of "history" as being that which simply happens in and of itself. He would consider her use of "tendency" (defined as change toward a better society) more applicable to philosophical considerations (and statistical laws) than that of history, yet he would admit that historical realignments do affect just who makes cigars at any given point in time.

23. Royce tried to transpose the logic of his philosophy of community into a novel, but *The Feud of Oakfield Creek* (1887) fails so abjectly as an expressive form that we as narratologists turn with relief to his vigorous vision of the statistical utopia offered by his 1914 essay.

24. Sinclair, *The Jungle,* 413: hereafter cited parenthetically in the text. The serialized version of Sinclair's narrative, which originally appeared in *Appeal to Reason* throughout 1905, was drastically revised in the Doubleday, Page book version. Sinclair's praise of socialism and the unions was greatly toned down, as were other criticisms of capitalism. Consider the final sentence of the *Appeal* version. After the stirring thrice-uttered cry "Chicago is ours!" the narrative closes with the brief mention that, within the hour, Jurgis is taken to prison to serve a two-year sentence for assault. This is not a defeat, one critic maintains, since Jurgis has been reborn and will emerge from prison an impassioned leader in the socialist cause. For this and other explanations of the tangled state of affairs linking the *Appeal* serial and the Doubleday, Page edition, see Sinclair, *The Lost First Edition of Upton Sinclair's The Jungle;* Harris, *Upton Sinclair;* and Folsom, "Upton Sinclair's Escape from *The Jungle.*" For an altogether different "telling," see "The Life Story of a Lithuanian," in *The Life Stories of Undistinguished Americans, as Told by Themselves.*

25. In the final chapter, Jurgis attends a gathering where there is "a young college student, a beautiful girl with an intense and earnest face" who remains silent, "drinking in the conversation" of the men arguing the merits of alternative modes of revolutionary action (Sinclair, *The Jungle*, 396). She contributes neither narrative power to the scene nor conceptual bite to the political debate. In contrast, Barrett's *Work and Community in the Jungle* describes the activism of the Packingtown women and their outspoken support of the strike of 1904.

26. See Boudon and Bourricaud, *A Critical Dictionary of Sociology*, 395–99, and Porter, *The Rise of Statistical Thinking, 1820–1900*, 69–69, 191, for Durkheim's use of suicide statistics to formulate a sociology based on theories of averages.

27. Dreiser, *Sister Carrie* [Norton Critical Edition], 28; hereafter cited parenthetically in the text. This edition reproduces the text of the version published by Doubleday, Page in 1900. The manuscript text that concludes with Hurstwood's suicide is contained in the Pennsylvania Edition (1981). Based on Doubleday, Page's record for tampering with authors' manuscripts (as demonstrated by Dreiser's novel of 1900 and Sinclair's of 1906), the editors believed in applying a strong managerial hand.

28. Donald Pizer, editor of the Norton Critical Edition, supplies the information that Dreiser had recently written "It Pays to Treat Workers Generously," an essay about John H. Patterson's welfare programs. Patterson was the industrialist who figures in chapter 4 above and in Updegraff's *Captains in Conflict*.

29. Carrie's fame and fortune are conventional by nature. The "exception" she provides comes from the fact that her success follows upon her earlier status as "a fallen woman," misdeeds that novels of the time preferred to punish. Perhaps Sinclair believed he had to "punish" Ona and Marija for their prostitution, although he wished to expose the prostitution exacted by the competitive system.

30. See, for example, Michaels, "*Sister Carrie*'s Popular Economy," *The Gold Standard and the Logic of Naturalism;* Fisher, "Acting, Reading, Fortune's Wheel"; and Banta, *Imaging American Women*, 669–71.

31. Carrie is not seated in a rocking chair when last seen in the original manuscript (the Pennsylvania Edition).

32. Lewis, *The Job*, 5; hereafter cited parenthetically in the text.

33. Back in Pennsylvania, Una had read "Walter Scott, Richard Le Gallienne, Harriet Beecher Stowe, Mrs. Humphrey Ward, *How To Know Birds, My Year in the Holy Land, Home Needlework, Sartor Resartus,* and *Ships That Pass in the Night*" (ibid., 5–6). In New York she reads "*The Outlook, The Literary Digest, Current Opinion, The Nation, The Independent, The Review of Reviews, The World's Work, Collier's,* and *The Atlantic Monthly*." Eventually she masters *System, Printer's Ink,* and *Real Estate Record* (195, 289). Just as one can trace Carrie Meeber's progress by noting the stage roles she plays, one can measure Una Golden's move from girl to manager by the literature she reads.

34. During this period, Una's high moment comes while living at a woman's

club, which is run on "a scientific basis" by a Mrs. Fike. Una is less influenced by Mrs. Fike's austere managerial style than by the time she spends among intelligent, energetic career women, whose friendship brings her "self-confidence and self-expression" (ibid., 178).

35. Carrie's tone is not this forceful when she tells Hurstwood to get out of his rocking chair and look for work, but at this crisis point she, like Una, sets out on her own "to master" life.

36. During this period, Edna Ferber wrote three best-sellers that relate the "business adventures" of Emma McChesney, divorced wife and single parent, who makes her way ever upward in the retail trade to success as manager of her own company and the further reward of a perfect husband. In *The Girl and the Job,* Hoerle and Saltzberg cite Emma as a perfect example how a young woman can "maintain a womanly and dignified bearing, and at the same time a bright and engaging cordiality of manner" (105). See Ferber's *Roast Beef, Medium* (1913), *Personality Plus* (1914), and *Emma McChesney and Company* (1915). Susan L. Albertine is completing a study of women of this period who achieved notable success in business yet continued to be caught up in "family" obligations and unsettling relations with their husbands.

37. Updegraff, "Captains in Conflict," in *System: The Magazine of Business* 49–50 (Jan.–Dec. 1926); this quotation and those immediately following are editorial notes attached to the opening episode (49:46). In November 1926 *System* ran an advertisement for "this gripping story" that cited letters from businessmen requesting copies "to present to every one of their executives" (50:602). In the final issue, another advertisement emphasized the double quality of the story: "full of practical ideas and sound business philosophy," it is also "a romantic story of American business" (50:742). When the story appeared in book form, the writer of "From the Editor's Desk" defended Updegraff's opus from the snide remarks that it had "all the literary merit of a good sales letter!" In rebuke, the editor asserted, "No wonder the thousands of business leaders . . . are so warm in their praise," since the story "is written for them in a language that echoes in the cash register and reflects itself favorably on the balance-sheet" (51:548, 550). Subsequent quotations from the serialized version are cited parenthetically in the text.

38. The word "dictator," as used in Clark's essay "Getting the Office Work Done—II," refers to the staffperson assigned to train novice stenographers to take dictation, but its constant application to designate the one in charge strikes an ominous note, as does the figure of "the driver" in factories committed to Taylorism.

39. Veblen, "The Industrial System and the Captains of Industry," *The Engineers and the Price System,* 32.

40. Sumner's 1906 *Folkways* is the classic study of habitual behavior that lingers on, continuing to color new systems. Throughout the year following their serialization of *Captains in Conflict, System* ran photo spreads illustrating business folkways by which tradition is carried on in the midst of business change (51:170–71, 626–27, 764–65). "In Stone & In the Hearts of Men" shows a half-dozen examples

of mottoes (cribbed from Milton, Ruskin, and others) carved into stone over the thresholds of corporate headquarters, including "Sum up at night what thou hast done by day" and "See this our Fathers did for Us." The segment titled "No Sentiment in Business?" gives lie to the notion that businessmen feel no attachment to their past. It depicts objects enshrined within modern-day plants: the bell that brought farmers from their fields to work at the Marmon Motor Car Company; the original office of the Hammermill Paper Company; the 1883 press placed in the corner of the vast W. F. Hall Printing Company plant. In "Battlefields of Strategy," photos of boardrooms display the decor chosen to represent company traditions, such as the figured cretonne and white-paneled woodwork of the Yale and Towne Manufacturing Company, which "reflects the New England traditions built into the company's policies."

41. Besides the Fowler Rowntree-John Rowntree-Hustus Lockhart configuration, several other father-son relationships receive emphasis throughout *Captains in Conflict*. Placed alongside the episode of January 1927 was "He's a Chip Off the Old Block," containing photographs of "eight sons who, in their management methods, reflect the sound training received from fathers ranking among the great builders of business" (51:30–31). Included are "the good sons" of the senior Wrigley, Edison, Ford, Firestone, Patterson, and Selfridge.

42. Echoes resonate from the Custom House prologue and the main text of *The Scarlet Letter,* but *The House of the Seven Gables* is also part of the unconscious intertextuality of Updegraff's romance.

43. Nelson's legend was reinforced by a doomed love relationship, but Louise Lockhart is a more pristine inspiration than Emma Hart.

44. John's justification for disclosing the family secret after all these years of silence is twofold: one, he has suffered and struggled enough to have won his private victory; two, it is the only way he can save the jobs of the hundreds of workers in Lockhart's employ. This overlooks the fact that, at several crucial points during the business life of John's company, his own employees face layoffs because of his refusal to reveal the hidden paper.

45. One scene reinforces John's role as a nurturer by placing his actions within his home in ways that displace Corinne, the nominal mother. Little John is gravely ill with pneumonia, and John takes over his care. He had once let business matters wait a few hours while foreign radicals threatened the stability of his work family at the time of Corinne's difficult childbirth. Now he keeps an "anxious vigil at the bedside of his baby," even as one of his plants burns down (50:200).

46. In 1922 Baruch's War Industries Board published *Simplification: What It Is Doing for Business,* a compilation of articles from journals such as *Factory* and *System.* Baruch and Herbert Hoover are the heroes of the wartime success story that inspires peacetime business to cut back on difference and diversity. Later, of course, major adjustments were made in the "simplification" program, once manufacturers learned that consumers desired more colors than black. See Hounshell, *From the American System to Mass Production 1800–1932,* and Marchand, *Advertising the American Dream.*

47. See Banta, *Imaging American Women,* 564–90.

48. We may doubt just how modern John Rowntree's marketing methods are and how alert he is to the changing world. In 1906 John *suddenly* recognizes that people are living in apartments, not single-family dwellings—a change "in living modes" that leads them to prefer gas stoves over coal ranges (49:676).

49. Chapter 7 discusses Christine Frederick's role in promoting Taylorism in the modern women's kitchen. As the author of *Selling Mrs. Consumer* (1929), Frederick was a leading supporter of the idea that women gain public power through the control they exert over the consumer market.

50. In contrast to the many scenes that depict Rowntree standing in the midst of his men, Lockhart is never seen to leave the bastion of his office. His presence at the center of a vast network of workers is filtered through a managerial staff primed with newfangled talk about "systematic production rhythms," stopwatches, check sheets, and autocratic memos sent down from on high—actions that incite slowdowns and strikes from the sullen work force (50:88).

Chapter Seven

1. See Lewis, *The Public Image of Henry Ford,* on the making of the Ford legend. Susman's essay "Culture Heroes: Ford, Barton, Ruth," in *Culture as History,* also examines the means by which Ford and others were elevated to special status in the public's view.

2. See Jacob, "The Rouge in 1927," 15. The caption *Vanity Fair* provided for Sheeler's photograph is given in Jacob's essay. Rubin discusses relations between Sheeler's art and Constance Rourke's effort to construct a theory of American culture based upon "a tradition of fantasy and mythmaking" in "A Convergence of Vision."

3. Sinclair, *The Flivver King,* frontispiece.

4. Niebuhr, "How Philanthropic Is Henry Ford?" 1508; my emphasis.

5. Subsequent pagination from Lane's *Henry Ford's Own Story* will be given within parentheses. The only surviving child of Laura Ingalls Wilder (herself a consummate mythmaker), Lane was born in 1886. She began as a telegrapher and was one of the first women to sell California real estate, but it was as a nationally known journalist that she made her name. During the 1930s, while her mother helped to reinstate the frontier myth with the "Little House" memoirs, Lane served as a major critic of Roosevelt's New Deal policies. Both mother and daughter preferred the domesticated America of "the Old Deal." See *Notable American Women,* 733.

6. This 1938 painting by Irving Bacon, the Ford Company artist (see Lewis, *The Public Image of Henry Ford,* 382), depicts the occasion in late 1895 when Ford clamped a one-cylinder engine to the kitchen sink, an act that agitated Clara since two-year-old Edsel slept in the next room and she feared he might be poisoned by the gasoline fumes (Nevins, *Ford,* 147).

7. See Nevins, *Ford,* 142–47, for the "correct" details of this night's events. In Nevins's account, Henry and Clara worked together over the engine in the Ford kitchen; the place is Bagley (not Edison) Avenue; it is Christmas Eve; Edsel has been born and is already seven weeks old; Clara is not having hysterics.

8. Arnold and Faurote, *Ford Methods and the Ford Shops,* 16.

9. *Helpful Hints and Advice to Employees,* 3; the following quotation is from 13.

10. See Higham, *Strangers in the Land,* 247–48; Nevins and Hill, *Ford,* 338–41; and Nelson, *Managers and Workers,* 144–45. General concern over the need to transform foreign elements into loyal American citizens was particularly intense at the start of World War I. See *A Brief Account of the Educational Work of the Ford Motor Company;* Rindge, "From Boss to Fore-Man." 511–12; and Burlingame, "Americanizing a Thousand Men." The latter piece, written in 1917 for *Industrial Management,* discusses methods used to show "who is with us and who against us in the world struggle." Such appeals to nationalistic spirit also came in response to perceived threats from socialism and other forms of radical thought based on class allegiances. See the entry on "Nationalism" in Bottomore, ed., *A Dictionary of Marxist Thought.* Links between "Americanization and Consumption" of the kind analyzed by the Ewens in their essay of the same name are set out in a memorandum of June 3, 1915, written by A. E. Gruenberg of the Ford Sociological Department (contained within the Marquis Papers). Titled "Progress among Foreigners since the Proclamation of Profit Sharing Plan," Gruenberg reports that at the time of home visitations, immigrants called the company inspectors' attention "to every piece of furniture purchased with great pride and pleasure." He also notes that several asked "what more could be bought in order that their home might not be inferior to those of Americans."

11. The implementation of the original initiatives of the Sociological Department, formulated by John R. Lee and Samuel Marquis, ended in 1921.

12. Ford Motor Company, Labor Policies, Sociological Department (Ford Archives, Account 62, Folder "Minneapolis"). It is interesting to note that John Reed's article, "Why They Hate Ford," in *The Masses* heaps scorn upon Big Business for opposing Ford's program of worker benefits. Even so, many workers resented the prying practices that followed them out of the shops into their houses. See Meyer, *The Five-Dollar Day,* chap. 6.

13. Company towns located in Pennsylvania and Colorado mining regions, as well as George Pullman's attempts to regulate his employees' lives in every detail, have received ample attention. So has their famous precursor, the Lowell works. Among the many writings on these examples, see Kasson, *Civilizing the Machine,* 55–106; Dal Co, "From Parks to the Region"; Sennett, *Authority;* Handlin, *The American Home;* and Brandes, *American Welfare Capitalism, 1880–1940,* chap. 5.

14. Recent scholarship verifies the authenticity of Sinclair's account. See Szuberla, "Dom, Namai, Heim."

15. Morawska, *For Bread with Butter,* 1–2.

16. Many attempts were made to duplicate Ford techniques in the mass pro-

duction of ready-made houses. See Hounshell, *From the American System to Mass Production*, 310–15.

17. For extended critiques of the American Dream of single-family housing, see Hayden, *Redesigning the American Dream*, and Wright, *Building the Dream*.

18. Glassie's classic *Folk Housing in Middle Virginia* details the rationalizing use of spatial squares in the eighteenth century.

19. Bullock, *The American Cottage Builder*, 13. Bullock and Thoreau were both concerned about house spaces adapted to "the peculiarities of the American people," since, in Bullock's words, "their desires, their occupations and wants must first be apprehended and understood before any Architect . . . can successfully and truly become an Architect for America."

20. Vaux, *Villas and Cottages*, 111–12.

21. The happy occupants of Vaux's cabin would enact the republican ideals advanced for the lives of all "industrious and intelligent mechanics and working men, the bone and sinew of the land"—words taken from *The Architecture of Country Houses* (1850), written by Vaux's mentor, Andrew Jackson Downing (40). Log cabin design had been an American political force since the 1840 presidential campaign, when William Henry Harrison's backers used it to image lower-class virtue.

22. Schindler's design is included in Sky and Stone's *Unbuilt America*. Wright's "prairie" style and Schindler's log idyll epitomize another strand of American housing history: that of the custom-designed home. Idiosyncratic features, as well as expensive labor and materials, prevented builders and architects from adapting the custom-made home for mass consumption. In regard to the at-each-others'-throats relations between professional architects and self-trained builders, see Hayden, *Redesigning the American Dream;* Wright, *Building the Dream;* and Fitch, *American Building*. By treating this antagonism as a political issue, house-plan designers and builders commended themselves for their practical skills while attacking elitist aesthetics, but the architectural profession gave as good as it got.

23. Barber, *The Cottage Souvenir, No. 2*, 7; the following quotation is from 12.

24. Kirstein, introduction to *The Hampton Album*, 10; the following quotation is by Samuel Chapman Armstrong, founder of the Hampton Institute (ibid., 6). See Guimond, "Frances Johnston's *Hampton Album*."

25. Riis, "The Genesis of the Tenement," in *How the Other Half Lives*. For an early "professional" definition of tenement housing, see ["Tenement Housing"] *The American Architect and Building News*. Lubove, *The Progressives and the Slums*, and Boyer, *Dreaming the Rational City*, examine attempts to introduce enlightened planning of model housing units into the chaos of the expanding urban scene. Lubove emphasizes the good intentions, albeit limited effectiveness, of Progressivist city planners. With her Foucauldian perspective, Boyer finds either conscious greed or ignorant ineptitude on the part of city designers. Also see Handlin, *The American Home*, both for the rise of tenements and the concept of planned cities. For the City Beautiful movement, see Atterbury, "Model Towns in Amer-

ica"; Hines, "The City Beautiful Movement in Urban American Planning, 1890–1920"; Kriehn, "The City Beautiful"; Machor, *Pastoral Cities;* and Robinson, *Modern Civic Art, or the City Made Beautiful.*

26. Editorial comments heading Julius's article "Roadtown" in the July 1911 issue of *The Masses.* Among the designers of utopian "cooperative ventures" are John Adolphus Etzler, Melusina Fay Peirce, Edward Bellamy, King Gillette, and others included in Sky and Stone *Unbuilt America,* Hayden's *The Grand Domestic Revolution* (which cites Chambless's Roadtown design, 246–47), and Handlin's *The American Home.*

27. The American Arts and Crafts movement was a crusade in the name of the simple life, but its products were one-of-kind pieces. They were characterized by an intricate simplicity only the affluent could afford to buy for their intricately simple and expensive houses. The tensions between collectivist socialist beliefs and individualistic aesthetic concerns, and the politicized relation of the mass products of the machine age to the handcrafted, unique forms, tensions William Morris's crafts movment kept alive in England, were largely absent from the American version; there was little commitment to socialist ideals and no commitment to socialist practices. See Shi, *The Simple Life;* Kaplan, *"The Art That Is Life";* Boris, *Art and Labor;* and Bowman, *American Arts and Crafts.* It is apparent that the Arts and Crafts movement was anathema to the goals of scientific management: complicated oppositions obtain between Morris's socialist aims and Gustave Stickley's furniture designs, spirit and materiality, the aesthetic and the political life, handwork and machine technology. Spokesmen for the prebuilt house business had no use for craftsman ideals. They were scathing in their critiques of the "appalling waste" that comes from "slow, inefficient hand labor" in contrast to the "fast, accurate machines" used to manufacture their house models. See *Pacific Houses,* 8.

28. The work of Frank Lloyd Wright and Richard Neutra is often approached from this angle. For recent appraisals of the political relations between house designs and machine processes, see McLeod, "'Architecture or Revolution'"; Hughes, "Gropius, Machine Design, and Mass Production"; and Herbert, *The Dream of the Factory-Made House.* Also see Handlin, "House Plans for Everybody," chap. 5 of *The American Home.* Two critics from the opening days of the Great Depression urged that proper housing be brought to the general public; see Wood, *Recent Trends in American Housing,* and Stowell, "Housing the Other Half." As for what "simplicity" means to people of wealth, anyone who lives, as I do, near both the Wrigley Mansion and the California Craftsman style Gamble House in Pasadena (built in 1914 and 1908, respectively) knows full well how variously the rich elect to represent their wealth in the form of personal dwelling space. The "mansion" that Wrigley Chewing Gum built does not extol "the simple life" as the Greene and Greene-designed "house" (built by Ivory Soap) does.

29. Whether Wright was born in 1867 or 1869 is still at issue; not in question is Wright's recollection of the importance of Froebel blocks. See Wright's autobiography; Spencer, "The Work of Frank Lloyd Wright"; and Manson, *Frank Lloyd*

Wright to 1910, 5–10. Compare William Ford's visit to the Philadelphia Centennial. The stories he brought home to his son Henry focused on the mighty Corliss engine that dominated Machinery Hall. See Nevins, *Ford,* 60.

30. The sampler of Froebel's birthplace was featured in Harper's two-volume encyclopedia of home management advice, *The Woman's Book* (1894), 1:334. Froebel (1782–1852) established the first kindergarten in 1837.

31. Dominated by men, but not entirely without women. See Cole, *From Tipi to Skyscraper;* Weimann, *The Fair Women,* 144–48; and Hayden, *The Grand Domestic Revolution,* 229–65.

32. It did not take the advent of Taylorism for rational design practices to be brought into the home. The oft-cited names in this field are Lydia Maria Child and Catharine Beecher. See Child, *The American Frugal Housewife* (1835), and Beecher, *Treatise on Domestic Economy* (1841); see also Beecher's *American Woman's Home,* written in collaboration with her sister, Harriet Beecher Stowe, in 1869. Much attention has been paid to Beecher's conservative gender politics, particularly in her designs for efficient cupboards and work spaces, which reinforce woman's traditional role as the hallowed manager of the family dwelling. See Fitch, *Architecture and the Esthetics of Plenty,* chap. 5; Hayden, *The Grand Domestic Revolution* and *Redesigning the American Dream;* and Handlin, *The American Home.* In the post-Civil War period, radical feminism and the scientific approach to domestic economy struck off in quite different directions. Melusina Fay Peirce and Charlotte Perkins Gilman urged that kitchens and laundry facilities be removed from the single-family household. They preferred cooperative housing plans as well as plans for apartment complexes and hotels; and envisioned a scientifically planned world in which women would be liberated through the availability of communal kitchens and laundries. Traditional spaces were coming under increased scrutiny, too, even by women unaware of or indifferent to the feminists' ambitious programs to correct the wrongs of women's material existence. There was a new insistence upon women being brought into line with the "scientific" and "efficient" use of time and motion exacted in other areas of the nation's work life. Hayden's *Grand Domestic Revolution* is the essential scholarly study of these issues. Handlin's chapter on "Good Housekeeping" in *The American Home* and Cowan, "The 'Industrial Revolution' in the Home," are also valuable. For contemporary statements, see Campbell, *The Easiest Way in Housekeeping and Cooking Adapted to Domestic Use or Study in Classes;* Leach, "Science in the Model Kitchen"; Salmon, *Progress in the Household;* and Wood, "The Ideal and Practical Organization of a Home."

33. The 1893 Columbian Exposition provided important display space to demonstrate the new "domestic science." See Weimann, *The Fair Women,* 463–68. *Cosmopolitan* (vols. 26–27) ran a series of articles in 1899 under the heading "The Ideal and Practical Organization of a Home," advocating the principles of domestic science. Also see McDougall, "An Ideal Kitchen," for another example of the contemporary interest in scientific management for the home, and Cowan, "The 'Industrial Revolution' in the Home," for a recent scholarly look at the issue.

34. Campbell, *The Easiest Way in Housekeeping and Cooking,* 18.

35. White, *Successful Houses and How to Build Them,* 92.

36. Frederick, *The New Housekeeping: Efficiency Studies in Home Management,* viii, 14; hereafter cited parenthetically in the text.

37. Christine McGaffey Frederick was born in 1883 and received a B.S. (and membership in Phi Beta Kappa) from Northwestern University in 1906. She married Justus G. Frederick in 1907—a business executive, writer, and editor active in advertising and marketing research—and bore four children between 1908 and 1917 (the years she was introduced to Taylorism). Her busy professional career continued until her death in 1970. See *Notable American Women,* 249–50.

38. Bunce, *My House: An Ideal,* 104–7.

39. Gilman's demand that women go "outside" first appeared in *Women and Economics: A Study of the Economic Relation between Men and Women as a Factor in Social Evolution* (1899), soon followed by *The Home: Its Work and Influence* (1903) and *The Man-Made World; or, Our Androcentric Culture* (1911).

40. Spencer, *Woman's Share in Social Culture,* 150, 158.

41. Richards, *Euthenics,* xx.

42. Tarbell, *The Business of Being a Woman,* 103. In the quote from *Woman's Share* above, Spencer rebukes Tarbell's belief that a woman's main "business" is to be "house-mother."

43. Marden, *Woman and the Home,* 22. He went on to say that the home had been extended into the world's "factories, stores, workshops, business and professional offices, laundries, bakeries, mines, railroads, wherever human industry is at work." Thus echoes Gilman: "what we need is not less home, but more; not a lessening of the love of human beings for a home, but its extension through new and more effective expression" (*Women and Economics,* 22).

44. See Leach, "Transformations in a Culture of Consumption."

45. Marx's thesis about the "syntax of the middle landscape" permeates his whole book; his reading of the Inness painting comes from *The Machine in the Garden,* 220–21.

46. Prefabricated houses figured in the earliest colonization of Australia and New Zealand and, later, in the settling of the American West. Excellent data has been gathered by Charles E. Peterson, who has traced prefabrication back to 1578 and 1624, to the use of corrugated iron prefabs in Hawaii in the early 1800s and to the gold rush camps of California. See Peterson, "'Prefabs for the Prairies,'" "Early American Prefabrication," and "Prefabs in the California Gold Rush."

47. The story of efforts made by Thomas Edison, Grosvenor Attenbury, and others to refine concrete ready-mades, together with later attempts to use Foster Gunnison's Van Guilder system, is described in Handlin, *The American Home,* 272–302, and in Bracken, *New Homes Series, Report No. 1—The Story of Prefabricated Houses.* Also see Bruce and Sandbank, *A History of Prefabrication,* and *Industrialized House Forum.* As previously noted, Hounshell surveys problems in the

mass manufacturing of housing units as part of his history of a system that edged ever closer to the goal of using completely interchangeable parts, efforts that linked the concepts (although not the actual practices) of automobile and housing manufacturers (*From the American System to Mass Production, 1800–1932*).

48. Copy for *Instructions for the Erection of Your Aladdin Home* states that the ready-mades were so easy to assemble "that many women have erected" them. "As one of them remarked: 'Any man should be ashamed to admit having any difficulty.'"

49. *The Famous Fifty*, 3.

50. Remarks about family virtue in 1915 differed in texture and tone from those of Downing and Vaux in the 1850s. The emerging market for ready-mades was not interested in lives patterned according to log cabin simplicity or regulated by the boxlike adobe shelters built by immigrant builders. Only the exceptions—like Rudolf Schindler, who had grown up in Vienna, most likely reading Cooper and the westerns concocted by Karl May—continued to dream of the good life promised by the log cabin. Houses associated with rustic poverty were out of date by 1895, as Robert Grant insists: "The American people . . . smiles to-day at the assumption that the owner of a log cabin is more inherently virtuous than the owner of a steam-yacht" (*The Art of Living*, 13).

51. *The Famous Fifty*, 3.

52. Quoted in Tuan, *Topophilia*, 53–54.

53. Remark made by the leader of the Cincinnati Women's Art movement in *The Ladies, God Bless 'Em*, 10.

54. Louis, *Decorum*, 288. House literature in the 1840s and 1850s argued that American males could not be counted on for moral stability; that was the obligation of the wife and mother. By the 1880s, however, emphasis was placed on the man's duty to protect the family's physical welfare (at least). R. Thomas Short's warning, in *Proper Homes and How to Have Them* (1887), stands for many such admonitions:

> If you have lost a child, a wife, or other relative from your household, whose death has been due to a preventable disease, or if the health of your family has suffered mysteriously, it is a duty, which you have no right to neglect, to at least make an attempt to discover the source of your trouble. . . . If you value the health of your wife, your children or yourself, see that you live in a Proper Home.

True, both "Fathers and Mothers" alike are "Guilty of Manslaughter" if they fail; true, blame is placed upon external forces of "speculative capitalism," which contribute to the construction of crowded, unsanitary housing; but the man is the one most painfully placed upon this rack of rhetoric (Short, preface).

The pressure did not let up. In 1919 an advertisement for a Connecticut ready-built house company featured a shack paired with a model home. The copy, which equates health, house pride, and home virtue, reads, "Take Your Choice. . . . If you and your wife and babies lived in this unhealthful hovel do you think you would work as cheerfully and well as you could if you all lived in this handsome modern home where you could hold up your head and your children would not be ashamed" (cited in Wright, *Building the Dream*, 179).

55. Adams, "The Primitive Rights of Women," 360. This Lowell Institute lecture was first published in 1891 *Historical Essays*.

56. *Home Builder's Plan Book*, 8. Excellent recent sources on the linkage of the "good home" and the "good house" are Clark, *The American Family Home, 1800–1960;* Gowans, *The Comfortable House;* Kwolek-Folland, "The Useful What-Not and the Ideal of 'Domestic Decoration,'"; McDannell, *The Christian Home in Victorian America, 1840–1900;* Schwartz, "Home as Haven, Cloister, and Winnebago"; and Wright, *Moralism and the Model Home*.

57. Gardner, *The House that Jill Built after Jack Had Proved a Failure*. In 1889 Gibson came out with *Convenient Houses with Fifty Plans for the Housekeeper*. His market was clearly targeted.

58. Male salesmen thought that the wives of prospective buyers were exceedingly hard to please, but their companies' promotional literature veiled the men's peevishness with praise for the women's "progressive" search for perfection. See *Modern Homes*.

59. The Sterling catalogue makes much of the fact that the company employed two full-time women consultants—one a "country woman," the other a "city" sophisticate. Together they form a single "complete woman," the composite Sterling Woman, who is ready to guide all American women into the fulfillment of their house needs (*The Famous Fifty*, 9).

60. Pagination for Gilman's sustained attack (which radiates out from its core in *The Home*, 51ff) is cited parenthetically in the text.

61. As exampled by Lasch, *Haven in a Heartless World*.

62. James, *The American Scene*, 11. Edith Wharton and Ogden Codman were in complete agreement, as their "reformist" views, presented in *The Decoration of Houses* (1897), make clear. The desire for privacy did not belong to American patricians alone. Gibson's *Beautiful Houses* (1895) speaks of the ordinary man's wish for a house that will "attract little attention" (allowing him "to sit quietly in its yard") and of his wife, the "bright and enthusiastic little woman," who also prefers to avoid "public applause" (234).

If lack of privacy was perceived as a growing problem by 1900, consider the title of an article by John R. Stilgoe, one of the deans of environmental design, about the problems that arise from linking technologies of efficiency to the psychology of privacy, problems we continue to face today: "Privacy and Energy-Efficient Residential Site Design: An Example of Context." Also see Handlin, *The American Home*, 176–97, and Hutner, "Modern Instances," an essay where "private life," which "registers the most pressing public anxieties," is examined through readings of novels by Howells, Abraham Cahan, John Updike, and Ann Beattie.

63. Humphreys, "House Decoration and Furnishing," *The Woman's Book,* 2:103–78; hereafter cited parenthetically in the text.

64. Ellwanger, *The Story of My House,* 79–81, describes "male" designs for a series of staircases and doors that channel the passage of "such tardy and bibulous friends as might meet the disapproval of madame" directly to the man of the house.

65. Gilman, *The Home,* 40–45.

66. Ibid., 64–65.

67. Stevenson and Jandl, *Houses by Mail,* 9. Further copy drawn from this compilation and from the Sterling System-Built Homes catalogue of 1915 will be cited parenthetically in the text. For the need to give careful study to mail-order catalogues, see Schlereth, "Mail-Order Catalogs as Resources in Material Culture Studies," 48–65.

68. Dalzell, *Homes of Moderate Size,* 6. The only way "moderns" could play out nostalgia for Currier & Ives images of large families gathering around festive tables was by crowding guests into all available space on December 25 before letting the house shrink back to its normal size for the remaining 364 days.

69. On the last point, see Lears, "Some Versions of Fantasy."

70. In January 1991 the *Ann Arbor Observer* featured a story on "Ann Arbor's Kit Homes," a look at the group of Bay City, Michigan, ready-made house companies as well as the designs offered by Sears and Montgomery Ward. It includes a current photograph of The Vernon described as "the city's best-known (and fanciest surviving) kit home" (32). Special thanks to Anne Gere for sending me this document.

71. Throughout the prolonged era when the single-family house was upheld as the American icon, debates over the pros and cons of apartment living were heated. In the beginning, "French flats" in particular were criticized as being un-American; see "New Apartment Houses" (1879). But by 1902 the brochure *Artistic Modern Homes,* published by the Associated Architects of America, contained a section on apartment houses, described as the form of modern design rapidly growing in favor; by the 1930s the apartment had become an economic imperative for most. For diverse attitudes taken toward apartment living, early and late, see Hancock, "The Apartment House in Urban America"; Wright, *Building the Dream,* 22–40; Handlin, *The American Home,* 216ff; Gilman, "The Passing of the Home in Great American Cities"; Stevenson, *Homes of Character;* Howells, *A Hazard of New Fortunes* (1890), and Fuller, *The Cliff-Dwellers* (1893).

72. One of the strongest statements for a return to the colonial style of architecture that instills proper "home" values is Dow's *American Renaissance* (1904).

73. Sears halted production in 1934 because of defaults on mortgage payments. It reestablished itself the next year but only to sell houses, not to deal in lots or financing as before.

74. Hoover, "Home Ownership," 3–5.

75. McElvaine, ed., *Down and Out in the Great Depression*, 105.

76. Beaux, *Background with Figures*, 48.

77. McElvaine, ed., *Down and Out in the Great Depression*, 84.

Chapter Eight

1. O'Connell, "The Taylor System in Government Shops," 559.

2. Weber, *Max Weber*, 286. For a scholarly analysis of turn-of-the-century critiques (offered by William James and others) of labor conditions that led to psychic fragmentation and alienation, see Gilbert, *Work without Salvation*.

3. See chapter 3 for details of Veblen's concerns.

4. See Sinclair's version of how Ford was forced to drop the Model T in *The Flivver King*, 17, 69.

5. Cooley, *Human Nature and the Social Order*, 375. For Meade, consult in particular the chapter titled "Society" in *Mind, Self, and Society from the Standpoint of a Social Behaviorist*. In "Nature" (1836), Emerson describes the one who "masters the world by a penny-wisdom" as "a half-man"—one whose power over nature is "through the understanding" alone, limited to "the economic use of fire, wind, water, and the mariner's needle; steam, coal, chemical agriculture; the repairs of the human body by the dentist and the surgeon" (*Complete Works* 1:72).

6. This and the following quotations are from Marquis, *Henry Ford*, 57, 118, 165–66.

7. Before Marquis became disaffected with the Ford method, he wrote, apparently without irony, "Mr. Ford's business is the making of men, and he manufactures automobiles on the side to defray the expenses of the main business" ("The Ford Idea in Education," 1). In notes he compiled for Ida Tarbell's use in 1916, part of his document "Hints to the Investigator," Marquis declared that the Sociological Department had as its sole task "the uplift of humanity." Its responsibility was "to restore [each worker] to the estate that is rightfully his."

8. The following quotations are from Niebuhr, "Mechanical Men in a Mechanical Age," 493–94. Niebuhr attacked Ford directly in "How Philanthropic Is Henry Ford?" and "Ford's Five-Day Week Shrinks."

9. James, *The American Scene*, 75; the following quotations are from 84, 199.

10. Although Zangwill (a founding father, with Theodor Herzl, of the Zionist movement) dedicated the 1914 book edition of *The Melting-Pot* to Roosevelt, his afterword makes his position clearer: "The process of American amalgamation is not assimilation or simple surrender to the dominant type, as is popularly supposed, but an all-round give-and-take by which the final type may be enriched or impoverished" (203).

11. Rabinbach, *The Human Motor*, 4.

12. See Hayden, *The Grand Domestic Revolution*, for running commentary. Peirce's remarks are from *Co-Operative Housekeeping*, 111.

13. Larsen, *Quicksand,* in *Quicksand and Passing,* 4. Also see Ellison, *Invisible Man,* chap. 10.

14. Sinclair's *The Flivver King* (1929) is a decent stab at writing yet another flip-flop of the Emerson/Alger myths. Lacking West's wit and malice, Sinclair's earnest parable gives us Abner Shutt, the boy who enters Ford's employment in 1903, already minus a finger due to his misadventures as a newsboy. He is one of the faithful who believes that "if you worked hard and lived a sober and God-fearing life, success was bound to come to you (10)." Alas, neither Abner nor his employer realizes that "Henry Ford was doing more than any man now alive to root out and destroy this old America"; Ford "had thought that men could have the machinery and comforts of a new world, while keeping the ideas of the old" (64). Once Abner is assimilated into the Ford production line, he becomes "the specialist in spindle-nut screwing," a routine he carries out like any "mule in industry, one that was hitched to a pole, and set to walking round and round, running a piece of machinery" (18, 95).

15. Twain, *Roughing It* (1872), chap. 53.

16. West, *A Cool Million; or, The Dismantling of Lemuel Pitkin,* epigraph; pagination hereafter cited parenthetically in the text.

17. We give credit here to the "cruel" style that marked Mark Twain's later writings and to the vinegary tongue Veblen would have used if he had written novels rather than essays. Credit for mordant wit should also be given to Dewey and Tufts, based on their comment that American courts insisted on the right of workers to be maimed (*Ethics,* 506).

18. Faulkner gives us a variation on Whipplean political maneuverings in his account of the race for state senate (mis)conducted by Clarence Snopes. Snopesian politics also utilizes the dismantled for its own gain. As Gavin Stevens sees it, "The surest way to be elected to office in America is to have fathered seven or eight children and then lost your arm or leg in a sawmill accident: both of which— the reckless optimism which begot seven or eight children with nothing to feed them by but a sawmill, and the incredible ineptitude which would put an arm or a leg in range of a moving saw—should already have damned you from any form of public trust. They cant beat him" (*The Mansion,* 310). Yet in the end the anti-Snopes party gets a "good" man—a legless veteran—elected by means of dirty tricks involving trousers, dogs, and uplifted legs.

19. Ford, *My Life and Work,* 108. See Norwood, *Ford,* chap. 10–12, for a glowing report on the company's ability to "salvage" all things, reconverting potential waste into gain. Also note Ford's remarks in "What I Have Learned about Management in the Last 25 Years." Ford's language emphasizes absences: "reduce," "eliminate," and "do away with" are operative terms for successful management.

20. Sinclair, *The Flivver King,* 20, 22; my emphasis.

21. See Mayr and Post's introduction to *Yankee Enterprise,* xv. Their volume, containing papers presented at a symposium on this much-debated subject, deflates myths like the one that credits Eli Whitney with making muskets with inter-

changeable parts prior to the War of 1812. Eugene S. Ferguson, in "History and Historiography," and David A. Hounshell, in "The *System:* Theory and Practice," urge that we avoid making "cross-cultural" equations between different kinds of manufactory—the Colt Revolver Factory, the Singer Sewing Machine Company, the Ford Motor Company. Such equations simplify the processes by which interchangeable parts became a part of advanced production methods. The following information incorporated into the text is based upon Ferguson's and Hounshell's essays in *Yankee Enterprise* as well as Hounshell, *From the American System to Mass Production, 1800–1932;* Hindle and Lubar, *Engines of Change,* chap. 13; and Giedion, *Mechanization Takes Command.*

22. The following studies provide background on the making of Civil War uniforms, the standardization of men's and boys' clothing, the women's dress pattern business, the success of the Singer sewing machine, and the rise of the ready-made garment industry: Brandon, *A Capitalist Romance* (to be read with caution, according to Hounshell); Daves, *Ready-Made Miracle;* Kidwell, *Cutting a Fashionable Fit;* Kidwell and Christman, *Suiting Everyone;* Marot, "Revolution and the Garment Trade"; Richards, *The Ready-to-Wear Industry, 1900–1950;* Ishbel Ross, *Crusades and Crinolines, The Life and Times of Ellen Curtis Demorest and William Jennings Demorest;* and "The Representative and Cosmopolitan Emporium of Demorest."

23. Whitman, "Walt Whitman in War-Time," 840; letter to his mother, 29 Dec. 1862.

24. Blotner's biography of Faulkner recounts the fact that one-fifth of the Mississippi budget went to pay for artificial limbs after the war (*Faulkner,* 1:34).

25. Systematized measure also had to take into account the dynamics of growth. *Human Proportions in Growth: Being the Complete Measurement of the Human Body, for Every Age and Size during the Years of Juvenile Growth,* compiled by Daniel E. Ryan in 1880, proclaims the value of a cutting method based on "nature," "the living subject," and "the law of growth." Ryan maintained that those cutting boys' clothing should not depend upon memory, as was true of cutters of men's garments, who relied upon the stabilized measurements of the adult. However, D'Arcy Wentworth Thompson's *On Growth and Form* (1917) revivified the Schoolmen's axiom *ignorato motu, ignoratur Natura,* which calls into question whether any living form can be fixed by memory-bound statistics at any stage.

26. Kidwell and Christman, *Suiting Everyone,* 43.

27. Hounshell, "The *System:* Theory and Practice," 129.

28. William Salisbury is clearly the leading nineteenth-century aesthetician of tailoring. In one of several such essays that appeared in his journal, *The Tailors' Intelligencer,* during 1870, Salisbury addresses the question, "Can the Science of Garment Cutting Be Considered Paramount to Realistic Art?" He concludes that tailoring can be equated with "Raphaelite art" only if the "originality" introduced by the cutter, his own "designer," expands upon the "beau ideal" of the paper pattern.

29. Affirmation of the Platonizing process by which design reaches cutter and contractor in the making of ready-made women's garments comes directly from Leon Stein. What Stein (son of a tailor, former editor of *Justice,* journal for the ILGWU, and author of *The ILGWU News-History, Labor's Story,* and *The Triangle Fire*) does not know about the garment industry is of little consequence. Thanks to him (and the conversation we had during a long working dinner), I was inspired to write this book. In his extensive remarks concerning the intricate moves between design and assembly, Stein emphasizes that every dress ever made is a replica of the designer's dummy, in his words, "the Platonic idea" of the human body. Also see *Efficiency and Incentives in the Cutting Room;* Rohr, *Pattern Drafting and Grading;* and Knoblaugh, *Modelmaking for Industrial Design.*

30. The MIT experiment is described (vaguely) in *Elements of Human Engineering* by Charles R. Gow, director of the "Humanics" program. See Schell, *The Million Dollar Lecture,* 3, 44–45.

31. See Brewer, *The Man-Building Process;* Cheley, *The Business of Living;* Myers, *Human Engineering.* As late as 1951, Butler University sponsored the Institute of Human Engineering; its program is carefully outlined in Casteller, *Fundamentals of Human Engineering.*

32. Hurlburt, *The Grid,* 24.

33. Rabinbach, *The Human Motor,* 23, 57.

34. In 1854 Helmholtz referred to the eighteenth-century technical fictions of Jacques de Vaucanson and the younger Jacquet-Droz as automata that did not aspire to possess "a soul gifted with moral perfection." He acknowledged the inventors' hope for a future in which men "would be willing to dispense with the moral qualities of their servants, if at the same time their immoral qualities could also be eliminated." These robotic servants would replace "the mutability of flesh and bone" with "the regularity of a machine and the durability of brass and steel" (ibid., 58). Helmholtz shared with Marx a conception of the human body linked to the cosmos, responsive to laws of nature and production, a happy condition that "dissolved the anthropomorphic body as a distinct entity and made the industrial body subject to a sophisticated analytics of space and time" (87).

35. The quotations above are from ibid., 4, 7, 76, 122. An essay by Dwight E. Robinson, "Fashion Theory and Product Design," indicates how model-making was expected to convey an "ethic," although not a full-fledged moral position. In the 1930s "streamlining" suggested "its own ethical justification," since it symbolized "the modern American's enlightened determination to cast off the encumbrances of convention in order to forge a new, vital, and dynamic civilization." Eventually, "the importance of ethical justification to support styling appeal . . . got to be a habit." Clients wanted more than an attractive product. As one industrial designer put it, whenever clients demanded an ethic, "'we give them an ethic. Ethic? That's a fashion, too'" (135). Far less cynical is Farnsworth, *The Art and Ethics of Dress* (1915). In its concentration upon "rational clothing," Farnsworth's book is an earnest example of feminist dress-reform literature. See also Riegel, "Women's Clothes and Women's Rights."

36. Informative studies on the development of industrial engineering and product design (and the importance of constructing design models) are: Cheney and Cheney, *Art and the Machine;* Knoblaugh, *Modelmaking for Industrial Design;* Meikle, *Twentieth-Century Limited;* Middleton, *Group Practice in Design;* Schaefer, *The Roots of Modern Design;* Schutte, ed. *The Uneasy Coalition;* Starr, *Product Design and Decision Theory;* and Wilson, Pilgrim, and Tashjian, eds. *The Machine Age in America, 1918–1941.*

37. Dreyfuss, *The Measure of Man,* 4. Figures 38 and 39 are reduced from the life-size sheets included in pockets at the side of the front cover of Dreyfuss's book. They bear out Etienne-Jules Marey's extensive use of graphic methods, which refined attempts to gauge the "space of the body" and "to map the body in space" (Rabinbach, *The Human Motor,* 94).

38. Rabinbach, *The Human Motor,* 24. In distinguishing between the (effective) designs executed by Gropius and the (relatively unsuccessful) designs of Le Corbusier, Hughes remarks that the latter's designs "were the products of modern technology, not the methods of modern technology." Instead of incorrectly defining "modern technology entirely in terms of form rather than of form and methodology," Le Corbusier should have studied "a Ford production line and a Taylor plant layout" (Hughes, "Gropius, Machine Design, and Mass Production," 173). Dreyfuss's efforts fall into the Gropius camp.

39. Stigler notes that F. V. Edgeworth "argued that Antoine Augustine Cournot's criticism of Quételet's average man (that an individual consisting of all average parts might be an unviable monster) could be dismissed on correlational grounds" (*The History of Statistics,* 325). Those whose trust in numbers is not as strong as Edgeworth's would side with Cournot.

40. Dreyfuss, *The Measure of Man,* 5. Observations have been made about the implied racism of product design—that airplane cockpits are said to be better suited to Caucasian bodies than to those of African Americans, for example. The managers argue, however, that the use of models like Joe and Josephine derives from theories of "the science of work" and "Social Helmholtzianism," theories in which "the body of the worker [is] a universal, degendered motor." Notwithstanding this denial of the importance of taking gender, race, and other particulars into account, the objections remain—as when Max Weber criticized Emil Kraepelin's laboratory setting because of lack of attention paid to "real workers," those "motivated by money and influenced by diet, sleep patterns, and sexuality" (Rabinbach, *The Human Motor,* 121, 194).

41. Dreiser, *An American Tragedy* 1:236; hereafter cited parenthetically in the text.

42. Like several of his contemporaries in the industrial design business, Dreyfuss's early connections were with the theater world. These experiences led him to respond, to some extent, to "the human factors" involved in the making of emotional as well as bodily work-environment narratives. See Meikle, *Twentieth-Century Limited,* 56–60.

43. Whether design models ultimately bring harm is currently a subject of debate. The models known as Sid, Biosid, and Eurosid figure in work narratives in which they are fated to "die" so that mortals might survive otherwise fatal side-impact car crashes. Such stories may not have happy endings for us, however, if the wrong protagonist is assigned the role of martyr. Barry Meier's article in the *New York Times* (22 Jan. 1990) examines the issue of which model—Sid, Biosid, or Eurosid—should be utilized in government and industry research. Differences in design (Sid is armless, Biosid and Eurosid have adjustible limbs, and Biosid has a flexible ribcage) is "the subject of intense dispute—a dispute that may well end up costing lives." The U.S. Government favors Sid, but General Motors Corporation (which favors Biosid) describes Sid as "an unreliable, technological has-been whose use will result in dangerous car designs." In the words of one car industry person, "The dilemma is whether [Sid] simulates what happens in the real world, and our answer is we don't think so."

44. Schaefer, *The Roots of Modern Design*, 3. It is the Cheneys, themselves among the first to set up offices as product designers, who refer to the new profession's wish to step in as the "divine designer" capable of making the product as "grace incarnate, the symbol of eager life" (*Art and the Machine*, 74). Also see the Bauhaus Proclamation, which called for "one single integrated creation . . . symbol of a new faith" and for the advancement of a "universally valid methodology" (Middleton, *Group Practice in Design*, 44). No one doubts the importance of using models, but there is a long history of concern (documented in part by *The Human Motor*) about whether models function within the world of "experience." Some argued that "theory" and "practice" are "interchangeable parts" of the same process. Still others found gaps between procedures performed in the laboratory and procedures enacted in the workplace. This disagreement led to the friction to which Rabinbach continually refers between advocates of European-based experiments in "the science of work" and those who praised American-style Taylorism for keeping its feet firmly on the factory floor.

45. Schaefer, *The Roots of Modern Design*, 199.

46. Meyer, *The Five-Dollar Day*, 17.

47. Meikle, *Twentieth-Century Limited*, 186. The "smoothness" sought by Walter Dorwin Teague and by "styling" engineers like Roy Sheldon and Egmount Areans was singled out as "an echo in the new politics, the politics of collectivism" (ibid.).

48. Other, more dynamic notions of "wholeness" were abroad in the land during the early decades of the twentieth century. In a writing style analogous to the process he describes, Louis Sullivan goes on "ceaselessly unfolding and infolding" his faith in forms that are "related, interwoven, intermeshed, interconnected, interblended," enclosing within a single dramatic spectacle "its appalling, its inspiring harmony of drift and splendor" (*Kindergarten Chats and Other Writings*, 45). In a less excitable style, D'Arcy Thompson leagues the biologist with the philosopher in comprehending "that the whole is not merely the sum of its parts." It is "an organisation of parts, of parts in their mutual arrangement, fitting one with

another, in which Aristotle calls 'a single and indivisible principle of unity' "; in what Goethe names "balancement of growth"; in what Driesch refers to as "entelechy"; and in what (the one Thompson favors most) Buffon describes as the combination "*qui conspirent toutes ensembles à produire cet effect général que nous nommons la vie*" (*On Growth and Form*, 264–65).

49. See chapter 6 for discussion of the Gilbreths' "The Effect of Motion Study upon the Workers."

50. See Eliot, "Content in Work," and Rodgers "Epilogue: Charles W. Eliot and the Quest for Joyful Labor," *The Work Ethic in Industrial America, 1850–1920*, 233–42.

51. Robert and Helen Lynd found many boys just like Clyde when they came to Middletown in 1924: boys just out of high school, who took shortcuts to the factory jobs that would put quick money into their pockets, not realizing until it was too late that they would peak early and then remain at low-level jobs for the rest of their working lives. The fact remained that Middletown's workplaces did not provide what they found "interesting."

52. The extent to which Dreiser imposes an inescapable fate upon Clyde (implying that there is no other life than the one controlled by the narrative terms of "an American tragedy") will be discussed later. Note, however, the figure of Ratterer, who comes and goes in the narrative. Ratterer shows that there are different options available. He had also been involved in the Kansas City hit-and-run incident, but when he shows up in Chicago, he has (dare we say it?) "chosen" a different kind of life: "a tale of only modest adventure . . . a tale which had less of nerves and worry and more of a sturdy courage and faith in his own luck and possibilities" (1:171–72). Ratterer disappears from Clyde's own narrative as quickly as he appears. We have no chance to see if that "sturdy courage and faith" will be rewarded or whether it will be crushed, as it has to be in a decently deterministic novel. He exists only as a footnote to the main text—perhaps faintly to propose that there *are* alternatives, perhaps ironically to underscore the naïveté of his "courage and faith." As for the quality of fatality with which Dreiser burdens Clyde, recall that Clyde says that he felt "more subdued, less romantic, more practical, certain that if he tried now, imitated the soberer people of the world, and those only, that some day he might succeed, if not greatly, at least much better than he had thus far" (1:173). But lest we think that through an imitation of "better" models of behavior Clyde might become a hero of a novel written by, say, William Dean Howells, look at the phrase immediately preceding these words: "within the precincts of the club itself, he felt himself different from what he really was" (ibid.). Clyde's fate as Dreyfuss's Joe would be less tragic only if he, like Joe, were kept within a protective work environment; only if his behavior (limited to being "more subdued, less romantic, more practical") were machine-tooled to fit the "precincts" of his labors.

53. Dreiser includes more information about conditions at the Griffiths factory: the labor is piecework; the hiring and firing system is keyed to retain only the speediest workers; rapid turnovers "make room for new blood and new energy"

(1:262); the labor force includes foreign-born workers, whom "the American types" consider "ignorant, low, immoral, un-American" (1:273).

54. In 1913 Leo Frank, manager of the National Pencil Company in Marietta, Georgia, supervised the accounts, payroll, and "quality control" of 103 young women. Although he insisted upon his innocence, Frank was tried for the murder of Mary Phagan, an employee about whom he knew nothing but her work number. His workplace detachment did not save him from conviction, nor from being dragged from jail and lynched as a Jew and Northerner.

55. Sondra Finchley's life is adumbrated, as it were, in William Hard's 1911 *The Women of Tomorrow*. The chapter titled "The Wasters" tells the story of "Marie of the smart set"—as "competent a little grafter as the town afforded," whose family "had trained her to deadhead her way through life." Although Marie is "The Nice Girl," she is a danger to the town males, whose efficiency is affected by any dissipation. (Hard is the journalist who caused Dorr such unhappiness over the terms of their coauthorship of the sad tales of working women.)

56. The doctor whom Roberta consults will not help her for the standard reasons: abortion is "too dangerous and ethically and socially wrong and criminal into the bargain" (1:412). He is also guided by the fact that Roberta is not of the same social class as other young women of "good family" whom he has helped in the past. The Griffiths factory has no provision for helping women workers in Roberta's situation.

57. In "An American Tragedy, or the Promise of American Life," Michaels discusses the effects of "drifting." That Clyde's life is ruled by "drift" once his hopes turn to desperation is reinforced by the way "drift" replaces "interesting" in the second half of the novel. Not that Clyde was not always adrift, but he initially drifts *toward* what is of interest.

58. The way Sondra handles Clyde, despite the self-revealing infantilism of her talk, is similar to the way Kate Croy handles Merton Densher in James's novel, *The Wings of the Dove*. Kate chides Densher for having delayed his coming to her after he returns from Venice where he "killed" Milly Theale; in his case, however, he follows Kate's well-laid plan to gain both money and sexual desire.

59. Two years after *An American Tragedy*, the January 1927 issue of *System: The Magazine of Business* ran an advertisement for the Pelman Institute of America. The headline is "Scattered-brained! No wonder he never accomplishes anything worthwhile!" The copy states: "His mind is like a powerful automobile running wild—destroying his hopes, his dreams, his POSSIBILITIES! . . . He pities himself, excuses himself, sympathizes with himself. And the great tragedy is that he has every quality that leads to success. . . . His trouble is that he does not know how to USE his brain." In order to achieve the "BALANCED, ORDERED MINDS" that guarantee success, consumers are urged to sign up for the "scientific Mind Training" offered by the Pelman system.

60. If Ford had had his way, Clyde would not have been "wasted" through execution. He is more valuable alive, furnishing labor power in a state prison

"turned into an industrial unit," which offers "excellent profit to the State" (Ford, *Today and Tomorrow,* 90). The Southern slavery system that Mark Twain attacks in *Pudd'nhead Wilson* had already shown the way. When Tom Driscoll is convicted of murder, he is not sent to languish in a prison cell as a white man; rather, he is sent as a black to do valuable slave labor in the fields. Ford simply conflates the conditions of slaves with those of white criminals, converting prisons into factories to assure there will be no waste of "the human motor."

Chapter Nine

1. "From Original Sin to Anomie" and "Desire, Wealth, and Value: Anomic Themes in Political Economy"—the first and second chapters of Herbert's *Culture and Anomie*—brilliantly set out the ways in which John Wesley's preachings on original sin found expression throughout the nineteenth century in cultural models contrasting wilderness and discipline, boundlessness and limits, the "free" individual and the "socialized" group. Herbert's book reads like a gloss on "Wild Palms," that perfect example of Faulkner's own imaginative love affair with the postlapsarian world; it also serves as an extended comment upon the evolutionary tales told by Taylor, Veblen, and Ford.

2. Faulkner, "Wild Palms," *The Wild Palms,* 83; hereafter cited parenthetically in the text.

3. Herbert's *Culture and Anomie* (which appeared too late for me to make as much reference to as I should have liked) explodes just this myth. He vividly documents the way both the nineteenth-century European city and the South Sea islands lived out the cultural erotics of bodies and money.

4. See Seltzer, *Bodies and Machines,* 20.

5. Clark emphasizes distinctions between "The Blot and the Diagram" in his essay of that name, but Kuntz, in "The Art of Blotting," suggests ways in which these two seemingly antagonistic designs for art and loving might be brought into combination. After recounting the gist of Norman Juster's "criteriological allegory," which Juster titles "The Dot and the Line: A Romance in Lower Mathematics," Kuntz acknowledges that lines that become squiggles—"airy and coarse," "untidy and graceless"—are not safe lovers for neat dots, which prefer closed and ordered forms. Yet he gives good reasons for living with squiggles, blots, and blobs, however intolerant management theorists might be of their irrationality and randomness. In the "romance" of "Wild Palms," Charlotte the blot draws Harry the dead dot into her energizing sphere.

6. D'Arcy Thompson writes in the opening pages of his treatise *On Growth and Form,* "As soon as we adventure on the paths of the physicist, we learn to *weigh* and to *measure* . . . and to find more and more our knowledge expressed and our needs satisfied through the concept of *number,* as in the dreams and visions of Plato and Pythagoras." He concludes his book by affirming with the ancients that number is "*le comment et le pourquoit des choses,*" adding, "Dreams apart, numerical pre-

cision is the very soul of science" (1–2, 327). Clearheaded precisionists like Charlotte never place "dreams apart."

7. Faulkner, *The Hamlet,* 5; hereafter cited parenthetically in the text.

8. On the eve of the American Revolution, when Hawthorne's young Robin sets out to make his fortune with or without the aid of his kinsman Major Molyneux, the operative word is already "shrewd." Snopesism-cum-the-American Way continues to find expression in Dorey's *The Daily Worker's Counsellor* (1923), which opens with a chapter on "Shrewdness," and in Casteller's *Fundamentals of Human Engineering* (1951) and its four interlocking terms: "American freedom," "capitalism," "bargaining," and "shrewdness." Casteller concludes, "In the process of making bargains, one who is mentally alert, a keen thinker, and shrewd in his methods makes better bargains than one who is mentally dull, a slow thinker, and never very clever. This is a main reason why the shrewd get control of the most wealth" (25).

9. Gavin Stevens muses that "*Snopes* were some profound and incontrovertible heramaphroditic principle for the furtherance of a race, a species, the principle vested always physically in the male . . . the Snopes female incapable of producing a Snopes." But "more than a mere natural principle: a divine one . . . else before now they would own the whole earth" (Faulkner, *The Town,* 136; hereafter cited parenthetically in the text.

10. The soul-depleting craving for money and respectability that Faulkner the author questions throughout the Snopes trilogy and "Wild Palms" was something from which Faulkner the man could not shake himself free entirely, at least according to evidence in Karl's biography.

11. Faulkner, *The Mansion,* 153; hereafter cited parenthetically in the text.

12. According to Pursell's historiography, Mink's personal work life would be seen as predating the "authoritarian" technologies; it is closer to the "democratic" technology of Jefferson "the craftsman or the farmer." In Pursell's schema, the one is "system-centered, immensely powerful, but inherently unstable" while the other is "man-centered, relatively weak, but resourceful and durable" ("The American Ideal of a Democratic Technology," 12).

13. Compare the fate Labove chooses for himself. He toils toward respectability along a narrow groove of labor. At last comes the moment he has worked for; all he has to do is "rise and walk out of the room and on, his face steady, in the direction he had chosen to set it. . . . And he could not do it" (*The Hamlet,* 113). Labove's faith in the ability to control time and effort in order to reach rational goals dissolves in the presence of Eula Varner. The acts of "labor" with which Labove "writes" his name yield to the insertion of "love" (rather, lust).

14. Before the opening of the "Wild Palms" narrative, Charlotte had submitted to the error of "buying" the duplicate of a prototype. In the face of the taboo against marrying one's brother, she had taken up Rat Rittenmeyer, a near likeness. But once she meets Harry, she discards the "model husband" procured according to the conventions by which nice young Southern women marry surrogate broth-

ers or fathers. She seizes upon Harry as raw material, which she, as designer-sculptor, shapes to her needs. Although it is the Platonistic ideal of Love she pursues, she needs his material body to incarnate that dream.

15. Eula Varner Snopes introduces an interesting distinction when she remarks, "Maybe men are just interested in facts too and the only difference is, women dont care whether they are facts or not just so they fit and men dont care whether they fit or not just so they are facts" (*The Town,* 330–31).

16. Charles Mallison says that Gavin Stevens "is a good man, wise too except for the occasions when he would aberrate, go momentarily haywire and take a wrong turn . . . and then go hell-for-leather, with absolutely no deviation from logic and rationality from there on, until he wound us up in a mess of trouble or embarrassment" (*The Mansion,* 230). The practice of human engineering is plagued by precisely this dangerous combination of logical illogic.

17. Slade's review of American writers vis-à-vis American inventions rejects the twin notions that Faulkner was unalterably opposed to modern technology and that he forever placed Nature/man in opposition to the machine. He concludes that Faulkner "aligns himself with Samuel Gompers in admitting that man and machine do resemble each other; the necessary qualification is that man is the more complex of the two—he is not, or should not be, 'single-purposed' " ("American Writers and American Inventions," 44).

18. Benjamin, "The Work of Art in the Age of Mechanical Reproduction," 220.

19. From Marx, *Capital,* vol. I, cited in Rabinbach, *The Human Motor,* 78.

20. Mink conducts his life according to the rules of labor that govern the universe, the natural world, and the individual. Notwithstanding his compliance with Parchman's regimen, he places no trust in man-made regulations, which are a shabby imitation of the all-encompassing work routine exacted by "Old Moster." Society's rules are motivated by wants; the code of the universe is a matter of imperatives. "*If a feller jest wants to do something, he might make it and he might not. But if he's GOT to do something, cant nothing stop him*" (*The Mansion,* 49). The way society manages Mink's life only compounds injustice; thus he attempts to manage his actions according to the justice (harsh and unmerciful as it is) handed down from the stars.

21. "That was the danger, what a man had to watch against: once you laid flat on the ground, right away the earth started in to draw you back down into it. The very moment you were born out of your mother's body, the power and drag of the earth was already at work on you. . . . As soon as you could move you would raise your head even though that was all, trying to break that pull, trying to pull elrect . . . to get away from the earth, save yourself." But all this time, "the old patient biding unhurried ground has already taken that first light holt on you" (*The Mansion,* 402–3).

22. Nietzsche, in *The Will to Power* (1988), quoted by Rabinbach, *The Human Motor* 19, distinguishes between the fatigue that results from pushing the body too

hard and fatigue that is "a sign of limit, of the point of rest, even of spiritual awakening." The *Journal des Goncourts* (1887) reports on longing for rest that leads to "an incredible indifference to the pinpricks of life, a detachment from reality" (Rabinbach, *The Human Motor,* 39). Freud's *Beyond the Pleasure Principle* (1920) "introduced the idea that the human organism resists the excess expenditure of energy and strives toward the elimination of tension, not unlike the principle of inertia" (ibid., 63). Eula Varner Snopes represents the vis inertia men both fear and delight in because it is the pleasure principle that pulls them back into the female body of the earth.

23. Marx, *Grundisse,* quoted by Rabinbach, *The Human Motor,* 80.

24. Rabinbach, *The Human Motor,* 82.

25. Snopesism gains its hold once "that outrageous belief that courage and honor are practical has had time to fade and cool so that merely the habit of courage and honor remain; add to that then that generation's natural heritage of cold rapacity as instinctive as breathing, and tremble at that prospect: the habit of courage and honor compounded by rapacity or rapacity raised to the absolute *nth* by courage and honor" (*The Town,* 35).

26. I. O. Snopes enters Varner's store, "still talking . . . his voice voluble and rapid and meaningless like something talking to itself about nothing in a deserted cavern" (*The Hamlet,* 65). He talks out of sheer pleasure. The rhetoric Clarence Snopes uses on the campaign trail has the practical end of manipulating people and things to suit his purposes: "the man who had used the Ku Klux Klan when he needed it and then used their innocence to wreck the Klan when he no longer did, who was using the Baptist Church as long as he believed it would serve him; who had used W.P.A. and N.R.A. and A.A.A. and C.C.C . . . , [then] he turned against the party which had fathered them, ringing the halls . . . with his own voice full of racial and religious and economic intolerance" (*The Mansion,* 306).

27. See *The Hamlet,* 149–53. In this fantasy interlude, Flem's managerial mastery is far superior to that of the Prince of Hell.

28. Actually (or as Ratliff would say, "actively") Linda is exceedingly passionate. This intensity does not show itself, however, through the spoken word.

29. Krauss, "Grids, You Say," *Grids,* 1; hereafter cited parenthetically in the text.

30. For a discussion of Janet's theories about life held to an "economy that is the result of a real feeling of poverty" (theories coinciding with studies by Théodule Ribot and William James, men who believed that diseases of the will have material causes), see Rabinbach, *The Human Motor,* 170–71.

31. One can have different views about pornography and Goldbergian machines. Both might seem liberating. I, for one, believe that the contemplation of Rube's marvels of wasted energy produces immense amounts of imaginative energy in the viewer. On the other hand, I go along with Steven Marcus's analysis of the repetitious production of pornography in *The Other Victorians: A Study of Sexuality and Pornography in Mid-Century England)* rather than with Leo Bersani in

his chapter, "Persons in Pieces." Bersani could be speaking of Lem Pitkin when he describes "a scattered or disseminated self," or of West's pleasure in "putting 'persons in pieces,'" an enterprise which, in certain pornographic writing, becomes an appropriate image for the process of violent deconstruction of the self" (*A Future for Astyanax*, x–xi). Fun for West, however, is not the same as fun for Lem or for the reader. Once again, my belief is that West's novella is "perfect" because *it closes out process;* therefore, the narrative is "dead," foregoing the chance for further fertile "violent deconstruction."

32. The diagrams essential to industrial model-making, discussed by Starr in *Product Design and Decision Theory* and by Knoblaugh in *Modelmaking for Industrial Design,* find visual parallels in Bal, "The Narrating and the Focalizing," 245; Genette, *Narrative Discourse Revisited,* 117–21; and Bremond, "The Logic of Narrative Possibilities," 390–99.

33. Belknap, one of the defense attorneys, hopes to replace Clyde's story with one that will "appear less cruel or legally murderous." Although he works to "concoct some other story," he will not do for Clyde what was once done for him. Involved in circumstances very like Clyde's (pregnant girl, social reputation to uphold), Belknap was saved by money and his father's aid, but his "happy ending" cannot be transferred to Clyde (Dreiser, *An American Tragedy,* 2:189). On the other hand, Clyde's parents hope to provide a good ending by putting up mission placards, which "proclaimed the charity, the wisdom, and the sustaining righteousness of God" (2:216). Clyde's mother—"this American witness to the rule of God upon earth," she who exists in "her six thousand-year-old world"—strives even harder (2:334–35). She tries to sell stories considered *interesting* by the press (2:340). She fails, however, because her "unauthorized" creed defies "the tenets and processes of organized" religion. Her "dream" of a lecture tour ends with loss of public interest (2:358, 368).

34. Benjamin, "The Author as Producer," 233, 237.

35. Interweaving his readings of early nineteenth-century legal documents with readings of the final chapter of Emerson's *Nature,* Christopher Newfield points to the burdens placed upon the myth of American individualism long before late capitalism became identified with "incorporation." Note in particular Newfield's remarks concerning Emerson's awareness that "in still-transcendentalist America, individuals compete in unending labors of self-differentiation while their social relations are managed from somewhere else." Emerson recognizes that no one can "possess" the self as promised by laissez-faire "freedom"; he also "insures that an individual's submission to a sufficiently gigantic and inaccessible collective instrument will seem like a spiritual triumph. This metaphysics also allows personal agency being directed by a 'transcendental' agency to seem coherent and individuating" ("Emerson's Corporate Individualism," 680).

BIBLIOGRAPHY

Basic Bibliographic References

The following list of short titles is provided for the convenience of those who wish to go directly to the heart of various aspects of "the cultures of management." Complete citations are given in the selected bibliography.

Taylor, Taylorism, Time-Motion Studies:
Aitken, *Scientific Management in Action;* Babcock, *The Taylor System in Franklin Management;* Bendix, *Work and Authority in Industry;* Beniger, *The Control Revolution;* Copley, *Frederick W. Taylor;* Giedion, *Mechanization Takes Command;* Gies, "Automating the Worker"; Haber, *Efficiency and Uplift;* Hounshell, *From the American System to Mass Production, 1800–1932;* Hoxie, *Scientific Management and Labor;* Hughes, *American Genesis;* Hunt, ed. *Scientific Management since Taylor;* Kakar, *Frederick Taylor;* Mayr and Post, eds. *Yankee Enterprise;* Mumford, *Technics and Civilization;* Nelson, *Managers and Workers* and *Frederick W. Taylor and the Rise of Scientific Management;* Rabinbach, *The Human Motor;* Segal, *Technological Utopianism in American Culture;* Taylor; *Scientific Management;* Thompson, ed. *Scientific Management;* Tichi, *Shifting Gears;* Waring, *Taylorism Transformed.*

Transatlantic Appropriation and Developments:
Bailes, "Alexei Gastev and the Soviet Controversy over Taylorism, 1918–24"; Beniger, *The Control Revolution;* Frost, "Assembly Lines and Vacuum Cleaners"; Hughes, *American Genesis;* McLeod, "'Architecture or Revolution'"; Merkle, *Management and Ideology;* Rabinbach, *The Human Motor;* Traub, "Lenin and Taylor."

The Extension of Managerial Control:
Alchon, *The Invisible Hand of Planning;* Baritz, *The Servants of Power;* Bendix, *Work and Authority in Industry;* Beniger, *The Control Revolution;* Brandes, *American Welfare Capitalism, 1880–1940;* Chandler, *The Visible Hand* and *Scale and Scope;* Ehrenreich, *The Altruistic Imagination;* Gilbert, *Designing the Industrial State;* Graebner, *The Engineering of Consent;* Hughes, *Networks of Power;* Kirkland, *Industry Comes of Age;* Ross, *The Origins of American Social Science;* Stabile, *Prophets of Order;* Weisberger, *The New Industrial Society;* Zunz, *Making America Corporate, 1870–1920.*

Developments in Technology (in addition to titles about Taylorism listed above):
Akin, *Technocracy and the American Dream;* Basalla, *The Evolution of Technology;* Clark, "The American Image of Technology from the Revolution to 1840";

Hindle and Lubar, *Engines of Change;* Kasson, *Civilizing the Machine;* Pursell, "The American Ideal of a Democratic Technology."

Progressivist Reform Movements:
Colburn and Pozzetta, eds. *Reform and Reformers in the Progressive Era;* Crunden, *Ministers of Reform;* Hofstadter, *The Age of Reform;* May, *The End of American Innocence;* Noble, *The End of American History;* Susman, "Ideology as Culture" in *Culture as History.*

The Politics of Language:
Bannister, *Social Darwinism;* Brown, "Professional Language"; Connolly, *The Terms of Political Discourse;* Dallmayr, *Language and Politics;* Edge and Wolfe, eds. *Meaning and Control;* Gilbert, *Work without Salvation;* Hofstadter, *Social Darwinism in American Thought, 1860–1915;* Moore, *The Post-Darwinian Controversies;* Rodgers, *Contested Truths* and *The Work Ethic in Industrial America, 1850–1920;* Russett, *Sexual Science;* Scott, *Gender and the Politics of History.*

Selected Bibliography

Abbott, Edith. "Are Women Business Failures?" *Harper's Weekly,* 8 Apr. 1905, 496.

———. "Employment of Women in Industries: Cigar-Making—Its History and Present Tendencies." *Journal of Political Economy* 15 (Jan. 1907): 1–25.

Adams, Brooks. "The Heritage of Henry Adams." Introduction to Henry Adams, *The Degradation of the Democratic Dogma,* ed. Brooks Adams. New York, 1919.

Adams, Henry. *History of the United States of America during the Administration of James Madison.* 1889–91; New York: Library of America, 1986.

———. *History of the United States of America during the Administration of Thomas Jefferson.* 1889–91; New York: Library of America, 1986.

———. "A Letter to American Teachers of History." In *The Degradation of the Democratic Dogma.*

———. *The Letters of Henry Adams. Vol. 6, 1906–1918.* Ed. J. C. Levenson et al. Cambridge, Mass., 1988.

———. "The Primitive Rights of Women." *The Great Secession Winter of 1860–61 and Other Essays,* ed. George Hochfield. New York, 1958.

———. "Recognition of Cuban Independence." ["Acknowledging Cuban Independence."] In U.S. Congress, Senate report 1160. 54th Cong., 2d sess., 21 Dec. 1896. Washington, D.C., 1897. (Submitted under the name of Senator Donald Cameron.)

———, and Henry Cabot Lodge. Review of Von Holst's *History of the United States. North American Review* 123 (Oct. 1876): 328–61.

Adorno, Theodor W. "Culture and Administration." *Telos* 37 (Fall 1978): 94–111.

Afanasyev, Viktor G. *The Scientific Management of Society.* Trans. L. Ilitskaya. Ed. R. Daglish. Moscow, 1971.

Aitken, Hugh G. J. *Scientific Management in Action: Taylorism at Watertown Arsenal, 1908–1915.* Princeton, N.J., 1985.

Akin, William E. *Technocracy and the American Dream: The Technocrat Movement, 1900–1941.* Berkeley, Calif., 1977.

Alchon, Guy. *The Invisible Hand of Planning: Capitalism, Social Science, and the State in the 1920s.* Princeton, N.J., 1985.

American Women Writers. Vol. 4. Ed. Lina Mainiero. New York, 1982.

Anderson, Mary. "Wages for Women Workers." *Annals of the American Academy of Political and Social Science* 81 (1919): 123–29.

Anderson, Perry. *In the Tracks of Historical Materialism.* Chicago, 1984.

"Ann Arbor's Kit Homes." *Ann Arbor Observer,* Jan. 1991, 29–37.

"Apartment Houses." In *Artistic Modern Homes.* New York, 1902.

"The Army of the Potomac." *Harper's Weekly,* 23 May 1863, 331.

Arnold, Horace Lucien, and Fay Leone Faurote. *Ford Methods and the Ford Shops.* New York, 1915.

Atterbury, Grosvenor. "Model Towns in America." *Scribner's Magazine* 52 (July 1912): 20–35.

Babcock, George D. *The Taylor System in Franklin Management.* New York, 1918.

Bailes, Kendall E. "Alexei Gastev and the Societ Controversy over Taylorism, 1918–24." *Soviet Studies* 29, no. 3 (July 1977): 373–94.

Baker's Twentieth-Century Homes. Racine, Wis., 1901.

Bal, Mieke. "The Narrating and the Focalizing: A Theory of the Agents in Narrative." *Style: Narratology* 17, no. 2 (Spring 1983): 234–69.

Bannister, Robert C. *Social Darwinism: Science and Myth in Anglo-American Social Thought.* Philadelphia, 1979.

Banta, Martha. "The Boys and the Bosses: Mark Twain's Double Take on Work, Play, and Democratic Ideals." *American Literary History* 3, no. 3 (Fall 1991): 487–520.

———. *Imaging American Women: Idea and Ideals in Cultural History.* New York, 1987.

Barber, George F. *The Cottage Souvenir, No. 2.* Knoxville, Tenn., 1891.

Baritz, Loren. *The Servants of Power: A History of the Use of Social Science in American Industry.* Middletown, Conn., 1960.

Barnes, Earl. "Women in Industry." *Atlantic Monthly* 110 (1912): 116–24.

Barrett, James R. *Work and Community in the Jungle: Chicago's Packinghouse Workers, 1894–1922.* Urbana, Ill., 1987.

Basalla, George. *The Evolution of Technology.* Cambridge, 1988.

"Battlefields of Business Strategy." *System: The Magazine of Business* 51 (June 1927): 764–65.

Battles and Leaders of the Civil War. Vol. 3. Ed. R. U. Johnson and C. C. Buell. New York, 1887–88.

Baym, Nina. "Early Histories of American Literature: A Chapter in the Institution of New England." *American Literary History* 1, no. 3 (Fall 1989): 459–88.

Beaux, Cecilia. *Background with Figures.* Boston, 1930.

Becker, O. M. "How to Increase Factory Efficiency: Conservation of Strength." *The Engineering Magazine* 51 (Sept. 1916): 813–26.

———. "The Square Deal in Works Management—IV." *The Engineering Magazine* 31 (Apr. 1906): 38–59.

Beeks, Gertrude. "What Is Welfare Work?" *National Civic Federation Monthly Review* 1, no. 6 (Aug. 1904): 5–6.

Bendix, Reinhard. *Work and Authority in Industry: Ideologies of Management in the Course of Industrialization.* New York, 1956.

Beniger, James R. *The Control Revolution: Technological and Economic Origins of the Information Society.* Cambridge, Mass., 1986.

Benjamin, Walter. "The Author as Producer." *Reflections: Essays, Aphorisms, Autobiographical Writings,* trans. Edmund Jephcott. New York, 1978.

———. "The Work of Art in the Age of Mechanical Reproduction." *Illuminations,* trans. by Harry Zohn. New York, 1969.

Bennett, Helen M. *Women and Work: The Economic Value of College Training.* New York, 1917.

Bersani, Leo. *A Future for Astyanax: Character and Desire in Literature.* Boston, 1976.

Blotner, Joseph. *Faulkner: A Biography.* 2 vols. New York, 1974.

Boelhower, William. *Through a Glass Darkly: Ethnic Semiosis in American Literature.* New York, 1987.

Boris, Eileen. *Art and Labor: Ruskin, Morris, and the Craftsman Ideal in America.* Philadelphia, 1986.

Borus, Daniel H. "Thorstein Veblen and the Distopia of Commodities." Unpub. paper.

Bottomore, Tom, ed. *A Dictionary of Marxist Thought.* Cambridge, Mass., 1983.

Boudon, Raymond, and François Bourricaud. *A Critical Dictionary of Sociology.* Select. and trans. Peter Hamilton. Chicago, 1989.

Bourget, Paul. *Outre-Mer: Impressions of America.* New York, 1895.

Bowman, Leslie Greene. *American Arts and Crafts: Virtue in Design.* Los Angeles and Boston, 1990.

Boyer, M. Christine. *Dreaming the Rational City: The Myth of American City Planning.* Cambridge, Mass., 1983.

Bracken, Lawrence E. *New Homes Series. Report No. 1—The Story of Prefabricated Houses. Highlights of Half a Century. Materials, Methods, Experiments.* Columbus, Ind., 1946.

Brady, Kathleen. *Ida Tarbell: Portrait of a Muckraker.* New York, 1984.

Brandes, Stuart D. *American Welfare Capitalism, 1880–1940.* Chicago, 1976.

Brandon, Ruth. *A Capitalist Romance: Singer and the Sewing Machine.* Philadelphia, 1977.

Brann, Henry Walter. "Max Weber and the United States." *The Southwestern Social Science Quarterly* 25, no. 1 (June 1944): 18–30.

Braybon, Gail. *Women Workers in the First World War: The British Experience.* London, 1981.

Bremond, Claude. "The Logic of Narrative Possibilities." *New Literary History* 11, no. 3 (Spring 1980): 387–41.

Brewer, C. P. *The Man-Building Process*. Missoula, Mont., 1925.

Brick, Howard. *Daniel Bell and the Decline of Intellectual Radicalism: Social Theory and Political Reconciliation in the 1940s*. Madison, Wis., 1986.

A Brief Account of the Educational Work of the Ford Motor Company. Detroit, 1916.

Brockett, L. P. *Men of Our Day; or, Biographical Sketches of Patriots, Orators, States-men, Generals, Reformers, Financiers and Merchants, Now on the Stage of Action*. Philadelphia, 1868.

Brooks, John Graham. "New Aspects of Employer's Welfare Work." *Journal of Social Science: Proceedings of the American Association, Boston Papers of 1904*. Boston, 1904.

Brooks, Peter. *Reading for the Plot: Design and Intention in Narrative*. New York, 1984.

Brown, JoAnne. "Professional Language: Words that Succeed," *Radical History Review* 34 (1986): 33–51.

Brown, Marshall. "Introduction: Contemplating the Theory of Literary History." *PMLA* 107, no. 1 (Jan. 1922): 13–25.

Bruce, Alfred, and Harold Sandbank. *A History of Prefabrication*. 1944; reprint New York, 1972.

Bruce, John H. "Comments." *Bulletin of the Society to Promote the Science of Manage-ment* 1 (Nov. 1915): 21–22.

Bullock, John. *The American Cottage Builder: A Series of Designs, Plans, Specifica-tions from $200 to $20,000. For Homes for the People*. New York, 1854.

Bunce, Oliver Bell. *My House: An Ideal*. New York, 1884.

Burlingame, Luther D. "Americanizing a Thousand Men." *Industrial Management: The Engineering Magazine* 53 (June 1917): 385–92.

Bush, Clive. *Halfway to Revolution: Investigation and Crisis in the Work of Henry Adams, William James, and Gertrude Stein*. New Haven, Conn., 1991.

Butler, Elizabeth B. *Women and the Trades: Pittsburgh, 1907–1908*. Vol. 1. *The Pitts-burgh Survey*. Ed. Paul Underwood Kellogg. New York, 1909.

Calkins, Earnest Elmo. *Business the Civilizer*. Boston, 1928.

Campbell, Helen. *The Easiest Way in Housekeeping and Cooking: Adapted to Domestic Use or Study in Classes*. Boston, 1893.

———. "In Home Life." *The Congregationalist* [Boston], 5 Jan. 1901, 14.

Carnegie, Andrew. *A Rectorial Address Delivered to the Students in the University of Aberdeen, 6th June 1912*. New York, 1912.

Carpenter, Charles U. "How We Trained 5000 Women: After Three to Ten Days They Do Precision Work on Fuses and Instruments." *Industrial Management: The Engineering Magazine* 55 (May 1918): 353–57.

Carpenter, Elizabeth. "More Truth about Women in Industry." *North American Review* 179 (Aug. 1904): 215–25.

Casteller, Luther L. *Fundamentals of Human Engineering*. Indianapolis, 1951.

Chandler, Alfred D., Jr. *Scale and Scope: The Dynamics of Industrial Capitalism*. Cambridge, Mass., 1990.

————. *The Visible Hand: The Managerial Revolution in American Business.* Cambridge, Mass., 1977.

Cheley, Frank H. *The Business of Living: Personal Engineering.* New York, 1936.

Cheney, Sheldon, and Martha Chandler Cheney. *Art and the Machine: An Account of Industrial Design in Twentieth Century America.* New York, 1936.

Clark, Clifford Edward, Jr. *The American Family Home, 1800–1960.* Chapel Hill, N.C., 1986.

Clark, Jennifer. "The American Image of Technology from the Revolution to 1840." *American Quarterly* 39, no. 3 (Fall 1987): 431–49.

Clark, Kenneth. "The Blot and the Diagram." *Encounter* [London] 20 (Jan.–June 1963): 28–36.

Clark, Sue Ainslie. "Editorial: Industrial Efficiency." *Life and Labor* 1 (May 1911): 131.

————, and Edith Wyatt. *Making Both Ends Meet: The Income and Outlay of New York Working Girls.* New York, 1911.

Clark, Wallace. "Getting the Office Work Done—II: Organizing a Stenographic Department." *Industrial Management: The Engineering Magazine* 60 (Aug. 1920): 116–21.

Cohen, Lizabeth. "What Kind of World Have We Lost? Workers' Lives and Deindustrialization in the Museum." *American Quarterly* 41, no. 4 (Dec. 1989): 670–81.

Colburn, David R., and George E. Pozzetta, eds. *Reform and Reformers in the Progressive Era.* Westport, Conn., 1983.

Cole, Doris. *From Tipi to Skyscraper: A History of Women in Architecture.* Boston, 1973.

Comstock, Sarah. "A Woman of Achievement: Miss Gertrude Beeks." *The World's Work* 26 (Aug. 1913): 444–48.

Connolly, William E. *The Terms of Political Discourse.* 2d ed. Princeton, N.J., 1983.

Cooley, Charles Horton. *Human Nature and the Social Order.* 1902, 1922; reprint, New Brunswick, N.J., 1983.

Coolidge, Mary Roberts. *Why Women Are So.* New York, 1912.

Copley, Frank Barkley. *Frederick W. Taylor, Father of Scientific Management.* 2 vols. New York, 1969.

Cowan, Ruth Schwartz. "The 'Industrial Revolution' in the Home: Household Technology and Social Change in the 20th Century." *Technology and Culture* 17, no. 1 (Jan. 1976): 1–23.

Crane, Stephen. *The Red Badge of Courage.* Vol. 2 of *The Works of Stephen Crane.* Charlottesville, Va., 1975.

————. *The War Dispatches of Stephen Crane.* Ed. R. N. Stallman and E. R. Hagemann. New York, 1964.

Crunden, Robert M. *Ministers of Reform: The Progressives' Achievement in American Civilization, 1889–1920.* New York, 1982.

Dal Co, Francesco. "From Parks to the Region: Progressive Ideology and the Reform of the American City." In *The American City: From the Civil War to the New Deal,* trans. Barbara Liugia La Penta. Cambridge, Mass., 1979.

Dallek, Robert. *The American Style of Foreign Policy: Cultural Politics and Foreign Affairs.* New York, 1983.

Dallmayr, Fred R. *Language and Politics: Why Does Language Matter to Political Philosophy?* South Bend, Ind., 1984.

Dalzell, Kenneth W. *Homes of Moderate Size.* New York, 1921.

Daves, Jessica. *Ready-Made Miracle: The American Story of Fashion for the Millions.* New York, 1967.

"Davis, Jessie." "My Vacation in a Woolen Mill." *The Survey,* 10 Aug. 1918, 538–41.

Davis, Richard Harding. *The Cuban and Porto Rican Campaigns.* New York, 1898.

———. *Real Soldiers of Fortune.* New York, 1918.

———. *Soldiers of Fortune.* New York, 1897.

De Forest, John. *Miss Ravenel's Conversion from Secession to Loyalty.* New York, 1939.

Dell, Floyd. "Mr. Dreiser and the Dodo." *The Masses* 5, no. 5 (Feb. 1914): 17.

———. "Talks with Live Authors: Theodore Dreiser." *The Masses* 8, no. 10 (Aug. 1916): 36.

Denning, Michael. "'The Special American Conditions': Marxism and American Studies." *American Quarterly* 38, no. 3 (1986): 356–80.

Dewey, John, and James H. Tufts. *Ethics.* New York, 1908.

Docherty, Thomas. *Reading (Absent) Character: Toward a Theory of Characterization in Fiction.* Oxford and New York, 1983.

Dorey, J. J. *The Daily Worker's Counsellor: Advice Worth a Ransom. A Book of Value on Attainments and Progress for the Worker and His Family. A Factor in the Making and Saving of Money.* New York, 1923.

Dorr, Rheta Childe. "Bullying the Woman-Worker." *Harper's Weekly,* 30 Mar. 1907, 458–59, 473.

———. *A Woman of Fifty.* New York, 1924.

Dorson, Richard M. *America Begins: Early American Writing.* New York, 1950.

Dos Passos, John. *The Big Money* and *Nineteen Nineteen, U.S.A.* New York, 1938.

Dow, Joy Wheeler. *American Renaissance: A Review of Domestic Architecture.* New York, 1904.

Downing, Andrew Jackson. *The Architecture of Country Houses.* 1850; reprint, New York, 1969.

Dreiser, Theodore. *An American Tragedy.* 2 vols. New York, 1925.

———. "It Pays to Treat Workers Generously," *Success,* 16 Sept. 1899, 691–92.

———. *Sister Carrie.* Norton Critical Edition. Ed. Donald Pizer. New York, 1970.

———. *Sister Carrie.* University of Pennsylvania Edition. Ed. John C. Berkey et al. Philadelphia, 1981.

Dreyfuss, Henry. *The Measure of Man: Human Factors in Design.* New York, 1959.

Drury, Horace B. "Democracy as a Factor in Industrial Efficiency." *The Annals of the American Academy of Political and Social Science* 65 (May 1916): 15–27.

———. *Scientific Management: A History and Criticism. Studies in History, Economics and Public Law.* 3d ed. New York, 1922.

Du Bois, W. E. B. *The Souls of Black Folk.* In *Three Negro Classics,* ed. John Hope Franklin. New York, 1965.

Eastman, Max. "Class War in Colorado." *The Masses* 5, no. 4 (June 1914): 5–8.

———. "Knowledge and Revolution." *The Masses* 4, no. 10 (July 1913): 3.

Edge, D. O., and J. N. Wolfe, eds. *Meaning and Control: Essays in Social Aspects of Science and Technology.* London, 1973.

Efficiency and Incentives in the Cutting Room. Great Neck, N.Y., 1963.

Ehrenreich, Barbara, and John Ehrenreich. "The Professional-Managerial Class." In *Between Labor and Capital,* ed. Pat Walker. Boston, 1979.

Ehrenreich, John H. *The Altruistic Imagination: A History of Social Work and Social Policy in the United States.* Ithaca, N.Y., 1985.

Eleventh Annual Meeting. The National Civic Federation. New York, January 12, 13, and 14, 1911. Welfare Workers' Conference. New York, 1911.

Eliot, Charles W. "Content in Work." *Journal of Social Science: Proceedings of the American Association. Boston Papers of 1904.* Boston, 1904.

Ellwanger, George Herman. *The Story of My House.* New York, 1890.

Emerson, Harrington. *The Twelve Principles of Management.* New York, 1924.

Emerson, Ralph Waldo. *The Complete Works of Ralph Waldo Emerson.* 12 vols. Centenary Edition. Boston, 1903–4.

Ewen, Stuart, and Elizabeth Ewen. "Americanization and Consumption." *Telos* 37 (Fall 1978): 42–51.

The Famous Fifty: Sterling System-Built Homes. Bay City, Mich., 1915.

Farnsworth, Eva Olney. *The Art and Ethics of Dress: As Related to Efficiency and Economy.* San Francisco, 1915.

Faue, Elizabeth. *Community of Suffering and Struggle: Women, Men, and the Labor Movement in Minneapolis, 1915–1945.* Chapel Hill, N.C., 1991.

Faulkner, William. *The Hamlet.* New York, 1940.

———. *The Mansion.* New York, 1959.

———. *The Town.* New York, 1957.

———. *The Wild Palms.* New York, 1939.

Feather, William. "A Fourth of July Speech—New Style." *Nation's Business* 14, no. 8 (July 1926): 13–14.

Fisher, Boyd. "How to Reduce Labor Turnover," *Bulletin of the U.S. Bureau of Labor Statistics* 27 (2–3 Apr. 1917): 29–47.

Fisher, Philip. "Acting, Reading, Fortune's Wheel: Sister Carrie and the Life History of Objects." In *American Realism: New Essays,* ed. Eric J. Sundquist. Baltimore, 1982.

———. "Democratic Social Space: Whitman, Melville, and the Promise of American Transparency," *Representations* 24 (Fall 1988): 60–101.

Fishkin, Shelly Fisher. *From Fact to Fiction: Journalism and Imagination in America.* New York, 1985.

Fitch, James Marston. *American Building: The Historical Forces that Shaped It.* New York, 1973.

———. *Architecture and the Esthetics of Plenty.* New York, 1961.

Fitzpatrick, Ellen. *Endless Crusade: Women Social Scientists and Progressive Reform.* New York, 1990.

Folsom, Michael Brewster. "Upton Sinclair's Escape from *The Jungle:* The Narrative Strategy and Surpressed Conclusion of America's First Proletarian Novel." *Prospects 4.* Cambridge, 1979.

Foner, Philip S. *A History of Cuba and Its Relations with the United States.* Vol. 2. New York, 1963.

Ford, Henry. *My Philosophy of Industry.* Authorized interview by Fay Leone Faurote. New York, 1929.

Ford, Henry, in collaboration with Samuel Crowther. *Moving Forward.* London, 1931.

———. *My Life and Work.* Garden City, N.Y., 1922.

———. *Today and Tomorrow.* Garden City, N.Y., 1926.

———. " What I Have Learned about Management in the Last 25 Years." *System: The Magazine of Business* 49 (Jan. 1926): 37–40, 103–04, 106.

Fox, Richard Wightman. "Epitaph for Middletown: Robert S. Lynd and the Analysis of Consumer Culture." In *The Culture of Consumption: Critical Essays in American History, 1880–1980,* ed. Fox and T. J. Jackson Lears. New York, 1983.

Frederick, Christine. *The New Housekeeping: Efficiency Studies in Home Management.* Garden City, N.Y., 1914.

"From the Editor's Desk." *System: The Magazine of Business* 51 (Apr. 1927): 548, 550.

Frost, Robert L. "Assembly Lines and Vacuum Cleaners: Exporting and Reinventing the American Dream in France, 1919–1930." Paper presented at the American Studies Association annual meeting, New Orleans, 1990.

Fuller, Henry B. *The Cliff-Dwellers: A Novel.* New York, 1893.

Fuller, Walter D. "Application of Scientific Principles to Office Management," *Bulletin of the Taylor Society* 4, no. 3 (June 1919): 8–28.

———. "Standardization in Office Work." *Industrial Management: The Engineering Magazine* 53 (July 1917): 503–7.

Gardner, Eugene C. *The House that Jill Built after Jack Had Proved a Failure: A Book on Home Architecture.* New York, 1882.

Genette, Gérard. *Narrative Discourse: An Essay in Method.* Trans. Jane E. Lewin. Ithaca, N.Y., 1980.

———. *Narrative Discourse Revisited.* Trans. Jane E. Lewin. Ithaca, N.Y., 1988.

Gerster, Georg. *Grand Design: The Earth from Above.* New York, 1976.

Gerstle, Gary. *Working-Class Americanism: The Politics of Labor in a Textile City, 1914–1960.* Cambridge, 1989.

Gibson, Louis H. *Beautiful Houses: A Study in House-Building.* New York, 1895.

———. *Convenient Houses with Fifty Plans for the Housekeeper.* New York, 1889.

Giedion, Siegfried. *Mechanization Takes Command: A Contribution to Anonymous History.* New York, 1969.

Gies, Joseph. "Automating the Worker." *American Heritage of Invention and Technology* 6, no. 3 (Winter 1991): 56–63.

Gilbert, James B. *Designing the Industrial State: The Intellectual Pursuit of Collectivism in America, 1880–1940.* Chicago, 1972.

———. *Work without Salvation: America's Intellectuals and Industrial Alienation, 1880–1910.* Baltimore, 1977.

Gilbreth, Frank B., and Lillian M. Gilbreth. "The Effect of Motion Study upon the Workers." *The Annals of the American Academy of Political and Social Science* 65 (May 1916): 272–76.

Gilbreth, Frank, Jr., and Ernestine Gilbreth Carey. *Cheaper by the Dozen.* New York, 1948.

Gilkeson, John S., Jr. *Middle-Class Providence, 1820–1940.* Princeton, N.J., 1986.

Gilman, Charlotte Perkins. *The Home: Its Work and Influence.* New York, 1903.

———. *The Man-Made World; or, Our Androcentric Culture.* New York, 1911.

———. "The Passing of the Home in Great American Cities." *The Cosmopolitan* 38 (Dec. 1904): 137–47.

———. *Women and Economics: A Study of the Economic Relation between Men and Women as a Factor in Social Evolution.* New York, 1975.

Gilman, Nicholas Paine. "The Laws of Daily Conduct." *Conduct as A Fine Art.* Boston, 1892.

Gilson, Mary Barnett. "The Relation of Home Conditions to Industrial Efficiency." *The Annals of the American Academy of Political and Social Science* 65 (May 1916): 277–89.

Glassie, Henry. *Folk Housing in Middle Virginia: A Structural Analysis of Historic Artifacts.* Knoxville, Tenn., 1975.

Glenn, Susan A. *Daughters of the Shtetl: Life and Labor in the Immigrant Generation.* Ithaca, N.Y., 1990.

Godden, Richard. *Fictions of Capital: The American Novel from James to Mailer.* Cambridge, 1990.

Goldmark, Josephine. *Fatigue and Efficiency: A Study in Industry.* New York, 1912.

Gow, Charles R. *Elements of Human Engineering.* Ed. F. Alexander Magoun. New York, 1932.

Gowans, Alan. *The Comfortable House: North American Suburban Architecture, 1890–1930.* Cambridge, Mass., 1986.

Graebner, William. *The Engineering of Consent: Democracy and Authority in Twentieth-Century America.* Madison, Wis., 1987.

Gramsci, Antonio. "Americanism and Fordism." In *Selections from the Prison Notebooks,* ed. Quintin Hoare and Geoffrey Nowell Smith. New York, 1971.

Grant, Robert. *The Art of Living.* New York, 1895.

Groneman, Carol, and Mary Beth Norton, eds. *"To Toil the Livelong Day": America's Women at Work, 1780–1980.* Ithaca, N.Y., 1987.

Grossman, Lionel. "History and Literature: Reproduction or Signification." In *The Writing of History: Literary Form and Historical Understanding,* ed. Robert H. Canary and Henry Kozicki. Madison, Wis., 1978.

Guimond, James. "Frances Johnston's *Hampton Album:* A White Dream for Black People." *American Photography and the American Dream.* Chapel Hill, N.C., 1991.

Haber, Samuel. *Efficiency and Uplift: Scientific Management in the Progressive Era, 1890–1920.* Chicago, 1964.

Hacking, Ian. *The Taming of Chance.* Cambridge, 1990.

Hall, Stuart. "Gramsci and Us." *Marxism Today* 31 (June 1987): 16–21.

Hampshire, Stuart N. Review of *Spinoza and Other Heretics* by Yirmiyahu Yovel. *New York Review of Books,* May 1990, 40–42.

Hancock, John. "The Apartment House in Urban America." *Buildings and Society: Essays on the Social Development of the Built Environment,* ed. Anthony D. King. London, 1980.

Handlin, David P. *The American Home: Architecture and Society, 1815–1915.* Boston, 1979.

Hard, William. *The Women of Tomorrow.* New York, 1911.

Harris, Leon. *Upton Sinclair: American Rebel.* New York, 1975.

Hayden, Dolores. *The Grand Domestic Revolution: A History of Feminist Designs for American Homes, Neighborhoods, and Cities.* Cambridge, Mass., 1981.

———. *Redesigning the American Dream: The Future of Housing, Work, and Family Life.* New York, 1984.

Haydu, Jeffrey. *Between Craft and Class: Skilled Workers and Factory Politics in the United States and Britain, 1890–1922.* Berkeley, Calif., 1988.

Healy, David. *Drive to Hegemony: The United States in the Caribbean, 1898–1917.* Madison, Wis., 1988.

Heller, Adele, and Lois Rudnick, eds. *1915, The Cultural Moment: The New Politics, the New Woman, the New Psychology, the New Art and the New Theatre in America.* New Brunswick, N.J., 1991.

Helpful Hints and Advice to Employees. 1919. Ford Motor Company Archives and Library. Henry Ford Museum and Greenfield Village, Dearborn, Mich.

Hendler, Glenn. "The Limits of Sympathy: Louisa May Alcott and the Sentimental Novel." *American Literary History* 3, no. 4 (Winter 1991): 685–706.

Herbert, Christopher. *Culture and Anomie: Ethnographic Imagination in the Nineteenth Century.* Chicago, 1991.

Herbert, Gilbert. *The Dream of the Factory-Made House: Walter Gropius and Konrad Wachsmann.* Cambridge, Mass., 1984.

Hernadi, Paul. "On the How, What, and Why of Narrative." In *On Narrative,* ed. W. J. T. Mitchell. Chicago, 1981.

Herreshoff, David. *American Disciples of Marx: From the Age of Jackson to the Progressive Era.* Detroit, 1967.

"He's a Chip Off the Old Block." *System: The Magazine of Business* 51 (Jan. 1927): 30–31.

Higham, John. *Strangers in the Land: Patterns of American Nativism, 1860–1925.* New York, 1981.

Hill, Thomas E. *Right and Wrong, Contrasted.* Chicago, 1884.

Hindle, Brooke, and Steven Lubar. *Engines of Change: The American Industrial Rev-olution, 1790–1860*. Washington, D.C., 1986.

Hines, Thomas S. "The City Beautiful Movement in American Urban Planning, 1890–1920." *Transactions* 7 (1985): 28–43.

Hobbs, Isaac H. *Hobbs's Architecture: Containing Designs and Ground Plans For Vil-las, Cottages, and Other Edifices. Both Suburban and Rural. Adapted to the United States*. Philadelphia, 1873.

Hoerle, Helen Christine, and Florence B. Saltzberg. *The Girl and the Job*. New York, 1919.

Hofstadter, Richard. *The Age of Reform: From Bryan to F.D.R*. New York, 1955.

———. *Social Darwinism in American Thought, 1860–1915*. Philadelphia, 1945.

Home Builder's Plan Book: Prize and Honor Designs of the National Small Home Com-petition. New York, 1921.

Hoover, Herbert. "Home Ownership." In *The Better Homes Manual*, ed. Blanche Halbert. Chicago, 1931.

Hopkins, Ernest Martin. "Democracy and Industry." *Annals of the American Acad-emy of Political and Social Science* 65 (May 1916): 57–67.

Hounshell, David A. *From the American System to Mass Production, 1800–1932: The Development of Manufacturing Technology in the United States*. Baltimore, 1984.

Houser, J. David. *What the Employer Thinks: Executives' Attitudes toward Employees*. Cambridge, Mass., 1927.

Hoxie, Robert Franklin. *Scientific Management and Labor*. 1915; reprint, New York, 1966.

Hubbard, Charles W. "Some Practical Principles of Welfare Work." *Journal of So-cial Science: Proceedings of the American Association. Boston Papers of 1904*. Boston, 1904.

Hughes, Thomas P. *American Genesis: A Century of Invention and Technological En-thusiasm, 1870–1970*. New York, 1989.

———. "Gropius, Machine Design, and Mass Production." *Jahrbuch (Wissenschafts Kolleg Zu Berlin), 1983–1984*. Berlin, 1984.

———. *Networks of Power: Electrification in Western Society, 1880–1930*. Baltimore, 1983.

Humphreys, Mary Gay. "House Decoration and Furnishing." *The Woman's Book*. Vol. 2. New York, 1894.

Hunt, Edward Eyre, ed. *Scientific Management since Taylor: A Collection of Authori-tative Papers*. New York, 1924.

Hurlburt, Allen. *The Grid: A Modular System for the Design and Production of News-papers, Magazines, and Books*. New York, 1978.

Hutner, Gordon. "Modern Instances: Intimacy and America's Crisis of Confi-dence." *Southern Review* 25, no. 3 (July 1989): 533–48.

"'I Make Cheap Silk': The Story of a Fifteen-Year-Old Weaver in the Paterson Silk Mills, as Told by Her to Inis Weed and Louise Carey." *The Masses* 5, no. 11 (Nov. 1913): 7.

Industrialized House Forum: Proceedings of Course Conference, January 6 and 7, 1950. Cambridge, Mass., 1950.

"In Stone and In the Hearts of Men." *System: The Magazine of Business* 50 (Feb. 1927): 170–71.

Instructions for the Erection of Your Aladdin Home. Bay City, Mich., 1912.

Jackson, John Brinckerhoff. *American Space: The Centennial Years, 1865–1876.* New York, 1972.

Jacob, Mary Jane. "The Rouge in 1927: Photographs and Paintings by Charles Sheeler." *The Rouge: Image of Industry in the Art of Charles Sheeler and Diego Rivera.* Detroit, 1978.

James, Henry. *The American Scene.* 1907; reprint, Bloomington, Ind., 1968.

———. *The Golden Bowl.* Vols. 22–23 of *The Novels and Tales of Henry James.* New York, 1909.

———. *The Wings of the Dove.* Vols. 19–20 of *The Novels and Tales of Henry James.* New York, 1909.

James, William. "Frederic Myers' Services to Psychology." In *A William James Reader,* ed. Gay Wilson Allen. Boston, 1971.

———. "The Hidden Self." In *A William James Reader,* ed. Gay Wilson Allen. Boston, 1971.

———. "The Moral Equivalent of War." In *A William James Reader,* ed. Gay Wilson Allen. Boston, 1971.

———. "The Moral Philosopher and the Moral Life." *Ethics: The International Journal of Ethics* 1, no. 3 (Apr. 1901): 330–54.

———. "The Philippines Tangle." *A William James Reader,* ed. Gay Wilson Allen. Boston, 1971.

Jordan, John M. "To Engineer a Modern America: The Romance of Rational Reform, 1911–1939." Unpub. book manuscript.

Julius, Emmanuel. "Roadtown: A Glimpse of the Future. A Scientific Prophecy of the Dwellings of Tomorrow." *The Masses* 1, no. 7 (July 1911): 5–6.

Kakar, Sudhir. *Frederick Taylor: A Study in Personality and Innovation.* Cambridge, Mass., 1970.

Kaplan, Amy. "Romancing the Empire: The Embodiment of American Masculinity in the Popular Historical Novel in the 1890s." *American Literary History* 2 (1990): 659–90.

———. "The Spectacle of War in Crane's Revision of History." In *New Essays on The Red Badge of Courage,* ed. Lee Clark Mitchell. Cambridge, 1986.

Kaplan, Wendy. *"The Art that Is Life": The Arts and Crafts Movement in America, 1875–1920.* Boston, 1987.

Karl, Frederick R. *William Faulkner: American Writer.* New York, 1989.

Kasson, John F. *Civilizing the Machine: Technology and Republican Values in America, 1776–1900.* New York, 1977.

Kemler, Edgar. *The Deflation of American Ideals: An Ethical Guide for New Dealers.* Seattle, 1941.

Kendall, Henry P. "Unsystematized, Systematized, and Scientific Managment." In *Dartmouth College Conferences. First Tuck School Conference. Scientific Management. Addresses and Discussions at the Conference on Scientific Management Held October 12, 13, 14, 1911.* Hanover, N.H., 1912.

Kessler-Harris, Alice. *Out to Work: A History of Wage-Earning Women in the United States*. New York, 1982.

Kidwell, Claudia B. *Cutting a Fashionable Fit: Dressmakers' Drafting Systems in the United States*. Washington, D.C., 1979.

――――, and Margaret C. Christman. *Suiting Everyone: The Democratization of Clothing in America*. Washington, D.C., 1974.

Kipnis, Laura. "'Refunctioning' Reconsidered: Toward a Left Popular Culture." In *High Theory/Low Culture: Analysing Popular Television and Film*, ed. Colin MacCabe. Manchester, 1986.

Kirkland, Edward Chase. *Charles Francis Adams, Jr. 1835–1915: The Patrician at Bay*. Cambridge, Mass., 1965.

――――. *Industry Comes of Age: Business, Labor, and Public Policy, 1860–1897*. Vol. 4 of *The Economic History of the United States*. New York, 1961.

Kirstein, Lincoln. Introduction to *The Hampton Album*. New York, 1966.

Kloppenberg, James T. *Uncertain Victory: Social Democracy and Progressivism in European and American Thought, 1870–1920*. New York, 1986.

Knapp, James F. *Literary Modernism and the Transformation of Work*. Evanston, Ill., 1988.

Knoblaugh, Ralph R. *Modelmaking for Industrial Design*. New York, 1958.

Knoeppel, C. E. "American Women in War Industry—I." *Industrial Management: The Engineering Magazine* 55 (June 1918): 480–83.

Krauss, Rosalind. *Grids: Format and Image in Twentieth-Century Art*. New York, 1978.

Kriehn, George. "The City Beautiful." *Municipal Affairs* 3, no. 4 (Dec. 1899): 594–601.

Kuntz, Paul Grimley. "The Art of Blotting." *Journal of Aesthetics and Art Criticism* 25 (Fall 1966–67): 93–103.

Kwolek-Folland, Angel. "The Useful What-Not and the Ideal of 'Domestic Decoration.'" *Helicon Nine: The Journal of Women's Arts and Letters* 3 (1983): 72–83.

"Labor Policies." Account 62, folder "Minneapolis." Ford Motor Company Archives and Library. Henry Ford Museum and Greenfield Village, Dearborn, Mich.

The Ladies, God Bless 'Em: The Women's Art Movement in Cincinnati in the Nineteenth Century. Cincinnati, 1976.

"Landmarks of Business." *System: The Magazine of Business* 51 (Mar. 1927): 312–13.

Lane, Rose Wilder. *Henry Ford's Own Story: How a Farmer's Boy Rose to the Power that Goes with Many Millions yet Never Lost Touch with Humanity*. Forest Hills, N.Y., 1917.

Lang, Robert. *American Film Melodrama: Griffith, Vidor, Minelli*. Princeton, N.J., 1989.

Larkin, W. "Reports of Our Business Agents—Bridgeport, Conn." *Machinists' Monthly Journal of the International Association of Machinists* 26, no. 3 (Mar. 1914): 274.

Larsen, Nella. *Quicksand and Passing.* Ed. Deborah E. McDowell. New Brunswick, N.J., 1986.

Lasch, Christopher. *Haven in a Heartless World: The Family Besieged.* New York, 1977.

Laurie, Bruce. *Artisans into Workers: Labor in Nineteenth-Century America.* New York, 1989.

Leach, Anna. "Science in the Model Kitchen." *The Cosmopolitan* 27, no. 1 (May 1899): 95–104.

Leach, William R. "Transformations in a Culture of Consumption: Women and Department Stores, 1890–1925." *Journal of American History* 71, no. 2 (Sept. 1984): 319–42.

Lears, T. J. Jackson. "The Concept of Cultural Hegemony: Problems and Possibilities." *American Historical Review* 90, no. 3 (June 1985): 567–93.

———. "Man the Machine." Review of *The Human Motor* by Anson Rabinbach. *The New Republic,* 15–22 July 1991, 43–45.

———. "Some Versions of Fantasy: Toward a Cultural History of American Advertising, 1880–1930." *Prospects 9.* New York, 1984.

Lenin, V. I. "Raising the Productivity of Labour." *Selected Works.* One vol. ed. New York, 1971.

Lentricchia, Frank. *Ariel and the Police: Michel Foucault, William James, Wallace Stevens.* Madison, Wis., 1988.

Lewis, David L. *The Public Image of Henry Ford: An American Folk Hero and His Company.* Detroit, 1976.

Lewis, Lawrence. "Uplifting 17,000 Employees." *The World's Work* 9, no. 5 (Mar. 1905): 5939–50.

Lewis, Sinclair. *The Job: An American Novel.* New York, 1917.

Lewis, Wilfred. "An Object Lesson in Efficiency." In *Scientific Management: A Collection of the More Significant Articles Describing the Taylor System of Management,* ed. C. Bertrand Thompson. Cambridge, Mass., 1914.

The Life Stories of Undistinguished Americans, as Told by Themselves. Ed. Hamilton Holt. New York, 1906.

Lipset, Seymour Martin. "Why Is There No Socialism in the United States?" In *Sources in Contemporary Radicalism,* ed. S. Bialer. Boulder, Colo., 1977.

Lloyd, Henry Demarest. "In New Applications of Democracy." *The Congregationalist* [Boston], 5 Jan. 1901, 14.

London, Jack. "The Sea-Wolf." *The Century* 67–69 (Jan.–Dec. 1904).

Lord, C. B. "How to Deal Successfully with Women in Industry." *Industrial Management: The Engineering Magazine* 53 (Sept. 1917): 838–45.

Louis, S. L. *Decorum: A Practical Treatise on Etiquette and Dress of the Best American Society.* Chicago, 1881.

Lubove, Roy. *The Progressives and the Slums: Tenement House Reform in New York City, 1890–1917.* Pittsburgh, 1962.

Lynd, Robert S., and Helen Merrill Lynd. *Middletown: A Study in Modern American Culture.* New York, 1929.

MacCabe, Colin. "Defining Popular Culture." In *High Theory/Low Culture: Analysing Popular Television and Film,* ed. MacCabe. Manchester, 1986.

Machor, James L. *Pastoral Cities: Urban Ideals and the Symbolic Landscape of America.* Madison, Wis., 1987.

McDannell, Colleen. *The Christian Home in Victorian America, 1840–1900.* Bloomington, Ind., 1986.

McDonnell, Lawrence T. "'You Are Too Sentimental': Problems and Suggestions for a New Labor History." *Journal of Social History* 17 (Summer 1984): 629–54.

McDougall, Isabel. "An Ideal Kitchen." *The House Beautiful* 13 (Dec. 1902): 27–32).

McElvaine, Robert S., ed. *Down and Out in the Great Depression: Letters from the "Forgotten Man."* Chapel Hill, N.C., 1983.

MacLean, Annie Marion. *Wage-Earning Women.* New York, 1910.

McLeod, Mary. "'Architecture or Revolution': Taylorism, Technology, and Social Change." *Art Journal* 43, no. 2 (Oct. 1983): 132–47.

McWhirter, David. *Desire and Love in Henry James: A Study of the Late Novels.* Cambridge, 1989.

Maland, Charles J. *Chaplin and American Culture: The Evolution of a Star Image.* Princeton, N.J., 1989.

Manson, Grant Carpenter. *Frank Lloyd Wright to 1910: The First Golden Age.* New York, 1958.

Marchand, Roland. *Advertising the American Dream: Making Way for Modernity, 1920–1940.* Berkeley, Calif., 1985.

Marden, Orison Swett. *Woman and the Home.* New York, 1915.

Marot, Helen. "Revolution and the Garment Trade." *The Masses* 8, no. 10 (Aug. 1916): 29.

Marquis, Samuel S. *Henry Ford: An Interpretation.* Boston, 1923.

——. Papers. Accession no. 293 (microfilm): "The Ford Idea in Education." "Hints to the Investigator." "Memo on the Ford Profit-Sharing Plan." "Progress among Foreigners since the Proclamation of the Profit-Sharing Plan." Ford Motor Company Archives and Library. Henry Ford Museum and Greenfield Village, Dearborn, Mich.

Martin, Ronald E. *American Literature and the Universe of Force.* Durham, N.C., 1981.

Martindale, Colin. *The Clockwork Muse: The Predictability of Artistic Change.* New York, 1990.

Marx, Karl. *Capital.* Vol. 1. Trans. Samuel Moore and Edward Aveling from the 3d German ed. New York, 1967.

Marx and Engels on the United States. Moscow, 1979.

Marx, Leo. *The Machine in the Garden: Technology and the Pastoral Ideal in America.* New York, 1964.

Marzio, Peter C. *Rube Goldberg: His Life and Work.* New York, 1973.

May, Henry F. *The End of American Innocence: The First Years of Our Own Time, 1912–1917.* New York, 1959.

Mayr, Otto, and Robert C. Post, eds. *Yankee Enterprise: The Rise of the American System of Manufactures.* Washington, D.C., 1981.

Meade, George Herbert. *Mind, Self, and Society from the Standpoint of a Social Behaviorist.* Vol. 1. of *Works of George Herbert Meade.* Ed. Charles W. Morris. Chicago, 1934.

Meikle, Jeffrey L. *Twentieth-Century Limited: Industrial Design in America, 1925–1939.* Philadelphia, 1979.

Meier, Barry. "Debate over Dummies Delays Car Safety Rule." *New York Times* [national ed.], 22 Jan. 1990.

Merkle, Judith A. *Management and Ideology: The Legacy of the International Scientific Management Movement.* Berkeley, Calif., 1980.

Meyer, Stephen, III. *The Five-Dollar Day: Labor, Management, and Social Control in the Ford Motor Company, 1908–1921.* Albany, N.Y., 1981.

Michaels, Walter Benn. "An American Tragedy, or the Promise of American Life." *Representations* 25 (Winter 1989): 71–98.

———. *The Gold Standard and the Logic of Naturalism.* Berkeley, Calif., 1987.

Middleton, Michael. *Group Practice in Design.* New York, 1967.

Milton, Joyce. *The Yellow Kids: Foreign Correspondents in the Heyday of Yellow Journalism.* New York, 1989.

"Minimizing the Controversy: Industrial Peace in Its Relation to Social and Industrial Efficiency." *Life and Labor* 3 (Apr. 1913): 105–7.

Mink, Gwendolyn. *Old Labor and New Immigrants in American Political Development: Union, Party, and State, 1875–1920.* Ithaca, N.Y., 1986.

"Miss Ten-A-Week's Plea." *Bulletin of the Taylor Society* 4, no. 4 (July 1919): 42.

Mitchell, John. "Efficiency Not Acceptable to Wage-Earners." In *Eleventh Annual Meeting, The National Civic Federation. New York, January 12, 13, and 14, 1911.* New York, 1911.

Modern Homes: A Collection of Practical Designs of Houses and Cottages. Cleveland, 1900.

Montgomery, David. *The Fall of the House of Labor: The Workplace, the State, and American Labor Activism, 1865–1925.* Cambridge, 1987.

Moore, James R. *The Post-Darwinian Controversies: A Study of the Protestant Struggle to Come to Terms with Darwin in Great Britain and America, 1870–1900.* Cambridge, 1979.

Morris, Edmund. *The Rise of Theodore Roosevelt.* New York, 1980.

Morawska, Ewa T. *For Bread with Butter: The Life-Worlds of East Central Europeans in Johnstown, Pennsylvania, 1890–1940.* Cambridge, 1985.

"Mr. Ford's Own Page." *The Dearborn Independent,* 20 Dec. 1919, 27 Dec. 1919, 7 Feb. 1920.

Mulcare, Terry. "Progressive Visions of War in *The Red Badge of Courage* and *The Principles of Scientific Management.*" *American Quarterly* 43, no. 1 (Mar. 1991): 46–72.

Mulvey, Laura. "Melodrama In and Out of the Home." In *High Theory/Low Culture: Analysing Popular Television and Film,* ed. Colin MacCabe. Manchester, 1986.

Mumford, Lewis. *Technics and Civilization*. 1934; reprint, New York, 1963.

Myers, Harry. *Human Engineering*. New York, 1932.

Nadworny, Milton J. *Scientific Management and the Unions 1900–1932: A Historical Analysis*. Cambridge, Mass., 1955.

National Civic Federation. Garment Trades Committee. New York and New Jersey Section. Woman's Department. *Welfare Work: Clothing Manufacturers, New York City. Some Deplorable Conditions. Investigations, 1908–9*. New York, 1909.

Nelson, Daniel. *Frederick W. Taylor and the Rise of Scientific Management*. Madison, Wis., 1980.

————. *Managers and Workers: Origins of the New Factory System in the United States, 1880–1920*. Madison, Wis., 1975.

————, and Stuart Campbell. "Taylorism Versus Welfare Work in American Industry: H. L. Gantt and the Bancrofts." *Business History Review* 46 (Spring 1972): 1–16.

Nestor, Agnes. "A Day's Work Making Gloves." *Life and Labor* 2 (May 1912): 137–39.

Nevins, Allan. *Ford: The Times, the Man, the Company*. New York, 1954.

————, and Frank E. Hill. *Ford: Expansion and Challenge, 1915–1933*. New York, 1957.

"New Apartment Houses." *The American Architect and Building News*, 31 May 1879, 175.

Newfield, Christopher. "Emerson's Corporate Individualism." *American Literary History* 3, no. 4 (Winter 1991): 657–84.

Niebuhr, Reinhold. "Ford's Five-Day Week Shrinks." *The Christian Century*, 9 June 1927, 713–14.

————. "How Philanthropic Is Henry Ford?" *The Christian Century*, 9 Dec. 1926, 1507–8.

————. "Mechanical Men in a Mechanical Age." *The World Tomorrow* 13, no. 2 (Dec. 1930): 493–94.

"No Sentiment in Business?" *System: The Management of Business* 51 (May 1927): 626–27.

Noble, David W. *The End of American History: Democracy, Capitalism, and the Metaphor of Two Worlds in Anglo-American Historical Writing, 1880–1980*. Minneapolis, 1985.

Norwood, Edwin P. *Ford: Men and Methods*. Garden City, N.Y., 1931.

Notable American Women. The Modern Period. A Biographical Dictionary. Ed. Barbara Sicherman et al. Cambridge, Mass., 1980.

O'Connell, James. "The Taylor System in Government Shops." *Machinist Monthly Journal* (June 1911): 559.

Otte, Frank R. "As Deever Does It." *System: The Magazine of Business* 51 (Apr. 1927): 476, 478, 480, 538, 540.

Pacific Houses. Ready-Cut and Factory-Built. The Ultimate Types. Los Angeles, 1918.

Parker, Cornelia Stratton. *Working with the Working Woman*. New York, 1922.

Patten, Simon N. *The New Basis of Civilization*. New York, 1912.

Patterson, John H. "Altruism and Sympathy as Factors in Work Administration." *The Engineering Magazine* 20, no. 4 (Jan. 1901): 577–602.

Peirce, Charles Sanders. "How to Make our Ideas Clear." *Popular Science Monthly* 12 (Jan. 1878): 286–302.

Peirce, Melusina Fay. *Co-Operative Housekeeping: How Not to Do It and How to Do It. A Study in Sociology.* Boston, 1884.

Peiss, Kathy. *Cheap Amusements: Working Women and Leisure in Turn-of-the-Century New York.* Philadelphia, 1986.

Petersen, Peter. "Henry Gantt's Work at Bancroft: The Option of Scientific Management." Paper on file in Hagley Museum and Library, Wilmington, Del.

Peterson, Charles E. "Early American Prefabrication." *Gazette des Beaux-Arts.* 6th ser., 33 (1948): 37–46.

———. "Prefabs for the Prairies." *Journal of the Society of Architectural Historians* 11, no. 1 (Mar. 1952): 28–30.

———. "Prefabs in the California Gold Rush." *Journal of the Society of Architectural Historians* 24 (Dec. 1965): 318–24.

Pinchot, Amos. "The Failure of the Progressive Party." *The Masses* 6, no. 3 (Dec. 1914): 9–10.

Porter, H. F. J. "Detroit's Plans for Recruiting Women for Industries." *Industrial Management: The Engineering Magazine* 53 (Aug. 1917): 654–57.

———. "The Higher Law in the Industrial World." *The Engineering Magazine* 29, no. 5 (Aug. 1905): 641–55.

Porter, Theodore M. *The Rise of Statistical Thinking, 1820–1900.* Princeton, N.J., 1986.

Posnock, Ross. "Henry James, Veblen and Adorno: The Crisis of the Modern Self." *Journal of American Studies* 21 (1987): 31–54.

———. "The Politics of Pragmatism and the Fortunes of the Public Intellectual." *American Literary History* 3, no. 3 (Fall 1991): 566–87.

———. "William and Henry James." *Raritan* 8, no. 3 (Winter 1989): 1–26.

Potter, David M. *People of Plenty: Economic Abundance and the American Character.* Chicago, 1954.

Purcell, Edward A., Jr. *The Crisis of Democratic Theory: Scientific Naturalism and the Problem of Value.* Lexington, Ky., 1973.

Pursell, Carroll. "The American Ideal of a Democratic Technology." In *The Technological Imagination: Theories and Fictions,* ed. Teresa de Lauretis, Andreas Huyssen, and Kathleen Woodward. Madison, Wis., 1980.

Rabinbach, Anson. *The Human Motor: Energy, Fatigue, and the Origins of Modernity.* New York, 1990.

Redfield, William C. "The Employment Problem in Industry." *The Annals of the American Academy of Political and Social Science* 65 (May 1916): 9–14.

Reed, John. "Why They Hate Ford." *The Masses* 8, no. 12 (Oct. 1916): 11–12.

Reinitz, Richard. "Niebuhrian Irony and Historical Interpretation: The Relation between Consensus and New Left History." In *The Writing of History: Literary Form and Historical Understanding,* ed. Robert H. Canary and Henry Kozicki. Madison, Wis., 1978.

"Reminiscences of Charles Sorensen." Accession no. 904, box 16. Ford Motor Company Archives and Library. Henry Ford Museum and Greenfield Village, Dearborn, Mich.

"The Representative and Cosmopolitan Emporium of Demorest." In *New York Illustrated*. New York, 1876.

Richards, Ellen H. *Euthenics: The Science of Controllable Environment. A Plea for Better Living Conditions as a First Step toward Higher Human Efficiency*. Boston, 1910.

Richards, Florence S. *The Ready-to-Wear Industry, 1900–1950*. New York, 1951.

Richardson, Dorothy. *The Long Day: The Story of a New York Working Girl, as Told by Herself*. New York, 1905.

Riegel, Robert E. "Women's Clothes and Women's Rights." *American Quarterly* 15 (Fall 1963): 390–401.

Riesman, David. "The Social and Psychological Setting of Veblen's Economic Theory," *Journal of Economic History* 13 (Fall 1953): 449–61.

Riffaterre, Michael. *Fictional Truth*. Baltimore, 1990.

Riis, Jacob. *How the Other Half Lives: Studies among the Tenements of New York*. 1890; reprint, New York, 1971.

Rindge, Fred H., Jr. "From Boss to Fore-Man." *Industrial Management: The Engineering Magazine* 53 (July 1917): 508–14.

Robbins, Bruce. "Death and Vocation: Narrativizing Narrative Theory." *PMLA* 107, no. 1 (Jan. 1992): 38–50.

Robins, Margaret Dreier. "Fatigue and Efficiency: A New Defense For Shorter Hours." *Life and Labor* 2 (Oct. 1912): 297–99.

Robinson, Charles Mulford. *Modern Civic Art, or the City Made Beautiful*. New York, 1904.

Robinson, Dwight E. "Fashion Theory and Product Design." *Harvard Business Review* 36, no. 6 (Nov.–Dec. 1958): 126–38.

Robinson, James Harvey. "Intellectual Radicalism." *The Masses* 8, no. 8 (June 1916): 21.

Rodgers, Daniel T. *Contested Truths: Keywords in American Politics since Independence*. New York, 1987.

———. *The Work Ethic in Industrial America, 1850–1920*. Chicago, 1974.

Rohr, Mayer. *Pattern Drafting and Grading: Women's and Misses' Garment Design*. N.p., 1934.

Roosevelt, Theodore. *The Autobiography of Theodore Roosevelt*. Vol. 22 of *The Works of Theodore Roosevelt, Memorial Edition*. New York, 1925.

———. *Citizenship, Politics and the Elemental Virtues*. Vol. 15 of *The Works of Theodore Roosevelt, Memorial Edition*. New York, 1925.

———. *The Naval War of 1812*. Preface by William S. Sims. Vol. 7. of *The Works of Theodore Roosevelt, Memorial Edition*. New York, 1925.

———. *The Rough Riders*. Vol. 13 of *The Works of Theodore Roosevelt, Memorial Edition*. New York, 1925.

———. *The Strenuous Life: Essays and Addresses*. New York, 1901.

Ross, Dorothy. *The Origins of American Social Science.* Cambridge, 1991.

Ross, Edward Alsworth. *Changing America: Studies in Contemporary Society.* New York, 1912.

Ross, Ishbel. *Crusades and Crinolines, The Life and Times of Ellen Curtis Demorest and William Jennings Demorest.* New York, 1963.

Rotella, Elyce J. *From Home to Office: U.S. Women at Work, 1870–1930.* Ann Arbor, Mich., 1981.

Rotundo, E. Anthony. "Boy Culture: Middle-Class Boyhood in Nineteenth-Century America." In *Meanings for Manhood: Constructions of Masculinity in Victorian America,* ed. Mark C. Carnes and Clyde Griffen. Chicago, 1990.

Rowe, John Carlos. "Henry Adams." In *Columbia Literary History of the United States,* ed. Emory Elliott et al. New York, 1988.

Royce, Josiah. "The Mechanical, the Historical, and the Statistical." *The Basic Writings of Josiah Royce.* Vol. 2. Ed. John J. McDermott. Chicago, 1969.

Rubin, Joan Shelley. "A Convergence of Vision: Constance Rourke, Charles Sheeler, and American Art." *American Quarterly* 42, no. 2 (June 1990): 191–220.

Russell, Charles Edward. "The Invisible Government." *The Masses* 4, no. 12 (July 1913): 3.

Russett, Cynthia Eagle. *Sexual Science: The Victorian Construction of Womanhood.* Cambridge, Mass., 1989.

Ryan, Daniel Edward. *Human Proportions in Growth: Being the Complete Measurement of the Human Body. For Every Age and Size during the Years of Juvenile Growth.* New York, 1880.

Salisbury, William. "Can the Science of Garment Cutting Be Considered Realistic Art?" *The Tailors' Intelligencer* 1, no. 1 (1870).

Salmon, Lucy Maynard. *Progress in the Household.* Boston, 1906.

Samuels, Ernest. *Henry Adams.* Cambridge, Mass., 1989.

Sayman, Isaac H. *Utilizing Our Waste Power.* Baltimore, 1922.

"Scatter-brained! No Wonder He Never Accomplishes Anything Worthwhile!" *System: The Magazine of Business* 51 (Jan. 1927): 119.

"Scenes in the War of 1812." *Harper's Monthly Magazine* 26 (May 1863): 721–36.

Schaefer, Herwin. *The Roots of Modern Design: Functional Tradition in the 19th Century.* London, 1970.

Schell, Erwin H. *The Million Dollar Lecture: Presented to the 1920, 1921, and 1922 Senior Classes in the Engineering Administration at the Massachusetts Institute of Technology.* Boston, 1923.

Schlereth, Thomas J. "Mail-Order Catalogs as Resources in Material Culture Studies." *Artifacts and the American Past.* Nashville, 1980.

Schofield, Ann, ed. *Sealskin and Shoddy: Working Women in American Labor Press Fiction, 1870–1920.* New York, 1988.

Scholes, Robert. "Language, Narrative, and Anti-Narrative." In *On Narrative,* ed. W. J. T. Mitchell. Chicago, 1981.

Schutte, Thomas F., ed. *The Uneasy Coalition: Design in Corporate America.* Philadelphia, 1975.

Schwartz, Joel. "Home as Haven, Cloister, and Winnebago." Review of *The American Family Home, 1800–1960* by Clifford E. Clark. *American Quarterly* 39, no. 3 (Fall 1987): 467–73.

"Scientific Management." *Life and Labor* 2 (Dec. 1912): 368–69.

Scott, Joan Wallach. *Gender and the Politics of History*. New York, 1988.

Segal, Howard P. *Technological Utopianism in American Culture*. Chicago, 1985.

Seltzer, Mark. *Bodies and Machines*. New York, 1992.

———. *Henry James and the Art of Power*. Ithaca, N.Y., 1984.

Sennett, Richard. *Authority*. New York, 1980.

Shi, David E. *The Simple Life: Plain Living and High Thinking in American Culture*. New York, 1985.

Short, R. Thomas. *Proper Homes and How to Have Them*. New York, 1887.

Sicherman, Barbara. "The Paradox of Prudence: Mental Health in the Gilded Age." *Journal of American History* 62, no. 4 (Mar. 1976): 890–912.

Silcox, F. A. "Discussion." In "Workers' Participation in Management." *Bulletin of the Taylor Society* 14 (Feb. 1929): 25.

Silk, Leonard, and David Vogel. *Ethics and Profits: The Crisis of Confidence in American Business*. New York, 1976.

Simplification: What It Is Doing for Business. N.p., 1922.

Sinclair, Upton. *The Flivver King: A Story of Ford-America*. Detroit, 1937.

———. *The Industrial Republic: A Study of the America of Ten Years Hence*. New York, 1907.

———. *The Jungle*. New York, 1906.

———. *The Lost First Edition of Upton Sinclair's The Jungle*. Ed. Gene DeGruson. Memphis, 1988.

Sky, Alison, and Michelle Stone. *Unbuilt America: Forgotten Architecture in the United States from Thomas Jefferson to the Space Age*. New York, 1976.

Slade, Joseph. "American Writers and American Inventions: Cybernetic Discontinuities in Pre-World War II Literature." In *The Technological Imagination: Theories and Fictions*, ed. Teresa de Lauretis, Andreas Huyssen, and Kathleen Woodward. Madison, Wis., 1980.

Sloan, Kay. *The Loud Silents: Origins of the Social Problem Film*. Urbana, Ill., 1988.

Scollors, Werner. "Immigrants and Other Americans." In *Columbia History of the United States*, ed. Emory Elliott et al. New York, 1988.

Spencer, Anna Garland. *Woman's Share in Social Culture*. 1912; reprint, New York, 1972.

Spencer, Robert C., Jr. "The Work of Frank Lloyd Wright." *Architectural Review* [Boston] 7 (June 1900): 61–72.

Stabile, Donald. *Prophets of Order*. Boston, 1984.

Starr, Martin Kenneth. *Product Design and Decision Theory*. Englewood Cliffs, N.J., 1963.

Stein, Gertrude. *Three Lives*. New York, 1909.

Stevenson, Katherine Cole, and H. Ward Jandl. *Houses by Mail: A Guide to Houses from Sears, Roebuck and Company*. Washington, D.C., 1986.

Stevenson, Robert. *Homes of Character: Illustrating One Hundred Designs.* Boston, 1923.

Stigler, Stephen M. *The History of Statistics: The Measurement of Uncertainty before 1900.* Cambridge, Mass., 1986.

Stilgoe, John R. "Privacy and Energy-Efficient Residential Site Design: An Example of Conduct." *Journal of Architectural Education* 37, no. 3–4 (Spring–Summer 1984): 20–25.

Still, F. R. "Women as Machinists." *Industrial Management: The Engineering Magazine* 53 (Aug. 1917): 650–54.

Stone, Warren S. "Railway Engineer Opposed to Efficiency." *Eleventh Annual Meeting. The National Civic Federation. New York, January 1, 12, and 13, 1911.* New York, 1911.

Stowell, Kenneth Kingsley. "Housing the Other Half." *Architectural Forum* 56, no. 3 (Mar. 1932): n.p.

Strum, Philippa. *Louis D. Brandeis: Justice for the People.* Cambridge, Mass., 1984.

Sullivan, J. W. *The Trade Unions' Attitude toward Welfare Work: Welfare Department of the National Civic Federation.* New York, 1907.

Sullivan, Louis. "Kindergarten Chats." *Kindergarten Chats and Other Writings.* Rev. ed. 1918; reprint, New York, 1979.

Sumner, William Graham. "The Conquest of the United States by Spain." *Essays of William Graham Sumner.* Vol. 2. Ed. Albert G. Keller and Maurice R. Davie. New Haven, Conn., 1934.

——. *Folkways: A Study of the Sociological Importance of Usages, Manners, Customs, Mores, and Morals.* Boston, 1940.

——. "The Forgotten Man." *Essays of William Graham Sumner.* Vol. 1. Ed. Albert G. Keller and Maurice R. Davie. New Haven, Conn., 1934.

Susman, Warren I. *Culture as History: The Transformation of American Society in the Twentieth Century.* New York, 1984.

Szuberla, Guy A. "Dom, Namai, Heim: Images of the New Immigrant's Home." *Prospects 10.* Cambridge, 1985.

Tarbell, Ida M. *The Business of Being a Woman.* New York, 1912.

——. "The New Place of Women in Industry—I: A Critical Study of the Newest Factor in Management Science." *Industrial Management: The Engineering Magazine* 60 (Oct. 1920): 265–66.

——. "The New Place of Women in Industry—II: The First Step in Employing Women." *Industrial Management: The Engineering Magazine* 60 (Nov. 1920): 329–30.

——. "The New Place of Women in Industry—III: The Second Step—The Manager Must Know His Material." *Industrial Management: The Engineering Magazine* 60 (Dec. 1920): 399–400.

——. "The New Place of Women in Industry—IV: Women of the International Harvester Company." *Industrial Management: The Engineering Magazine* 61, no. 1 (Jan. 1921): 51–57.

——. "The New Place of Women in Industry—V: The Forewomen." *Industrial Management: The Engineering Magazine* 61, no. 2 (Feb. 1921): 135–37.

Taylor, Frederick Winslow. *Scientific Management: Comprising Shop Management; The Principles of Scientific Management: The Testimony Before the Special House Committee.* New York, 1947.

———. "No. 1003—Shop Management." *Transactions of the American Society of Mechanical Engineers* 24 (1903): 1337–480.

———. "Workmen and Their Management." Typescript of 1909 lecture delivered at Harvard University. Stevens Institute of Technology, Hoboken, N.J.

Taylor, Graham. "The Policy of Being Human in Business." *Chicago Daily News,* 16 June, 1906, 8.

"The Taylor System—Report." *Life and Labor* 2 (May 1912): 156.

["Tenement Housing"] *The American Architect and Building News* 14 Sept. 1878, 96.

Thompson, C. Bertrand. "Classification and Symbolization." In *Scientific Management: A Collection of the More Significant Articles Describing the Taylor System of Management,* ed. Thompson. Cambridge, Mass., 1914.

Thompson, D'Arcy Wentworth. *On Growth and Form.* Abridged ed. Ed. John Tyler Bonner. Cambridge, 1966.

Thompson, Flora MacDonald. "The Truth about Woman in Industry." *North American Review* 178 (May 1904): 751–60.

Tichi, Cecelia. *Shifting Gears: Technology, Literature, Culture in Modernist America.* Chapel Hill, N.C., 1987.

Traub, Rainer. "Lenin and Taylor: The Fate of 'Scientific Management' in the (Early) Soviet Union." *Telos* 37 (Fall 1978): 82–92.

Trescott, Martha M. "Women Engineers in History: Profiles in Holism and Persistence." In *Women in Scientific and Engineering Professions,* ed. Violet B. Haas and Carolyn C. Perrucci. Ann Arbor, Mich., 1984.

Tuan, Yi-Fu. *Topophilia: A Study of Environmental Perception, Attitudes, and Values.* Englewood Cliffs, N.J., 1974.

Tucker, Robert C., ed. *The Marx-Engels Reader.* 2d ed. New York, 1978.

Turner, Victor. "Social Dramas and Stories about Them." In *On Narrative,* ed. W. J. T. Mitchell. Chicago, 1981.

The Universal Self-Instructor and Manual of General Reference. New York, 1883.

Updegraff, Robert R. "Captains in Conflict." *System: The Magazine of Business* 49–50 (Jan.–Dec. 1926).

Updike, John. "Better than Nature." Review of Albert Pinkham Ryder exhibition. *New York Review of Books,* 8 Nov. 1990, 17–18.

U.S. Bureau of Labor. "Intensity of Labor." *Report on Condition of Woman and Child Wage-Earners in the United States.* Vol. 9, *History of Women Workers in the United States.* Washington, D.C., 1911.

———. "Speed Rate." *Report on Condition of Woman and Child Wage-Earners in the United States.* Vol. 3, *The Glass Industry.* Washington, D.C., 1916.

U.S. Congress. *Report of the Industrial Commission on Relations and Conditions of Capital and Labor Employed in Manufacturers and General Business.* Vol. 14, 1901. H. Doc. 183.

Van Kleeck, Mary. "The Social Meaning of Good Management." In *Classics in*

Scientific Management: A Book of Readings, ed. Donald Del Mar and Rodger D. Collons. University, Ala., 1976.

Van Vlissingen, Arthur, Jr. "Ardsley Thinks Out His Problem." *System: The Magazine of Business* 51 (June 1927).

Van Vorst, Mrs. John, and Marie Van Vorst. *The Woman Who Toils: Being the Experience of Two Gentlewomen as Factory Girls.* New York, 1903.

Vaux, Calvert. *Villas and Cottages.* New York, 1857.

Veblen, Thorstein. *The Engineers and the Price System.* New York, 1921.

———. "The Instinct of Workmanship." In *Essays in Our Changing Order.* New York, 1934.

———. *The Instinct of Workmanship and the State of the Industrial Arts.* New York, 1919.

———. *The Place of Science in Modern Civilisation, and Other Essays.* New York, 1932.

———. *The Theory of Business Enterprise.* New York, 1932.

———. *The Theory of the Leisure Class: An Economic Study of Institutions.* New York, 1899, 1912.

Vreeland, Herbert H. *Welfare Work.* New York, 1905.

Walling, William English. "Class Struggle within the Working Class." *The Masses* 4, no. 4 (Jan. 1913): 12–13.

Ward, Geoffrey C. *A First-Class Temperament: The Emergence of Franklin Roosevelt.* New York, 1989.

Ward, Hetta. [on women architects and builders] *The Independent,* 17 Nov. 1892, 1623.

Ward, Lester, F. *Applied Sociology: A Treatise on the Conscious Improvement of Society by Society.* Boston, 1906.

Waring, Stephen P. *Taylorism Transformed: Scientific Management Theory since 1945.* Chapel Hill, N.C., 1991.

Washington, Booker T. *Up from Slavery.* In *Three Negro Classics,* ed. John Hope Franklin. New York, 1965.

Watts, Steven. *The Republic Reborn: War and the Making of Liberal America, 1790–1820.* Baltimore, 1987.

Weber, Marianne. *Max Weber: A Biography.* Trans. and ed. Harry Zohn. New York, 1975.

Weber, Max. *The Protestant Ethic and the Spirit of Capitalism.* Trans. Talcott Parsons. New York, 1958.

———. *The Sociology of Religion.* Trans. E. Fischoff. Boston, 1963.

Weimann, Jeanne Madeline. *The Fair Women: The Story of the Woman's Building, World's Columbian Exposition, Chicago, 1893.* Chicago, 1981.

Weiner, Lynn Y. *From Working Girl to Working Mother: The Female Labor Force in the United States, 1820–1980.* Chapel Hill, N.C., 1985.

Weisberger, Bernard A. *The New Industrial Society.* New York, 1969.

West, Nathanael. *A Cool Million: or, The Dismantling of Lemuel Pitkin.* New York, 1934.

West, Thomas D. *The Competent Life: A Treatise on the Judicious Development, Di-*

rection and Employment of Man's Inherited Ability to Aid in the Betterment of Labor. Cleveland, 1905.

White, Charles E., Jr. *Successful Houses and How to Build Them.* New York, 1912.

White, Hayden. "The Historical Text as Literary Artifact" and "The Narrativization of Real Events." In *The Writing of History,* ed. Robert H. Canary and Henry Kozicki. Madison, Wis., 1978.

———. "The Value of Narrativity in the Representation of Reality." In *On Narrative,* ed. W. J T. Mitchell. Chicago, 1981.

White, Morton G. *Social Thought in America: The Revolt against Formalism.* New York, 1949.

Whitman, Walt. *Complete Prose Works.* Philadelphia, 1897.

———. "Walt Whitman in War-Time: Familiar Letters From the Capitol." *The Century* 46, no. 6 (Oct. 1893): 840–50.

Wilhelm, Donald. "Cyrus H. McCormick, of the Harvester Trust." In series "The 'Big Business' Man as a Social Worker: A Series of Personal Portraits." *The Outlook,* 23 Sept. 1914, 196–201.

———. "Judge Gary, of the Steel Trust." In series "The 'Big Business' Man as a Social Worker: A Series of Personal Portraits." *The Outlook,* 22 Aug. 1914: 1005–9.

Wilson, Christopher. *The Labor of Words: Literary Professionalism in the Progressive Era.* Athens, Ga., 1985.

Wilson, Richard Guy, Dianne H. Pilgrim, and Dickran Tashjian, eds. *The Machine Age in America, 1918–1941.* New York, 1986.

Wood, Edith Elmer. "The Ideal and Practical Organization of a Home." *The Cosmopolitan* 26 (Apr. 1899): 659–64.

———. *Recent Trends in American Housing.* New York, 1931.

Woods, Robert A., and Albert J. Kennedy. *Young Working Girls: A Summary of Evidence from Two Thousand Social Workers. Edited for the National Federation of Settlements.* Boston, 1913.

Wren, Daniel A. "Industrial Sociology: A Revised View of Its Antecedents." *Journal of the History of the Behavioral Sciences* 21, no. 4 (Oct. 1985): 311–20.

Wright, Gwendolyn. *Building the Dream: A Social History of Housing in America.* Cambridge, Mass., 1981.

———. *Moralism and the Model Home: Domestic Architecture and Cultural Conflict in Chicago, 1873–1913.* Chicago, 1980.

Yezierska, Anzia. "America and I." In *Women Working: An Anthology of Stories and Poems,* ed. Nancy Hoffman and Florence Howe. Old Westbury, N.Y., 1979.

Yost, Edna. *Frank and Lillian Gilbreth, Partners for life.* New Brunswick, N.J., 1949.

Zangwill, Israel. *The Melting-Pot.* New York, 1923.

Zunz, Oliver. *Making America Corporate, 1870–1920.* Chicago, 1990.